COMING TO

COMING TO

Consciousness and Natality in Early Modern England

TIMOTHY M. HARRISON

THE UNIVERSITY OF CHICAGO PRESS

CHICAGO AND LONDON

The University of Chicago Press, Chicago 60637
The University of Chicago Press, Ltd., London
© 2020 by The University of Chicago
Published 2020
Printed in the United States of America

29 28 27 26 25 24 23 22 21 20   1 2 3 4 5

ISBN-13: 978-0-226-72509-3 (cloth)
ISBN-13: 978-0-226-72512-3 (paper)
ISBN-13: 978-0-226-72526-0 (e-book)
DOI: https://doi.org/10.7208/chicago/9780226725260.001.0001

The University of Chicago Press gratefully acknowledges the generous support
of the Division of the Humanities at the University of Chicago toward the
publication of this book.

Library of Congress Cataloging-in-Publication Data

Names: Harrison, Timothy M., author.
Title: Coming to : consciousness and natality in early modern England /
    Timothy M. Harrison.
Description: Chicago ; London : The University of Chicago Press, 2020. |
    Includes bibliographical references and index.
Identifiers: LCCN 2020001837 | ISBN 9780226725093 (cloth) |
    ISBN 9780226725123 (paperback) | ISBN 9780226725260 (ebook)
Subjects: LCSH: English poetry—17th century—History and criticism. |
    Consciousness in literature. | Experience in literature. | Fetus in literature. |
    Milton, John, 1608–1674—Criticism and interpretation. | Traherne,
    Thomas, -1674—Criticism and interpretation. | Locke, John, 1632–1704. |
    Infant psychology—England—History—17th century. | Philosophy,
    English—17th century.
Classification: LCC PR438.C66 H37 2020 | DDC 821/.409353—dc23
LC record available at https://lccn.loc.gov/2020001837

♾ This paper meets the requirements of ANSI/NISO Z39.48–1992
(Permanence of Paper).

For Christina

CONTENTS

Beginnings

As the concept of consciousness emerged in the mid-seventeenth century, English poets shaped its meaning by imagining the moment when an individual human being's thought first flared into existence. The poetic attempt to represent the consciousness of birth enabled the birth of consciousness, that concept which is so central to how we understand ourselves today. To be sure, human beings have probably always pondered what philosophers now call "mindedness"—the fact that we are *minded* creatures, capable of perceiving, thinking, understanding, and generating meaning in ways that are uniquely human.[1] Philosophers, theologians, and poets from ancient India and Greece, the medieval Islamic world, and many other traditions have developed a wide variety of concepts through which mental life can be divided and organized: mind, soul, spirit, sensation, memory, imagination, thought, and experience, among others, proliferating across languages. Never completely adequate to the phenomena they invoke or conjure into existence, these concepts provide different ways of expressing and understanding mindedness. And the belief that human beings possess a mind, say, precipitates questions, truth claims, representational strategies, and social practices that are subtly different from those precipitated by the belief that human beings possess, say, a soul. Such concepts came into being at a particular moment within a particular culture, and each has changed over time as it was brought to bear on new circumstances and as it was translated into different languages, transposed into different discourses. Concepts are historical entities.[2] Such concepts as soul, mind, memory, and thought are ancient, but *consciousness*, perhaps the dominant concept powering modern questions about mindedness, is a historically recent conceptual achievement.

Readers familiar with how philosophy of mind or cognitive science has discussed consciousness in recent years might be primed to associate it with rationality, self-reflexivity, knowledge, and other putatively higher-order mental states. These were not considered integral to consciousness at its conceptual inception. Before it entered later histories of philosophy and literature or was deployed by psychology and the other new sciences that developed between seventeenth- and twenty-first-century theories of mind-edness, the concept of consciousness was simpler, unburdened by many of the meanings it has since come to possess. In the seventeenth century, the concept indicated mental presence. Far from an explicitly reflexive, ratio-nally structured property of mind, consciousness was understood to be a necessary feature of everything that might be said to *show up* or to *appear* to someone: from the outermost reaches of intellectual speculation, through the varied forms of memory, imagination, sensation, and dream, down to even the faintest phenomenal quiver. In seventeenth-century Europe, consciousness indexed whatever was present to mind. The concept emerged when, through an entangling of historical circumstances, the Latin *conscientia*, which had meant something like "moral conscience," began to index mental presence—the fact that self and world show up, that the various contents of mental life are present to us in and through the fact of their appearance.

By using consciousness to capture mental presence, seventeenth-century writers expressed firmly and clearly a division that has, in actual human experience, probably never been so clear cut. The concept enabled a new way of depicting and understanding human life; namely, dividing it in two along a breathtakingly simple line of demarcation so that a given percep-tion, state, act, or event is either conscious or not.[3] If it is conscious, then it is present to someone in a seemingly unmediated way. If it is not conscious, then it can be present only in a mediated way. To use an example favored by several of the writers we will encounter in this book, when a given person suffers from food poisoning, although she is immediately conscious of the pain and general unpleasantness that accompanies the condition, she will, according to this line of thought, never be immediately conscious of how the stomach itself perceives the poison; such bodily perceptions will only ever appear in a mediated way. This line between presence and absence has not gone uncontested. For well over a century, many philosophers, psycho-analysts, and critics have argued that the idea of mental presence is flawed, that the picture of mindedness afforded by and organized around conscious-ness is based on fictions that distort human self-understanding.[4]

Although mental presence may be an inadequate way of grasping mind-edness, it has nevertheless exerted a powerful influence. This book provides a new account of the conceptual emergence of consciousness in order to explain how a modern vision of mental presence first came to acquire a position of epistemological privilege.[5] Previous scholars have argued that the concept of consciousness was invented by philosophers.[6] Sometime between René Descartes's *Meditationes* (1641) and the second edition of John Locke's *Essay Concerning Human Understanding* (1694), or so the story goes, philosophers developed the concept of consciousness to advance epistemological theories about the role of the subjective observer in the scene of knowledge production.[7] *Coming To* revises this narrative by arguing that poetry—sensuous mimetic fiction enhanced by verse—played a major, even necessary role in the emergence of consciousness as a concept.[8]

The poets John Milton (1608–74) and Thomas Traherne (1636–74) clarified this concept by doing something that no previous European writer had attempted: they crafted recognizably human speakers capable of representing memories from the moment consciousness first arises. In Milton's *Paradise Lost* (1667, 1674), Adam and Eve are able to remember and describe what it was like to awaken newly created and suddenly mature: when she "first awaked," Eve later recalls, she existed in a state of "unexperienced thought."[9] Although Milton's Adam and Eve begin their remembered life without experience, they are nevertheless able to actualize all of their physical and mental capacities from the moment of creation. Unlike their descendants—who will be born, not created—Adam and Eve can recall their *prima naturae*, or "first impressions," a phrase used by ancient thinkers to invoke the initial but unremembered encounter between a new living being and its surrounding milieu.[10] Seizing on Milton's profoundly original treatment of human mindedness *ab initio*, Traherne appropriates this Edenic memory as his own. In a series of lyric poems and prose treatises, which I understand to be composed in response to *Paradise Lost*, Traherne draws on what he claims are his own memories in order to depict what it is like for an embryo to encounter itself and its world, the moment it first becomes minded, when "I in my Mothers Womb was born."[11] By constructing a verbal decorum adequate to the experience of absolute novelty, these poets responded to the ongoing seventeenth-century integration of consciousness and what Milton's Adam calls "human life" (8.250). Their poetry clarifies what was at stake in the conjunction of consciousness with prenatal and infant life for later thinkers, especially Locke, who, in a feat of philosophical imagination all but undiscussed by intellectual historians, grounds his epistemology in the first conscious impressions of embryonic minds.

Milton and Traherne summon a primal encounter with human nature in the absence of the multiple contingencies that shape each new life as it is normally lived: mother tongue, historical moment, cultural inheritance, family circumstances, socioeconomic standing, geographical position, and so on. Through poetic experimentation, they attempt to isolate what, in the most fundamental sense, it is like to be human. Milton and Traherne return to beginnings in order to develop accounts of human nature prior to the distortions of nurture and culture. Modeled on the experience of Adam, who was for many seventeenth-century writers the paradigm of what it should be like to be human, these poetic accounts bypass human limits by expressing what we cannot know with any certainty. Both poets project a representation of human nature onto the blank screen of origins, thereby weaving fiction into the fabric of the real. These fictions combat the profound helplessness of human infancy by actualizing adult capacities in the earliest stages of development. Milton and Traherne intertwine two of the great recurring obsessions that dominated the period of Renaissance and Reformation in Western Europe: first, the question of origins (rehearsed in debates about theology and political legitimacy, in arguments surrounding religious practice, textual studies, and natural philosophy); and, second, the question of experience (brought to prominence by such writers as Francesco Petrarch and Michel de Montaigne, and further elevated by the developing sciences and a proliferation of writing about the inner life in lyric poetry and devotional literature). To highlight this intertwining, I am calling the phenomenon imagined by Milton and Traherne *originary experience*, an experience of the earliest glimmerings of consciousness. It should go without saying that the memory of such an experience is, for most if not all human beings, impossible. When Locke and his followers drew out the implications of consciousness as a concept, they smuggled originary experience into the heart of modern epistemology. These philosophers deployed an idea hatched in the poetic imagination: to understand mindedness one must examine the birth of consciousness insofar as it intersects with the consciousness of birth.

NATALITY AND CONSCIOUSNESS

To illustrate why it is important to attend to conceptual history, we may turn to Hannah Arendt's conjoining of natality and consciousness. By assuming the stability of consciousness as a concept, Arendt misreads Saint Augustine and, at the same time, points to the role played by birth in the historical emergence of consciousness. By coining the term *natality* to name the fact that birth is, alongside death or mortality, "the most general condition of human existence," Arendt created an enduring puzzle.[12] A pivot away from what she saw as the connection between mortality and metaphysics, natality opened a new way of understanding politics through the category of action: since human beings are, she writes in *The Human Condition* (1958), "newcomers and beginners by virtue of birth," as adults they therefore "take initiative" and "are prompted into action."[13] Birth bestows on all who are born the capacity to begin, a capacity that may be actualized later in life through action—taking initiative, beginning something new.[14] The conceptual silhouette of what would become *natality* first emerges through Arendt's search for the "promise" of a "new beginning" in the wake of the Holocaust and other horrors. In *The Origins of Totalitarianism* (1951), she argues that birth guarantees the capacity for beginning because it gives rise to individuals uniquely able to act in new ways.[15] The possibility for historical and political novelty is grounded in the existential fact of birth and the uniqueness of each new human life. This is an attractive idea. But, as others have noted, Arendt's natality is riven by a paradox: the concept folds active beginnings into the passivity of birth: "Being-born is not something we *do*," as Rémi Brague puts it. "It happens to us."[16] It is, after all, difficult to see why the passivity of being born—an event that involves intensive labor and extreme motherly effort but nevertheless seems to *begin* passively, often in spite of the most carefully laid parental plans, according to natural promptings over which one has no control—should ground actively initiated beginnings.

In the years after the publication of *The Human Condition*, Arendt reoriented the meaning of natality in a revision to her dissertation that she undertook between 1958 and 1962.[17] The original dissertation, a study of love in the work of Saint Augustine that was completed in 1929, did not focus on birth or employ the term *natality*. When she returned to it, however, Arendt reexamined her concept in light of Augustine's theories of mind and in ways that illuminate the nexus of historical and conceptual concerns to which this book is dedicated: "The decisive fact determining man as a conscious, remembering being is birth or 'natality,' that is, the fact that we have entered the world through birth."[18] In *The Human Condition*, Arendt had looked forward in time, treating birth as a guarantor for the possibility of new beginnings. In the revisions to *Love and Saint Augustine*, she looks backward, drawing on Augustine's sense of the bond between memory and individual: *ego sum, qui memini, ego animus*, "I am, who remember, I the mind," he writes in the *Confessiones* (c. 397), identifying ego and mind with memory in a way that Arendt picks up when she describes Augustinian "memory as the seat of consciousness."[19] With this turn toward mind, Arendt excavates the grounds of political action with a phenomenologically oriented formulation: the uniqueness of each individual's memories guarantees the uniqueness that subtends action.

But a version of the earlier paradox remains. Just as the beginning of action does not spring in any straightforward way from the passive beginning of birth, so natality seems to exclude memory. Jean-Luc Marion uses the phrase "negative certainty" to gloss this idea: although "birth gives me to myself," it does not "appear to me or show itself to me," and the absence of remembered originary experience is nothing less than an existential "certainty."[20] Milton and Traherne attempt to glean positive knowledge about the human condition by imagining the contents of this experiential absence—a strategy that Arendt does not entertain. Why, then, does she claim that it is "birth or 'natality'" that determines "man as a conscious remembering being"? This question is especially pressing given that Augustine's *Confessiones* opens with the denial of any connection between "birth" and "remembering being." Augustine insists that he "cannot remember" his time in the womb, that he "know[s] not whence [he] came hither into this" life, and that he "cannot remember" how he drank milk or began to articulate his desires. Since he does not "remember having lived" this "period of [his] life," it does not properly belong to his account: "I do not wish to reckon this as part of the life that I live in this world" (6; 1.6.7), Augustine writes of infancy, "for it is lost in the darkness of my forgetfulness, and is on the same level as the life I lived in my mother's womb" (10; 1.7.12). When Traherne claims to remember how "I in my Mothers Womb was born" (6:4, 38), he deliberately flouts this aspect of Augustine's thought. Arendt, by contrast, wants to understand Augustine. Why, then, does she focus on how memory relates to natality?

The answer to this question lies in a double historical misalignment between Arendt and Augustine's horizons of expectation, one that reveals how philosophical inquiry can be frustrated when the conceptual historicity of consciousness is ignored.[21] On the one hand, as Arendt's analyses in fact reveal, Augustine focuses not on birth but on creation. Arendt claims that for Augustine the *differentia* distinguishing human beings from all other creatures is that "the former possesses consciousness, hence memory, and therefore can relate back to its own origin." To relate back to one's origin involves an "act of recollection" that is "identical to a return to the Creator": "The source as Creator antedates the created object and has always existed. Since the creature would be nothing without its source, its relation to its origin is the very first factor establishing it as a conscious entity."[22] It is this dependence of human creature on creator that prompts Arendt's claim that the "decisive fact determining man as a conscious, remembering being is birth or 'natality.'" As this slippage from creation to birth suggests, Arendt's commitments drive her to transfer ideas from Augustine's theological dis-

course of createdness into her own philosophical discourse of natality, a substitution that runs up against the absence of infant memory and, at the
same time, erases the presence of motherly effort and care.[23] If it makes
sense for Augustine to argue that recollection returns one to God, the connection Arendt draws between memory and birth is far more fraught.

This strain is exacerbated by a second historical misalignment that illuminates the central concerns of this book: Arendt treats memory in terms of
consciousness. In Augustine's *Confessiones*, *memoria* is coterminous with
mind: *animus sit etiam ipsa memoria*, "mind is the very memory itself"
(191; 10.14.21). *Memoria* recalls what can become present to mind, but it
also "retains forgetfulness [*oblivionem*]" (193; 10.16.24); it exceeds the parameters of what the mind can conjure into mental presence.[24] Since consciousness, understood in its most basic sense, separates what is conscious
from what is not, Augustine's *memoria* cannot be understood in light of this
concept. Although some scholars have aligned *memoria* with the unconscious, this too misses the mark, for the concept of consciousness did not
exist in late antiquity and the concept of the unconscious only comes into
being as a way of explaining what either exceeds or fails to enter consciousness.[25] This is not to say that something approximating what we call the unconscious did not exist or that Augustine was incapable of thinking about it;
concepts are, after all, never fully adequate to the phenomena they invoke or
bring into being. The point is rather that Augustine could not have deployed
a nonexistent concept. Augustine's *memoria* evades the distinction between
what is conscious and what is not, and this is why he can argue that the
human creature relates to origins through *memoria*. When Arendt claims
that Augustine sees memory "as the seat of consciousness," she projects a
modern view back onto his *memoria* and reads Augustine through a concept
that reorders mindedness in ways that invalidate his own arguments.[26] By
misaligning birth with creation and consciousness with *memoria*, Arendt
transforms a possible relation (of creature to creator through *memoria*) into
an impossible relation (of memory to birth through consciousness).

Arendt's pairing of natality and consciousness clarifies this book's topic:
the historical circumstances that gave rise to an intersection of birth, memory, and consciousness that has long been integral to modern theories of
mindedness but has nevertheless remained all but invisible to intellectual
historians and philosophers alike. Before the invention of consciousness,
mindedness was organized otherwise; it was understood in a way that produced a different set of affordances and limitations. If Augustine's conception of *memoria* surpasses the limits of consciousness, the same holds, as
Daniel Heller-Roazen has argued, for Aristotle's *koine aisthesis*, or common

sensation: the sense of one's own sensation indexes a phenomenal field that is distinct from consciousness.[27] It is not an exaggeration to remark that the same observation would apply to all theories of mindedness developed prior to the emergence of consciousness. The specificity of concepts is irreducible, and this specificity affects the warp and woof of human knowledge. The concept of consciousness changed understandings of mindedness in ways both far-reaching and subtle.

Previous scholars have traced aspects of how consciousness transformed philosophical inquiry. *Coming To* examines a key but overlooked change that consciousness brought to the intersection of natality and mindedness. Ancient and medieval thinkers were, of course, profoundly interested in infancy. Consider the words of Piso, student of Antiochus of Ascalon in Cicero's *De finibus*, who claims, "All the ancient philosophers . . . turn to cradles [*incunabula*] because it is in childhood that they think we can most easily recognize the will of nature [*naturae voluntatem cognoscere*]."[28] Many were likewise interested in prenatal life.[29] But up until the mid-seventeenth century, the official discourse of embryological inquiry was shaped by a powerful consensus more than two millennia old: embryos and fetuses do not so much as sense, let alone think consciously. Although fetuses possess the capacity to sense and to think, they do not, according to this view, actualize these capacities until after birth. I argue that it was not until the emergence of the concept of consciousness that philosophical or scientific accounts of mindedness needed to consider natality in any serious way. With the arrival of consciousness, natality unexpectedly became central to epistemological concerns, and this shift changed how fetal life was understood. Aspects of the current debates over reproductive rights—particularly the reliance of interest groups on a certain strain of scientific research into embryonic sensitivity—find their origin in the seventeenth-century introduction of actualized fetal sensation into natural philosophical discourse.[30]

This shift also changed the role played by the mother in philosophical, embryological, and poetic accounts of natality. Since, as we will see in chapter 4, embryologists often pitched the denial of fetal sensation against unnamed interlocutors who held that the fetus moved itself and could in fact sense, it is likely that this developing scientific discourse stood in opposition to the many mothers who, no doubt, felt the movements of their unborn children responding to external stimuli.[31] If the voices of these mothers were thus dismissed, the new seventeenth-century attention to embryonic mindedness altered the position of the mother in the scene of knowledge production in ways that continued to reinforce gender hierarchy. For centuries, official discourses had reduced the mother to an object: a body entangled in a patriarchal drive to gain a totalizing view of and power over women, a body observed from the outside by natural philosophers, physicians, and anatomists.[32] Mothers were understood to shape prenatal life both positively and dangerously.[33] The emergence of the concept of consciousness opened the possibility of fetal sensation to the many men who studied reproduction and fetal development. When embryonic consciousness became a topic of philosophical speculation, the mother's body was approached not from the outside but from within, through the imagined perspective of the fetus living within her womb. In this discourse, the mother remains a vessel, but has ceased to be an object of inquiry and has instead become an environing space, the background for originary experience, a milieu fit for the initial flickering light of a newly conscious prenatal mind.

To get a preliminary sense of how the emergence of consciousness opened embryonic mindedness to philosophical speculation and, at the same time, reduced the mother's body to a phenomenal backdrop, consider Descartes, who is often hailed as the founder of modern epistemology and is usually described as the first major thinker to position consciousness as the "mark of the mental," the defining feature of human mindedness.[34] In Descartes's view, human beings think only insofar as they are conscious of their thought. "By the term 'thought' [cogitationis], I understand everything which we are conscious [consciis] of as happening within us, insofar as we have consciousness [conscientia] of it," he writes in the Principia philosophiae (1644): "Hence thinking is to be identified not merely with understanding, willing, and imagining, but also with sensing."[35] If any thought is to count as thought, it must be accompanied by consciousness. Since thought is always structured by the mode through which it appears—understanding, will, imagination, memory, and sensation, among others—thought can be said to exist if and only if a given ego is conscious of a particular idea (a pleasure, a pain, an imagined entity, and so on).[36] This view of conscientia altered how mindedness was understood. What was for Plato, Aristotle, Plotinus, Augustine, Aquinas, and many others a vertical hierarchy stretching from lowly sensation up toward intellectual intuition became, in Descartes's hands, a horizontal plane: whatever appears exists as thought and is marked as such by the presence of consciousness. Descartes helped to transform an ancient and variegated mental landscape populated by features both exposed and hidden—recall Augustine's memoria, which includes the oblivion of forgetfulness within it—by wrenching all mental acts (at least those that count as such) up onto a plane of luminosity unified by the conscientia through which things appear. We are, Descartes argues, res cogitantes, thinking things whose essence is exhausted in the activity of thought. As such, one's mental life—even the most basic sensation—exists only insofar as it is conscious.

Descartes's interlocutors argued that this position entailed an untenable intersection of consciousness and natality.[37] Attacking the claim that consciousness is necessary for thought, the polymath Antoine Arnauld argues that Descartes "lays it down for certain that there can be nothing in him, in so far as he is a thinking thing, of which he is not conscious [*conscia*], but it seems to me that this is false. . . . [A]ll of us can surely see that there may be many things in the mind of which the mind is not conscious [*conscia*]. The mind of an infant in the mother's womb has the power of thought, but is not conscious [*conscia*] of it" (CSM 2:150; AT 7:214). Arnauld is sure that we are not conscious of everything within the mind. Fetuses are a privileged example because they are capable of thinking but have not yet actualized this capacity. They possess minds, but do not think. And they are certainly not conscious. Descartes rejects Arnauld's views about the nonexistence of fetal thought:

> As to the fact that there can be nothing in the mind, in so far as it is a thinking thing, of which it is not conscious [*conscia*], this seems to me self-evident. For there is nothing that we can understand to be in the mind, regarded in this way, that is not a thought or dependent on thought. If it were not a thought or dependent on thought it would not belong to the mind *qua* thinking thing; and we cannot have any thought of which we are not conscious [*conscii*] at the very moment when it is in us. In view of this I do not doubt that the mind begins to think as soon as it is infused in the body of an infant [*non dubito quin mens, statim atque infantis corpori infusa est*], and that it is immediately conscious of its thoughts [*simulque sibi suae cogitationis conscia sit*], even though it does not remember this afterwards because the impressions of these thoughts do not remain in the memory. (CSM 2:171–72; AT 7:246)

Since the mind is "infused" by God while the child remains in the womb, since the mind cannot help but think, and since all thought requires *conscientia*, fetuses must be conscious.

Descartes does not, however, hold that fetuses think with any complexity.[38] In his view, being born a baby is nothing less than a "philosophical disaster."[39] In the *Discours de la méthode* (1637), Descartes observes that we "were all children before being men." This unfortunate fact means that it is "virtually impossible that our judgments should be as unclouded and firm as they would have been if we had had the full use of our reason from the moment of our birth" (CSM 1:117). In the *Principia*, he goes further with a section entitled "The chief cause of error arises from the preconceived opinions of childhood." There, he argues that in "our early childhood the mind was so closely tied to the body that it had no leisure for any thoughts except those by means of which it had sensory awareness of what was happening to the body" (CSM 1:218). Descartes's fetus thinks, but only in a limited way. "It is true that the mind does not work so perfectly when it is in the body of an infant" (CSM 2:245), Descartes concedes in response to Pierre Gassendi's plea that he "bear in mind how obscure, meager and virtually non-existent your thought must have been during those early periods of your life" (CSM 2:184). If the soul is always thinking, and thought is necessarily conscious, then fetuses must be conscious. This much is true. But, Descartes admits, sensation is the only mode of thought accessible to embryonic minds. He clarifies his position in a 1641 letter to a respondent known as Hyperaspistes. Although Descartes holds that fetuses think, "this does not mean, however, that I believe that the mind of an infant meditates on metaphysics in its mother's womb; not at all." He continues:

> We know by experience [*experiamur*] that our minds are so closely joined to our bodies as to be almost always acted upon by them; and although when thriving in an adult and healthy body the mind enjoys some liberty to think other things than those presented by the senses, we know there is not the same liberty in those who are sick or asleep or very young; and the younger they are, the less liberty they have. So if one may conjecture on such an unexplored topic, it seems most reasonable to think that a mind newly united with an infant's body is wholly occupied in perceiving in a confused way or feeling the ideas of pain, pleasure, heat, cold and other similar ideas which arise from its union and, as it were, intermingling with the body. (CSM 3:189–90; AT 3:424)

Descartes maintains that fetuses perform the act of thought. Even if this thought exists only in the mode of sensation, it is nevertheless accompanied by the *conscientia* of "pain, pleasure, heat, cold, and other similar ideas" arising from its contact with the womb of a mother it does not yet know exists. Descartes's conception of consciousness forced him to account for prenatal mindedness. But the philosopher can say next to nothing about this "unexplored topic." It is as if consciousness requires an account of natality that philosophy is unable to provide.

OF CONCEPTS AND POETS

When Descartes positioned *conscientia* as the defining feature of all thought, he used an old Latin word in a new way. In a seventeenth-century semantic shift in which Descartes played an important role, *conscientia* came to signify a form of "self-referential non-evaluative knowledge."[40] By *nonevaluative*, scholars mean a mode of knowing that apprehends all phenomena regardless of moral status. Since one can possess consciousness of anything at all—a tree, a mathematical problem, the idea of a unicorn, a memory of something that happened years ago, a temptation, a virtuous action—it is a nonevaluative field insofar as it includes any form of appearance whatsoever. By using *conscientia* in this way, Descartes participated in an important semantic transition. Used as a translation of the Greek *syneidesis* (the state of possessing knowledge, often together with others), in classical Latin *conscientia* possessed evaluative connotations: knowledge that one has done something well or ill.[41] For instance, in *Pro Cluentio*, Cicero claims that "*conscientia* is God's gift to us all and cannot be wrested from us, and if it [*conscientia*] testifies throughout our lives to good intentions and good deeds, those lives will be wholly fearless and entirely virtuous."[42] In *De senectute*, Cicero reinforces this evaluative sense by stating, "It is most delightful to have the *conscientia* of a life well spent and the memory of many deeds worthily performed."[43] Similarly, Seneca often writes of a *bona conscientia* and *mala conscientia* in much the same way that English speakers talk about a good or bad conscience.[44] *Conscientia* was important to medieval theories of mind and natural law, but in the hands of such thinkers as Bonaventure and Aquinas the term remained evaluative, about determining the actions proper to one's knowledge.[45] When Descartes used *conscientia* in a nonevaluative way, he broke with a long tradition.

In French, this new, nonevaluative sense of *conscientia* was translated as *conscience*.[46] Consider the *Traité de l'esprit de l'homme* (1667), in which the physician Louis de La Forge claims that the "essence of thought consists in that *conscience* and that perception that the mind has of all that passes in it" and that thought should be defined as "that perception, *conscience*, or internal knowledge that each of us feels immediately by himself when he perceives what he does or what passes in him."[47] While French still uses *conscience* in both evaluative and nonevaluative ways, seventeenth-century English underwent what C. S. Lewis calls "a notable example of desynonymisation" in which *conscience* continued to perform its evaluative function, and *consciousness* became aligned with nonevaluative meanings.[48] In English, *consciousness* was first used as a synonym for *conscience*—what, in 1596, the theologian William Perkins defines as the "natural power, faculty, or created quality" used to "judge of the goodness or badness of things or actions done."[49] Debuting in 1605, the word *consciousness* was used infrequently until the 1650s, when its usage began to pick up before taking off toward the end of the century.[50] Early uses were mostly evaluative, with writers invoking the "consciousness" of "guilt" or "sin" or "inability," drawing on Calvin's sense in the *Institutio* that everyone is "stung by the *conscientia* of his own unhappiness."[51] Some writers grappled with how *consciousness* related to *conscience*. In *True Happiness* (1633), the Scottish preacher William Struther claims that each moral choice is "accompanied with a conscience of itself; for our conscience goeth along all this work, and maketh us conscious, both of our *seeking* and our *finding*: God hath joined it to the reasonable soul, as a witnesse of all actions, yea even the least motion of our affections: the conscience making us sensible of our own consciousnesse'."[52] Here *conscience* is a witness to what is revealed through "our own consciousnesse." Similarly, the lectures on *Humane Conscience* (1660) delivered in 1647 by Robert Sanderson, Bishop of Lincoln, translate Saint Bernard's aphorism *Conscientia quasi cordis scientia* as "The Conscience is the hearts consciousness."[53] If Sanderson holds that *conscientia* is best translated as *conscience*, he renders *scientia* (knowledge) as *consciousness*, thereby placing the new term in a nonevaluative position.

If, in its earliest usages, *consciousness* was a synonym for *conscience*, the reverse also held true: *conscience* was used in nonevaluative ways. Consider the *Epistles* (1608) of Joseph Hall, bishop of Exeter, in which the "fruit of study" is equated with the "conscience of knowledge," which seems to mean the awareness of knowledge.[54] The same idiom obtained in philosophy. In the first English translation of Descartes's *Meditationes* (1680), William Molyneux rendered Descartes's *conscientia* as *conscience*. Replying to Hobbes's attack on the term *res cogitans*, Descartes writes (in Molyneux's translation): "There are other Acts, which we call *cogitative* or *thinking*, as *understanding, will, imagination, sense,* &c. All which agree under the common notion of *thought, perception,* or *Conscience* [*qui omnes sub ratione communi cogitationis, sive perceptionis, sive conscientiae, conveniunt*]; And the *substance* wherein they are, we say, is a *thinking thing,* or *mind.*"[55] All acts of thought, from sensation through to understanding, can, Molyneux asserts, be understood under the rubric of a nonevaluative "*Conscience.*" Even toward the end of the century, *conscience* was still used in an evaluative, moral sense as well as in the nonevaluative sense of awareness in general.

Although nonevaluative uses of *consciousness* were rare in the first half of the seventeenth century, they were common in later decades; nonevaluative

uses outstripped evaluative uses in the 1670s.[56] Although this nonevaluative
sense sometimes appeared in relation to *conscience*, it was also used to translate ancient Greek. In his *History of Philosophy* (1656), Thomas Stanley uses
consciousness to translate Diogenes Laertius's *syneidesis*: "The first appetite
of a living creature is to preserve it self, this being from the beginning proper
to it by nature, as Chrysippus in his first Book of Ends, who affirmes that
the care of our selves, and consciousness thereof, is the first property of all
living Creatures."[57] In the *True Intellectual System of the Universe* (1678),
Ralph Cudworth uses *consciousness* to translate Plotinus's *synaisthesis* (the
sensation of one's affections, the state of being aware of one's acts). For Cudworth, "consciousness," which is "essential to cogitation," is founded on
"that duplication, that is included in the Nature of *synaisthesis*, 'con-sense
and consciousness,' which makes a being to be present with it self."[58] When,
a decade later, Locke defined consciousness as "what passes within a Man's
own mind" and used it to explain personal identity ("whatever has the consciousness of present and past Actions, is the same Person to whom they both
belong"), his views powered controversies in which nonevaluative uses of
consciousness increased exponentially.[59] As we will see in chapter 5, Locke
drew on many resources for thinking through the nonevaluative nature of
consciousness, including Descartes and Cudworth. He also relied on a semantic shift that was decades in the making.

In England, the word *consciousness* was not used in a broadly Cartesian
sense—as a self-referential property accompanying all thought—until late
in the 1670s. Such usage did not become common until the 1690s. But even
if English writers working in the first half of the century did not use the
word *consciousness* in this way, they nevertheless used the *concept* that
corresponds to the meaning this word came to possess. The nonevaluative
meaning of *consciousness* came into being as a way of naming changes that
had taken place in the concept of *thought*; consciousness named a feature
of thought that many had come to see as necessary. The word solidified and
clarified a new concept that parsed how thought was organized and thereby
helped to make sense of mindedness as such. When, in *An Essay upon Reason* (1694), the philosopher Richard Burthogge draws on Descartes in claiming that "Cogitation," or thought, "is conscious Affection," that "Conscious
Affection, is Affection with Consciousness of that Affection," and that
"Consciousness [is] nothing but a Sense of Alteration made by the Mind,
by some new Affection of it, that is, by a new Thought," the addition of
the term *consciousness* does not add much to earlier definitions of thought
such as that advanced in Thomas Wilson's *Christian Dictionary* (1612):
"Thought"—a category that includes passion, reasoning, and will—is noth-

ing more than "the least motion and stirring of our minde."[60] Descartes's nonevaluative use of *consciousness* made legible and intelligible shifts in the meaning of *thought* that had already taken place. This is why Descartes's early reception in England from the 1640s to the 1670s involved discussions of *thought* and not one mention of *consciousness*. As I show throughout this book, the concept of consciousness emerged in England before the semantics of the word were fully ironed out to express this concept.[61]

By *concept*, I mean something distinct from a word.[62] I mean a shared cultural product that is visible in the interstices between idea and word.[63] Drawing on Peter de Bolla's sense that concepts are collectively generated ways of thinking that come with a "grammar and syntax that situates them in a network of linked concepts," this book focuses on the scene of natality as an ideational space in which such a "network" develops, showing how *thought, ego, experience,* and *self* intertwine before being pulled into the "orbital drag" of *consciousness.*[64] To frame this in the terms supplied by Arnold Davidson, the emergence of consciousness as a nonevaluative concept entailed the advent of a new "style of reasoning," a new way of linking terms and fitting them together. If *conscientia* and its vernacular cognates were once joined with such evaluative terms as *good, bad, virtue, vice,* and so on, in seventeenth-century Europe this conceptual arrangement remained in place, but *conscientia* and its vernacular cognates also began to "fit together" with such nonevaluative terms as *thought, ego, experience, self,* and so on. This new style of reasoning enabled a "conceptual space" in which different kinds of statements—utterances subject to truth or falsity—were stabilized and acquired meaning, thereby enabling different social practices and mimetic representations.[65] Although Cicero and Descartes use the same word (*conscientia*), this "lexical continuity hides," as Davidson would put it, "conceptual discontinuity."[66] This is why some of the "most remarkable moments in the history of thought are precisely those in which an old phrase or word is stabilized in a new way, resulting in the production of a new set of concepts and a new realm of statements."[67] By the end of the seventeenth century, *consciousness* was newly stabilized at the center of a network of interlinked terms that enabled human life to be articulated in novel ways—including a new relationship between mindedness and natality that prompted Milton and Traherne's depictions of originary experience.

While in 1694 it was not unusual to read the claim that "the peculiar excellency of Man" over other animals is the extent to which the human "Sense of Knowledge include[s] an immediate Consciousness of Perceptions," such turns of phrase were almost nonexistent prior to the 1670s.[68]

Indeed, as the century came to a close, it became increasingly common to claim that the *differentia* separating human beings from other creatures was a special, expansive form of consciousness. Descartes held that the distinction between human mindedness and animal existence was best articulated as a difference of kind. By contrast, most thinkers—including Cudworth and Locke—held that this distinction was one of degree: when compared with other animals, human beings were simply conscious of more things in different ways. After all, consciousness indexed nothing other than minimal mental presence; surely animals were also capable of, say, sensing warmth in a way that made it present to them. These differences aside, however, all thinkers focused on the *perspectival* nature of consciousness, and many argued that consciousness is, in Locke's words, whatever "happens within" and is apparent to a given "mind." Put another way, the concept came to be grounded in the perspectives of particular beings living singular lives. Unlike, say, *mind, soul, self*, or *subject*, it is not easy to abstract *consciousness* from the conditions of life as it is lived; it exists only when a thought is actualized, only insofar as something shows up for someone. Consciousness possesses a necessary quality of "mineness," a perspective, however minimal, that opens onto the appearance of a given phenomenon.[69] Whatever is conscious appears to and for someone or something, a quality captured in Thomas Nagel's claim that consciousness marks "what it is like" for a given being to exist.[70] The meaning of the concept of consciousness is exhausted in and through the structure of what appears to or within particular individuals. To adopt a general formula, *consciousness indexes the appearance of the various somethings that show up for someone.*

In the web of seventeenth-century discourse, poetry was uniquely positioned to address the extreme perspectival quality of consciousness as a nonevaluative concept. After all, consciousness seems to be a concept fit for mimesis, the practice or art—often translated as *imitation* but best understood as *representation*—famously criticized by Plato for its allegiance to the finite particular over the universal idea.[71] As Guido Mazzoni argues, the cultures indebted to Greek antiquity are characterized by a split between two discursive regimes through which "legitimate knowledge" might emerge: "imitation versus abstract thought, mimesis versus concept."[72] Mimesis "inhabits the realm of particularities," individual lives with their biographical trajectories, states of mind, pleasures, pains, and circumstances strung along between beginning and end: *this* particular being, finite and mutable, in all of its idiosyncrasy and uniqueness.[73] Concepts, on the other hand, are ways of thinking that aspire to universality and address the general. If poetry, novels, and other literary forms tend toward mimesis (a representation of *this* person or *this* thought), philosophy and the natural, social, and human sciences tend toward concepts (an examination of *person* or *thought*). Consciousness indexes the appearance of the various somethings that show up for someone. This means that even though, *qua* concept, it exists in the abstract space of universals examined by philosophy, it is most at home on the horizon of particularity, in the world of singular things, unique individuals, fleeting thoughts, and temporally situated events that poetry and various forms of narrative put into words.

Drawing out the implications of this intuition, Milton and Traherne weld mimesis to concept.[74] By returning to beginnings and imagining an originary experience of human nature without nurture, these poets conjure scenarios in which mimetic representation captures the concept of consciousness. When Milton's Adam or Eve describe what it was like to awaken for the first time, or when Traherne recounts his experiences in the womb, these poets describe a moment in human life when the particularity of experience becomes adequate to the generality of a concept. Since it is prior to cultural and familial differentiation, prenatal life is perhaps as close as fallen human beings can come to the shared sameness of our species being. Even more radically, the unfallen Adam and Eve live as human beings in whom the category of humanity is exhausted.[75]

Comparing the "universal archetype of man" presented in Milton's *De idea Platonica* (c. 1628) with Adam of *Paradise Lost*, Gordon Teskey claims that the "first is an abstract universal, disengaged from the world," while the second is a "finite universal," a "universal ideal [that] is not merely abstract but rather exists by subsuming the finite and the factual."[76] Adam and Eve embody this universal real and thereby radicalize a distinction made famous in Aristotle's *Poetics* and elaborated by such Renaissance theorists as Lodovico Castelvetro, Torquato Tasso, and Sir Philip Sidney: if history "describes the thing that has been" and poetry "a kind of thing that might be," then "poetry is something more philosophic and of graver import than history, since its statements are of the nature rather of universals, whereas those of history are of singulars."[77] Focusing on a period prior to history and its endless series of contingent "singulars," the "statements" of *Paradise Lost* are "of the nature of universals" in a sense deeper than Aristotle intended: Milton's poem represents the first-person existence of "finite universals," *the experience of human nature itself*.[78] Traherne recognized Milton's achievement and widened its scope, using poetic fiction to capture the universal experience of each particular human being prior to his or her departure from the womb and entry into the historical world. Whereas Milton aims to bring readers back to the phylogenetic origins of experience in an unfallen Paradise, Traherne attempts to capture the ontogenetic origins of experience in embryonic thought.

Milton and Traherne use the mimetic power of poetry to depict consciousness as a finite universal form. They work through the implications of a new and inchoate concept by situating it on the horizon of particularity proper to mimesis. To be sure, in and of itself, this accomplishment is not especially novel. From antiquity onward, concepts had entered regimes of mimetic representation through the procedures of allegory, personification, the *exemplum*, or the Theophrastian character. To take an example that Milton and Traherne knew well, in the *Faerie Queene* (1590, 1596), Edmund Spenser deploys this literary mode by subsuming concepts within characters, at one point baring the architecture of his allegory when the jealous Malbecco transforms into a personification of the concept of jealousy: "through priuy griefe, and horrour vaine, / [Malbecco] Is woxen so deform'd that he has quight / Forgot he was a man, and *Gelosy* is hight."[79] Milton and Traherne similarly capture the concept of consciousness in the nets of mimesis, but, as we will see, they eschew reliance on types or personifications. Adam, Eve, and Traherne's authorial persona are cast not as personifications or *exempla* but as real, finite, unique human beings. Milton and Traherne use the fictions of poetry to draw the concept of consciousness into the contours of the imagined real, where its affordances and limitations as a mode of organizing human mindedness can be tested. Poetry provided a discursive space in which a new way of thinking about thinking could be thought through.

FICTION, MIMESIS, AND THE WORLD REVEALED

What do I mean by *poetry*? If, as I argue in *Coming To*, poetry was central to the emergence of consciousness as a concept, and if the story I tell in this book differs from more familiar accounts about the discovery of consciousness in philosophy, how do I understand the distinction between poetry and philosophy? This distinction does not lie in the ostensibly easy gap separating prose from verse, for, as Aristotle remarks in the *Poetics*, it is a mistake to associate poetry with verse: "Homer and Empedocles," he claims, "have really nothing in common apart from their metre; so that, if the one is to be called a poet, the other should be termed a natural philosopher rather than a poet" (2:2316; 1447b). Aristotle's rejection of this distinction was rearticulated in the Renaissance, with such writers as Sidney arguing in the *Defence of Poesy* (1595) that Xenophon and Heliodorus had composed "heroical poem[s]" despite the fact that both "wrote in prose." Milton and Traherne would have agreed: "it is not riming and versing that makes a poet."[80]

Although the equation between poetry and fiction was common—Sidney, for instance, argues that since the poet "nothing affirms," the reader of "poesy [is] looking but for fiction"[81]—it is equally true that fiction as such cannot be the *differentia* separating poetry from philosophy. After all, from Plato's myths to the zombies and brains in vats of contemporary thought experiments, fictions regularly animate philosophical inquiry. Drawing out the implications of what was sometimes seen as the equation between fiction and poetry, early modern writers and contemporary critics have both understood the philosophical use of fiction to be fundamentally poetic. Taking inspiration from the sixteenth-century recovery and dissemination of Aristotle's *Poetics* and the Greek understanding of *poiesis* as a process of making, Sidney elaborates a theory of poetry *as* fiction, a thing made in either prose or verse. The best poets, Sidney argues, imitate not what nature has produced—"nothing of what is, hath been, or shall be"—but rather "range, only reined with learned discretion, into the divine consideration of what may be and should be."[82] Poetry *qua* fiction is an activity undertaken by poets and also, at times, by philosophers. Following Sidney's lead, a number of scholars have brilliantly explored how, in seventeenth-century Europe, the category of poetry (understood to be coterminous with fiction) was central to many of the historical developments associated with early modernity. Victoria Kahn has argued for the importance of the early modern elaboration on the idea that human politics is a thing made, a form of poetically inspired organization articulated both by philosophers like Thomas Hobbes and poets like Milton.[83] Frédérique Aït-Touati has claimed that the seventeenth-century sciences were powered poetically, through a revolution in the use of fictions at play in the natural philosophy of, say, Johannes Kepler and the narrative fiction of, say, Margaret Cavendish.[84] Ayesha Ramachandran has argued for poetry as a mode of fiction-making that was used with equal aplomb in poems like Milton's *Paradise Lost* and philosophical treatises like Descartes's *Le monde* (1633).[85] Poets and philosophers alike deployed the powers of poetry *qua* fiction, and the critics who see poetry in this way have helped to make visible a power of human making that inspired many early modern thinkers.[86] But although the relationship between poetry and fiction was unquestionably important, it was not, I argue, an isomorphic relation. In this book, I attend to the specificity of poetry as a discourse that overlaps with but is not exhausted by fiction.[87] In crafting visions of originary experience, Milton and Traherne drew on poetry not only as a way of producing fictions. They also deployed two qualities related to but importantly distinct from fiction-making: first, poetry's mimetic dedication to particular beings, lives, thoughts, and speech acts; and second, poetry's role as a vehicle for praise and blame. In making this argument, I aim not to devalue poetry by shrinking its purchase but to show how its cultural importance rested on its specificity.

Sidney was certainly invested in poetry as fiction, but he defines it as "an art of imitation, for so Aristotle termeth it in the word *mimesis*, that is to say a representing, counterfeiting, or figuring forth."[88] As Stephen Halliwell has argued, from Plato onward, mimesis could be understood to operate in a "world-reflecting" mode (think of realism in all of its forms) or in a "world-simulating" mode (think of, say, utopian literature).[89] But whether it reflects or simulates a world, mimesis always, as I argued above, exists on the horizon of particularity: individual lives, finite objects, temporally located events.[90] Put otherwise, mimesis aims to represent a fictionally ordered, probable phenomenal world. For Aristotle, poetry exists between the contingent particularities of history and the abstracted universals of philosophy, offering a representation of "fictive particularities" that, in Halliwell's words, "work together, through the requisite degree of causal and explanatory unity" in order to "make exceptionally intelligible patterns of human experience."[91] In a Renaissance context, the mimesis of phenomenal worlds could center on the world of actions and speech that characterizes epic from Tasso through Milton, tragedy from Shakespeare to Calderón, romance from Ariosto through Spenser, and prose narrative fiction from Boccaccio through Aphra Behn. It could also be the world of thoughts, desires, memories, and intentions articulated in verse from the troubadours, through Petrarch, and on to Marvell, or the transfer of this expressive form into narrative prose by such writers as Madame de La Fayette.

Of course, this is a loose set of oppositions.[92] For Renaissance and early modern poets, all poetic forms provided different affordances for articulating the relationship between mindedness and the phenomenal world. When Sidney claims that the "golden" world of the poets exceeds the world maintained by nature, he argues that poets, working in verse or prose, meld fiction with mimesis: "Nature never set forth the earth in so rich tapestry as diverse poets have done," he writes, "neither with so pleasant rivers, fruitful trees, sweet-smelling flowers, nor whatsoever else may make the too-much-loved earth more lovely: her world is brazen, the poets only deliver a golden."[93] If this world is fictional insofar as it is "more lovely" than the world in which the poet lives—compare Milton's Eden with Restoration London, for example—it is nevertheless a world of particularities, one situated on the horizon of mimesis, in the realm of phenomenal appearances. In other words, poetry represents a world made available through revelation—space- and time-bound particulars revealed in specific contexts by the senses, by memory, by the imagination, or by the influence of some higher power, whether the muse or God himself.

This is part of what Milton means when, in *Of Education* (1644), he claims that the language of poetry is "simple, sensuous, and passionate."[94] In a proposed curriculum that includes grammar, agriculture, mathematics, natural philosophy, ethical philosophy, politics, church history, logic, and rhetoric, poetry is the final discipline because, Milton argues, poetry returns one to the world. This argument is predicated on the basic assumption— shared, as we will see, by Aristotelians, Socinians, and empiricists alike— that human "understanding cannot in this body found it selfe but on sensible things, nor arrive so cleerly to the knowledge of God and things invisible, as by orderly conning over the visible and inferior creature."[95] Education brings students up from the "sensible" and the "inferior" toward the "invisible." Poetry is the final and best discipline because it uses the resources of mimesis to bring one back to the world with a heightened understanding derived from the arduous effort of lifting oneself up from the sensible world toward the ideal. In Balachandra Rajan's words, Milton sees poetry as "superior" because "its intelligence shines into the senses" and because "its transforming intelligence permeates even the frontiers of reality."[96]

Poetry reveals the world as it is lived by particular beings, in all of its "simple, sensuous, and passionate" density, but it also *evaluates* this revealed world by offering praise and dispensing blame. Following a long history of medieval and Renaissance criticism, Milton held that poets are supposed to represent what is worthy of praise or blame and celebrate God's works so as to "set the affections" of their readers "in right tune."[97] As we will see in chapters 1 and 2, this is what Milton attempted to do in *Paradise Lost*, a poem that, among other things, reveals a teeming phenomenal world and expresses the sensuous truth of human life as organized by and through the new concept of consciousness. Although Milton's epic is traditional in its praise of God and creation, it is daring in how it praises human thought by celebrating the joyous affect that structures Adam's and Eve's originary experiences. Both of these stories express wonder at the brute fact of existence: Eve awakes "much wondering where / And what I was" (4.451–52), and Adam turns his "wondering eyes" skyward (8.257). This praise of conscious life radicalizes how previous poetic theory had understood the place of thought in poetry. Whereas, in the *Poetics*, Aristotle classified "thought" as one of the "formative elements" in tragedy (2:2320; 1450a), Castelvetro and Tasso also considered it central to the epic form.[98] By thought, Aristotle means the "power of saying whatever can be said" (2:2321; 1450b). In the *Discourses on the Heroic Poem* (1594), Tasso expands this point by

defining thought as the "qualitative component of poetry" able to "demonstrate, to solve, [and] to arouse emotions" by "force of speech, which is the
index of this power of mind [that is, thought]."[99] When, in *Paradise Lost*,
Eve informs Adam about what, in her initial moments of life, it was like
to encounter the world with "unexperienced thought" (4.457), her speech
serves as what Tasso would call an "index" of Eve's thought and, at the
same time, describes the structures of thought at the moment when human
mindedness first appeared. Tasso claims that poets compose epics "with
the purpose of moving the mind to wonder," and Milton accomplishes this
end by directing the mind back to itself so that it can "wonder" at its own
existence.[100] A writer who dedicated multiple lyrics to wonder and in praise
of thought, Traherne radicalizes Milton's depiction of originary experience
by turning poetry into a form of thought that praises the act of thinking.
Traherne celebrates mindedness by describing the beginnings and epigenetic development of prenatal and infant thought.

Whereas poets tend to deploy mimetic fictions in order to praise or blame
particular beings, deeds, or thoughts that exist in the revealed, phenomenal
world, philosophers, by contrast, tend to deploy nonmimetic or minimally
mimetic fictions to open up unfamiliar abstract corners in the space of reason.[101] For example, although the world of contract theory is a thoroughly
fictional world, it does not fully exist on the horizon of mimesis. When, in
De cive (1642), Hobbes asks readers to "consider men as if but even now
sprung out of the earth, and suddenly, like mushrooms, come to full maturity, without all kind of engagement with each other [*consideremusque ho-
mines tanquam si essent iamiam subito e terra (fungorum more) exorti &
adulti, sine omni unius ad alterum obligatione*]," he produces a fiction that
opens up the space of reason so that such concepts as dominion and consent
can be clarified.[102] However, conceptually illuminating as these fictional
mushroom men might be, they exist as abstractions. They are not represented as particular beings living in a world of singular things, and they are
certainly not developed in order to articulate praise or blame. The scope of
fiction exceeds that of poetry, for whereas fictions in general may be capable
of complementing concepts in the space of reason, the fictions of poetry are
situated in a revealed world, a world represented through mimesis. Poets
and philosophers deploy fiction to achieve different ends.

Consider a limit case, a famous thought experiment that, like the poetry of Milton and Traherne, evokes originary experience. Avicenna's treatise on the soul, written around 1027 and translated into Latin as *Liber de
anima* between 1150 and 1160, includes a startling invitation.[103] The reader
is asked to "suppose" [*putare*] that someone was "created all at once and in

a perfect state" [*subito creatus esset et perfectus*].[104] What would appear to someone so fashioned? The answer is complicated, since Avicenna's Flying Man, as he is known, enters the world in a state of sensory deprivation: he cannot see, he is created hanging in a void so that not even the air touches his body, and his limbs are separated so that they cannot so much as brush each other. Bereft of all sensory contact, Avicenna's Flying Man cannot "affirm any outer organs, such as his limbs [*membrorum*], nor anything inside, such as his inner organs, neither the heart, nor the brain, nor any of the things existing outside." He can, however, "affirm the existence of his own essence" [*affirmat esse suae essentiae*], which is nothing less than a soul inherently separate from the body: "The essence that he affirms to exist is specific to him because it is he himself; [it is] beyond his body and his limbs, which he does not affirm" [*essentia quam affirmat esse est propria illi, eo quod illa est ipsemet, et est praeter corpus eius et membra eius quae non affirmat*].[105] Avicenna places his Flying Man in a fictional void so as to demonstrate that neither the whole body nor such parts as limbs are included in his essence. Since even without sensation the Flying Man would still be able to "affirm the existence of his essence," that essence cannot be bodily. Avicenna attempts to prove the independence of soul from body by weaving the powers of fiction into the space of reason, which he literalizes as a void of abstraction.[106]

Descartes followed Avicenna, using fictions of isolation to arrive at the conclusion that the ego is "entirely distinct from the body" (CSM 1:127). Although scholars have only recently begun to link Descartes and Avicenna, the philosopher Kenelm Digby made the connection in 1644, three years after the publication of the *Meditationes*:[107] "Avicenna in his booke *de Anima & Almahad*, and Monsieur des Cartes in his Methode, do presse upon the same occasion"; namely, that "when all body is abstracted in us, there still remaineth a *substance*, a *thinker*, an *Ego*, an *I*, that in it selfe is no whitt diminished, by being . . . stripped out of the case it was enclosed in."[108] By recognizing Descartes's appropriation of Avicenna, Digby flags the extent to which both philosophers defamiliarize human thought by using fictions to abstract that thought from the conditions of life as it is lived. Although Descartes's use of fictions was dismissed by contemporaries like Christiaan Huygens—"Mr. Descartes has found a way to have his conjectures and fictions taken for truths"—these fictions were necessary both to his physics and to his epistemology.[109]

In the *Discours*, Descartes is explicit about the extent to which fictions enable his discovery of the necessary relationship between thought and existence: "I resolved to pretend [*feindre*] that all the things that had ever entered my mind were no more true than the illusions of my dreams. But immediately I noticed that while I was trying thus to think everything false, it was necessary that I, who was thinking this, was something" (CSM 1:127; AT 6:32). By "pretend[ing]" that his relationship with the world and with other human beings is nothing but an illusion, Descartes arrives at certain truth: *je pense, donc je suis*. As Digby saw, the complete bracketing of the world undertaken by Avicenna illuminates the solitude in which Descartes begins his philosophical project: "Finding no conversation to divert me and fortunately having no cares or passions to trouble me, I stayed all day shut up alone in a stove-heated room, where I was completely free to converse with myself about my own thoughts" (CSM 1:116). Descartes's discovery that his ego is distinct from his body parallels that made by Avicenna both in content and by virtue of the fact that it emerges in complete solitude, cut off from the world, with its "cares or passions." Although Descartes does not follow Avicenna into the void, like many other philosophers, he employs fictions to enter the space of reason by bracketing the background of self-world relations against and within which human thought occurs.

Whereas Avicenna's and Descartes's philosophies employ fiction to illuminate concepts (mind, self, ego) in the space of reason, Milton's and Traherne's poems similarly isolate human thought, but do so by situating newly conscious life on the horizon of mimesis, by employing the full resources of poetic language to express the vibrant richness and idiosyncratic particularity of life in the revealed world. Although, as we have seen, verse is not what separates poetry from other forms of discourse, it nevertheless remains integral to Milton and Traherne's efforts. Both poets draw on the affordances of verse to loosen syntax, elevate diction, and generate meaning through rhyme, meter, and the play between syntax and line break. My claim is not that verse is *necessary* for the depiction of originary experience. After all, Mary Shelley transfers Adam's verse account of awakening in *Paradise Lost*—"For man to tell how human life began / Is hard" (8.250–51)—into the prose narrative of the newly conscious creature in *Frankenstein* (1818): "It is with considerable difficulty that I remember the original era of my being: all events of that period appear confused and indistinct. A strange multiplicity of sensations seized me, and I saw, felt, heard, and smelt at the same time; and it was, indeed, a long time before I learned to distinguish between the operations of my various senses."[110] But in late seventeenth-century England, prose fiction was not yet adequate to the birth of consciousness. Prior to the temporal innovations brought about by Samuel Richardson's technique of writing to the moment, and prior to the eighteenth-century work of Daniel Defoe and Henry Fielding, among others, English prose was ill-equipped to produce a first-person account capable of capturing what it was like to emerge into existence. English verse, by contrast, was more than ready for such a task, with many centuries of poetic experimentation in narrative structure and the intricacies of first-person expression on which to draw. One can debate the relative merits of William Wordsworth's versified "spots of time" in the *Prelude* or his treatment of infancy in "Ode: Intimations of Immortality" and Shelley's contemporary depiction of originary experience in *Franken-stein*, but such a comparison is impossible in seventeenth-century England.

Although Locke wrote in prose and was, in the *Essay*, notoriously opposed both to the fictions produced by the imagination (he defines "*Fantastical or Chimerical*" ideas as those that have "no Foundation in Nature, nor have any Conformity with that reality of Being" [372, 2.30.1]) and to figurative language itself (which is, he claims, "an imperfection or abuse" of language, a "perfect cheat" [508, 3.10.34]), I argue that his repeated exploration of originary experience in the *Essay* and in the *Two Treatises* (1689) in fact appropriates the strategies of poetry and tilts his philosophy toward the discursive realm of the poets. Part of Locke's rejection of Cartesian speculation involves his recognition that consciousness—the various somethings that appear to someone—is best articulated not in the space of reason but through an examination of the world as it is revealed. As we will see in chapter 5, Locke's analysis of consciousness pulls philosophy toward mimesis by harnessing the power of poetic thinking.[111] To be sure, Locke is not a poet. He uses fiction and the techniques of mimesis in the service of abstraction, and his focus remains on concepts rather than particulars: *person* as opposed to *this* person. Yet, as his examinations of originary experience reveal, Locke moves philosophy away from the space of reason and toward the world revealed by developing a mode of inquiry best described as philosophical *poiesis*.

WHAT THIS BOOK THINKS IT IS DOING

Coming To tells the story of how consciousness came to be necessarily, however improbably, intertwined with natality. It does so by analyzing and contextualizing the writings of one of England's most famous poets (Milton), the work of an understudied poet and theologian the bulk of whose writings were not discovered until centuries after his death (Traherne), and the argumentation of one of England's most well-known philosophers (Locke). This is an unusual group. It is my hope that by the end of this book, what might seem to be an unnatural adjacency will come to seem not only sensible but inevitable, for each of these figures responded to the heightened importance accorded the first-person perspective by thinking about the origins of thought. For all of their admittedly vast differences, Milton, Traherne, and Locke all share a profound interest in how human thought began. Taken together, they shed new light on the emergence of the concept of consciousness by revealing how this concept was born alongside an important and unnoticed shift in the meaning of human natality.

Paradise Lost was first printed in 1667, around the time Traherne began his great burst of writing that generated hundreds of poems and nearly a dozen treatises. Milton and Traherne were both survivors of the Civil War and the Interregnum, and they both responded to the Restoration by rethinking the meaning of Paradise. But these poets have not been studied together, perhaps because their careers were remarkably different and their respective reception histories present a study in contrasts.[112] On the one hand, Milton is arguably England's greatest poet, famous in his own lifetime both for his poetry and for his political views—particularly his defenses of regicide and divorce, and his position within the regime that ran England's short-lived republican experiment. On the other hand, Traherne lived a quiet life, spent most of his career as rector of the tiny parish of Credenhill in Herefordshire, sent only two largely ignored treatises to the press in his short lifetime, and was not really known as a writer at all until some of his poetry and devotional prose was rediscovered in 1896 by William Brooke, who purchased the manuscripts from a "penny or two penny stall."[113] Whereas Milton's works have been pored over and debated by generations of critics and historians, Traherne's corpus of poetry and prose is still being uncovered, with new manuscripts coming to light even as the project of editing his works remains ongoing.[114]

I argue that Traherne was a careful reader of Milton. In fact, Traherne was perhaps Milton's most creative contemporary reader, for he drew an entire philosophical agenda from a sustained engagement with *Paradise Lost*. Milton provided Traherne with the idea that one could write a first-person account of the beginnings of one's own experience, and the deepest impulses in Traherne's intellectual life emerge from this Miltonic insight. Traherne took Milton's treatment of originary experience and routed it through his reading of and appreciation for Descartes. In this sense, Traherne's poetry is similar to Locke's philosophy, which involved a close engagement with Cartesian ideas coupled with a return to origins—both Adamic and embryonic—that resonates in remarkable ways with Milton. The first four chapters of this book unpack how these two poets arrived at and elaborated on the idea that originary experience could be remembered and described, a strategy that has, as we will see, complex implications for how each poet understands and represents such topics as human nature, gender, sociality, and animal life. The final chapter demonstrates how Locke's *Essay* works around the fact that what is possible in poetry is all but impossible in philosophy. My analyses of Milton and Traherne illustrate how each poet crystalizes ideas that Locke would later develop in his own terms as he transformed poetic modes of thinking into philosophical commonsense.

I begin with *Paradise Lost*, showing (in chapters 1 and 2) how Milton's depiction of Adam's and Eve's first waking moments reworks biblical, Greco-Roman, medieval, and Renaissance antecedents in order to develop a truly original first-person account of human nature experienced at its beginning. Arguing that Milton's epic charges the meanings of *experience* and *thought* so that they verge on the sense of *consciousness* that was developing in the late 1660s, I demonstrate that Adam's and Eve's accounts of awakening enable Milton to paint a picture of human nature capable of underwriting his understanding of gender relations, political community, and God's existence. In chapter 3, I turn to Traherne, showing how the younger poet repeatedly reworks Milton's scenes of awakening in his poetry and prose. If Traherne imported his own, vastly different vision of human nature into the phenomenological perspective Milton invented, he also developed a new account of consciousness by transferring the Edenic ability to remember beginnings into his own prenatal and infant experience. Relating the long history of the embryologists who argued against the possibility of fetal sensation, in chapter 4 I show how Traherne's representation of neonatal thought draws on and differs from the discussions of embryonic consciousness advanced by William Harvey and Descartes. Chapter 5 explores Cudworth's consolidation of the English word *consciousness* and examines how Locke synthesized Descartes's notion of thought and the natality depicted by Milton so as to develop an account of consciousness that requires but also denies a vision of originary experience.

In each chapter, I intertwine two modes of scholarly practice. In the first mode, I deploy a form of literary criticism that is both phenomenologically inflected and historically sensitive.[115] This means using all available formal modes of analysis—rhetorical, grammatical, metrical, structural, or philological techniques: whatever works best in response to the particularities of a given passage—in order to bring to light how a given writer manipulates language so as to conjure conscious experience.[116] At the same time, this approach also requires rich contextualization, a thick description of the literary, philosophical, scientific, theological, devotional, political, anthropological, and juridical sources and antecedents that were available to a given writer and that informed the production of a given text. My aim is to situate

Milton, Traherne, and Locke in the density of their historical intellectual worlds. Bringing formal analysis into dialogue with overlapping and interpenetrating contexts, I demonstrate both how and why poetry is, to borrow a phrase from Theodor Adorno, a "philosophical sundial telling the time of history."[117] In the second mode, I intertwine this literary critical approach with an excavation of the conceptual history of *consciousness* that traces how this concept intersects with understandings of *experience, thought,* and *ego*—each of which consolidated important new meanings in the latter half of the seventeenth century. Taking inspiration from two approaches that deepen the work of Michel Foucault—the historical epistemology of Arnold Davidson and the philosophical archaeology of Alain de Libera—as well as the *Begriffsgeschichte* of Reinhart Koselleck and the methodological innovations employed by such scholars as Quentin Skinner in the history of ideas, I develop a conceptual history that is sensitive to semantic shifts, alert to the emergence of new philosophical ideas, and, perhaps most innovatively, alive to the importance of poetry and mimetic representation to the currents of conceptual change.[118]

The mingling of these two scholarly modes generates what might be described as two voices. On the one hand, in unearthing the rich historicity of the texts I study, I work to establish the nature of the temporal and cultural distances that separate us from Milton, Traherne, Locke, and others. On the other hand, by delving into the formal structures of the seventeenth-century texts and the experiences they evoke, I ventriloquize the experiences they articulate as genuine positions that one might take up and with which one might identify. Double-voiced, this book is written so that historical distance fuses with phenomenological identification.

My attempt to inhabit various depictions of originary experience is rooted in a deeply held conviction about the human condition. We are—against staggering odds—richly and wondrously minded beings. But the shape, contour, and form of that mindedness remain a mystery. We are creatures that cannot help but reflect on our own mental capacities, beings that have, throughout our historical existence, developed a number of overlapping but nonidentical mental maps for indexing and organizing those capacities. Disparate European traditions have explained mindedness using such concepts as mind, soul, spirit, thought, experience, imagination, memory, and so on. In the seventeenth century, *consciousness* was added to the mix and became a powerful new tool for grasping the properties of mindedness.

In the twenty-first century, many neuroscientists, psychologists, biologists, and philosophers of mind are still struggling to understand what consciousness in fact is. From my perspective, one reason for the extreme difficulty of this scientific project lies in a very simple fact: *consciousness is a concept*, a culturally crafted historical entity that names and points toward a vital feature of human and perhaps all sentient life but that does not exist in the same way that, say, brains and other organs exist. Although the set of phenomena that scientists now associate with what we currently call *consciousness* is, without doubt, related to brain processes and can therefore be studied scientifically, whatever it is that emerges from the brain is importantly distinct from consciousness as I understand it in this book. The concept of consciousness has become naturalized to such an extent that it has all but lost many of its cultural and historical properties; it now seems to many researchers to be a physiological property emergent from the brain.

But the concept of consciousness was made in and continues to circulate through human culture, and this is why, if we are to understand consciousness as such, we must use the resources of historically-oriented and literarily-sensitive humanistic thinking as a necessary complement to other modes of philosophical and scientific inquiry. Like all mental entities—imagination, thought, emotion, and will, among others—consciousness does not possess a reality equivalent to that of, say, a table, or a tree, or even a brain. But that does not make it any less real. As Markus Gabriel puts it, "The human mind makes an image of itself and thereby engenders a multiplicity of mental realities."[119] If the mind does not exist without its self-images, and these images are irreducibly historical, then there is nothing to prevent one from inhabiting or trying on even the most historically distant and ostensibly dusty notions of mindedness. This is what I attempt to do in this book: to ventriloquize a seemingly outmoded, distant way of understanding what it is to be human and alive, while at the same time preserving and working to explain the historical conditions responsible for this understanding—and the social and political consequences (both positive and pernicious) that flow from it. *Coming To* attempts to bring to life the views of Milton, Traherne, and Locke in order to portray consciousness at the moment of its conceptual emergence, when it was still strange and new.

The story of how seventeenth-century English poets and philosophers attempted to articulate the birth of consciousness is the story of an effort to isolate an experience of human nature. Since experience is nothing other than openness to the world—to the influence of nurture, to the realm of engagement with other things and persons—an experience of one's own nature is, strictly speaking, impossible.[120] But Milton, Traherne, and Locke set themselves the task of articulating precisely such an experience. These writers thus clarify, on the one hand, an important and still-prevalent cultural logic that emerged in the seventeenth century and, on the other hand, the necessity of poetic thinking to this logic. According to this logic, if we need to retreat into the period of genesis when we were not yet what we have become in order to understand the sorts of beings we are, then, insofar as we are beings defined by a certain type of consciousness, the only way to truly understand ourselves is to imagine our way inside an experience that is, for most of us at least, impossible to access.

PART I

Milton and the Birth of Consciousness

CHAPTER ONE

Unexperienced Thought

MILTONIC MINDEDNESS

From its opening scene, *Paradise Lost* inhabits the perspectives of its characters; most of the poem takes place among the appearance of the various somethings that show up for someone. After describing his intention to "justify the ways of God to men," Milton relates how Satan and his companions launched an unsuccessful rebellion and then tumbled from heaven into the "fiery gulf" (1.26, 52). At this point, Milton's swift movement across space and time suddenly slows as the poet strives to occupy the perspective of Satan at the moment he awakens, utterly changed, into his fallen condition:

> now the thought
> Both of lost happiness and lasting pain
> Torments him; round he throws his baleful eyes
> That witnessed huge affliction and dismay
> Mixed with obdúrate pride and steadfast hate:
> At once as far as angels' ken he views
> The dismal situation waste and wild. (1.54–60)

Milton's "now" plunges the reader into a field of "thought" that includes memories of the "happiness" Satan once enjoyed and the anticipation that his current pain will be "lasting," projected into the future. The "now" of "thought" combines memory and anticipation with the sensory impressions generated by burning body and roving eyes (the "affliction and dismay" of his companions) along with Satan's emotional states, which shape what he sees (the landscape he views is "Mixed with obdúrate pride and steadfast hate"). Although Milton makes it impossible to fully see through

Satan's eyes—how far does the visual field of "angels' ken" extend?—the poet invites readers to enter a familiar form of mindedness in which sensation, perception, emotion, memory, and anticipation mingle synchronically in the phenomenal field of "thought."

In *Paradise Lost*, Milton imagines his way inside myriad and astoundingly different perspectives—those of Satan, God, Adam, Eve, and a variety of angels, among others. The poem grapples with the question of what it is like to be a minded creature. Milton occupies the first-person scene of thought in order to examine and represent the conditions of possibility that underpin free choice.[1] How, the poem asks, do minded creatures make up their minds? How do they decide to obey or to rebel? What sort of phenomenal goings-on lead a given creature to do what it does? This set of questions is not unique to Milton. Many of the poets, philosophers, and theologians that he studied so assiduously also explore what it means to be minded and how various mental states enable virtuous or vitiated action.[2] The mimesis of Satanic "thought" in *Paradise Lost* is likewise indebted to tragic and epic conventions for rooting narratives in a given speaker's perspective.[3] What sets Milton apart from his predecessors is the truly radical nature of his ambitions. *Paradise Lost* develops mimetic representations of minded freedom that begin at the very beginning.

Although *Paradise Lost* provides four narratives of originary experience—Satan, Sin, Adam, and Eve each relate such a story—Milton's most daring innovation lies in his depiction of humanity's first waking moments. As I argue in chapter 2, these stories mark the first attempts in European literature to describe originary experience in recognizably human terms, an effort to unveil an experience of human nature in the absence of nurture. Such an experience is difficult to articulate: "For man to tell how human life began / Is hard," Adam admits, "for who himself beginning knew?" (8.250–51). Yet both Adam and Eve tell stories that capture the wonder, joy, and strangeness of this initial moment. The early stages of every normal human life are, to borrow a phrase from Augustine's *De civitate Dei* (c. 426), "sunk in oblivion" [*demergit oblivio*], but Adam and Eve enter the world without the delay between capacity and actualization that characterizes postlapsarian human development.[4] Their memories stretch back to their own beginnings. Eve reveals what it was like to appear in Paradise, how she awoke "much wondering where / And what I was, whence thither brought, and how" (4.451–52). Her initial encounter with the world raises questions that anticipate those asked by Adam after he awakens, when he puzzles over "who I was, or where, or from what cause" (8.270).

For readers accustomed to Milton's poem, it is easy to miss the novelty of these scenes.[5] But Milton's early readers felt it. In *Annotations on*

Milton's Paradise Lost (1695)—the first work to treat English poetry with the philological rigor that had been reserved for the Bible and such select authors as Homer, Virgil, or Dante—Patrick Hume states about Eve's narrative: "Our Author, in this Place and its Parallel, . . . Where *Adam* relates the first Thoughts and Sentiments he had of himself, . . . has litt upon something so new and strange, that as it cannot square with any Persons but those of our two first Progenitors, so it is exactly suitable to them, created certainly at full growth, perfect in Body, Mind and Memory. . . . It had not only been *hard, but impossible for any other Man, to have given a Relation of his Beginning.*"[6] Given that Hume loved finding sources for *Paradise Lost*, his claim that Milton has "litt upon something . . . new and strange" should be taken seriously. After all, the creation of Adam and Eve was often depicted in the Middle Ages and the Renaissance.[7] Recall the luminous gaze of the awakening Adam in Michelangelo's painting in the Sistine Chapel or consider Petrarch's invocation of the "day when Adam opened his eyes" [*dì ch' Adamo / aperse gli occhi*] in the *Canzoniere*.[8] What Hume found so astonishing was not Milton's depiction of Adam's and Eve's creation, but rather that these scenes present the "first Thoughts and Sentiments" of human beings that are "created certainly at full growth, perfect in Body, Mind and Memory." Adam and Eve do not grow slowly into the world, from helplessness toward sufficiency. From their first moments, they are able to stand, walk, perceive, feel, imagine, judge, reason, and remember everything that has happened since they first felt the pleasurable shock of existence. As Hume points out, the experience that Adam and Eve relate should be "impossible." What Hume sees as "new and strange" is the first-person expression of humanity's "first Thoughts."

Milton is able to accomplish this feat because his Adam and Eve are created in a state of what I am calling *neonatal maturity*—a mode of being that is just beginning but nevertheless draws on a full complement of human capacities ready for immediate actualization.[9] To be sure, Adam and Eve were created, not born. But Milton is careful to bring out the neonatal qualities of Adam's creation from the earth: the first man awakens covered in "sweat" (8.255), the vernacular term used by anatomists like Helkiah Crooke and midwives like Jane Sharp for amniotic fluid.[10] Both Adam and Eve undergo what Milton elsewhere calls a "birth mature" (5.862).[11] They are, from the beginning, mature in the seventeenth-century sense of "perfect." According to William Harvey, "an animal is called 'perfect' [*perfectum*] when it has the power to beget its like" and is fully grown, which is why such writers as Locke refer to childhood as an "imperfect state."[12] But Adam and Eve are not mature in the sense that they come into the world knowing what needs to be known. They must learn about themselves and the world and recognize their incompleteness: human life in Milton's Eden is dynamic, a process of education.[13] My use of *maturity* should not, therefore, evoke stasis or completion. Adam and Eve begin their lives in a state of neonatal maturity because, although they are without experience, they are able to apprehend themselves and the world with the physical and mental powers of fully formed adults.[14]

Although scholars have long recognized Milton's interest in origins, no one has adequately addressed the beginnings of mindedness in *Paradise Lost*.[15] This critical neglect is, at least in part, due to the radical novelty at work in Milton's representation of the birth of consciousness. Most of the other moments in *Paradise Lost* rework existing traditions. Based on the early books of Genesis, Milton's epic is in dialogue with many literary, theological, and philosophical works that account for beginnings: medieval and Renaissance dramas about creation and Satan's temptation of Adam and Eve; hexameral literature stretching from Basil's *Hexaemeron* (c. 379) to Torquato Tasso's *Il mundo creato* (1607); Greek genealogies of the gods, including Hesiod's *Theogony* and humanist commentaries on ancient religions from Giovanni Boccaccio to Gerardus Vossius; and philosophical accounts ranging from Plato's *Timaeus* through Lucretius's *De rerum natura* to Galileo's *Dialogi* (1632). But although much of *Paradise Lost* gains its power in relation to previous accounts of creation, there is no true precedent for Milton's description of the birth of human consciousness, which Hume rightly saw as "new and strange." Not recognizing the novelty of Milton's efforts, previous critics have not fully grappled with the imaginative labor and conceptual innovation that underpins the stories of personal beginning in *Paradise Lost*. But one cannot truly grasp Milton's project without analyzing and contextualizing these stories. When Milton's characters describe what it is like for mindedness to begin, they both consolidate and contribute to the emergence of the concept of consciousness. They also provide an important point of entry into the poem. Since *Paradise Lost* is grounded in the perspectives of its characters, Milton's treatment of what it is like to begin opens a window not only onto his understanding of conscious life but also onto the nature of the poem itself.

MIMESIS AND ORIGINS: FROM MYTH TO VERISIMILITUDE

The first account of originary experience in *Paradise Lost* is related by Sin. Far from Edenic splendor and the attempt at mimetic verisimilitude that characterizes Milton's scenes of human interaction, this initial foray reworks the mythic birth of Athena through a first-person remembered narration voiced by an allegorical personification of Sin.[16] Though rife with incest, rape, and deformation, Sin's story shadows the poem's later descriptions of human beginning. Milton invites comparison between Greek myth and biblical truth.[17] The birth of Sin is a damaged sketch: without illuminating details, and twisted by outlandish circumstances, this story only vaguely resembles the fully realized originary experiences of Adam and Eve. But Sin's account remains vital for grasping Milton's project; it outlines a tradition he works against.

When Satan encounters Sin, he does not recognize her and demands that she reveal "What thing" she is, "thus double-formed" (2.741–44). She jogs his memory:

> at the assembly, and in sight
> Of all the seraphim with thee combined
> In bold conspiracy against heaven's king,
> All on a sudden miserable pain
> Surprised thee, dim thine eyes, and dizzy swum
> In darkness, while thy head flames thick and fast
> Threw forth, till on the left side opening wide,
> Likest to thee in shape and countenance bright,
> Then shining heavenly fair, a goddess armed
> Out of thy head I sprung: amazement seized
> All the host of heaven; back they recoiled afraid
> At first, and called me Sin, and for a sign
> Portentous held me[.] (2.749–61)

A "goddess armed" from the moment "Out of thy head I sprung," Sin emerges as a neonatally mature agent capable of remembering her own entrance into the world.

Milton's stress on the first-person perspective distinguishes this scene from its mythic sources. In *Theogony*, Hesiod relates how "by himself, out of his head, [Zeus] fathered the pale-eyed Tritogeneia [Athena], the fearsome rouser of the fray, leader of armies, the lady Atrytone [Athena], whose pleasure is in war and the clamor of battle."[18] The focus here is not on Athena's perspective but on the powers of Zeus, who appears to birth Athena "by himself."[19] The same holds true for Homeric Hymn 28, which is, to my eyes, the closest precedent for Milton's treatment of the theme but has not, so far as I know, been suggested as a source:

Zeus himself begot her
From his divine head, holding weapons of war,
Golden and wide-gleaming; and awe
Seized all who were watching, immortal as they were.[20]

Athena emerges from Zeus's head "holding weapons of war," just as Sin
enters the world a "goddess armed." In the Homeric hymn, "awe / Seized"
(or "held") "all" of the Olympian gods "who were watching" the scene unfold: σέβας δ' ἔχε πάντας ὁρῶντας / ἀθανάτους reads the original Greek, which
is rendered into Latin by Jean de Sponde in the 1583 edition of Homer consulted by Milton as *stupor [autem] habebat omnes uidentes / Immortales*.[21]
Milton translates this Homeric hymn: "Amazement seized all the host of
heaven." But whereas the Greek poem describes the awestruck audience in
the third person, it is Milton's Sin herself who witnesses the "amazement"
seizing the angelic host.

Milton's use of the first-person perspective dramatizes the phenomenological valences implicit in Athena's birth. Satan's description of Sin as
"double-formed" retrospectively describes how she was created through
doubling. Sin's genesis ends with the appearance of a "fully armed" personification sprung from Satan's head but the process begins within, when
Sin feels her own emergent individuality *through* her father's experience:
"All on a sudden miserable pain / Surprised thee, dim thine eyes, and
dizzy swum / In darkness, while thy head flames thick and fast / Threw
forth." The fire darting from Satan's head is public, visible to others. By
contrast, the "sudden miserable pain" he feels is private. In describing the
war in Heaven, Raphael will later claim that Satan "first knew pain" when
he is publicly wounded by Michael's sword (6.327), but Sin knows about
Satan's earlier headache because she herself felt this "sudden miserable
pain." She also saw through his dimming eyes and felt Satan's vertigo as
he "dizzy swum / In darkness." Beginning her existence as someone else,
Sin describes the experience of one ego emerging from and through the experiences of another. Milton's syntax registers this separation. "All on a
sudden miserable pain / Surprised thee": although the line break performs
the unexpectedness of this surprise and suggests how the painful genesis of
Sin divides Satan from himself, the objective personal pronoun *thee* nevertheless provides a grammatical anchor for that self. But the following
phrases—"dim thine eyes, and dizzy swum / In darkness"—progressively
eliminate self-coherence, moving from the dimming of a body part ("eyes")
to a state of being that is relatively untethered from the implied subject: a
verb ("swum") and an adjective ("dizzy") both situated "In darkness." With

the line break separating "swum" from "In darkness," the verse performs the generation of an independent *I* capable of springing "armed" from the sinister "left side" of her father's head.

To be sure, Sin is "Likest to [Satan] in shape and countenance bright" (2.756), a double fit for Satan's narcissism: "Thyself," Sin recalls, relating how her father's incestuous erotic interest began, "in me thy perfect image viewing / Becam'st enamored" (2.764–65). She is a personification or allegorical representation of Satan's sin—his pride and his unwarranted belief in the self-sufficiency of his own powers. Summarizing a theory propounded by Ernst Cassirer and recently revised by Boris Mazlov, the *Princeton Encyclopedia of Poetry and Poetics* claims that personification "replaced mythical figures when rational attitudes superseded the primitive imagination."[22] Milton enacts this transition from myth (the birth of Athena, an event that simply happens) into a rationally oriented personification (the birth of Sin, an event that responds to and represents Satan's inner states and moral choices).[23] Milton furthers this process by using the mimetic gulf separating Sin and Death from such characters as Satan and Adam and Eve to suggest that his epic exists on a literary plane entirely distinct from the realm of allegory inhabited by its greatest English precursor, Spenser's *Faerie Queene*. Milton inserts a bubble of allegorical personification into an epic structured by the conventions of what Alastair Fowler calls "Renaissance realism."[24] Yet as the phenomenological valences of Sin's initial emergence suggest, she is also more than a personified vice; her being quivers at the edges of verisimilitude.

As Steven Knapp has argued, this ambivalence in Milton's portrayal of Sin and Death unsettled later eighteenth-century readers of *Paradise Lost*. On the one hand, the two figures are allegorical personifications, concepts situated on the horizon of mimesis, endowed with feeling and agency. On the other hand, they exist in the "essentially realistic and classical world of the epic" and interact with such "ostensibly literal agents" as Satan. "The trouble with Milton's power to transform abstract concepts into animated beings," Knapp writes, summarizing the reservations of eighteenth-century critics, "was not merely its inherent primitiveness and irrationality, but its *reversibility*. Once the boundaries between literal and figurative agency were erased, it seemed that nothing could prevent the imagination from metaphorizing literal agents as easily as it literalized metaphors."[25] If the personification of Sin lives the life of a person, this struck the eighteenth-century readers studied by Knapp as dangerous insofar as such a situation implied that the literary persons of *Paradise Lost*—especially Adam and Eve—could, through a figurative reversal, be reduced to personifications.

It is Milton's depictions of Edenic originary experience that most explicitly court this risk. After all, like Sin, both Adam and Eve emerge into the
world fully formed and they each tell a remembered story that describes
their first moments of existence. Sin's story transforms the mythic power
of Athena's birth into the first person, and Adam's and Eve's recollections
of awakening seem to share a similar source. Perhaps, that is, Milton's depiction of Edenic neonatal maturity is, in part, a retelling of archaic Greek
myth. Milton flirts with such a position. While the structure of Eve's creation resonates with that of Sin—a female character made from a body part
(rib and head respectively) of a male character—Milton's language ties Sin's
story to Adam's. After Sin, having fallen through chaos with the rest of the
defeated angels, is given the keys to Hell, she sits alone in her new and unfamiliar home. Relating her story to Satan, she recalls: "Pensive here I sat /
Alone, but long I sat not, till my womb / Pregnant by thee, and now excessive grown / Prodigious motion felt and rueful throes" (2.777–80). Shortly
after this moment of respite, Sin will give birth to Death, who almost immediately rapes her. This sexual violence leads, Sin relates, to the birth of
vicious "hell hounds" (2.654) who hourly "return" to "gnaw" within the
"womb / That bred them" before "bursting forth / Afresh with conscious
terrors vex me round, / That rest or intermission none I find" (2.798–802).
It would be hard to imagine a more allegorical episode: Death is born from
the union of Satan and Sin, and the consequences of that union are enacted
through ceaseless torment. However, Sin's existence is not exhausted by
her thematic role. Milton inserts a brief moment of contemplation, prior
to the onset of Sin's suffering, into an otherwise allegorical plot. As Knapp
points out, Sin's "speculative leisure endows her with an empirical consciousness wholly inexplicable in allegorical terms," and this moment "anticipates" both Adam's and Eve's accounts of awakening.[26] "Pensive here I
sat / Alone": Sin's language provides the model for Adam's later recollection
of how, after asking the creation for the name of his creator, "On a green
shady bank profuse with flowers / Pensive I sat me down" (8.286–87).

Why does Milton connect Sin's story with Adam's? Does he want to flag
the mythological source for his accounts of Edenic awakening? Or is he using the shared scene of "Pensive" stillness in order to wrest his treatment
of Paradise away from archaic Greek sources? Any answer must address
the word that binds Sin to Adam: "Pensive." Etymologically connected to
the French *penser* (to think), *pensive* could mean "sorrowful," but in these
passages it comes closer to the more general sense: "full of thought; medi-
tative, reflective."[27] Puzzled by his sudden appearance in the world, Adam
thoughtfully considers the meaning of his condition, the possible explana-

tions behind his coming to "feel that I am happier than I know" (8.282). Although Sin does not find herself in Paradise, her brief moment of contemplative peace is nonetheless untroubled by the "conscious terrors" that will, after the birth of Death, "vex" her ceaselessly. Sin exists as a newly generated individual, all alone, caught up in thought. Both Sin and Adam are, then, portrayed as thinkers, beings capable of conscious thought. By animating the myth of Athena's birth from within, by granting Sin a glimmer of personal existence and access to her own originary experience, Milton situates the gods of pagan antiquity on the horizon of first-person experience. But in doing so, he demonstrates the poverty of these sources. Milton gets behind ancient myth and suggests that what the Greeks assumed was a story about Athena's birth is in fact a distorted way of relating the genesis of Sin. Employing a strategy that Gordon Teskey calls "*capture*," Milton appropriates "the beauty and psychological appeal of classical myth for the promotion of Christian truth."[28]

Despite this moment of contemplative potential, Sin's account of originary experience is all but emptied of content. She may engage with such realistic characters as Satan, but she remains a personification, a figure who does not quite belong in the poem's world. Real enough to possess her own perspective, to be "Pensive" and think her own thoughts, Sin's experience is not mimetically verisimilar. Her story does not reveal a world but rather indexes her present circumstances with a series of deictic markers. After emerging a "goddess armed" (2.757), Sin falls "down / Into *this* deep," is given "*this* powerful key" in order "to keep / *These* gates for ever shut," and then relaxes for a moment: "Pensive *here* I sat / Alone" (2.772–78). Although she is a character in the poem's world, she cannot conjure a scene adequate to the verisimilar depiction of her experience. Contrast this formulation to Adam's: "On a green shady bank profuse of flowers / Pensive I sat me down" (8.286–87). If Sin indexes a place ("here"), Adam reveals a world: a milieu full of clearly differentiated spatial features (a "bank" raised from the ground), colors ("green"), variations of light and heat ("shady") that imply the presence of trees overhead, and a rich abundance of other life forms ("flowers"). While Milton's treatment of Greek myth generates nearly empty space, his use of the Bible leads to the detailed textures of reality, to embodied life as it is lived and captured through mimesis pitched toward verisimilitude. This bifurcation of rhetorical and stylistic strategies—allegorical personification as opposed to realistically depicted persons—cultivates different sorts of relationships between poem and reader. Although Sin relates her story in the first person, and the violence that she suffers is terrible, her account of her first moments of existence does not foster readerly identification. No one

can identify with directly feeling the pain of another being, or leaping, fully
formed, from someone else's head. By contrast, Milton invites readers into
Adam's and Eve's first moments: everyone knows what it is like to wake
up, move around, explore an environment, and ask questions. When Milton
articulates Edenic waking, he describes the beginning of human thought as
a phenomenological scene in which rationality is in harmony with feeling,
desire sidles up to intellect, and we are presented with a heightened version
of our own conscious thought.

NEONATAL MATURITY

Milton intensifies the realism of Adam's and Eve's stories by making sure
that, despite their many differences, each narrative conjures a shared and
fundamentally human sense of experience. Adam starts his account of how
"human life began" (8.250) by recalling, "As new waked from soundest
sleep, / Soft on the flowery herb I found me laid / In balmy sweat, which
with his beams the sun / Soon dried" (8.253–56). This sentence recalls Eve's
"That day I oft remember, when from sleep / I first awaked, and found myself reposed / Under a shade of flowers" (4.449–51). The differences between
these passages are well known: Eve straightforwardly claims she awakened
from sleep, while Adam compares nonexistence with sleep; Eve awakens in
the shade, while Adam is placed in the sunshine.[29] Less frequently discussed
are the parallel reflexive constructions—Adam's "I found me laid" and Eve's
"I . . . found my self reposed"—through which Milton articulates the shared
strangeness of mature birth.

   What sort of thoughts do Adam and Eve encounter upon awakening?
What are their first impressions like? Most importantly, Adam's and Eve's
formulations reveal the relation between thought and creation. Grammatically, these phrases turn the first-person pronoun in on itself: when the *I*
(subject) first awakens into activity, it finds the *me* (reflexive object, now
archaic) or the *my self* (reflexive object, still in use) already there, awaiting discovery.[30] Milton's phrases express a relation in which the self lags
behind itself: the relationship between active pronoun and reflexive object
includes within it the belatedness made explicit in Adam's "laid" and Eve's
"reposed." To find oneself laid or reposed is to have the presence of some
prior force (that which does the laying or reposing) built into one's sense of
self. At the same time, Adam and Eve are, from the beginning, embedded in
a world, tied up in a preexisting situation marked by prepositional phrases:
they find themselves "*on* the flowery herb," "*In* balmy sweat," "*Under* a
shade of flowers." Although Adam is, in Thomas Browne's words, the man

"without a navel," in Milton's poem, he is far from autonomous.[31] In *Paradise Lost*, human dependence runs all the way down into originary experience, which is both constitutively belated and completely given.[32]

In Adam's "I found me laid" and Eve's "I . . . found my self reposed," the verb *find* marks the form of thought that connects the subjective and objective cases of the first-person pronoun. For Milton, this self-finding is isomorphic with feeling, an assertion that is borne out both by the fact that *find* can mean to "feel" or to "perceive" and by the shared sense of the expressions "to find one's feet" or "to feel one's feet," two early modern formulations that mean to be "conscious of one's powers."[33] *Find* traces its ancestry back through Old English to Old German, and the same meanings are at work in the German verb. For example, in *Being and Time* (1927), Heidegger capitalizes on the linguistic richness of *find* to express how it is through feeling that the human being "finds itself" [*es befindet sich*] in what it does.[34] For Heidegger, the "primary orientation" of human being is "not a *knowing*, but a *finding oneself*."[35] Thrown into a world, one finds oneself like Adam or Eve, caught up in a preexisting situation. One orients or attunes oneself to this situation by means of what Heidegger calls *Befindlichkeit*, a word literally translated as "the feeling in which one finds oneself."[36] While Milton uses a similar linguistic strategy, he does not maintain a strict division between knowing and finding. In *Paradise Lost*, feeling cannot be disentangled from knowing. In Milton's view, the fundamental form of human consciousness is a self-feeling that is distinct from but nevertheless fastened to self-knowing.

Feeling saturates Adam's self-finding. It is prioritized both sequentially and thematically: "As new waked from soundest sleep / Soft on the flowery herb I found me laid / In balmy sweat" (8.253–55). A hinge between nonbeing and waking awareness, *soft* syntactically occupies the initial position of this sentence's second clause. The early deployment of this adverb creates an expansive halo of significance. Since *soft* is positioned in advance of whatever term it modifies, it permeates the scene with an ambience that encompasses verb, subject, object, and atmosphere. *Soft* invokes the loving care with which Adam was "laid" upon the vegetation, the tenderness of newly created skin, the tactile quality of the flowery herb, and the feel of the world as it appears to and encompasses emergent thought. Milton emphasizes the importance of *soft* by using it to close off Adam's first fully conscious moments: "there gentle sleep / First found me, and with soft oppression seized / My drowsèd sense, untroubled, though I thought / I then was passing to my former state / Insensible" (8.287–91). As waking awareness fades, grammatical agency shifts, and Adam (who had only just "found" himself "laid") is now "found" by sleep, which "seiz[es]" him and causes him to feel a "soft oppression."[37] This paradoxical formulation, which echoes Eve's earlier account of how Adam's "gentle hand / Seized mine" (4.488–89), tempers what should be the violence of oppression so that bodily necessity becomes pleasurable. Recalling both Adam's discussion with Eve about how the "soft slumberous weight" of sleep "inclines / Our eyelids" (4.615–16) and Milton's description of Adonis's "slumber soft" in the *Masque Presented at Ludlow Castle* (1634), the adjective in Adam's account suggests that the texture of the waking world is best disclosed at its borders.[38] The softness of sentient feeling greets Adam as he awakens and waves farewell as he fades into sleep.

Milton inherits this connection between softness and the edges of waking thought from previous English poets—recall, for instance, Spenser's Morpheus "in his slumber soft" or Shakespeare's Antony, who anticipates when "wine hath steeped our sense / In soft and delicate Lethe"[39]—but Adam's "soft" awakening and "soft" descent into sleep are also tied up with a gentle tactility that suffuses all of *Paradise Lost*. Spirits, we are told in book 1, possess an "essence pure" that is "soft / And uncompounded" (1.424–25), and this is one of the main reasons why the fallen angels want to get out of Hell. Satan's suggestion that they find "soft delicious air, / To heal the scar of these corrosive fires" (2.400–401) is more appealing than Mammon's hope of acclimatization: "Our torments also may in length of time / Become our elements, these piercing fires / As soft as now severe" (2.274–76).[40] Eden, by contrast, presents a perfect alignment of environment and inhabitant. Eve is the epitome of "softness" (4.298), and even if Adam is "less winning soft" (4.479), he wakes her with "soft touching" (5.17) and the two participate in "soft embraces" (4.471). All of this nuptial softness takes place against what Joe Moshenska calls the "pleasurably tactile backdrop" of Eden.[41] When Satan first encounters the pair, they are sitting on "the soft downy bank damasked with flowers" (4.334) beneath a "tuft of shade that on a green / Stood whispering soft" (4.325–26). Adam awakens in a soft world the tactility of which Milton invokes in order to conjure a felt sense of atmosphere.[42]

This ambience is intensified by the "balmy sweat" that covers Adam, a residue from creation that lingers on the skin and tethers the body to an environment that makes its presence felt through an accumulation of tactile impressions: the softness of flowers, the dampness of sweat, the warmth of the air, the power of the sun's beams as they dry his skin. The feeling of the sun's warmth recalls Milton's tactile awareness in blindness: "thee I revisit safe, / And feel thy sovereign vital lamp" (3.21–22), he writes in the invocation to book 3.[43] Milton draws on his familiarity with the feeling of atmospheric warmth against flesh in order to place Adam in the primal human situation of bodily immersion. I stress the tactility of Adam's first encounter with the sun because this detail militates against the common position that the first thing Adam does upon awakening is stare at the heavens. Usually pairing this direct and ostensibly immediate vision of light—"Straight toward heaven my wondering eyes I turned" (8.257)—with Eve's mediated and more earthly encounter with a lake that "seemed another sky" (4.459), critics tend to see Adam's awakening as a direct and masculine movement into rationality.[44] Implicitly continuing a tradition of biblical commentary begun in the first century CE by Philo Judaeus, these critics depict Milton's Adam as a figure of reason and Milton's Eve as a figure of sensuality.[45] Yet despite the fact that Adam claims that his "wondering eyes" turned "Straight toward heaven," his account begins not with the vocabulary of sight, but in the register of touch.[46] Only after Milton establishes the primacy of feeling does Adam invoke vision.

Adam's self-finding begins in the register of feeling, shuttling between outer and inner tactility. After gazing at the "ample sky," Adam is "raised / By quick instinctive motion" to stand upon his feet (8.258–59). The word *quick* refers to both speed and life, linking motion and vitality.[47] The spontaneity at work here is registered by Milton's use of *instinctive*. Early modern English lexicographers associated *instinct* with an "inward motion, or stirring."[48] From Aquinas onward, *instinctus* was tethered to the innate responses of animal life.[49] Milton's invocation of animal powers suggests a quasi-embryological development from the powers of the vegetative soul toward those of the animal soul. Adam emerges into awareness "on the flowery herb" with his skin covered in a dew-like "balmy sweat" (8.254–55) that allies his still-immobile body with plants, much like the trees of Eden that "wept odorous gums and balm" (4.248).[50] Standing with "quick instinctive motion," Adam occupies the sentience of animal life.[51] His movement upward marks the stirring of an embodied teleological force that he cannot help but feel.

Once on his feet, Adam surveys his surroundings, paying attention to the "Creatures that lived, and moved" (8.264). The close relationship between Adam's life and that of other animals is solidified in his first speech act, when he inquires of the "fair creatures" that "live and move" if they can tell him about the source of the gift he has just received: "From whom I have that thus I move and live" (8.276–81). Self-movement was thought to be coterminous with animal life.[52] What is most striking about Milton's chiastic formulation, however, is how Adam recognizes life in other creatures by implicitly appealing to his own sense of felt movement.[53] Humans

feel themselves to be living, and perceive this life in the motion of other
bodies. Milton captures this reflexive felt vitality by linking Adam, who
"move[s] and live[s]" with the other creatures that "live and move." This
creaturely attunement is felt: "all things smiled, / With fragrance and with
joy my heart o'erflowed" (8.265–66). Gazing at creation, Adam is saturated
with the "joy" of living in a living world. The near identity between Adam's
emotional response and the world affecting him is registered in Milton's
syntax, which renders Adam's feeling of joy as one with the "fragrance"
of the world.[54] Adam's waking thought is grounded in a feeling of self and
world that opens toward the knowledge of both:

> My self I then perused, and limb by limb
> Surveyed, and sometimes went, and sometimes ran
> With supple joints, and lively vigour led:
> But who I was, or where, or from what cause,
> Knew not. (8.267–71)

Milton uses ocular verbs to structure the movement toward knowledge
that shapes Adam's story. When Adam first opens his "wondering eyes,"
he "gazed a while the ample sky" (8.257–58). The verb *to gaze* suggests that
Adam is dazzled with wonder.[55] Once on his feet, he takes in his surroundings: "about me round I saw / Hill, dale, and shady woods, and sunny plains, /
And liquid lapse of murmuring streams," all populated with living, moving
creatures (8.261–63). Now Adam simply *sees* the world in all of its variety,
progressing away from the astonishment implied by *gaze* and toward the
detailed discernment with which he attends to his own body, when he *peruses* himself and *surveys* his limbs. These last two verbs indicate a scrutiny that combines perception with discrimination and sets up the turn to
unanswered intellectual questions: "But who I was, or where, or from what
cause, / Knew not."[56]

Adam's drive to know begins with "wondering eyes" (8.257), a phrase
that echoes Aristotle's famous claims about philosophy's origins in both
wonder and vision.[57] "It is owing to their wonder," Aristotle states in the
Metaphysics, "that men both now begin and first began to philosophize"
(2:1554; 982b). The *Metaphysics* opens by linking the human urge for knowledge to vision: "All men by nature desire to know. An indication of this is
the delight we take in our senses; for even apart from their usefulness they
are loved for themselves; and above all others the sense of sight, [which,
more than the other senses] makes us know and brings to light the many

differences between things" (2:1552; 980a). Human beings move from wonder toward knowledge by moving from perception, through memory, to experience, toward art or science (2:1552; 980a–981a). Adam's story follows
this *telos*: his desire to know the answers to basic questions is spurred by
his sense of sight, which peruses and surveys his body, marking the "differences between things." He shares this affective orientation toward knowledge with Eve, who awakes "much wondering where / And what I was,
whence hither brought, and how" (4.451–52). But even if Adam's desire to
know is encoded in Milton's narrowing visual vocabulary, the movement
toward knowledge remains integrated with Milton's insistence on Adam's
embodied feeling. Adam is "led" by his "lively vigour" to walk and run,
exploring a capacity for movement the felt quality of which is registered in
the adjective *supple*, which could mean pliable but also meant *soft*.[58]

The sort of propositional knowledge that might allow one to answer
the questions "who," "where," or "from what cause" is important both to
Adam and to Milton—it is, after all, what the story is moving toward—but
this kind of knowing is not, in Milton's view, the primordial form of human thought. The transition from wondering *gaze* to critical *survey* suggests
that Adam's intellect is coming into focus. But the continued insistence on
felt vitality—on "supple joints" and "lively vigour"—also suggests that the
sentient softness into which Adam awakens continues to hum beneath the
first stirrings of rationality.[59] By positing a self-feeling that precedes and subtends intellectual self-knowing, Milton draws on a medieval tradition that
is exemplified by the Franciscan Pierre Jean Olivi, whose thirteenth-century
commentary on Lombard's *Sentences* articulates a theory of self-knowledge
that illuminates how feeling and intellect intertwine in Adam's account.[60]
"The soul knows or is able to know itself by two modes," claims Olivi:

> The first mode is an experiential and almost tactile sensation [*sensus
> experimentalis et quasi tactualis*] by which the soul undoubtedly senses
> that it is, lives, cognizes, wills, sees, hears, moves the body, and likewise
> for all its other acts, whose principle and subject it knows and senses
> itself to be [*scit et sentit se esse principium et subiectum*]. And this to
> such an extent that it cannot actually know or consider any object or any
> act without always knowing and sensing itself to be the subject of the
> act by which it knows and considers [*quin semper ibi sciat et sentiat se
> esse suppositum illius actus quo scit et considerat illa*]. . . . The other
> mode of knowing itself is through reasoning, by investigating the genera
> and differences it doesn't know by the first mode.[61]

This passage seems to theorize Adam's first apprehensions, which begin suf-
fused with a *sensus experimentalis et quasi tactualis*—a felt knowledge of
self and world bound up with motion, perception, and affect—before moving toward a mode of knowing that seeks rationally to answer those questions that are inaccessible through the first mode: "But who I was, or where,
or from what cause, / Knew not" (8.270–71).[62]

Adam's first speech act moves even further into this second mode, reasoning about how he came to be while still emphasizing felt vitality:

> Thou sun, said I, fair light,
> And thou enlightened earth, so fresh and gay,
> Ye hills and dales, ye rivers, woods, and plains,
> And ye that live and move, fair creatures, tell,
> Tell, if ye saw, how came I thus, how here?
> Not of myself; by some great maker then,
> In goodness and in power pre-eminent;
> Tell me, how may I know him, how adore,
> From whom I have that thus I move and live,
> And feel that I am happier than I know. (8.273–82)

Fully actualizing his *logos*, Adam's address to the unresponsive creatures
begins to solve the puzzle he presents—"how came I thus, how here?"—by
employing discursive rationality. Since he did not make himself, Adam reasons that "some great maker" must stand behind his sudden emergence
into awareness. But this rational argument veers back into a consideration
of how he feels. Milton stresses that it is the affective force of Adam's
existence—the gift of moving, living, and feeling that one is happier than
one knows—that drives him to seek to "know" and "adore" his maker as
well as to praise and celebrate his condition and the forces responsible for it.

Adam's catalogue of capacities invokes Saint Paul's sermon at the Athe-
nian Areopagus, in which the apostle explains that God "gives to all mortals life and breath," made all nations "from one ancestor," and enabled us
to "search for God and perhaps grope for and find him." This groping toward
God—as Milton's Adam, the ancestor invoked in this passage, does in his
first speech act—is possible, Paul suggests, because "he is not far from each
one of us. For 'in him we live and move and have our being'; as even some of
your own poets have said, 'For we too are his offspring.'"[63] Adam's desire to
"know" and "adore" a "great maker" "From whom I have that thus I move
and live" invokes Paul's claim that "'in him we live and move and have
our being,'" which is, in turn, a line from a pagan thinker. Milton notes the

importance of this quotation in *Areopagitica* (1644), where he remarks that Paul "thought it no defilement to insert into holy Scripture the sentences of three Greek Poets."[64] Although Paul takes the phrase "we too are his off-spring" from the Stoic poet Aratus's *Phaenomena* (second century BCE), the exact origin of "live and move and have our being" is not known.[65] Scholars now think it comes from Posidonius, but Theodor Beza's edition of the New Testament (1598)—a text Milton used—links the phrase to Virgil's *Eclogues* (c. 38 BCE): "of Jove all things are full" [*Iovis omnia plena*].[66] Whatever Paul's source, or Milton's understanding of it, Adam's appeal to his power to "move and live" while reasoning about God's existence demonstrates the very point that Paul makes through his quotation: God's existence is available to all.

If Milton takes this logic back to Paul's "one ancestor," he also moves this Pauline idea in a new direction. Whereas Paul describes a God "in [whom] we live and move and have our being," Adam wants to know a God "From whom I have that thus I move and live, / And feel that I am happier than I know." With this shift in word order Milton reorients an ancient conceptual hierarchy captured in Edward Herbert's *De veritate* (1624): "In man movement follows upon existence, life follows upon movement, sensation follows upon life, and free will follows upon sensation," with reason trailing behind, only able to manipulate the evidence of life's foundational orders "as far as it can."[67] Paul's sermon is ontologically oriented, burrowing down from life, through movement, toward that in which "we have our being." But Adam's account of the reason why he wants to know his maker drives not toward his ontological source (Paul's God "*in* [whom] we live and move and have our being") but rather away from that source toward conscious thought: he wants to know "*From* whom I have that thus I move and live, / And feel that I am happier than I know." Milton begins by spacing his terms through an even-keeled polysyndeton ("move and live, / And feel") that echoes Paul's syntax, but then breaks from this pattern as Adam's feeling opens onto the vibrant excess of emotional states (registered in the comparative *happier*) and, at the same time, the capacity to know.

Milton's line break ("move and live, / And feel") stages a leap away from established hierarchies—being and movement and life—into the bewildering complexity of human thought. Adam's variegated awareness is perfectly captured by the word *feel*, which in this line suggests a sophisticated activity, capable of making fine-grained discriminations. If one can "feel that" something is the case, then feeling is not simply the passive registration of stimuli but a complex form of relation. Adam feels a happiness that outstrips his knowledge of that state. He also feels that he cannot know how happy he is. This is feeling as multiply directed mediation: it registers happiness, connects knowledge to happiness, enables a comparison between happiness and knowledge, and facilitates the recognition that intellectual knowledge cannot properly grasp the happiness being felt. Feeling in this line is a form of self-knowledge—much like Olivi's *sensus experimentalis et quasi tactualis*—that allows one to know oneself and one's state of being in a mode distinct from more intellectual or discursive forms of knowledge. "I . . . feel that I am happier than I know": this phrase perfectly captures the complexity of first-person thought as it is lived, an ebb and flow in which intellectual activity remains distinct from but nevertheless mingles with feeling. Adam's articulation of nescience complements the narrator's earlier warning to the "blest pair" as they sleep: "yet happiest if ye seek / No happier state, and know to know no more" (4.774–75). Feeling that one is happier than one knows remains a kind of lived knowledge, one that is "happiest" if the urge to know intellectually is not pushed beyond proper bounds. Adam's phrase captures what, in response to Raphael's admonition to be "lowly wise" (8.173), he calls "the sweet of life," a conscious state removed from the "perplexing thoughts," "wandering thoughts, and notions vain" (8.183, 187) enabled by untethered rational inquiry. Adam's first impressions are thus characterized by a combination of felt vitality and the desire for appropriate knowledge: of himself, of his world, and of his maker.

EVE AND THE PRIVILEGE OF INEXPERIENCE

Critics have long addressed the literary techniques, rhetorical strategies, and intertextual borrowings on which Milton draws for his verisimilar representation of life in Eden.[68] Yet many have missed the innovation at the heart of this portrait: a reconceptualization of experience that Milton initiates through a depiction of *inexperience*.[69] This latter term tends to be thought of as simply the "want of experience," the state of being unskilled or inept.[70] Eve undoes this meaning when she claims that, after awakening, she approached herself and the world with "unexperienced thought" (4.457). In this phrase, Milton evokes a mode of apprehension that exists prior to the procedures of habit and the stable knowledge or knowhow that comes with experience.[71]

The roots of *experience* stretch back through the Latin *experientia* to the Greek *empeiria*, which is derived from the prefix *em-* (to go into) and *peira* (attempt) or *peras* (limit). The term connotes "both a breaking-through and an advancement into the world, a gain of knowledge or acquired expertise."[72] In early modernity, both the meanings and the uses of *experience*

were revised. From Giacomo Zabarella to Isaac Newton, from Michel de
Montaigne to John Locke, from Martin Luther to William Perkins—across
European languages and fields of learning, the concept of experience was
used to push the boundaries of human knowledge and practice.[73] When Milton wrote *Paradise Lost*, *experience* could refer to hard-won knowledge or
knowhow accumulated over time, describe an encounter with the world
sufficient to disprove the claims of reason or inherited authority, invoke an
experiment, or conjure the broadening of one's horizons through travel. But
the term did not come to mean *consciousness* until the end of the seventeenth century.[74] *Paradise Lost* registers early traces of the semantic shift
that would lead to the synonymization of *thought*, *experience*, and *consciousness*. In repurposing *inexperience* as a positive term enabling an unfamiliar perspective on self and world, Milton performs a subtle dialectical
maneuver: "unexperienced thought" sidles up to consciousness.[75]

Throughout his career Milton drew on the semantic power of *conscientia* and its cognates.[76] In *Defensio secunda* (1653), for example, Milton answers the "slanderers" who saw his blindness as punishment for his defense
of the 1649 regicide; he claims that he repents nothing, stating: "I would not
exchange my own consciousness [*mei conscientiam*] of what I have done,
for any act of theirs however well performed, or lose the recollection [*recor-
dationem*] of it, which is always delightful to me."[77] What he holds in his
mind is more valuable to him than anything his opponents have done. But
this "consciousness" is not synonymous with the memory of what he did,
for if Milton would not "exchange" his "own consciousness," he would also
not want to lose his "recollection." As Joshua Scodel has argued, Milton
here draws on Cicero, who describes "the good man rejoicing in the 'consciousness [*conscientia*] of a life well spent.'"[78] Milton often uses the term
in this Ciceronian evaluative manner. For example, in *Pro se defensio* (1655),
he claims that when a "good man" is "assailed by slander" he "entrenches
himself in his own integrity, and in the impregnable consciousness [*conscientiam*] of righteous deeds."[79] When he translates such views into English, Milton uses *conscience*. Consider the 1655 poem to Cyriack Skinner,
in which Milton addresses his blindness and its attendant circumstances:
"What supports me dost thou ask? / The conscience, friend, to have lost
them overplied / In liberty's defence."[80] This "conscience" does not invoke
what, in *Paradise Lost*, Milton calls the "umpire conscience," which God
claims he will "place within" Adam and Eve as a "guide" (3.194–95). Instead,
in the Skinner poem, "conscience" translates a Ciceronian *conscientia*.

In *Paradise Lost*, Milton employs this cluster of terms in a similar way.
When Satan is "raised / Above his fellows" as the angel selected for the

mission to earth, he reacts "with monarchal pride / Conscious of highest worth" (2.427–29). However misguided, Satan's consciousness of his "highest worth" remains a fact. The same holds true of Eve, who in Adam's recollection of their first meeting held back from his initial invitations because her "virtue and the conscience of her worth" dictated that she should "not unsought be won" (8.502–3). What Adam here describes as Eve's "conscience" is the consciousness of her value, the fact that she is aware of "her worth." Milton usually uses *conscientia*, *conscience*, and *conscious* in the Ciceronian way. But he does not use these words in descriptions of human mindedness such as Adam's story. Milton's accounts of mindedness point toward the emerging concept of consciousness, but they do so by using *thought* and *experience* in novel ways. Milton's depictions of neonatal maturity defamiliarize first-person life as it is lived, and Eve names the phenomenological correlate of neonatal maturity when she recalls moving through the world with "unexperienced thought." This phrase captures the state of being expressed in both Adam's and Eve's remembered accounts of their first waking moments.

Eve uses this phrase during a response to Adam, who has just described how God has "raised us from the dust and placed us here / In all this happiness" with only one "easy charge," the prohibition on the fruit being the "only sign of our obedience left / Among so many signs of power and rule / Conferred upon us" (4.416–17, 421, 428–30). In her reply, Eve describes her first moments to the person "for whom / And from whom I was formed" (4.440–41):

> That day I oft remember, when from sleep
> I first awaked, and found myself reposed
> Under a shade on flowers, much wondering where
> And what I was, whence thither brought, and how.
> Not distant far from thence a murmuring sound
> Of waters issued from a cave and spread
> Into a liquid plain, then stood unmoved
> Pure as the expanse of heaven; I thither went
> With unexperienced thought, and laid me down
> On the green bank, to look into the clear
> Smooth lake, that to me seemed another sky.
> As I bent down to look, just opposite,
> A shape within the watery gleam appeared
> Bending to look on me, I started back,
> It started back, but pleased I soon returned. (4.449–63)

Eve "found" herself in a state approximating a blank slate. She does not know what or where she was, from whence she arrived, or how she came to be where she "found herself reposed." Without any experience, she has no way of knowing anything about herself or the world. But she is nevertheless able to think—to perceive, feel, use her will, and exercise her reason. She possesses "unexperienced thought."

What does this phrase mean? At first blush, it seems straightforward. Since Eve did not yet have any experience of self or world, her initial actions and state of mind should be described as "unexperienced." This is reinforced by what she does: lie down next to a "clear / Smooth lake, that to me seemed another sky" (4.458–59). To Eve, the reflection in the lake "seemed" to be "another sky" and, similarly, her own reflected image "seemed" to be a different creature responding to her movements: "A shape within the watery gleam appeared / Bending to look on me" (4.461–62). If she were experienced, she would not have mistaken lake for sky or reflection for person. Since her radical newness means that she is unable to test the properties of the world, everything she does is untested. Framed negatively, this scene highlights a firm connection between error and inexperience: Eve makes mistakes of comprehension because she lacks experience.

Framed positively, however, Eve's "unexperienced thought" enables a faithful account of phenomena as they show up. To see the world as it "seem[s]" is to see the world as it appears. If someone is experienced, they need not engage with or even notice the full spectrum of available phenomena. Living in the world is smoother if one has a clear sense of what is most relevant. Such knowledge, gleaned by experience and transformed into habit, is clearly vital to human survival: although it might be a shame that one does not notice the details of one's milieu during a routine commute, a habitual focus on what matters significantly increases the chances of making it home unscathed. But the very experience that aids the procedures of everyday life minimizes one's receptivity to what might be disclosed. Through experience, Eve learns that her reflection in the water is not a real entity. By the time she relates the story of that day she "oft remember[s]," she has gained the experience requisite for a proper categorization of things in the world. This acquired knowledge represents a gain and a loss.

On the one hand, distinguishing between a being and a reflection is important. The divine admonition—"What thou seest, / What there thou seest fair creature is thyself, / With thee it came and goes" (4.467–69)—is helpful: it lays down the distinctions that will enable Eve to understand her reflection in the water as an image manifesting the surfaces of her own body. Eve's living body, which comes and goes with her, is different from all other bodies she encounters. Reflective surfaces are the only way she can see her body in the same way she sees all other objects. It is an accomplishment to grasp that one's bodily "self" is both a means of disclosing the world and, at the same time, an object in the world that appears to others *as an object*. Since she "turn[s]" away from Adam "back" toward "that smooth watery image" (4.480), it is unclear whether Eve learns this lesson immediately. Does she turn back because she wants to gaze on the reflection with the explicit awareness that it is an image? Or does she want to continue experimenting with the "shape within the watery gleam" (4.461)?

On the other hand, the accumulated experience through which Eve learns to distinguish self from reflection brings about a loss. This loss works in two ways. First, as Mary Nyquist and others have noted, Eve's experience amounts to an introduction into a patriarchal worldview in which her playful interaction with the "watery" image is recast as "pin[ing] with vain desire" (4.466), a social hierarchy in which she comes to "see / How beauty is excelled by manly grace / And wisdom, which alone is truly fair" (4.490–91).[81] Eve's account presents an inexperienced encounter with the world as retrospectively retold through a patriarchal understanding of that world. Although Eve awakens without any preconception of hierarchy, she now sees that she lives in a space made for Adam: "He for God only, she for God in him" (4.299). The first couple is "Not equal, as their sex not equal seemed" (4.296), and Eve's experience of her social world teaches her this lesson. It is no wonder that she "oft remember[s]" the "day" she first awoke (4.449); she knows she came from Adam's rib, and every time she looks at him, she cannot help but connect the beginnings of her own autonomous, subjective life with the body of the man "for whom / And from whom" she was made (4.440–41). The first form of loss brought about by Eve's experience of sociality, then, is the loss of her originary freedom through a gendered hierarchy that subordinates her to Adam's "manly grace / And wisdom" (4.490–91).

The second form of loss is phenomenological. In her initial waking moments, Eve's "unexperienced thought" discloses the world not as it is understood but as it appears. The "clear / Smooth lake" really does seem to be "another sky" (4.458–59). The state of inexperience in which Eve finds herself makes possible an apprehension of appearance *qua* appearance. Similarly, in this initial encounter, Eve sees her own reflection just as it appears, as a "shape within the watery gleam" that "appeared" "just opposite" to "look on" her (4.460–62). The "shape" mirrors her own movements in ways Milton captures through intricately repeated diction and the flow of verse across line-breaks: "I started back, / It started back, but pleased I soon returned, / Pleased it returned as soon with answering looks" (4.462–

64). If the fate of Ovid's Narcissus threatens in Eve's later reevaluation of this moment—"there I had fixed / Mine eyes till now, and pined with vain desire" (4.465–67)—in the initial encounter there is only joyous experimentation.[82] Her actions produce reactions in the shape, and this pleasing play is predicated on her ability to see an appearance as it is, to see the shape without recognizing it as her own reflection. Milton attaches to inexperience an unfamiliar meaning: the manifestation of a more expansive phenomenal field, the ability to see a "shape" for what it is.

Eve's inexperience reveals certain aspects of the phenomenal world and also leads her to mistake reflection for substance. But she does not, for all that, have trouble categorizing. She sees the difference between plants, sky, and so on. Like Adam, who in his first moments is able to address a multitude of creatures, Eve also distinguishes hills from rivers. The details of her story, with its "flowers" and "liquid plain" (4.451–55), indicate that her perceptual capacities for discrimination are as finely tuned as Adam's. For Milton, as for Aristotle, knowledge begins with perception (which is, in the *Posterior Analytics*, a "connate discriminatory capacity" [1:165; 99b]) and especially with sight, which, in the words of the *Metaphysics*, "brings to light the many differences between things" (2:1552; 980b). Neonatally mature, both Adam and Eve wield this capacity effectively.

Yet if Adam and Eve are equally effective as perceivers, they have different relationships to language, the God-given tool through which the "many differences between things" revealed by perception are named, manipulated, and understood. Although they each come into the world equipped with a capacity for language, they actualize that capacity in different ways. Eve's initial encounter with her reflection involves an exchange of "answering looks" and not, as John Leonard has noted, "answering words."[83] Her first contact with language comes from the outside, when a mysterious "voice" warns her away from her reflection and corrects her error: "What there thou seest fair creature is thyself" (4.468). By contrast, Adam's first encounter with language is a spontaneous upwelling of speech. After realizing that he "knew not" who he was in the moments after his awakening, Adam quickly actualizes his verbal capacities: "to speak I tried, and forthwith spake, / My tongue obeyed and readily could name / Whate'er I saw" (8.271–73). His ability to "readily . . . name" the sun, earth, and other creatures anticipates the later scene of naming, when Milton follows Genesis 2:19—God brought the animals "unto Adam to see what he would call them: and whatever Adam called every living creature, that was the name thereof"—and lets Adam recall this process: "I named them, as they passed, and understood / Their nature" (8.352–53).

There is no doubt that this biblical scene was important for Milton's understanding of the unfallen intellect.[84] He returns to it repeatedly in his prose. In *Tetrachordon* (1645), Milton relies on Edenic naming in order to argue that the meaning of Adam's biblical "This is now bone of my bones, and flesh of my flesh" (Genesis 2:23) is that Eve is his image "not so much in body, as in unity of heart and mind": "But *Adam* who had the wisdom giv'n him to know all creatures, and to name them according to their properties, no doubt but had the gift to discern perfectly, that which concern'd him much more; and to apprehend at first sight the true fitness of that consort which God had provided him."[85] Milton returns to this Adamic "wisdom" in *De doctrina Christiana* when he claims that when "man had been shaped after God's image, he must also have been endowed with natural wisdom [*naturali . . . sapientia*], holiness, and righteousness. . . . And indeed without very great wisdom [*Sine permagna autem sapientia*] he could not have given names to the animate beings so instantaneously [*subito*]."[86] But if the instantaneous naming of the creatures requires "natural wisdom" and even "very great wisdom," what exactly does Milton mean by "wisdom"?

As the pairing of "natural wisdom" with "holiness" and "righteousness" in *De doctrina* suggests, and as Richard Strier has argued, Milton certainly meant that Adam possessed the ability to act appropriately, to respond to situations correctly and without extensive deliberation.[87] Indeed, Milton stresses Adam's ability to orient himself with regard to action: since "man, made after God's image, had the whole law of nature born with him [*totam naturae legem ita secum natam*] and implanted in him in such a way that he needed no directive toward it, it also follows from this that if he received any further commands either about the tree of knowledge or about marriage, they applied not to the law of nature" (1:360–61). Born with the "whole law of nature" within him, Adam knew what to do. This is why the "one thing" banned in Paradise, the forbidden fruit, needed to be something "neither good nor bad in itself," for only in this way could "man's obedience be established." Since, Milton argues, "by his own disposition man behaved well, and was by nature good and holy [*essetque naturâ bonus et sanctus*]," this must mean that Adam did the right thing "without any command" and "entirely by a natural inclination" (1:358–59). Adam possessed "natural wisdom" insofar as he knew how to act.

How did Milton understand Adam's epistemological abilities? In *Tetrachordon*, Milton suggests that Adam's "wisdom" included a real understanding of things in the world: Adam "had the wisdom giv'n him to know all creatures, and to name them according to their properties."[88] When Adam recalls this moment in *Paradise Lost*, Milton reformulates this claim:

"I named them, as they passed, and understood / Their nature, with such knowledge God endued / My sudden apprehension" (8.352–54). As Leonard argues, the order—naming followed by understanding—suggests that speech precedes knowledge, that God endows "Adam and Eve with the reason to form an accurate language for themselves."[89] Adam's spontaneous speech helps him arrive at an understanding of the disparate creature's "nature[s]," a process that is aided by the "knowledge" latent in Adam's "sudden apprehension." This all sounds very impressive. But what does Adam really know? He has named such animals as the "lion," the "ox," and the "ape" (8.393–96), but has he "understood / Their nature[s]"?

Although Milton certainly thought that Adam was extremely intelligent, he did not hold that the first man came into the world equipped with innate knowledge. Like Eve, Adam begins with nothing more than "unexperienced thought." His keen perception and intelligence enable him to see "the many differences between things." And, when paired with his natural rationality, Adam's immediately actualizable linguistic capacities enable him to name and therefore *begin* to understand those disparate "things." But no matter how perfect they may be, perception, rationality, and language only go so far. There are many things Adam cannot know without experience. Consider Adam's first speech act once more. To be sure, in this speech Adam "readily could name" many of the creatures: "Thou sun, said I, fair light, / And thou enlightened earth, so fresh and gay, / Ye hills and dales, ye rivers, woods, and plains, / And ye that live and move" (8.272–76). But this act of naming does not mean that he "underst[ands] / Their nature[s]." In fact, he makes a profound error about the nature of the creatures.

After addressing the creatures by name, Adam repeatedly asks them to speak: "fair creatures, tell, / Tell, if ye saw, how came I thus, how here? . . . Tell me, how may I know him" (8.276–80). This request is not a rhetorical flourish, for "when answer none returned," Adam recalls with disappointment, "Pensive I sat me down" (8.285–87). Although Adam can name the creatures, without experience he has no way of knowing whether they can speak. Adam is just like Eve: his first attempt to engage the world is an error, for only experience can help one make difficult judgments about which creatures can speak or about the difference between body and reflection. In this sense, then, Milton's understanding of unfallen human thought anticipates David Hume's argument in *An Enquiry Concerning Human Understanding* (1748): if he were "unassisted by experience," Adam, "though his rational faculties be supposed, at the very first, entirely perfect, could not have inferred from the fluidity, and transparency of water, that it would suffocate him, or from the light and warmth of fire, that it would consume him."[90] Much like Hume's Adam and all other human beings, Milton's unfallen Adam and Eve require experience to know most things worth knowing.

EXPERIENCE IN THE *ARTIS LOGICAE*

In order to grasp how Milton uses *inexperience* in *Paradise Lost*, we need to know what he meant by *experience*. His fullest account of the term appears in a textbook published in 1672 but written in the 1640s, the *Artis logicae*, which is dedicated to logic, an art that was, in the seventeenth century, deeply connected to experience.[91] Although logic was dedicated to syllogism and deductive reasoning, it also focused on what, following the Latin *inventio* (discovery), was called "the inventive method"—the path by which one passes from the particulars perceived by the senses, through experience, to universal concepts.[92] Milton models his own logic on Ramus's *Dialecticae institutiones* (1543). Cutting through the complexities of Aristotle's logic as presented by the scholastics, Ramus reframed how logic was taught.[93] Ramist logic was central to British pedagogy in the 1570s but saw its influence wither long before Milton wrote his treatise.[94] Milton's sympathy for Ramus was cultivated as an undergraduate at Christ's College, for logic was central to undergraduate education and Christ's was the center of Ramist thought in England. When he wrote *Artis logicae*, Milton drew on a commentary on Ramus written by George Downame, a Fellow at Christ's and a professor of logic at the university from 1585 until 1616.

Critics often reduce Milton's *Artis logicae* to a gloss on the work of Ramus and Downame, but the text is more complex than that. Although Milton draws on these authorities, he rewrites them and adds his own examples. The text is Ramist in approach, but mirrors Milton's education in logic insofar as it draws on many sources. Among the tutors at Christ's was Joseph Mede, who demanded that his students read a wide range of logic textbooks, including Aristotle and Ramus, along with a host of English and Continental sources. Broadly Aristotelian in orientation, these books were written by such figures as the German pedagogue Bartholomeus Keckermann and the English logician Robert Sanderson. As an undergraduate, Milton was taught to move between these authors, searching for the places in which their ideas came into conflict or overlapped. As Harris Fletcher argues, years later Milton carried this comparative method into his own pedagogical practice as recorded in *Artis logicae*: "He used Ramus, certainly, as a base; but the real system of logic was Aristotle plus Ramus plus Milton (the tutor) plus several other textbooks."[95]

If Milton's tutors exposed him to Ramus's methods, they also opened his eyes to the empiricist revolution that was rewriting how Aristotle should be read and that would, as Marco Sgarbi has argued, lay the groundwork for the empiricism propounded by later thinkers such as Locke.[96] At the close of the sixteenth century, a new form of Aristotelian logic eclipsed Ramism. Propounded by the Paduan professor Giacomo Zabarella, this school of thought saw logic as an instrument of the sciences, the central task of which was to outline the inventive method. In the mid-seventeenth century, Zabarella's views were circulated by an ever-growing group of scholars. Since these views saturated the textbooks used to teach Milton at Christ's, it is not surprising that Aristotelian empiricism is central to Milton's account of experience in the *Artis logicae*.[97] This account is part of a broader treatment of logic that is, in turn, grounded in a discussion of art in general. Following Downame, Milton argues that men "eminent for ability" and "natural logic"—which is "the very faculty of reason in the mind of man"—discovered [*invenerunt*] the arts. "Reason or logic" [*Ratio autem sive Logica*] is, in Milton's view, that through which art first came into being, a view he inherits from Cicero: "All things which now are summed up by the arts formerly were dispersed and scattered, until this art was applied to bring them together and bind by some reason things scattered and separate." Milton argues that the "art" Cicero had in mind was "the art of logic, either that merely natural logic with which we are born [*vel haec saltem naturalis, quam ingenitam habemus*], or that artificial logic which we learn later, for logic finds [*invenit*] and teaches the precepts of the art."[98] The arts came to exist through the "bind[ing]" properties of reason or logic, which organized what was previously "dispersed and scattered."

According to Milton's *Artis logicae*, reason or logic "binds" scattered material into arts by using "four helpers," which aid the movement from sensible particulars to universals:

> Reason or logic—first the natural reason we just spoke of, then trained reason—attaches to itself, according to Aristotle [*Metaphysics* 1.1], four helpers: sense, observation, induction, and experience [*experientiam*]. For since the precepts of the arts are general, these cannot be gathered except from specific instances, and specific instances can be observed only by the senses; without observation, which commits individual examples to memory, the senses avail nothing; without induction, which by working on individuals rather than on large numbers sets up some general rule, observation is useless; without experience, which judges the conformity with one another and as it were agreement of all individuals,

induction is useless [*inductio sine experientia, quae singulorum om-nium convenientiam in commune & quasi consensum judicet, nihil juvat*]. Hence Polus comments correctly in Plato's *Gorgias*: "Experience has brought forth art; inexperience fortune," that is fortuitous and indeed unreliable statements. (10–13)

Milton follows Downame in claiming that reason operates according to "four helpers"—"sense, observation, induction, and experience"—and then departs from his source in claiming that this is true "according to Aristotle (*Metaphysics* 1.1)."[99] Downame does not align his own "four helpers" with Aristotle's text, probably because *Metaphysics* does not discuss knowledge production in these terms.

In addition to placing this discussion in the *Artis logicae* under the auspices of the *Metaphysics*, Milton includes a quotation from Aristotle's *Prior Analytics* and quotes from Manilius's *Astronomica*, which poeticizes Aristotle's claim that "astrologic experience has furnished the principles of that science" (10–11). The thoroughgoing Aristotelianism of experience as presented in the *Artis logicae* is highlighted by how Milton follows Downame's misattribution to Plato's *Gorgias* of a quotation by the Greek sophist Polus: "Experience has brought forth art; inexperience fortune." This line comes from the first chapter of Aristotle's *Metaphysics*. To be sure, Polus is a major interlocutor in the *Gorgias*, where he makes a similar argument. But Polus's claim means something different for Plato. In the *Gorgias*, Socrates discredits rhetoric by claiming that it is not the greatest existing art, or *techne*. According to Socrates, a *techne* is a purposive discipline that requires knowledge of causes and principles. Since rhetoric does not possess such knowledge, it is, Socrates concludes, an *empeiria*, a mere "knack" for producing "gratification and pleasure"—much like pastry baking.[100] This attack on rhetoric works by degrading *empeiria*. It also responds to Polus's yoking of *empeiria* to *techne*: "Many among men are the arts experientially devised by experience [*ek ton empeirion empeiros euremenai*]. . . . Yes, it is experience [*empeiria*] that causes our times to march along the way of craft [*techne*], whereas inexperience [*apeiria*] causes them to march along the way of chance [*tuche*]" (794; 448c). Polus binds the production of *techne* to experience, positioning *empeiria* as that which leads toward art and away from inexperience and chance, from *tuche* to *techne*. By breaking this connection, Socrates eliminates experience as a player in the genesis of human knowledge. Aristotle reverses Plato's position, and makes experience central by arguing for Polus's alignment of experience with art and inexperience with luck. When Milton follows Downame in attributing Aristotle's

Polus to Plato, he effectively replaces the arguments of the *Gorgias* with those of the *Metaphysics*.[101]

In the first chapter of the *Metaphysics*, Aristotle argues that all animals are "born with the faculty of sensation" but that only some are able to produce memory from sensation. These creatures are "more intelligent and apt at learning than those which cannot remember." Although traces of experience may be found in advanced forms of animal life, experience is a higher-order development most noticeably present in human beings:[102]

> The animals other than man live by appearances and memories, and have but little of connected experience; but the human race lives by art and reasonings. And from memory experience is produced in men; for many memories of the same thing produce finally the capacity for a single experience [*empeiria*]. Experience seems to be very similar to science and art, but really science and art come to men *through* experience; for "experience [*empeiria*] made art [*techne*]," as Polus says, "but inexperience [*apeiria*] luck [*tuche*]." And art arises when from many notions gained by experience one universal judgment about similar objects is produced. (2:1552; 980b–981a)

Since, as Aristotle writes in the *Posterior Analytics*, "one necessarily perceives an individual both at a place and at a time," since "it is impossible to perceive what is universal and holds in every case," and since "it is not possible to understand through perception," Aristotle requires a bridge from perception to understanding: experience (1:144; 87b, translation modified).[103]

One "single experience" arises from "many memories of the same thing," and this experience is that which produces art and science. If, to use Aristotle's example, I remember that a medicine helped Calias, Socrates, and others when they suffered from a given illness, this is a "matter of experience." To take the next step and "judge that [this medicine] has done good to all persons of a certain constitution, marked off in one class, when they were ill of this disease . . . this is a matter of art" (2:1552; 981a). Experience is a synthesis of memories that enables one to combine past cases and recognize when, say, a given medicine should be administered to an individual here and now. By contrast, art is the skill, derived through experience, of applying a universal judgment—all people with *X* condition require *Y* treatment—to a particular case. For Aristotle, "experience is knowledge of individuals, art of universals" (2:1552; 981a). To possess an art is to know a given universal, which amounts to having a causal knowledge of the thing in question: "*knowledge* and *understanding* belong to art rather than to experience [because] men of experience know that the thing is so, but do not know why, while the others know the 'why' and the cause" (2:1553; 981a). For Aristotle, experience consolidates multiple memories of perceived events into a unit ("a single experience") upon which the edifices of art and science might be built.[104]

Aristotle does not mention "four helpers." Milton borrows these from Downame, who lists the human faculties that lead to discovery [facultas inveniendi] as sensus, observatio, inductio, and experientia, and argues that one cannot arrive at "universal precepts" [praecepta universalia] without drawing on the increasing powers of discovery and consolidation captured by these terms.[105] The closest precedent for Downame's "four helpers" appears in Robert Sanderson's Logicae Artis Compendium (1618), which provides a parallel account of the Methodi inventionis by which one comes to know things about the world. According to Sgarbi, Sanderson shifted the English study of logic "radically towards empiricism" by "focusing on the cognitive process of knowing particulars more than [Aristotle] himself ever dared do" and by doing so with such clarity that "all subsequent logicians considered and discussed his approach."[106] Sanderson's method expands Aristotle's program in a manner followed by Downame and Milton: beginning with the "sensation" of "singular" things, Sanderson ascends to observatio (a process that connects singular sensations and situates them in the mind) and experientia (the collection of disparate observations in order to preserve them for future use) before concluding with inductio, which uses the accumulation of experience to infer universal conclusions. In Sanderson's model, experience collects observations (experientia; qua collectas plures observationes . . .), and then induction draws on a range of collected experiences (inductio; qua collectas plures Experientias . . .).[107]

This is how one moves from experience to universals. In a move with important consequences for Paradise Lost, Milton follows Downame in reordering the relationship between induction and experience. The Artis logicae argues that induction works not with "large numbers" but sets up a "general rule" based "on individuals." Experience is the mechanism of judgment that checks the general rule recommended by induction against the "conformity of all individuals" (10–11). For Milton, experience guarantees that induction's treatment of individuals holds true, so that a general claim can be advanced. By collecting and cross-checking, experience becomes the bridge between universal judgments and the work performed on "individuals" by sensation, observation, and induction. Since experience produces "conformity" and "agreement," it is, by definition, always of many things.

Developed by Aristotle, advanced by Zabarella, and tweaked by such English logicians as Sanderson, this notion of experience lies behind Milton's treatment of the concept in *Paradise Lost*. This sense of *experientia* is the horizon of expectation against which *experience* in Milton's Eden gains its meaning.

EXPERIENCE, EXPERIMENT, AND "UNEXPERIENCED THOUGHT"

Adam and Eve are the paragons of what, in the *Artis logicae*, Milton calls "natural logic," or the "very faculty of reason in the mind of man" (10–11). Without any training in the "artificial logic which we learn later," Adam and Eve argue brilliantly, drawing on the "merely natural logic with which we are born" to infer the existence of God and to arrive at a Ptolemaic understanding of the cosmos, among other accomplishments (12–13). Of course, Adam and Eve are not born but created. This means that their reason or logic is more than "merely natural." Whereas, in Robert Burton's words, "a child is rational in power, not in act," Adam and Eve are neonatally mature, rational in both power and act from the moment they are created.[108] But this does not mean that their knowledge is acquired in some superhuman way. Like all other human beings, Adam and Eve follow the inventive method Milton outlines in the *Artis logicae*.

Adam suggests that experience emerges only over time, from multiple encounters with a particular phenomenon. During a conversation with Raphael, Adam responds to the angel's advice to avoid astronomical speculation, to "be lowly wise," and to be concerned only with "what concerns thee and thy being" (8.173–74) by thanking the angel for having "taught" him "to live, / The easiest way, nor with perplexing thoughts / To interrupt the sweet of life" (8.182–84). Adam now knows that he should avoid "wandering thoughts, and notions vain" (8.187), and that trouble arises from speculative drift:

> But apt the mind or fancy is to rove
> Unchecked, and of her roving is no end;
> Till warned, or by experience taught, she learn,
> That not to know at large of things remote
> From use, obscure and subtle, but to know
> That which before us lies in daily life,
> Is the prime wisdom, what is more, is fume. (8.188–94)

Raphael's admonitions lead Adam to realize that the mind's endless "roving" can only be contained by what he learns. This learning can occur through experience or by being warned. The narrative of *Paradise Lost* is grounded on this distinction. Must humans be "by experience taught"? Genesis suggests that we do not learn well through warning alone. This is implicit in Eve's story: "unexperienced," she innocently returns to her reflection despite being warned by a divine voice about the "shadow[y]" qualities of her own "image" (4.457, 467–72).

Paradise Lost refuses William Blake's distinction: Milton's song of innocence is, simultaneously, a song of experience. Still unfallen, Milton's Adam and Eve come to possess experienced innocence.[109] Resisting a long tradition within which Adam and Eve remained virgins in Paradise, Milton insists that they were sexually experienced.[110] By the time readers encounter Adam and Eve, they have also gained experience in the arts of gardening, the preparation of food, and astronomical speculation, among other practices. When Adam and Eve first wake up in *Paradise Lost*, they are simultaneously innocent and inexperienced. As they come to know themselves and the world, they gain experience but remain innocent—right up until the moment they bite into the forbidden fruit. In *Paradise Lost*, innocence is not coterminous with inexperience, nor experience with fallenness.

The Fall is predicated on a desire to eliminate time and a parallel attempt to revise the meaning of experience. When Raphael instructs Adam on the nature of things, the angel suggests that human "bodies may at last turn all to spirit, / Improved by tract of time, and winged ascend / Ethereal" (5.497–99). It is this "tract of time" that Eve hopes to bypass when she eats the fruit. Satan inspires this idea. He conjures for Eve a dream in which she is told that if she eats the forbidden fruit she will be "henceforth among the gods / Thyself a goddess, not to earth confined, / But sometimes in the air, as we, sometimes / Ascend to heaven" (5.77–80). While Raphael suggests that it is possible that humans might in "tract of time" "ascend / Ethereal" (5.498–99), Satan convinces Eve that if she eats the fruit she will "Ascend to heaven," "henceforth" (5.77–80). In the dream, when she tastes the fruit, she enjoys a "high exaltation": "Forthwith up to the clouds / With him I flew" (5.86–90). This dynamic is replayed when Satan tempts Eve in waking life. Since the serpent has, Satan argues, eaten the fruit and gained the capacity to speak, if a human did the same then he or she would become divine: "I of brute human, ye of human gods" (9.712). And this is precisely what Eve has in mind when she eats. "[N]or was godhead from her thought" (9.790), Milton observes just before he reinforces the point by having Eve speak to the tree: "dieted by thee I [will] grow mature / In knowledge, as the gods who all things know" (9.800–804). There are many causes for Eve's fall, but this pivotal event is, at least in part, grounded in a desire to compress Raphael's "tract of time."

Although this reading of Milton's treatment of time is commonplace, so far as I know, his parallel treatment of experience has gone unremarked.[111] Until the Fall, the meaning of *experience* in *Paradise Lost* corresponds with the sense of the term outlined in the *Artis logicae*. When Adam claims that he can be "by experience taught" to curb the mind's drive toward obscure speculation (8.190), or when Abdiel states that the angels are "by experience taught" about God's goodness (5.826), both stress that they have been or can be "taught" by iterated events judged to be in conformity with one another. In the moments after her fall, Eve twice invokes experience. In each case, she eliminates or significantly compresses the "tract of time" necessary for experience. In her first fallen speech act, after addressing the tree that she believes will enable her to know "all things," Eve turns to experience, the "guide" that she believes has led her to this discovery: "Experience, next to thee I owe, / Best guide; not following thee, I had remained / In ignorance, thou op'nst wisdom's way, / And giv'st accéss, though secret she retire" (9.807–10). At the end of the epic, when Adam and Eve are expelled from the garden and the world lies "all before them," their "guide" will be "providence" (12.646–47). Just after the Fall, however, Eve insists that experience is her best guide. But what experience of the fruit could she possibly have? She has only eaten it once. Eve is wrong to think she has experience in the sense of the term that has been operative in the poem. She wants to "grow mature / In knowledge" (9.803–4) but bypass the required steps.

The conditions for this error lie in Milton's understanding of the inventive method. In the *Artis logicae*, Milton follows Downame in revising Sanderson's order of induction and experience. For Sanderson, induction is based on observations collected by experience, while for Downame and Milton it is based on singular observations and then cross-checked by experience. Induction now precedes experience. In *Paradise Lost*, Eve falls prey to a difficulty opened by this reordering. She reasons inductively from singular observations but believes that she has acquired experience. In Milton's view, even when following the inventive method, one can make inductive leaps from singular events. Moving from the particular to the universal through induction may *seem* to provide something like knowledge, but by activating this shortcut one is claiming to have knowledge *without experience*. This is precisely the mental operation that Eve performs in the moments leading to her fatal decision. She encounters a speaking serpent who informs her that eating the fruit has enabled him to live a "life more

perfect" than "fate / Meant me" (9.689–90). Following her tempter's reasoning, from this individual encounter Eve induces a general rule: all creatures
that eat the fruit will become "more perfect." If the fruit "Gave elocution to
the mute, and taught / The tongue not made for speech to speak [its] praise"
(9.748–49), then Eve will gain something greater when she eats, becoming
"as the gods who all things know" (9.804). She vaults inductively from individual to general. Compressing the "tract of time" required for knowledge,
she acts without experience.

In this way, Eve exposes one of the grave dangers of "unexperienced
thought." She now possesses abundant experience of her general relation to
the world, but she is completely inexperienced (of course!) when it comes
to speaking serpents. To follow Polus, inexperience can generate nothing
but luck. Applied without experience, the success of inductive reasoning
depends on chance: a given act of inexperienced induction could be right
or very wrong. Eve's invocation of experience as her "Best guide" is thus
terribly mistaken: she has no experience to confirm her inductive leap. To
frame this point in terms of a distinction available in German, Eve possesses *Erlebnis* (experience in the sense of a lived encounter, living through
a given situation) without *Erfahrung* (experience in the sense of *empeiria*,
knowledge or skills gathered over time). Crucially, she acts as though she
wields the authority of the latter state. Eve's mistake begins to transfer the
semantic force of *experience* into the orbit of something approximating
consciousness.

When Eve tempts Adam, she again speaks of experience in the sense
of *Erlebnis* as though it were experience in the sense of *Erfahrung*. If she
"thought" that "death menaced" after her forbidden snack, Eve would
not, she informs her husband, "persuade thee," but "rather die / Deserted"
(9.977–80). But her own experience suggests that her act has given not death
but rather, in Satan's words, a "life more perfect" (9.689):

> I feel
> Far otherwise the event, not death, but life
> Augmented, opened eyes, new hopes, new joys,
> Taste so divine, that what of sweet before
> Hath touched my sense, flat seems to this, and harsh.
> On my experience, Adam, freely taste,
> And fear of death deliver to the winds. (9.983–89)

Adam can eat without fear, Eve asserts, because he can trust her experience,
which has revealed the fruit to be a source of intense pleasure. Had she

followed God's prohibition instead of taking experience as her guide, Eve would have "remained / In ignorance" (9.808–9). This experience, which she hopes to share, has shown that "the event" of breaking the prohibition did not lead to the expected consequences. Here, Eve uses experience to invoke one of its standard effects: the disruption of inherited but untested views.[112] Eve positions her experience against an inherited prohibition; instead of death, she discovers "life / Augmented." Caught up in the thrill of "new hopes" and "new joys," Eve claims that her "experience" reveals that the fruit's "divine" taste makes "what of sweet before / Hath touched my sense, flat . . . and harsh." Milton positions this claim for experience against Adam's earlier hope that his fancy might, "by experience taught," learn how what "before us lies in daily life" excels "obscure and subtle" speculations (8.190–93). Adam anticipates the fruit of experience, while Eve claims that a single encounter replaces these old ambitions with "new hopes" (9.985).

In the aftermath of the defining "event" of human history, Eve realizes the enormity of her semantic error: "Adam, by sad experiment I know / How little weight my words with thee can find, / Found so erroneous, thence by just event / Found so unfortunate" (10.967–70). Eve suggests that Adam has every reason to find "little weight" in her speech. After all, her words—"On my experience, Adam, freely taste" (9.988)—have proven "erroneous" and, through the "just event" of the Fall, "unfortunate." Eve mistook her inexperience (and its necessary connection to chance and error) for experience. But she has learned a lesson: the difference between *experience* and *experiment*.[113] Eve employs a distinction made by Bacon and other experimentalists between a single experiment and accumulated experience.[114] The event of the Fall was a "sad experiment" and did not, as she previously thought, emerge from experience. When Eve understands a single encounter in terms of "Experience" (9.807, 9.988), she makes a mistake that she later corrects with her use of "experiment" (10.967).

With this background in place, we can now fully appreciate what is at stake in Eve's "unexperienced thought" (4.457). When Eve recalls what it was like to first encounter the world, she claims that she did not, at that time, possess the ability to judge what Milton calls the "conformity" or "agreement" of individual observations. To operate in a state of inexperience is to approach oneself and the world with only the resources of perception and the scattered memories of previous perceptions that have not yet coalesced into a single experience. This is not an abject position. Perception is intelligent. But to live without experience, with only perception and memory, is nevertheless to live, at best, as an intelligent animal. According to Aristotle, animals have "but little of connected experience," and it is

precisely the capacity to make connections, to perform consolidations between and among memories, that marks the threshold of the human. This
capacity allows humans to develop the power of reason, or *logos*, the ability
to give an account of *how* and *why* such and such is the case. All animals
perceive, but only some are able to retain memories or "grasp [a given per-
ception] in their minds." When many memories accumulate in the minds of
such animals "a difference comes about" such that some of them—humans
preeminently—"come to have *logos* [reason or an account] from the retention
of such things [that is, remembered perceptions]" (1.165–66; 100a, translation modified).[115] The "difference" that produces the potential for *logos* is
nothing less than *empeiria*.

Eve's account of awakening draws on experience she has since accumulated but recalls a moment prior to experience. Since she is neonatally
mature, the usual order of things is upended; Eve possesses *logos* prior to
experience. Milton stresses the topsy-turvy nature of Edenic epistemology
by noting that Eve approaches the world with "unexperienced *thought*."
In Aristotle's *De anima*, the activity of thinking—*noein* or *dianoeisthai*—
includes imagination, judgment, opinion, knowledge, and understanding
(but not, as Descartes will later argue, sensation or perception). The precondition for error, thought is a mental activity that "is found only where there
is discourse of reason [*logos*]" (1:680; 427b). At the same time, *logos* emerges
from experience. If Aristotle's views on *empeiria* are harmonized with his
understanding of thought, then *logos* connects these two terms: experience
is required for *logos* and *logos* is required for thought. Eve's phrase lays bare
what Patrick Hume found "new and strange" about Edenic awakening: she
emerges into the world with thought and *logos* but without experience—
without, that is, the very ground for postlapsarian *thought* (understood in
an Aristotelian sense). Insofar as Milton's use of *thought* can be understood
as similarly Aristotelian, then Eve's "unexperienced thought" conjures the
strange condition of neonatal maturity.[116]

But this phrase also captures a larger shift in seventeenth-century con-
ceptions of the inner life. When Eve recalls encountering the world with
"unexperienced thought," Milton uses a positive valuation of *inexperience*
to bring the Aristotelian understanding of *experience* into contact with
thought, which was acquiring a distinctively modern meaning. If, for Aristotle, thought occupied one of the upper rungs on a vertical hierarchy
of mental acts stretching from perception up to intellection, for Descartes
(as we saw in the introduction), thought is the horizontal plane on which
things appear. This sense of thought includes beneath its umbrella acts of

reasoning, memory, imagination, judgment, will, and, most importantly, perception and sensation. In *Paradise Lost*, Milton uses thought in this sense.

It is not an exaggeration to claim that much of *Paradise Lost* occurs in the landscape of thought. Satan claims that the "mind is its own place, and in itself / Can make a heaven of hell, a hell of heaven" (1.254–55). To be sure, Satan is wrong about his ability to control his state of mind, for he cannot escape his troubled interiority: "horror and doubt distract / His troubled thoughts, and from the bottom stir / The hell within him, for within him hell / He brings" (4.18–21). A similar idea is captured in Michael's comforting promise, delivered to Adam and Eve as they prepare to enter the wider world: if they will live virtuously, "then wilt thou not be loath / To leave this Paradise, but shalt possess / A paradise within thee, happier far" (12.585–87). Milton uses *thought* over a hundred times in *Paradise Lost* to index a mixture of intellectual and affective activities. This mixture is evident in the passage describing how Satan's thoughts are "distract[ed]" by both "horror" (an affective response to an unpleasant situation) and "doubt" (an epistemological indecision about what is true). In this epic, *thought* captures the full complexity of inner life: Satan has the "thought / Both of lost happiness and lasting pain" (1.54–55); Eve feels how "thoughts in my unquiet breast are risen" (10.975); Adam "promise[s]" "great joy" to "his thoughts" (9.843); the serpent claims to recall how he "turned [his] thoughts, and with capacious mind / Considered all things visible in heaven" (9.603–4); and Adam acknowledges that "All human thoughts come short" of God's "eternal ways" (8.413–14). *Thought* covers the full range of phenomenality, all of the somethings that might appear to someone. Consider Raphael's warning to Adam. "Solicit not thy thoughts with matters hid," the angel commands: "joy thou / In what [God] gives thee, this Paradise / And thy fair Eve; heaven is for thee too high / To know what passes there; be lowly wise: / Think only what concerns thee and thy being" (8.167–74). Using the reflexive construction "joy thou" to suggest how Adam's "thoughts" should enjoy his Edenic milieu, Raphael stresses that Adam should "Think only what concerns thee and thy being." Both as a noun ("thought") and as a verb ("think"), Milton's use of this term suggests that the act of thinking tends toward abstraction but should be grounded in perception and affect.

Adam's response shows that he shares Raphael's broad understanding of thought as something that participates in perception, feeling, and speculative reasoning. Raphael has, Adam claims, "taught" him "to live" the "easiest way":

> nor with perplexing thoughts
> To interrupt the sweet of life, from which
> God hath bid dwell far off all anxious cares,
> And not molest us, unless we ourselves
> Seek them with wandering thoughts, and notions vain. (8.182–87)

Milton here modifies "thoughts" with adjectival present participles ("per-plexing," "wandering"). These modifiers distinguish the kinds of thought one should avoid, the thoughts that "interrupt" life by generating "anxious cares." But when thought is not "perplexing" or "wandering," it is nev-ertheless still *there*; it is that through which "the sweet of life" is made manifest. One can think in healthy or problematic ways, but so long as one is conscious, one is always thinking. Even when Adam describes his first encounter with sleep, he emphasizes his own thought:

> there gentle sleep
> First found me, and with soft oppression seized
> My drowsèd sense, untroubled, though I thought
> I then was passing to my former state
> Insensible, and forthwith to dissolve:
> When suddenly stood at my head a dream,
> Whose inward apparition gently moved
> My fancy to believe I yet had being,
> And lived: one came, methought, of shape divine[.] (8.287–95)

Fading into sleep, Adam "thought" he was becoming "insensible," about to "dissolve." He cannot find the language for describing the state in which he found himself—"suddenly stood at my head a dream" is a profoundly strange phrase—but he is certain that it occurs through thought: "one came, methought, of shape divine." From dreams, through perception, affection, passion, and abstraction: *thought* in *Paradise Lost* covers all of the some-things that might show up for someone.

In Eve's "unexperienced thought," then, Milton's use of inexperience sutures this historically novel sense of *thought* on the Aristotelian notion of *experience*, thereby discovering the plenitude of thought in the absence of experience. This revaluation of inexperience brings "unexperienced thought" right up to the edge of consciousness, which by the end of the cen-tury will come to designate nothing other than the experience of thought. Poised between an old Aristotelian paradigm and what Arnold Davidson would call a new "conceptual space" generated by a subtly different "style

of reasoning" that was reordered when *consciousness* took on a nonevaluative meaning and became linked with such terms as *thought, self, ego,*
and so on, Milton's brilliant phrase illuminates a late seventeenth-century
mutation in the meaning of *experience*.[117] When the word begins to mean
what we would call consciousness, it continues to bind disparate events or
encounters together, but this binding function now operates synchronically
(linking multiple, simultaneous perceptions, affects, and ideas under one
rubric) as opposed to diachronically (linking multiple, repeated instances
across time). Experience as *empeiria* is mobilized over time; consciousness
in its modern sense is, as we will see in more detail in the following chapters, rooted in a given moment from which it stretches back in time and out
into the world. In other words, the emerging seventeenth-century sense of
conscious experience runs parallel to the Cartesian redefinition of thought
in terms of *conscientia*: both thought and experience came to index a phenomenal field in which objects, environs, sensations, affects, memories,
and other sorts of ideas could, through the concept of consciousness, be
described as appearing at the same time.

CHAPTER TWO

Human Nature Experienced

ADAMIC AWAKENING: A GENEALOGY

In "De l'experience," Michel de Montaigne discusses his kidney stones in a way that sheds light on one of the greatest differences separating fallen from unfallen life: the fact that Edenic pleasure does not exist in dialectical tension with pain. "But is there anything so sweet," Montaigne asks, "as that sudden change, when from extreme pain, by the voiding of my stone, I come to recover as if by lightning the beautiful light of health, so free and so full, as happens in our sudden and sharpest attacks of colic? . . . How much more beautiful health seems to me after the illness, when they are so near and contiguous [*si voisine et si contiguë*] that I can recognize them in each other's presence in their proudest array, when they vie with each other, as if to oppose each other squarely!"[1] In human life as it is normally lived, pleasure is felt most acutely in the aftermath of pain, and the former gains meaning in light of the latter. The same holds true for the relationship between life and death. But this is not the case in Milton's Eden, for, as Eve rightly claims, prior to the Fall, she and her husband are "not capable of death or pain" (9.283). In Paradise, Adam and Eve live without death and feel pleasure without pain. They are, in fundamental ways, completely different from their descendants. Unlike all of us—who are born in tears, who live often with pain and always toward death—Adam and Eve are created as neonatally mature, nonmortal beings whose lives play out in sentient softness. This difference is central to Milton's poem, which is, after all, about how paradise was lost. Yet, as I argue in this chapter, Milton also wants to extend an invitation to his readers, to elicit a quiver of recognition through his mimetic representation of the unfallen Adam and Eve. *Paradise Lost* aims to show its readers what has been lost but also, at the same time, to show them the extent to which their lives remain paradisal.

In this chapter, I explore how Milton maintains this balance between estrangement and recognition in his depiction of originary experience. Milton's depiction of these moments was, as Patrick Hume maintained, "new and strange," but he also makes sure that Adam's and Eve's first impressions remain recognizably human.[2] Although most of us have not reasoned ourselves toward the existence of God, almost everyone knows what it is like to wake up, open our eyes, stand, feel our bodies lead us in unanticipated ways, explore our environments, and desire to know something we do not yet know. Milton describes the impossible perspective of neonatal maturity, but this perspective discloses actions and forms of awareness that are disarmingly ordinary. In this section, I survey the various sources and analogues that may have been available to Milton when he wrote *Paradise Lost*. This genealogical work presents a negative image of what Milton *did not do* in order to reveal more clearly the extent of Milton's accomplishment. I make two interrelated arguments: first, that Milton is one of the first writers in the Genesis tradition to present originary experience in Eden; and second, that Milton is the first writer to describe this experience as a recognizably human event. This pair of claims forces a confrontation with the question at the heart of this chapter: *why* did Milton portray neonatal maturity and "unexperienced thought" in the first place? As we will see, the answer is bound up with his deepest anthropological conviction (humans are thoroughly embodied creatures), his most firmly held political opinion (human communities are bound together through an instinctive desire for society), and one of his fundamental theological assumptions (God's existence is evident through the most basic elements of everyday experience). Milton's extraordinary literary innovation offers an invitation to readers: *Come, enter into this vision of unfallen human life, and find yourself already at home in Eden.* And if we accept this alluring offer, we discover Milton's core beliefs naturalized, bundled together in the finite universal lives of the unfallen Adam and Eve.

Since there is not, so far as I can tell, a precedent for Milton's description of Eve's waking moments, my foray into his predecessors leans on what the Genesis tradition says about Adamic subjectivity. Such hexameral poems as Guillaume de Salluste Du Bartas's *Sepmaine* (1578) and Torquato Tasso's *Il mundo creato* (1607) use Adam's creation as an opportunity to discuss the human body and soul. These writers set up their analyses of Adam as an inventory of parts viewed externally. Du Bartas goes so far as to frame his description of Adam's form as an anatomy. He describes himself as making "incision[s]" in the body to access its "inward parts," and allies his poetic technique with such surgeons as Hippocrates and Galen.[3] Yet even when

they dig into Adam's entrails in search of his soul, these hexameral writers
present the first man as a series of surfaces, an object of knowledge. Milton's
great innovation was to adopt Adam's perspective *ab initio*. Of course, first-
person accounts of life in Eden are central to dramas based on Genesis. Milton drew inspiration from the long history of Middle English and neo-Latin
dramas that participate in what J. M. Evans calls the "Genesis tradition."[4]
Even such sophisticated late humanist dramas as Hugo Grotius's *Adamus
Exul* (1601), Serafino della Salandria's *Adamo caduto* (1647), and Joost van
den Vondel's *Adam in Ballingschap* (1664)—all of which feature moving
depictions of Adam's and Eve's inner lives—do not give Adam and Eve the
chance to describe their emergence into life from their own perspective.[5]

To be sure, *Paradise Lost* is not the first text to record Adam's subjective experience at the moment of awakening. But the versions of this experience that Milton may have encountered all stress Adam's prelapsarian
difference. The kernel for the idea of exploring Adam's early experiences
might have originated in the *Zohar*, a compilation of Jewish myth and scriptural exegesis—discovered (and perhaps written) in medieval Spain—that
describes how after "the spirit of life was poured upon him, as is said: *He
blew into his nostrils the breath of life* (Genesis 2:7)," Adam "rose and realized he was of above and below; he grasped and knew supernal wisdom."[6]
The *Zohar* thus probes prelapsarian awareness. This stress on Adam's ex-
ceptionality is expanded in the *Chronicles of Jerahmeel*, a medieval compendium of Jewish legends. After the Adam of *Jerahmeel* has been created,
he immediately reacts to his sudden arrival in the world:

> Adam then stood up and gazed above and below, saw all the creatures
> which God had created, and was amazed with wonderment, and he be-
> gan to extol and praise his Creator, and said: "How great are Thy works,
> O Lord!" He stood upon his feet, and was in the likeness of God; his
> height extended from the east to the west, as it is said, "Behind and in
> front Thou has formed me." Behind, that is the west, and in front, that is
> the east. All the creatures saw him and were afraid of him; they thought
> he was their creator and prostrated themselves before him.[7]

As the passage begins, this Adam resembles Milton's. He awakens, stands,
and observes his new environment, wonderstruck, then immediately praises
his creator. But the Adam of *Jerahmeel* is in command of himself and his
situation. Less hesitant and unsure than Milton's character, this Adam is
something more than human, a fact that becomes emphatically clear when

we learn of his enormous height and the fear with which the other creatures worship him. One other possible predecessor for Adam's originary
experiences in *Paradise Lost* is Giambattista Andreini's *L'Adamo* (1613).
Upon awakening, the eponymous hero of *L'Adamo* addresses God in already-
knowing language: "O great and peerless Monarch." This Adam does not
notice his environment or himself; he is automatically directed toward the
unearthly. He seems to dwell in the heavens: "Already, Lord, in ecstasy de-
vout / My mind flies upwards, soars beyond the clouds, / Past every sphere,
yea, enters even heaven / And there beholds the stars, a throne for man."
More mystic than man, he "merge[s]" with and becomes "part" of God.[8] The
Adams of the *Zohar*, the *Jerahmeel*, and *L'Adamo* are given first impressions
that light up exotic scenes. They foster the impossibility of identification. By
contrast, Milton's Adam invites readerly recognition.

Had he so desired, Milton could have made Adam's waking just as alien
as Andreini's. The opening scene of *Paradise Lost*, discussed in chapter 1
above, provides a perfect counterpoint. When Satan first opens his eyes, he
sees a scrambled, almost incomprehensible world. Milton gives readers a
scene of awakening that is all but unintelligible. Satan may witness "huge
affliction and dismay" (1.57), but what he sees is not only mixed with the
distorting effects of "pride" and "hate" (1.58); it is viewed through a perceptual apparatus that sees "as far as angels' ken" (1.59)—whatever that
might be! The reader confronts a strange environment disclosed by "darkness visible." Milton possessed an expansive poetic repertoire for depicting
the strange and unfamiliar. Adam's and Eve's recollections are "new and
strange" not because they are fantastic but because they provide a radically
fresh perspective on the everyday experience of being alive and in the world.
They perform the function that Victor Shklovsky ascribes to the work of
art, which exists, he claims, "that one may recover the sensation of life; it
exists to make one feel things."[9]

Milton renders Adam's and Eve's first thoughts as recognizable as possible because he wants to provide a perspective through which readers can
see themselves and the world as if for the first time. *Paradise Lost* thus does
what Traherne recommends to readers of his *Centuries*: "Were we to see [the
world] only once, the first Appearance would amaze us," Traherne claims,
"But being daily seen, we observe it not" (5:57, bk. 2, sec. 21)—a situation
that might be remedied by placing yourself in "the midst of the World as if
you were alone" (5:52, bk. 2, sec. 7), as if you were "the Adam or the Eve" for
whom the world was created (5:54, bk. 2, sec. 54). This is the heart of Milton's accomplishment: the use of a startlingly novel first-person perspective

to apprehend afresh the profoundly quotidian yet all but forgotten joy of existence. By employing a strategy that assumes that the effects of the fall have not fully ruined human nature, Milton reveals how far removed his account of human awareness is from the anthropologies of fallen humanity propounded by Calvin and Augustine, among others.[10] If Milton's aim is to invite the reader to inhabit the neonatally mature perspectives of Adam and Eve, then, as Joanna Picciotto, Sharon Achinstein, David Simon, and other scholars have recently argued, prelapsarian life cannot be alien, and post-lapsarian life cannot be irredeemably fallen.[11] This is why Milton stresses Adam's and Eve's sensual interaction with the world, their innocent errors, and the fact that they too require experience in order to gain knowledge: he wants readers to see glimmers of themselves in his depiction of the unfallen human condition.

THE EGO EMBODIED: MILTON'S SUBJECT

The extent of Milton's attempt to minimize the difference made by the Fall becomes fully visible through his depiction of the prelapsarian human body. As we saw in chapter 1, Milton suggests that Adam's and Eve's knowledge of self and world depends on and is necessarily interwoven with the feeling of self and world. This privileging of feeling emerges from Milton's conviction that the human being is a *totus homo* in which soul is inseparable from body.[12] Milton held clear beliefs about human nature: human beings are fundamentally embodied, the human body is necessarily ensouled, and the human soul has no existence before, beyond, or after the life of the body.[13] These beliefs determine how Milton interprets and rewrites the Genesis account of Adam's and Eve's creation in both *Paradise Lost* and *De doctrina Christiana*. They also shape Milton's sense of what it is like to be a human being. The centrality of feeling to Adam's first impressions is a consequence of the importance that Milton ascribes to embodiment. In this section I examine Milton's anthropological beliefs, their impact on Edenic experience in *Paradise Lost*, and their relationship to both Milton's exegetical practices and his poetic production. I begin by showing how Milton frames Adam's and Eve's first thoughts as inhering in their embodied individuality—how, that is, Milton positions Edenic thought as an *accident* (in the sense used in early modern logic) belonging to a *subject*.

The meanings of the term *subject* were in the midst of a profound shift when Milton wrote *Paradise Lost*. As a concept, the *subject* received its foundational treatment in Aristotle's *Categories*, in which *hypokeimenon*

(translated into Latin as *subjectum* and into English as *subject*) is a term sig-
nifying *ground* or *substratum*.[14] Some things, Aristotle argues, are "*said of
a subject but are not in any subject*" (the generic term *human being* is "said
of a subject, the individual man, but is not in any subject"). Other things are
"in a subject but are not said of any subject"; the "individual knowledge-of-
grammar is in a subject, the soul, but is not said of any subject" (1:3; 1a). For
Aristotle, *hypokeimenon* unites two registers of meaning: first, the logical
subject, the part of a proposition on which other terms are predicated (*human being* is predicated of an individual person); and second, the physical
subject, the substratum in which accidents inhere (knowledge-of-grammar
inheres in the soul). In the *Categories*, *hypokeimenon* brings these registers together in the term *ousia* (translated into Latin as *substantia* and into
English as *substance*): "A substance—that which is called a substance most
strictly, primarily, and most of all—is that which is neither said of a subject
nor in a subject, e.g., the individual man or the individual horse" (1:4; 2a).
Through this double negation ("neither said of . . . nor in"), *ousia*, or substance, becomes the privileged example of the *hypokeimenon*, or subject;
the "individual man" is both the logical subject of which things are said and
the physical subject in which things inhere. The use of *subject* in this sense
is far removed from the term's modern meaning—the *I* that is the subject of
feeling, perception, imagination, reason; the subject as ground of subjectivity. Even Augustine, the ancient thinker who most deeply pondered something like what we now call subjectivity, refused the conceptual power of the
subjectum. In *De trinitate*, he argues that because knowledge and love are
directed both toward the self and to what is beyond the self, they must be in
the soul "substantially" [*substantialiter*], not "as in a subject, as color, or
shape, or any other quality are in the body" [*non tamquam in subjecto, ut
color, aut figura in corpore, aut ulla alia qualitas*] (28; 9.4.5).[15]

   But if, for Aristotle, Augustine, and other ancient thinkers, *hypokeimenon* or *subjectum* were never terms for subjective awareness, by Milton's
time *subjectum* had come to mean precisely that. It gained this meaning
as early as the thirteenth century, when Pierre Jean Olivi argued that my
perception of my own acts—seeing, thinking, and so on—presupposes "my
prior perception of myself as subject of those acts." In other words, all acts
depend on "the perception of the subject itself," the "me" that subtends
those acts.[16] If this meaning was new in Olivi's time, it was already familiar
when, in an objection to Descartes's *Meditationes*, Hobbes claimed that
the French thinker had run together "the thing which understands with the
intellect" and had therefore failed to do what "all philosophers" do; namely,

"make a distinction between a subject and its faculties and acts [*distin-gunt subjectum a suis facultatibus & actibus*]" (CSM 2:122; AT 7:172).[17] In seventeenth-century England, the term *subject* possessed both its ancient meanings and the newer connotations of subjectivity. Milton was alert to the relationship between subject-as-*hypokeimenon* and subject-as-ego. This relationship subtends Adam's and Eve's first thoughts.

Milton employed Aristotle's sense of *hypokeimenon* from the beginning to the end of his career. He explicitly invokes the term in *De doctrina* when he reconciles his definition of sin as "Actual" with the traditional idea that sin is nothing more than privation by stating that "the action itself is not the material out of which sin [is made], but simply and solely the underlying thing [*subjectum*] and *hypokeimenon* in which [it exists]."[18] This late claim that action is the subject of sin follows an Aristotelian logic that Milton internalized in Cambridge and expressed in his "At a Vacation Exercise in the College" (1628), which pokes fun at Aristotle's *Categories*. In this poem, *Ens*, or being, as the father of the categories, recalls a prophecy made about his eldest son, *Substance*:

> [He] Shall subject be to many an accident.
> O'er all his brethren he shall reign as king,
> Yet every one shall make him underling,
> And those that cannot live from him asunder
> Ungratefully shall strive to keep him under,
> In worth and excellence he shall outgo them,
> Yet being above them, he shall be below them;
> From others he shall stand in need of nothing,
> Yet on his brothers shall depend for clothing.[19]

The joke depends on the near identity of *ousia*, "substance," and *hypokeimenon*, "subject."[20] Since a given substance—say, an individual person—is the subject of which things are said and in which accidents inhere, substance is, despite its position of importance, "subject to many an accident." If substance is "king" of the other categories—quantity, quality, and so on—it is also the *hypokeimenon*, or substrate, that supports them and so is an "underling," "under" them, "below them," and "cloth[ed]" by them. Milton is alert to the multiple meanings of *subject*, playing with the word's political connotations by drawing out the paradox of a king who is a subject and a ruler who is an underling.

He also invokes the term's modern sense of subjectivity. The poem opens with a meditation on the subjective experience of acquiring and using language, of the accident that is language coming to inhere in the first-person awareness of a human subject:

> Hail native language, that by sinews weak
> Didst move my first endeavouring tongue to speak,
> And mad'st imperfect words with childish trips,
> Half unpronounced, slide from my infant lips,
> Driving dumb silence from the portal door,
> Where it had mutely sat two years before. (79, 1–6)

Much like the accounts of Adam and Eve, this poem begins by recalling pre-linguistic experience, how speech emerges from "dumb silence" when an active "endeavouring tongue" is passively moved by a preexisting language. If the poem begins with a "childish" subject acquiring the attribute of language and experiencing that acquisition as it "slide[s] from [his] infant lips," it continues by reinforcing how language clothes subjective thought in exactly the same way that accidents provide "clothing" for Aristotle's *hypokeimenon* in the poem's second half. Milton bids his "native language" to "from thy wardrobe bring thy chiefest treasure"; namely, those "richest robes and gayest attire" that will help to dress his "naked thoughts," which need to be "decked" in the "best array" English has to offer (79, 18–26). Poetic composition requires that the subject's "naked thoughts" (79, 23)—the inner, creative, minded life of the speaking *I*—"depend" on the accident of language "for clothing" (82, 82). When Milton claims that he would rather be pursuing a more ambitious poetic project than the treatment of Aristotle's *Categories* he is about to deliver, he marks his own position as subject of language by appealing to yet another meaning of *subject*: "Yet I had rather, if I were to choose, / Thy [English's] service in some graver subject use" (79, 29–30). Repeating the first-person pronoun that is the grammatical subject of these lines, Milton stresses that his position as speaking subject is what unites the poem. The subject as *hypokeimenon*, the political subject, the subject as poetic topic: all are subtended by the speaking *I* as locus of subjectivity, as the self-aware subject in which language inheres.

In *Paradise Lost*, Milton explores the multiple meanings of *subject*. Adam and Eve describe the moment when a subject in the sense of *hypokeimenon* acquires consciousness. Adam's "I found me laid" and Eve's "I . . . found my self reposed" give readers the moment when first-person consciousness—the emergence of the subjective *I*—first inheres in individual human beings, the *ousiai* that are the subjects in which attributes or accidents inhere. In seventeenth-century English, *laid* and *reposed* were synonyms.[21] Beyond implying the actions of a God who places the first human beings in Eden, these verbs also mark the extent to which Milton had internalized the vocabulary of logic. In the *Artis logicae*, Milton claims that an effect "absolutely argues a cause, so that in whatever way the cause has been laid down, the effect is laid down; thus when the effect has been laid down, the cause is laid down, for as the causes give being to the effect, so the effect has its being from causes [*causam absolutè arguere; ita ut quemadmodum posita causa, ponitur effectum; sic posito effecto, ponatur causa: ut enim causae dant esse effecto, ita effectum esse suum habet à causis]*" (70–71). Employing a syntactical chiasmus that interweaves cause with effect through iterations of the verb *ponere* (to lay or put in place), Milton performs the closeness with which effect and cause are knit in ways that resonate with the creation of Adam and Eve. The first humans are effects of a divine cause. If Adam's *laid* translates *ponere*, Eve's *reposed* traces its etymological roots back to that Latin source. The moment when effect emerges from cause is also the moment when the *subject* first appears. In the *Artis logicae*, something becomes a *subjectum* "when, after it has already been constituted by its causes, something as a sort of addition besides its causes is adjoined to it" (78–79). One way that an effect turns into a subject is "when the subject receives ingrafted or inherent adjuncts" [*subjectum recipit adjuncta insita sive inhaerentia*]; as when the soul becomes the "subject of knowledge," for knowledge is "added over and above [the soul's] essence" (80–81).

Hypokeimenon is etymologically derived, as Milton knew well, from *hypokeisthai*, which literally means "to be laid or placed somewhere."[22] Adam's "I found me laid" and Eve's "I . . . found my self reposed" thus signal the moment when an effect becomes a subject, when an attribute—here the first glimmering of subjective experience—is added to a newly caused effect that, at that moment, transforms into a subject. Milton's *laid* and *reposed* are unobtrusively technical terms that position the emergence of Adam and Eve into waking life as the emergence of a subject from a newly caused effect that is, at the same time, the emergence of subjectivity. Adam's and Eve's accounts of awakening give Milton's readers imagined access to the moment when the subject as *hypokeimenon*, which has just been laid down, first acquires consciousness and the human being transforms into the sort of subject (an ego) capable of finding itself.

The idea that first-person experience is an accident of human *ousia* would have been deeply attractive to Milton because of Aristotle's insistence that an attribute that inheres "in a subject . . . cannot exist separately from what it is in" (1:3; 1a). Milton captures this notion in "At a Vacation

Exercise in the College" where he claims of substance that accidents "cannot live from him asunder" (*Shorter Poems*, 82, 77). This is Augustine's reason for rejecting the subject-accident relation as an explanatory model for the soul-understanding relation. When color (accident) inheres in a body (subject), Augustine claims, color does "not have its own proper substance in itself"—and he wants such states as understanding and love to be substantial, able to stand on their own.[23] Milton, on the other hand, denies the separability of soul from body and rejects the possibility of life after death. For Milton, there is no experience without embodied individuality. Human thought is an accident of human being and is therefore profoundly dependent on and shaped by that in which it inheres.

In *Paradise Lost*, this relation of dependence is conveyed by how Milton positions Adam's account as an outgrowth from Raphael's narration of how God created humankind on the sixth day. "Thee I have heard relating what was done / Ere my remembrance," Adam tells Raphael, "now hear me relate / My story, which perhaps thou hast not heard" (8.203–5). When Adam begins his "story," he has already learned from Raphael about where he came from and the materials from which he was made.[24] Raphael's version of Adam's creation, which is the foundational account of human substance in the poem, is based on a careful harmonizing of the Priestly text, Genesis 1:26 ("Let us make man in our image") and the Jahwist text, Genesis 2:7 ("And the Lord God formed man of the dust of the ground, and breathed into his nostrils the breath of life; and man became a living soul").[25] Raphael's words combine both versions, weaving the fact that Adam was made "in the image of God" with a story about how God "breathed / The breath of life" into Adam's nostrils so that he "becam'st a living soul" (7.525–28). Most early modern commentators thought that the Priestly text was an epitome, while the Jahwist text offered an expanded version of the same story.[26] Raphael's intertwining of Genesis 1:26 and 2:7 rewrites scripture, but the angel also lays down the nature of the human subject from which Adam's subjectivity will emerge in book 8.

Raphael's account subsumes the main mark of human privilege from Genesis 1:26 (being made in God's image) into the tripartite Jahwist story of Adam's creation: the formation of dust, the inspiration of the breath of life, and the becoming of a living soul. Whereas the Priestly text features an immediate creation both for humans (Genesis 1:27: "male and female created he them") and animals (consider Genesis 1:21: "God created great whales"), the Jahwist text offers an Adam who seems crafted in time. This process of creation was considered a sign of human privilege. Calvin claims that the "purpose" of the process described in Genesis 2:7 was "to put a

difference betweene man and brute beasts. For these had their beeing out of
the earth in a moment. But in that, man was fashioned by little and little,
his dignitie herein is shewed to be speciall. For why doth not God com-
maund him to come out of the earth alive straight away, but onely bycause
he might by a certeine privilege excel all the thinges whiche he brought out
of the earth."[27] Du Bartas makes the same point in the *Sepmaine*. In Joshua
Sylvester's 1604 translation, God

> both at-once both [*tout d'un coup*] life and body lent
> To other things; but when in Man he meant
> In mortall limbs immortal life to place,
> He seemed to pause, as in a weighty case:
> And so at sundry moments [*momens divers*] finished
> The Soul and Body of Earth's glorious head.[28]

The other creatures are given body and life "at once."[29] Milton follows this
understanding of nonhuman creation. In Raphael's account, the earth brings
forth "Innumerous living creatures, perfect forms, / Limbed and full grown"
(7.455–56) to dramatic effect: "grassy clods now calved, now half appeared /
The tawny lion, pawing to get free" (7.463–64).[30] Even while half covered
by the earth, the lion is already an individuated living being with an urge
for independence.[31]

Unlike Milton's "tawny lion," the Adam of *Paradise Lost* does not (in
Calvin's words) "come out of the earth alive straight away." He is formed
according to the process suggested by Genesis 2:7. Milton inherited a variety of views on the nature of this process. Aquinas rejected the notion that
"man's body was formed first in priority of time, and that afterwards the
soul was infused into the formed body," and argued that God made both
at the same time, a conclusion that finds in Genesis an Aristotelian truth:
"The soul is the form of the body." For Aquinas, the "breath of life" in
Genesis is merely an "exposition" of how God formed man from the dust.[32]
By contrast, Calvin saw in Genesis 2:7 a tripartite process involving the
formation of an inanimate body from dust, the addition of a living soul, and
the inspiration of the divine image.[33] When Milton provides his own interpretation in *De doctrina Christiana*, he emphatically insists that in creating
Adam, it was "the soul as much as the body that [God] made then." Adam
was created as a whole man, a *totus homo*:

> When man had been created in this way, it is at last said: *so man became
> a living soul* [*sic factus est homo anima vivens*]; from which it is under-

stood (unless we prefer to be taught what the soul is by pagan authors) that man is an animate being [*hominem esse animal*], inherently and properly one and individual, not twofold or separable—or, as is commonly declared, combined or composed from two mutually and generically different and distinct natures, namely soul and body—but that the whole man is soul, and the soul is man [*sed totum hominem esse animam, et animam hominem*]; namely a body or substance [*corpus nempe sive substantiam*] which is individual, animated, sensitive, and rational; and that the breath of life was neither part of the divine essence, nor was it even the soul, but a certain breeze or divine power wafted out, suitable only for the power of life and reason and instilled in an organic body; since man himself when finally made—the whole man himself, I say—is in distinct words called "a living soul." Hence the word Soul [*Anima*] in the Apostle's interpretation, I Cor. 15:45, is rendered as 'animate being' [*animal*]. (1:303)

Milton has no interest in the dualism invented by such "pagan authors" as Plato, Christianized by Augustine and others, modified by Descartes, and propounded by such English contemporaries as Henry More.[34] In Milton's view, human substance—the individual human being with a full range of vital capacities who is the subject of lived experience—is a fully embodied soul. Milton aligns this view with "that dictum of Aristotle—a very true one, I think—that if the soul is wholly within the whole body, and wholly in whatever part of it," then the human seed and the "power of matter" through which it produces new human souls carries everything requisite for the development of rational human substance (1:307).

Adam was created as an "animate being," the unity of which Milton captures with the Latin *animal*, a lexical choice that gets behind a tradition of privileging soul over body that had developed around Latin translations of scripture. Tremellius translates the Hebrew of Genesis 2:7—*nephesh chaya*—as *anima vivens* (living soul), a translation that could be read as supporting body-soul dualism. In Genesis 2:7, *nephesh* is best translated as "that which breathes, the breathing substance or being" or as "the man himself."[35] Milton's use of *animal* instead of *anima* brings out the Hebrew meaning. The term highlights the extent to which the Greek of Paul's epistles is in conformity with Hebrew usage. In 1 Corinthians 15:45, Paul writes, "The first man Adam was made a living soul." Paul's Greek for "living soul"— *psychen zosan*—was usually translated into Latin as *animam viventem*, a translation that stresses soul, used in the Vulgate and followed by Erasmus.[36] Theodor Beza's 1598 multilingual edition of the New Testament, on which

Milton here relies, rejects this reading. Beza translates Paul's phrase as *animal vivens* and thus eliminates the language of soul, stressing creaturely unity instead.[37] Milton replaces the traditional Latin *anima* of Genesis and Corinthians with Beza's *animal* (a Latin translation of Paul's Greek *zosan* that is also better suited to the Hebrew *nephesh* of Genesis), and in so doing presents an Adam who was always and necessarily an individual "whole." To be a human is to be an animated, sensitive, and rational substance. The breath of life cannot, then, be the addition of a soul, for in Milton's reading human soul and body are an indissoluble unity. An animate, individual whole came into being the moment God formed Adam from the dust.[38]

Indeed, Milton's reading of Genesis 2:7 in *De doctrina* renders the breath of life oddly superfluous. For Milton, the phrase "[God] breathed into his nostrils the breath of life" is not an "exposition" of what came before, as Aquinas contends, but signals instead a vague "certain breeze or divine power wafted out [*auram quandam sive virtutem divinum afflatum*], suitable [*habilem*] only for the power of life and reason and instilled in an organic body"—precisely the body that, as we have just seen, *already has* both life and reason.[39] It is unclear what role the breath of life plays in this scenario, but what is clear is that Milton wants to deflate its importance. He moves from the grammatically active, emphatic blowing of divine breath portrayed in Genesis 2:7 (*sufflavitque in nares ipsius halitum vitae* in Tremullius's Latin) to the undirected wafting of a "certain breeze" conveyed by the grammatically passive *afflatum* (1:302–03). Milton facilitates this transformation by mobilizing other scriptural passages against Genesis 2:7. Drawing on Zechariah 12:1, which claims that God "shapes man's spirit inside him," Milton claims, "Nor did he merely blow [*inflavit*] that spirit in, but in each actual person he shaped it, inwardly implanted it, and enhanced and distinguished it with its own faculties" (1:300–301). The spirit is not "merely" blown into the nostrils but is "inwardly implanted" [*penitùs indidit*], "shaped" within the human being, the *totus homo*, as he is created. This spirit, Milton continues, is not "part of the divine essence" but "only something human." Milton thus minimizes the "breath of life" or *halitum vitae* in Genesis 2:7 so that, only a few sentences later, these words are transformed; *halitum vitae* has become little more than the breath of life that we and all other creatures routinely "take in" (1:300, 302).[40]

In *De doctrina*, Milton returns to the unity implicit in the Hebrew *nephesh*. He rejects the Latin interpretive tradition that stressed Adam's movement from inanimate body to living man and schematized this as a tripartite process. But Milton's beliefs about the nature of humankind stand in tension with the narrative propulsion of Genesis 2:7: "And the Lord God formed man of the dust of the ground, and breathed into his nostrils the breath of life; and man became a living soul."[41] The repeated conjunction *and* suggests a temporal process: God formed man, *and then* breathed the breath of life into his nostrils, *and then* man became a living soul. The final *and* may be read either as introducing a third temporal stage in the process or as signaling the instantaneous culmination of the first two stages.

Milton's interpretation of Genesis militates against both of these options. He navigates this tension between scriptural source and anthropological conviction in *Paradise Lost*, when Raphael tells of Adam's creation:

> [God] formed thee, Adam, thee O man
> Dust of the ground, and in thy nostrils breathed
> The breath of life; in his own image he
> Created thee, in the image of God
> Express, and thou becam'st a living soul. (7.524–28)

Raphael does not simply deliver a harmonized version of Genesis 1:26 and 2:7. These lines infuse the Genesis narrative(s) with Milton's belief that Adam was created as an inseparably whole human being.[42] In Genesis, God forms Adam *out of* the dust of the ground (*ex pulvere terrae*, in Tremullius's Latin), but in *Paradise Lost* Adam *is* the dust of the ground: God "formed thee, Adam, thee O man / Dust of the ground." Registering more than the etymological connection between the name Adam and the Hebrew *adamah* (ground or earth), this identification suggests that Adam's personhood remains tethered to the "Dust of the ground." It is not the dust but Adam who is formed. Milton insists on this point by interposing a string of pronouns and names—"thee, Adam, thee, O man"—between the verb *formed* and the noun *dust*. To be sure, Raphael is addressing Adam, hailing him as he whose creation is being discussed. But the angel's collection of terms positions Adam's *thee* as that which is initially formed, so that the stages of the Genesis narrative no longer suggest a process of hominization but different ways of expressing the same act: God "formed *thee*, Adam, *thee*," "and in *thy* nostrils breathed," "in his own image he / Created *thee*," and "*thou* becam'st a living soul." The introduction of the breath of life in *Paradise Lost* works in a manner akin to the *afflatum* of *De doctrina*: it adds some flair to Adam's creation, but appears only after the *totus homo* has come into being.[43]

If Milton's anthropological convictions inflect Raphael's retelling of Genesis, they also influence Adam's and Eve's first impressions. Indeed, the insistence in *De doctrina* that Adam was created as a "body or substance [*corpus nempe sive substantiam*] which is individual, animated, sensitive, and rational" recalls the ancient use of *subjectum*. Milton's use of *substantia* in *De doctrina* draws on Aristotle's definition of *ousia* and its overlap with *hypokeimenon* in the *Categories*. Adam and Eve are individual, animate, sensitive, and rational substances that tell stories about the moment in which they became *subjects*, both in the Aristotelian and the modern sense. Consider the moment when Adam becomes a subject and is given subjectivity: "Soft on the flowery herb I found me laid / In balmy sweat" (8.254–55). The composition of the line makes it impossible to disentangle body from soul. There can be no question that both *I* and *me* are one with the body: the *I* nestles "on the flowery herb" while the *me* is bathed "In balmy sweat," and the same holds true for Eve, who was "reposed / Under a shade on flowers" (4.450–51). When Adam feels himself and his environment, it is *as* a body that lies on the ground and then instinctively stands up on two feet (8.261); when he runs, it is with "supple joints" (8.269); when he speaks, it is with a tongue (8.272); and so on. The body is a requirement for human thought. Slightly later, Adam solidifies this point when, after having explored his environment, he is once more reflexive: "Myself I then perused, and limb by limb / Surveyed" (8.267–68). He can peruse himself by surveying his body because he is an "individual, animate, sensitive, and rational" being. God himself corroborates this view when, in Eve's story, he attempts to correct her mistaken appreciation for her reflection: "What there thou seest fair creature is thyself, / With thee it came and goes" (4.468–69). The "self" implicit in "thyself" and that "came and goes" must, I think, be understood as what the water reflects. The self simply *is* the living body.

Adam and Eve awaken into first apprehensions thoroughly shaped by Milton's anthropology. In these accounts, Milton attempts to represent a form of consciousness that provides the subjective counterpart to his anthropological conviction that the human being is an *animal*. This is why, as we saw in chapter 1, Milton takes such care to make sure that knowledge is felt, and that feeling is related to knowing: all forms of human awareness carry within them the ineluctable necessity of embodiment.

PRIMA NATURAE FROM GROTIUS TO MILTON

Milton depicts Adam's and Eve's originary experience to provide an account of what it is like to be a living human body, and does so in order to elicit readerly identification with the unfallen human condition. But *Paradise Lost* also rethinks the experience of embodied human life in Edenic terms. Following ancient and scholastic writers, many seventeenth-century thinkers stressed the extent to which the drive to self-preservation is the basic principle underpinning all human activity. According to Hobbes, Spinoza, Locke, and many others, the innate urge to preserve one's body from harm is the bedrock on which human community and all political order stands.[44] Milton took advantage of the affordances of unfallen life in Eden in order to dispute this view. The primacy of self-preservation is based upon the fact of mortality, but, in Eden, the relation of Adam and Eve to death remains very different from that of mortal beings. Milton used this minimized role played by death in the lives of Adam and Eve to replace the centrality of self-preservation with a different principle that he saw at the core of human existence: the desire to live a life in common with other human beings. In *Paradise Lost*, Milton dramatizes the felt revelation of this principle by exploiting Adam's and Eve's neonatally mature ability to recollect the first impressions of their own natures—what ancient thinkers called *prima naturae*.[45]

Milton places his own political convictions at the core of human nature by situating Adam's and Eve's life stories in dialogue with the Dutch polymath Hugo Grotius. Milton's admiration for Grotius is well known. A famous humanist and jurist, Grotius wrote elegant neo-Latin lyric poetry, three biblical tragedies, a number of theological polemics, histories of republicanism, irenic defenses of Christianity, biblical commentaries, and one of the founding texts of international law, *De jure belli ac pacis* (1625, 1631).[46] Milton mentions him approvingly in the *Doctrine and Discipline of Divorce* (1643) and *Tetrachordon* (1645). In Milton's view, Grotius, "yet living," was "one of prime note among learned men."[47] In addition to admiring Grotius's learning, it is likely that Milton esteemed the Dutchman's politics. As the pensionary of Rotterdam, Grotius had advocated both for the Remonstrants and for Republican principles during the Arminian controversy of 1618–19. Grotius's role in the affair led to his imprisonment and then—after a daring escape—his exile in France, where he served as the Swedish ambassador. When Milton arranged to meet Grotius in Paris during the summer of 1638, they had many common interests to discuss, including Arminianism, natural law, and the new philological methods propounded by Joseph Scaliger, Daniel Heinsius, and Gerardus Vossius.[48] No doubt, they would also have discussed poetry and perhaps even the nature of the lives of Adam and Eve prior to the Fall.

Shortly after his 1639 return to England from his continental trip, Milton generated a number of drafts for biblical dramas in a notebook now known as the Trinity Manuscript. Among these were four outlines for a drama based on the fall of Adam and Eve, one of which was a five-act play entitled "Adam unparadiz'd"—a title that resonates with one of Grotius's

earliest works, *Adamus exul*, a five-act tragedy about the Fall. Published
alongside a number of Latin religious poems in a volume entitled *Sacra in
quibus Adamus exul* (1601) when Grotius was only eighteen, this tragedy
exerted a strong influence on *Paradise Lost*. Milton likely read *Adamus
exul* quite early in his life. Christian Gellinek has demonstrated that Milton's youthful "Paraphrase of Psalm 114"—ostensibly written when he was
only fifteen—is in fact a paraphrase of Grotius's poem "*In exitu Israel de
Aegypto*," which was published in the *Sacra*.[49] If this is true, then Milton
would have read Grotius's Edenic tragedy even before he entered Cambridge
in 1625 and would have known the work for well over a decade before he
met Grotius in 1638. Perhaps their conversation in Paris included a discussion of *Adamus exul* that led Milton to begin brainstorming about his
own literary projects after his return. In any case, it is clear that Grotius's
drama left its mark on *Paradise Lost*. From the mid-eighteenth century onward, many critics have noted the verbal echoes and structural similarities
between the two works.[50] But this intertextual relationship is most often
simply presupposed; *Adamus exul* is often mentioned but rarely analyzed.
In this section, I argue that, when read in light of the treatment of Adam and
Eve in *Adamus exul*, Milton's relationship to Grotius's juridical thought
offers a key for understanding the treatment of originary experience in *Paradise Lost*. Milton's scenes of Edenic awakening rework Grotius's influential
understanding of human nature from a first-person perspective and illuminate it through the affordances of neonatal maturity.

Across his career, Grotius attempted to balance two primary but distinct impulses in his account of human nature. On the one hand, he advances robust claims about the primordial force of self-preservation. A living creature is, by definition, a being that cares for itself and pursues its
own self-interest. Human beings are necessarily invested in their own self-
preservation, and this fact is at the root of natural law. On the other hand,
Grotius also advances claims about what he calls the *appetitus societatis*
in human beings, their innate desire for society or social instinct. Insofar as
we are rational animals, human beings are naturally motivated to seek out
each other's company and cooperate with one another. At different points
in his career, Grotius posits either self-preservation or some version of sociality as the fundamental principle on which the study of human nature
and natural law must be grounded: as I will show, the early *De jure praedae* (1604–06) evinces a much stronger interest in self-preservation than the
mature *De jure belli ac pacis*. I argue that the extent of Grotius's youthful
investment in self-preservation is visible even in the Eden of *Adamus exul*.
This is surprising. After all, the unfallen Adam and Eve cannot suffer pain,

let alone die. But if the necessity of self-preservation only makes sense in light of mortality and its attendant ills, Grotius's Edenic characters nevertheless understand themselves and the world in terms of this principle. After exploring the tensions in *Adamus exul* between an acknowledgment that unfallen human life exists without death and a simultaneous insistence that self-preservation is meaningful in Eden, I argue that *Paradise Lost* represents the nonmortal life of the unfallen Adam and Eve by eliminating the dominance of self-preservation from Edenic life and, at the same time, stressing the extent to which the *appetitus societatis* is fundamental to human nature. Employing the privileged principle of Grotius's mature juridical thought, Milton scrubs Grotius's Eden clean of self-preservation.

In the Prolegomena to *De jure praedae*, a posthumously published text written to defend the seizure of Portuguese goods in the Straight of Singapore by merchants from the Dutch East India Company, Grotius privileges self-preservation:

> Since God fashioned creation and willed its existence, every individual part thereof has received from Him certain natural properties whereby that existence may be preserved and each part may be guided for its own good, in conformity, one might say, with the fundamental law inherent in its origin. From this fact the old poets and philosophers have rightly deduced that love, whose primary force and action are directed to self-interest, is the first principle of the whole natural order. . . . For all things in nature, as Cicero repeatedly insists, are tenderly regardful of self, and seek their own happiness and security.[51]

Nature is "fashioned" by a God interested in the preservation of what he has made. In forceful language that prompts Richard Tuck to situate *De jure praedae* in a lineage of modern thought leading directly to the principles of Hobbes's political philosophy, Grotius claims that the "fundamental law inherent in [the] origin" of each creature is an impulse to preserve its own existence.[52] This "self-love" or "self-interest" leads each creature to be "tenderly regardful of self." The "happiness and security" of that self is the "primary force and action" for all natural things; it subtends the promptings of "aversion and desire" (22). "Implanted by nature" in "all living creatures," these impulses to pursue or flee are first and foremost concerned with what is "good and evil" for the body: "for example, among the ills, death, mutilation of the members (which is akin to death) and disease; among the blessings, life with the body whole and healthy" (22). Further, these desires and aversions lead to the first "precept of the law of nature";

namely, "It shall be permissible to defend [one's own] life and to shun that
which threatens to prove injurious" (23).

Self-preservation also preoccupies Grotius in his later revision of these
ideas in *De jure belli ac pacis*. For instance, when considering whether it
is "ever Lawful to make War," Grotius argues that "the first Impression of
Nature" [*prima naturae*] is "that Instinct whereby every Animal seeks its
own Preservation, and loves its Condition, and whatever tends to maintain it; but on the other Hand, avoids its Destruction, and every Thing that
seems to threaten it" so that it is the "first Duty of every one to preserve
himself in his natural state."[53] From this it follows that among "the first
Impressions of Nature [*prima naturae*] there is nothing repugnant to War;
nay, all Things rather favor it: For the End of War (. . . the Preservation of
Life and Limbs . . .) is very agreeable to those first Motions of Nature; and
to make use of Force, in case of Necessity, is in no wise disagreeable there-
unto; since Nature has given to every Animal strength to defend and help
itself" (1.182–83; 1.2.3).

But Grotius also strenuously modifies this view in *De jure belli ac pacis*.
As Benjamin Straumann has shown, Grotius draws on the Stoic arguments
advanced by Marcus Cato in Cicero's *De finibus*.[54] In this text's second iteration of what Jacques Brunschwig calls the "cradle argument," Cicero writes,
"Immediately upon birth (for that is the proper point to start from) a living
creature feels an attachment for itself, and an impulse to preserve itself and
to feel affection for its own constitution and for those things which tend to
preserve that constitution" (232–33; 3.5).[55] But although this drive for self-
preservation is first chronologically, it is not first in order of importance, for,
Cicero continues, as human beings develop, they graduate from the self-love
shared by all animals and enter, with the help of rationality, a sphere of
progressively refined choices, from "choice conditioned by 'appropriate action'" to "choice fully rationalized and in harmony with nature," which is
the point at which "the Good properly so called first emerges" (238–39; 3.6).
This is precisely the position Grotius adopts in *De jure belli ac pacis*, for immediately after laying out what is entailed by the *prima naturae*, he claims
that the "Knowledge of the Conformity of Things with Reason, which is a
Faculty more excellent than the Body," should be "preferred to those Things,
which mere natural desire first prompts us to." After all, "right Reason
should be dearer still to us than that natural Instinct" (1:181; 1.2.2). This
position is already visible in "The Preliminary Discourse" with which the
book begins, for in his refutation of the ancient skeptic Carneades's claim
that "Nature prompts all Men, and in general all Animals, to seek their
own particular Advantage," Grotius argues that human beings "excel all the

other Species of Animals" especially insofar as "amongst the Things peculiar to Man, is his Desire of Society [*appetitus societatis*], that is, a certain
Inclination to live with those of his own Kind, not in any Manner whatever,
but peaceably, and in a Community regulated according to the best of his
Understanding. . . . Therefore the Saying, that every Creature is led by nature
to seek its own private Advantage, expressed thus universally, must *not* be
granted" (1:79–81; *prolegomena* 6). In Grotius's view, this "Sociability" or
"Care of maintaining Society in a manner conformable with the Light of human Understanding, is the Fountain of Right, properly so called" (1:85–86;
prolegomena 8).

Self-preservation plays a larger and more unambiguously important role
in *De jure praedae*, written earlier in Grotius's life. To be sure, the text also
modifies its stress on self-preservation: "God judged that there would be
insufficient provision for the preservation of His works, if He commended
to each individual's care only the safety of that particular individual," Grotius writes around 1604, "without also willing that one created being should
have regard for the welfare of his fellow beings." The "love for oneself" necessarily runs alongside the "love of others" (24). But the stress falls differently in each text. *De jure praedae* opens with a focus on self-preservation
and modifies that view later on, while *De jure belli ac pacis* opens with a
focus on the *appetitus societatis* and introduces self-preservation only well
into the book. Scholars have explained this shift in a variety of ways. Tuck
holds that the stress on sociality only fully emerges in the 1631 revisions,
when Grotius reissued his text in the hope of returning to the Netherlands;
the stress on the *appetitus societatis* was, Tuck argues, added to appease
Dutch authorities.[56] By contrast, Hans Blom sees the later appeal to the *appetitus societatis* as a more theoretically sophisticated amplification of Grotius's earlier account of *fides* in *De jure praedae*.[57] For my purposes, the reason for this shift is unimportant. What matters is that in 1604 Grotius was
deeply interested in the extent to which the notion of self-preservation and
the avoidance of death played a principle role in the life of any and all creatures—human beings included.

Grotius's early fascination with self-preservation plays a crucial role in
Adamus exul.[58] A rich, psychologically complex drama about the Fall of
Adam and Eve, four of this play's five acts dwell on prelapsarian life in Eden.
For Grotius, the advent of human mortality is perhaps the most important
consequence of the Fall. In the biblical prohibition of Genesis 2:17, God
states, "Of the tree of the knowledge of good and evil you shall not eat, for
in the day that you eat of it you shall die." At the end of act 3, the Chorus
of Grotius's play reframes the prohibition so that the lived consequences of

mortality are even further stressed: God "forbids to pluck" the fruit "lest condign death / Avenge the fault that [God] admonishes / For pain, and Toil, and wretched Care and Age, / and Death, and every other ill of life / Lurk hidden in the fair, forbidden bark."[59] Prior to the fall, human life existed purely *as life*, in the absence of any dialectical tension with death. Grotius is explicit on this point, which sparks Satan's anger in act 1: "with impunity both [Adam and Eve] scorn / The wounds of Death [*mortis ambo vulnera / Impune temnut*]; Disease, and deadly Pain, and Fear [*metus*] / (Itself more horrible than all the pangs of Pain) / Flee from them [*Fungiunt ab illis*]" (102–3). The Edenic couple has no concern for death. Moreover, all of the difficulties associated with mortal life—disease, pain, fear—"flee" from their bodies. Prelapsarian human life has nothing to do with the ills of mortality.

This is a difficult thought. How can we—defined as we are by our mortality—even imagine a human life without death? After all, in the tradition in which Grotius wrote, the verb *to live* was all but synonymous with the verb *to die*. This is a point made by Augustine's *Confessiones*, in which to be born is equated with entering a "dying life" [*vitam mortalem*] or a "living death" [*mortem vitalem*] (6; 1.6.7). The degree to which human life is bound up with death and, more deeply, an awareness of death means that everything we do is implicitly connected to the fact that we will die. My decision to write these words here and now is *meaningful* precisely because I have chosen to be here at my desk instead of at home with my family or on vacation or at the bar or skydiving. Of course, even if I were immortal, I could not do all of these things simultaneously. But given that I will die, I can never do all the many things I would like to do, and my choice to be *here, now* derives its meaning from the fact that mortality forces me to select what I will do at the expense of other options. If I were immortal, these choices would be far less charged, for, with world enough and time, I could do almost everything.

As mortal beings, we can be injured, become ill, or die: these existential facts mean that we need to care for ourselves—to be, as Grotius, cribbing Cicero, puts it in *De jure praedae*, "tenderly regardful of self." Self-preservation is thus constitutive of creaturely life because mortality is part of fallen life. We possess an innate drive to preserve ourselves by avoiding things that are bad for us, which Grotius lists as, "among other ills, death, mutilation of the members (which is akin to death) and disease" (22): precisely the "ills" that, in *Adamus exul*, our first parents "with impunity both scorn" (102–3). Satan laments that, compared with Adam and Eve, the fallen angels "Now scarcely live as slaves; our life is less than life. / Death, which the fear of mankind knows not yet," Satan laments, "Is my supreme desire" [*Mancipia poenae vivimus, nec vivimus. / Mors una, quam nec novit humanis timor / Mihi summa voti est*] (104–5). If the fallen angels live a life that is not fully life, Adam and Eve live a life that simply *is* life—precisely, Grotius suggests, because they do not yet know the fear of death.

But this is not the end of the story. Grotius's Eden is carefully designed so that it *includes* death and pain, so that even if Adam and Eve do not yet know the *fear* of death, they nevertheless have insight into the workings of death, a natural part of the life of all nonhuman creatures. In act 2, an angel instructs Adam on the great chain of being. Plants are different from other living creatures, the angel avers, because "pleasure [*voluptas*] can delight no plant, / No pain can lacerate its senses to the quick [*nullus excruciat dolor*]" (118–19). Pleasure and pain begin with animals, which

> perceive the smells of things, and prove their food by taste,
> And touch with them performs its function; they have learned
> To flee from things that harm and follow after good [*Nocitura discunt fugere, quae prosunt sequi*]
> But they are drawn by the senses, lacking Mind as guide, [*Sensu trahuntur: Non habent mentem ducem*]
> Nor do they, as in mutual conversation, grasp
> And render rational thought. Religion shows them not
> That God exists. All weal for them is in brief life [*omnis in brevi vita est salus*].
> To thee, beyond these, is assigned a soul, exempt
> From death and sin, and mistress of the body's senses. (118–19)

Although Adam's and Eve's "soul[s]" are "exempt / From death and sin" [*mortis expers et mali*], the lives of all other living creatures are "brief." Animal life is structured by the drive toward self-preservation; animals "flee from things that harm and follow after good." All animals likewise reproduce—"Each duly brings to birth those like to it in form"—so that the "kind" will not "perish" with the individual (128–29). Living creatures perform the "act of sex" so that they can "preserve" their form of life, a drive rooted in the fact that they will die (134–35). At the end of the second act, the Edenic Chorus pulls no punches: "All living creatures wait upon [God's] nod; / Destined to Death abhorr'd, / They die in mute accord," their "spirits into empty air depart / And leave the senseless bodies in dismay; / So, suddenly the heart / Is stilled, the lung knows not its vital gust, / And soon the flesh is but a little dust" (144–45). Grotius's Eden is a place in which animals can be harmed, suffer pain, and die. Although human beings live outside the law of self-preservation, this principle is nevertheless at work in Eden and informs Adam's and Eve's understanding of the world.

In dramatizing an Eden in which animals suffer and die, Grotius weighs in on a debate. The account of creation in Genesis suggests that in the beginning all creatures were vegetarian: "Behold," God states in Genesis 1:29–30, "I have given you every herb bearing seed of their own kind, to be your meat: And to all beasts of the earth, and to every fowl of the air, and to all that move upon the earth, and wherein there is life, that they may feed upon." Many medieval and early modern commentators understood this passage to imply that prelapsarian animals did not prey upon one another. In his thirteenth-century *Hexameron*, Robert Grosseteste claims that in Eden "No animal would have been an enemy of others, nor would have eaten the flesh of others."[60] Du Bartas articulates this widespread view when he describes how, after Adam's fall, the harmony of the world was undone such that "the woolf the trembling sheep now pursues."[61] But this view was not universal. As Alastair Minnis has argued, many medieval thinkers insisted that, even in paradise, animals died and suffered pain. In *De genesi ad litteram*, Augustine claimed that some Edenic animals lived "by plunder," an idea picked up by Aquinas, who argues that, while in Eden, "clashes and antipathy would have been natural between certain animals" and that carnivorous creatures sought out paradisal blood.[62] In choosing this side of the debate, Grotius makes it possible for Adam and Eve to know death without fearing it. They know what death is because they have seen it happen, but do not fear death because they know human beings are immune. In Grotius's Eden, Adam and Eve understand the demands of self-preservation as they pertain to other animals but not in a first-personal way. This means that they are equipped to think through the implications of what, in *De jure belli ac pacis*, Grotius calls "private war"—violent conflict among individual creatures that is consistent with the law of nature and by means of which all creatures are able to "repel injuries of force" (1:240; 1.3.1).

When Satan first approaches Adam in act 3 of *Adamus exul*, he is rebuffed by "grim wrath." The ocean would, Adam claims, "bring forth ardent flames" before he would "offer peace or love" to Satan: "Between us there will be joined the sort of like-minded society [*concors societas*] that characterizes the relationship between"—and here one should recall Du Bartas—"the wolf and the sheep." Animal self-preservation provides Adam with a model for understanding his relationship with Satan as one of war. Adam sees himself as the wolf in this scenario, a position that Satan brings out in his response:

Let the brave fight against the powerful. But he
Who wars [*bella*] against the wretched must be mean of soul.

The lion, king of beasts, is never known to rage
Against the timid lamb, nor does his maw crave kine.
Rather against the bear he rears his warlike mane
And opes his gaping mouth and gnashes his grim teeth.
If thou believest I can harm thee, then with fear
Abandon war [*Depone bellum*]. If thou believest not, nevertheless
Abandon war [*Depone bellum*]. Think me not worth thy hate,
But rather, freely take my pledge of proffered peace [*pacis*]. (150–51)

While the wolf will eat the sheep, a noble animal like the lion will not
deign to feast on a "timid lamb." The lion only "gnashes his grim teeth"
in the face of such proper foes as bears. Given that, in this analogy, Adam
is the lion and Satan is the lamb, the noble human should "abandon war"
and accept an offer of "peace." But the repeated imperative "Abandon war"
works, Satan insinuates, even if the terms of the analogy are reversed: "If
thou believest I can harm [*nocere*] thee, then with fear [*metu*] / Abandon
war." Here, Satan attempts to corroborate his initial judgment—that Adam
is without fear [*metus*] (102–3)—by seeing if there is any chance that the
human will "abandon war" because he fears [*metu*] harm (150–51). Adam
is not afraid. With no concern for his own bodily self-preservation, Adam
responds to Satan's claim that "It is no one's advantage to wage endless
war" [*Perpetua gerere bella*] with a firm rebuttal. "What thing can harm
me? Fearing naught, I wish for naught" [*Mihi quod nocebit? nil timens,
spero nihil*], Adam claims, a sentiment that he repeats when he replies to
Satan's threat of war—"No day henceforth for thee shall lack its plot of
war"—with absolute clarity: "I do not refuse / Thy terms of warfare, neither
do I fear thy threats / About my human heart, impervious to thy shafts" [*nec
bellicas / Leges recuso, nec tuas metuo minas, / Cui sagittis cor tuis imper-
vium*] (152–55). Grotius's Adam knowingly and fearlessly undertakes perpet-
ual war because the worst consequence of war—death—is not built into his
horizon of expectation.

Milton's *Paradise Lost* responds to the ambivalent presence of Edenic
self-preservation in *Adamus exul*. Among the ideas that Milton took from
Grotius's play was a reworked answer to the question, How might one best
represent Edenic human life? How, in other words, could one depict life that
is not governed by self-preservation? In *Paradise Lost*, Milton steps back
from Grotius's vision. Whereas the Edenic protagonists of *Adamus exul*
know death but do not fear it, Milton's Adam and Eve know next to nothing
about death. Recalling the "easy charge" of the divine prohibition, in *Paradise Lost* Adam comments that the "tree / Of knowledge" is "planted by the

tree of life, / So near grows death to life, whate'er death is, / Some dreadful
thing no doubt" (4.421, 423–26). Adam and Eve cannot have perceived what
death might be—they do not, that is, have any way of developing experience
with death—for they have never witnessed one animal flee from another, let
alone die. All creatures live in harmony: "About them frisking played / All
beasts of the earth, since wild . . . / Sporting the lion ramped, and in his paw /
Dandled the kid; bears, tigers, ounces, pards, / Gambolled before them"
(4.340–45). There is no predation in Milton's Eden; predators frolic with the
creatures that will, in a fallen world, become their prey. Not until after the
Fall are death and the drive for self-preservation instilled in earthly life: "but
Discord first . . . / among the irrational / Death introduced through fierce antipathy: / Beast now with beast gan war, and fowl with fowl, / And fish with
fish; to graze the herb all leaving, / Devoured each other; nor stood much
in awe / Of man, but fled him" (10.707–14). In Milton's poem, the drive for
self-preservation is a principle that applies only to postlapsarian animal life.

When Milton describes Satan sitting "like a cormorant" in the "tree of
life," watching Adam and Eve while "devising death / To them who lived"
(4.194–198), the line break is significant. Adam and Eve truly live. They
are those "who live," without a relationship to death beyond the notional
"whate'er that is." To be sure, Adam admits that God's threat of death as a
consequence for breaking the prohibition "resounds / Yet dreadful in mine
ear" (8.334–35). Similarly, Adam responds in horror when he discovers that
Eve is "now to death devote" (9.901), and Eve encourages Adam to deliver his
"fear of death . . . to the winds" and eat the fruit with her (9.989).[63] Adam and
Eve are minimally aware of death, and they fear it insofar as God has established it as a punishment (insofar as it was part of a warning), but they live a
life that is nonmortal, and they know as much (they cannot learn about death
through experience).[64] When Eve attempts to convince Adam that she should
be able to labor by herself despite the Satanic threat about which Raphael has
recently warned them, she quickly picks through her husband's logic:

> But that thou shouldst my firmness therefore doubt
> To God or thee, because we have a foe
> May tempt it, I expected not to hear.
> His violence thou fearst not, being such,
> As we, not capable of death or pain,
> Can either not receive, or can repel.
> His fraud is then thy fear, which plain infers
> Thy equal fear that my firm faith and love
> Can by his fraud be shaken or seduced. (9.279–87)

Fear exists in Eden: Adam might, Eve claims, be afraid of fraud or he might fear that Eve's love or faith would fall short. But such fears are not intimately entwined with the maintenance of bodily life. After all, Adam and Eve are "not capable of death or pain." Eve does not understand why this is—it might be that they cannot *passively* receive such ills, or it might be that they *actively* repel them. She is, however, certain that it is true. Of course, all of this will change with the transformation brought about by the Fall. But at this moment, Adam and Eve remain nonmortal.

Milton tries to imagine Edenic human life without the pressure of self-preservation as a central and determining fact, in two senses: first, the need for such a relation to self is unnecessary if one cannot die or suffer pain; second, there is nothing in the world of Eden that lives according to such rhythms. What, then, does Milton imagine the basic principle of human life to be? What organizes its existence? The answer is Grotian. Recall that Grotius's discussion of self-preservation in *De jure belli ac pacis* is framed around the Stoic "cradle argument" in Cicero's *De finibus*. In Cicero's account, from the very moment of its birth, a living creature "feels an attachment for itself, and an impulse to preserve itself" (232–33; 3.5), an originary impulse that is, in human beings who have acquired reason and language, subsequently superseded by the ability to make choices "rationalized and in harmony with nature" (238–39; 3.6). In *De jure belli ac pacis* Grotius follows this pattern, noting that the "first Impression of Nature"—the "Instinct whereby every Animal seeks its own Preservation"—is superseded once the advent of "Right Reason" makes possible the "Knowledge of the Conformity of Things with Reason" (1:180; 2.1.1), a state evident in the "exquisite Desire of Society, for the satisfaction of which [human beings] alone have received from Nature a peculiar Instrument, viz. the Use of Speech" (1:84–85; *prolegomena* 7). In the Stoic view presented by Grotius, human infancy and childhood necessitate a delay between the instinct toward self-preservation with which life begins and the "exquisite" and "rational" *appetitus societatis* facilitated by human language.

In *Paradise Lost*, Milton revises this cradle argument. If, as we saw in the introduction, Piso, the student of Antiochus of Ascalon in *De finibus* claims that "all the ancient philosophers . . . turn to cradles [*incunabula*]," this is because it is "in childhood that they think we can most easily recognize the will of nature [*naturae voluntatem posse cognoscere*]" (456–57; 5.20, translation modified). Observing the behavior of infants in cradles, ancient Stoics understood self-love and a drive toward self-preservation as the primary "will of nature."[65] But the Epicureans also observed the behavior of infants in cradles, and they claimed that this behavior revealed pleasure to be the first principle of life.[66] In the absence of direct evidence—one cannot remember one's own time as an infant, and one cannot ask an infant in the cradle here and now what its own first impressions are like—philosophers relied upon arguments that became increasingly untethered from the cradle that ostensibly grounded their claims. Milton cuts through such squabbles by using mimetic fiction to describe the birth of human consciousness. When approached from the vantage point of Adam's and Eve's neonatally mature originary experience, Cicero's cradle arguments take on new, first-person significance. Adam and Eve *can recall* what Grotius, following Cicero, calls *prima naturae*. The first human beings can reconstruct, from within, the "will of nature" as it first became manifest in their lives.

Since Milton's Adam and Eve are created into pure life—"not capable of death or pain"—their first impressions are unrelated to self-preservation. But Milton nevertheless follows the basic idea of the "cradle argument" outlined by Cicero and expanded by Grotius. Since Adam and Eve enter the world as fully rational beings equipped with language, they begin their lives at the highest stage of human development, impelled not by self-preservation but by what Grotius describes in *De jure belli ac pacis* as "a Desire of Society, that is, a certain Inclination to live with [other human beings], not in any Manner whatever, but peaceably, and in a Community regulated according to the best of his Understanding" (1:79–91; *prolegomena* 5–6). Consider once again Adam's account of his first moments. After waking up, he is "raised" upward by a "quick instinctive motion" that brings him to his feet and enables him to interact with the various creatures around him. As Sharon Achinstein has argued, this is not an instinct oriented inward but an instinct that directs Adam outward, toward others—an instinct that is initially expressed through his first speech act, in which he asks the world around him about the "great maker" responsible for his existence.[67] When Adam realizes that the other creatures cannot answer him, he sits down, "pensive."

Driven by a desire for society, to converse with others like himself, Adam's first request to God is for another human being: "with me / I see not who partakes. In solitude / What happiness, who can enjoy alone" (8.363–65)? After God presses back, Adam responds, driven by his *appetitus societatis* for companionship based on rational communication. Although he is happy to interact with animals, Adam tells God,

> Among unequals what society
> Can sort, what harmony of true delight?
> Which must be mutual, in proportion due

Given and received . . .
. . . of fellowship I speak
Such as I seek, fit to participate
All rational delight, wherein the brute
Cannot be human consort. (8.383–92)

Adam's first impressions are structured by a desire for human society, properly proportioned and harmonious, full of "rational delight." Milton plays out a variation of this theme in Eve's pleasing play with the shape in the water that returns her gaze with "answering looks / Of sympathy and love" (4.464–65). In this way, as Mary Nyquist has argued, Milton's depiction of Adam's and Eve's first moments demonstrates the truth about human existence that Milton saw in the words of Genesis 2:18—"It is not good that the man should be alone"—and deployed in the 1640s in order to justify divorce on the basis of spiritual incompatibility.[68] Since the *appetitus societatis* is the impulse underpinning human life, marriage and the communities it will engender are present from the beginning, implicit in Adam's and Eve's first impressions. What Adam and Eve remember is not a love of self or a drive for self-preservation; rather, it is what Grotius calls "an exquisite desire for society."

HUMAN NATURE AND THE IDEA OF GOD

In *Paradise Lost*, Adam and Eve are nonmortal and neonatally mature, but they are otherwise recognizably human. Milton's vision of life in Eden is thus very different from how it was imagined by his contemporaries, many of whom were obsessed with the exotic nature of Adam's prelapsarian cognitive powers. To take an example of this tendency, on 9 November 1662, Robert South—an up-and-coming divine and a public orator to Cambridge University—delivered a sermon that epitomizes the claims often made on Adam's behalf: "He came into the world a philosopher." It may, South admits, be "difficult for us who date our ignorance from our first being" to "raise our thoughts, and imagination to those intellectual perfections that attended our nature in the time of innocence." However, if we could imagine Adam's first impressions, we might gain an appreciation for how he could "view essences in themselves" and see "Consequents yet dormant in their principles, and effects yet unborn in the womb of their causes." Until the Fall, Adam was "ignorant of nothing but sin."[69]

This celebration of Adam's cognitive powers is part of a larger argument pitched against the Aristotelian epistemological program: "An Aristotle was

but the rubbish of an Adam, and Athens but the rudiments of Paradise."
South ridicules Aristotle for affirming "the Mind to be at first meer *Rasa
tabula*" and for insisting that all human "notions" are "imprinted" by the
"languid impressions of sense; being only the Reports of observation, and the
Result of so many repeated Experiments" (10–11). Aiming to bypass the experiential demands of the inventive method, South claims that such notions
as "the *Whole is bigger than a Part*" or "*God is to be worshipped*" are "in-
genite" or "born with us" (9–11), universal truths "imprinted" into "humane
Nature" that form the "rules by which men take their first apprehensions
and observations of things" (15). If these innate notions shape, opaquely, the
thought of every fallen human being, "it was *Adams* happinesse in the state
of innocence to have these clear and unsullied" (11). South's all-knowing
Adam—whose discourse "did not so properly apprehend, as irradiate the
Object; not so much finde, as make things intelligible" (9)—is far from the
vision of unfallen life offered by Milton, with its insistence on finding, on
sensing, on gathering experience, and on making mistakes.

When Milton imagined Adam's and Eve's waking moments, he may have
had South's sermon in mind. On 30 January 1663, South delivered another
sermon before King Charles II, in which he denounced the "Latin advocate,
Mr. Milton, who, like a blind adder, has spit so much poison upon the King's
person and cause."[70] Such a remark would have brought the young South
to Milton's attention, and Milton may have addressed his differences with
South by reframing the younger man's notion that Adam could see "effects
yet unborn in the womb of their causes" as a Satanic temptation: when
wooing Eve in *Paradise Lost*, the first benefit the serpent attributes to the
"wisdom-giving plant" is the power to "discern / Things in their causes"
(9.679–82). Milton presents South's vision of Edenic cognition as a Satanic
temptation. Eve's fall occurs in part because she succumbs to the illusory belief that prelapsarian humans might possess Edenic superpowers, and Milton
frames the desire for such superpowers as the fantasy behind the Fall. The
Satanic temptation to easily and directly "discern / Things in their causes"
marks an attempt to gain knowledge—recall that, in Aristotle's *Metaphysics*, knowledge of universals requires an understanding of "the 'why' and the
cause"—without passing through the steps of the inventive method (2:1553;
981b). Since, as we saw in chapter 1, Aristotelian empiricism provides the
model according to which Milton's Adam and Eve acquire knowledge of self
and world, Milton's Aristotle is quite far from South's "rubbish of an Adam."

In framing Adam's and Eve's unfallen epistemology in this way, Milton
risks aligning himself with Socinianism, the theological position against
which South argues most strenuously. Developed in the late sixteenth-

century writings of the Italian theologian Faustus Socinus, who was based in the Polish city of Racow, the positions associated with this school of thought included a radical reading of prelapsarian Adam. Based on Socinus's teachings, translated into English by John Biddle in 1652, and controversially licensed for printing in England by Milton himself, the *Racovian Catechism* argues that "there is no such thing as Original sinne" and that Adam's transgression did not alter anything fundamental about human nature: "the fall of Adam being but one act, could not have such power to deprave his own nature, much lesse the nature of all his posterity." Adam and his descendants possess the same "free will" or "power to obey God."[71] Socinus was intent on eliminating all marks of Adamic distinction. In the Socinian view, Adam was, from the beginning, mortal.[72] And Adam learned about the world in the same way as his descendants. As Socinus writes in *De statu primi hominis ante lapsum* (1610), Adam understood his own mortality through *experientia*, just as we do, since "nothing is in the mind or the intellect that was not first in the senses."[73]

South takes aim at these ideas through mockery. The first step of his argument, South writes, is "to remove the erroneous opinion of the *Socinians*," who "deny that the Image of God consisted in any Habitual Perfections that adorned the Soul of *Adam*: But as to his Understanding bring him Void of all Notion, a rude unwritten Blanck; making him to be created as much an Infant as others are born; sent into the World onely to read and spell out a God in the Works of Creation, to learn by degrees, till at length his Understanding grew up to the stature of his Body" (5).[74] These formulations had a long life in seventeenth-century anti-Socinian literature. Consider Jonathan Edwards, the principal of Jesus College at Oxford, who, in the *Preservative Against Socinianism* (1693), treats as dangerous Socinus's idea that "*Adam* was born a frail, mortal Creature, having only the bare faculties of understanding and will, but without the accomplishments of either; being neither endued with wisdom nor holiness: a pure *rasa Tabula*, capable indeed of any impressions, but having no characters either of wisdom or Righteousness, engraven upon his mind, by the finger of God, when he first dropped out of his hands."[75] Even at the turn of the eighteenth century, Edwards, who, as we will see in chapter 5, also accused Locke of being a Socinian, remained shocked by the idea that Adam could have entered the world with only "the bare faculties of understanding and will." This characterization comes eerily close to the view I ascribed to Milton in chapter 1.

Like the Socinians, Milton aimed to minimize the differences between pre- and postlapsarian life. But although Milton may have been sympathetic to aspects of the Socinian position, as his licensing of the *Racovian*

Catechism suggests, he did not subscribe to Socinus's understanding of Adam's unfallen cognitive powers. After all, in *Tetrachordon* Milton claims that
if we understand Adam's "insight concerning wedlock" ("This is bone of
my bones, flesh of my flesh") as pertaining to the body and not to the mind,
"we shall make him as very an idiot as the Socinians make him; which
would not be reverently don of us."[76] Milton would not refer to Adam, in
South's caricature of the Socinian position, as "a rude unwritten Blanck,"
but he *did* insist on the degree to which Adam's neonatally mature thought
was a perfected version of that possessed by all subsequent human beings.
In Milton's view, for Adam, Eve, and all of their fallen descendants, human
knowledge is rooted in empirical contact with self and world. He expressed
this view as early as 1644 in *Of Education*: "The end of learning is to repair
the ruins of our first parents by regaining to know God aright. . . . But because our understanding cannot in this body found it selfe but on sensible
things, nor arrive so cleerly to the knowledge of God and things invisible as
by orderly conning over the visible and inferior creature, the same method
is necessarily to be followd in all discreet teaching."[77] One condition for
being able to "repair the ruins of our first parents" is that all human beings (including Adam and Eve) live in "this body," which "found[s]" all
human "understanding" (including knowledge of God) on its apprehension
of "sensible things." Education here and now can work toward repairing the
damage wrought by the Fall, because we come to know everything we know
through bodies that are—with the exceptions of mortality and navels—like
those of the unfallen Adam and Eve.

  The limit case for this claim is Milton's depiction of prelapsarian
knowledge of God's existence. After all, Adam seems to grasp the fact of
God's existence almost immediately upon awakening: "how came I thus,
how here? Not of myself; by some great maker then, / In goodness and in
power pre-eminent" (8.277–79). How does Adam come to know about this
"maker"? If, as I have been arguing, Milton depicts Adam and Eve as thoroughly embodied human beings in need of an education based on external
stimuli, then they do not possess an innate idea of God. They must reason
toward God's existence based on what they perceive of themselves and the
world around them. In presenting Adam and Eve in this way, Milton cuts
in half the usual set of Protestant sources for proving the existence of God.
Whereas such medieval thinkers as Aquinas had favored evidence based
upon rational argument—appeals to an unmoved mover, to a first cause,
and so on—Protestant writers focused on two sources of evidence: first, the
innate idea of God implanted in every human mind; second, the coherence,
order, and beauty of the created world.[78] Most thinkers agreed on the latter,

since this point was laid out by Paul in Romans 1:20–21, which argues that all human beings "knew God" through the glories of creation and are therefore "without excuse": "Ever since the creation of the world his eternal power and divine nature, invisible though they are, have been understood and seen through the things he has made." But there was a great deal of disagreement about the former.

Despite their insistence on the degree to which all human life is vitiated by the Fall, many early Reformers argued for an innate knowledge of God's existence. For example, in the *Loci communes* (1555), Philip Melanchthon argues both that the knowledge of God is "innate in the human mind" and that since "all confess naturally that there is a God, therefore this idea is true."[79] Articulating a stronger position, Calvin begins the third chapter of the *Institutio*—entitled "The Knowledge [*notitiam*] of God has been Naturally Implanted in the Minds of Men"—by claiming,

> There is within the human mind, and indeed by natural instinct, a sense of divinity [*Quendam inesse humanae menti, & quidem naturali instinctu, divinitatis sensum*]. This we take to be beyond controversy. To prevent anyone from taking refuge in the pretense of ignorance, God himself has implanted [*indidit*] in all men a certain understanding of his divine majesty. Ever renewing its memory, he repeatedly sheds fresh drops. Since, therefore, men one and all perceive that there is a God and that he is their Maker [*opificem*], they are condemned by their own testimony because they have failed to honor him and to consecrate their lives to his will.[80]

A "natural instinct" provides all human beings with a "sense of divinity" that cannot be eradicated. Indeed, "actual godlessness is impossible," Calvin contends, for the "conviction" of God's existence is "naturally inborn in all." It is "not a doctrine that must first be learned in school, but one of which each of us is master from his mother's womb and which nature itself permits no one to forget."[81]

But if Calvin clearly and influentially argued for the innate idea of God, another strand of Protestant thought denied its existence. Socinus inveighed against an innate idea of divinity and, more deeply, against any conception of natural religion. Contending that revelation was the only way to know God, in *Praelectiones theologicae* (1609) Socinus argues that it is impossible for either the created world or the form of the human mind to guarantee the knowledge of God's existence. If such an idea were true, Socinus avers, it would not be the case that "entire peoples" in places as far-flung as

Brazil and India seem to possess "no inward sense or notion of any deity."
Although "it is quite an accepted opinion nowadays that by nature there
is in man an implanted idea of some divinity," this opinion is "false."[82]
Socinus argues against the innate idea of God not only because there is anthropological evidence to suggest that there are many humans who do not
possess this idea but also because of a fundamental conviction about the
centrality of human freedom. Natural actions are not free; one cannot, for
instance, freely control the beating of one's heart. If the belief in God is natural, then, according to Socinus, that belief is not freely chosen. In order for
religion to be free and therefore virtuous, the source of religious belief must
not be woven into the fabric of one's being but rather revealed through revelation, which one is free to accept or reject.[83] This is why Socinus took such
pains to deny both the innate idea of God and the notion that the order of
the natural world provided evidence for God's existence.

Others argued that natural knowledge of God might be obtained from
observation of oneself and the world, but not from any innate ideas. Such
a position was held by both of the theologians selected by the Province of
Holland to fill the chair at Leiden University that had formerly belonged
to Jacobus Arminius—the leader of the Dutch Remonstrants and the theologian whose views Milton's most resemble—until his death in 1609. The
first of these was Conrad Vorstius, a Remonstrant theologian who generated
so much controversy that he was unable to take up the position at Leiden.
Written while he was still teaching in the German city of Steinfurt, Vorstius's *Tractatus theologicus de Deo* (1606) argues against the innate idea of
God: "We do not hold that there is any innate knowledge of God in us: for,
speaking strictly, no knowledge of anything appears to be innate in human
beings. Such knowledge is instead acquired over time through the operations of sensation and the intellect."[84] Vorstius defended this view in an
apology directed against a blistering Calvinist attack that sought to smear
him as a Socinian and prevent his appointment. In his *Apologetica* (1611),
published just after he arrived in the Netherlands, Vorstius argues that "just
like knowledge of all other things, the knowledge of God is acquired little
by little through the senses and the use of reason. And so, properly speaking
it cannot be said to be innate [*innata dici non potest*]."[85] This position was
rooted, Vorstius is quick to note, not in theological polemic but in philosophical conviction. Although the organs and capacities that will enable
thought are "innate in us from the outset," no intellectual *act* is "innate,"
for "these acts require, from the outset, not only appropriate sense organs,
but also a rational exercise of them, as can be seen both from the very constitution of human nature and continuing general experience [*tum ex ipsa*

humane naturae constitutione, ac generali perpetuaque experientia], and also from the received teaching of Aristotle's *Posterior Analytics*, . . . where he teaches that all knowledge arises from the senses."[86] Since human beings begin as blank slates, the idea of God cannot be innate.

Simon Episcopius, the Remonstrant theologian who finally took up Arminius's position at Leiden in 1612, was similarly committed to the view that humans did not possess an innate knowledge of God. Although Episcopius held that the mind begins as a tabula rasa, his denial of the innate knowledge of God was rooted, like that of Socinus, in a theological conviction that human beings must, in principle, freely choose their belief in God. In the *Institutiones theologicae*, published posthumously in his *Opera Theologicae* (1650), Episcopius held that natural knowledge of God emerged from the intersection of rationality and scrutiny of the world's order: "The knowledge of God is not so natural that by necessity it entirely inheres in man as flowing from the principles of nature, but is natural only in this way, that if a man is willing only to use reason he can find certain principles in nature through which, with the help of right reason [*recta . . . ratio*], he may arrive at the knowledge of God."[87] If one examines nature and brings the powers of *recta ratio* to bear on one's observations of the world, then it is possible to "arrive at the knowledge of God" even though that knowledge is not innate. This means that one can acquire natural knowledge of God, but that such knowledge is not assured; most people require revelation, and even then the decision to believe is not necessitated by one's own nature.

As a thinker partial to Remonstrant views, Milton likely knew about Vorstius's denial of the innate idea of God. He also seems to have read Episcopius's *Institutiones*.[88] Milton did not follow the Socinian path and eliminate natural religion altogether, but he did come close to the position advocated by Remonstrant theologians. In *De doctrina*, he advances an argument similar to that formulated by Episcopius: human beings can derive natural knowledge of God by pairing *recta ratio* with careful observation of the natural world around them. "As to God's existence," Milton writes in *De doctrina*, "God has imprinted [*impressit*] so many clear signs [*clara indicia*] of himself in the human mind, and so many traces [*vestigia*] of himself throughout all nature, that no sane person can be unaware of God's existence." Milton addresses the latter source of evidence first, making a strong claim for natural religion based on what one sees of the natural world: "Surely all the world's contents, made in orderly beauty [*pulcherrimo ordine*] for some purpose or benefit, attest [*testantur*] the pre-existence of a superlatively great being [*summum aliquem*] that, in all these things, sets itself a purpose" (1:24–25, translation modified).[89] If the order of the

natural world testifies to the existence of an intelligent maker of some kind,
Milton also insists that human mindedness likewise suggests that some
higher power exists. But he does not argue for the existence of an innate
idea of God. Instead, he argues that *conscientia*, which he equates with
recta ratio, works in such a way that the notion of God's existence will
occur to all those who are "not insane" [*non insanus*]. "But *conscientia* or
right reason [*sive eadem recta ratio est*] . . . also testifies to God's existence
[*esse Deum testificatur*]," Milton writes, arguing that there would be no
"distinction between right and wrong," that all assessment of virtue and
vice would be based only on mere opinion, and that "no one would abstain
from vices through shame [*pudore*] or through fear of the laws, unless *conscientia* or right reason often, inwardly, and even unwillingly reprehended
each person about the existence of some God that is controller and Lord of
all things [*nisi conscientia sive recta ratio subinde unumquemque vel in-
vitum intus redargueret esse Deum aliquem rerum omnium moderatorem
ac Dominum*], to whom each creature will one day provide an account of
their deeds, whether right or wrong" (1:24–27, translation modified). We
feel shame at immoral behavior because *conscientia*—that is, *recta ratio*—
reprehends us. And this inner reprehension—the Latin *redarguo* means
both argumentative refutation or legal conviction—makes us feel shame in
a way that points our right reason toward some sort of God capable of judging the rightness and wrongness of our actions.

    This does not point to the existence of what Calvin calls an inner "sense
of divinity." In Milton's view, human beings are naturally able to apprehend
God's existence by bringing right reason to bear on two sources of evidence:
the beautiful order of the natural world external to us and the inner feeling
of being reprehended for wrongdoing. God has "imprinted" signs "in the
human mind" and left traces "throughout all nature," but the knowledge
about His existence generated from these two sources is not innate. Such
knowledge emerges, rather, from the workings of reason on the inner and
outer phenomena made available through the sentient body.

    If human rationality generates a situation in which "no sane person can
be unaware of God's existence," how much more certain must the knowledge of God's existence be for Adam and Eve, both of whom possess reason
unsullied by prejudicial customs and social norms? In *Paradise Lost*, Milton
depicts how the ideal human being might, by nature and without any revelation, come to an understanding of God's existence. His account of Adam's
first waking moments suggests how human rationality works together with
impressions gathered both from affective bodily experience and from sen-

sory encounters with the surrounding natural world in order to deduce the existence of a God without the benefits of innate ideas.

To be sure, Adam's verticality gives him a direct connection with heaven unavailable to other creatures. In Raphael's words, Adam was created

> not prone
> And brute as all other creatures, but endued
> With sanctity of reason, might erect
> His stature, and upright with front serene
> Govern the rest, self-knowing, and from thence
> Magnanimous to correspond with heaven,
> But grateful to acknowledge whence his good
> Descends, thither with heart and voice and eyes
> Directed in devotion, to adore
> And worship God supreme. (7.506–15)

Adam's "reason" runs parallel to his power to "erect" himself "upright" so that he can "correspond with heaven" and direct his praise to God "thither." But if this is the purpose toward which Adam's bodily form is directed, in his first moments he must learn that this is the case. After gazing at the "sky," Adam stands: "raised / By quick instinctive motion up I sprung, / As thitherward endeavouring, and upright / Stood on my feet" (8.258–61). On the face of it, the "instinctive motion" that propels Adam up to his feet and toward the sky seems to resonate with Calvin's claim that humans possess a "sense of divinity" through a "natural instinct" [*naturali instinctu*].[90] Many other thinkers shared this view. In *Summa theologica*, Aquinas claims that human beings apprehend the need to worship God by means of a "divine instinct" [*instinctu divino*] that induces them heavenward like a "private law" [*privata lege*].[91] Edward Herbert champions a similar view in *De veritate* (1624 in Paris, 1633 in London), turning *instinctus* into the fundamental mode of human apprehension: "Natural instinct occupies the first position among our faculties, discursive reason the last" (139). For Herbert, such "common notions" as "that there is a first cause" (126) are manifest through the "universal feelings" of instinct (176).[92]

But Milton's use of instinct in *Paradise Lost* does not work this way. As I argued in chapter 1, Milton understands Adam's "quick instinctive motion" as the sort of natural bodily impetus shared by all animals. As an "erect" animal, Adam's body instinctively adopts its natural position. Milton does not suggest that Adam's instinctive upward movement provides

Adam with any awareness of God's existence, however. It is not until, standing on his feet, Adam looks "about me round" and sees the happy, living,
beautifully ordered world that surrounds him (8.261), that he arrives at the
conclusion—generated by his rational response to his experience of his own
body and its ambient environs—that he was created by a "great maker."
Milton's Adam discerns God's existence in a manner akin to that put forward by Episcopius, in the way South ascribes to the Socinians: by applying
his right reason to his own lived experience (understood here in the sense of
Erlebnis, which chapter 1 argued Milton was developing in *Paradise Lost*)
and thereby "read[ing] and spell[ing] out a God in the Works of Creation."
Milton portrays Adam's originary experience as one that is recognizably
human to anyone and everyone, even those who do not believe they have
access to the innate idea of God's existence. This is important to Milton because he aims to draw out the implications of this moment in Adam's story
in order to disarm the specter that, in Regina Schwartz's words, "haunts a
poem persistently engaged in inquiring into origins": Satan's claims about
his own "birth mature" (5.862).[93]

WHY ADAM KNOWS HE CANNOT BE SELF-BEGOT

Augustine's claim about the noncoincidence of memory and infancy in the
Confessiones is a claim about the ontological distinction between creature
and creator. Beings that cannot remember their origins cannot, as Augustine puts it, be the "cause of [their] own making" (8; 1.6.10). When Satan
responds to Abdiel's suggestion that the angels were "made," "formed," and
"circumscribed" by God (5.823–25), the new rebel invokes his capacious
memory:

> who saw
> When this creation was? Remembrest thou
> Thy making, while the maker gave thee being?
> We know no time when we were not as now;
> Know none before us, self-begot, self-raised
> By our own quickening power, when fatal course
> Had circled his full orb, the birth mature
> Of this our native heaven, ethereal sons. (5.856–63)

Critics have long recognized the centrality of this speech to Milton's epic.
John Rogers has given convincing reasons for taking Satan's claims seriously; they reflect a cosmic ontology strikingly similar to that presented in

Milton's vitalist account of creation.[94] My interest lies in Satan's slippery treatment of phenomenological possibility.

Satan attacks Abdiel with polemical questions the only answers to which can be "No one saw when this creation was" and "No, I do not remember my making." These questions are framed such that they *must* be answered negatively. No one can see "when" creation occurred, because the subject capable of seeing is not yet in existence "when" creation takes place. Likewise, while the maker is in the process of giving "being," that "being" is not yet there. It is impossible to remember an event prior to the generation of one's being, and Milton stresses this impossibility with a line break that separates the "thou" who could now remember from the "thy" undergoing "making." Satan claims the privilege of neonatal maturity. If the angels had lived through the inchoate becoming that is characteristic of infancy and childhood, they would remember a "time when [they] were not as now." Satan thus extracts from infancy's absence a claim about his nature that is also a claim about origins. Playing with the etymological connection between the Latin *origo* (origin) and *oriri* (to rise), Satan argues that the angels are "self-raised" by an immanent "quickening power." This self-begetting takes place "when" the cosmos renews itself, and a process akin to the Platonic great year begins anew: "when fatal course / Had circled his full orb," the angels' "native heaven" undergoes a "birth mature," coming into (or back into) existence fully formed.[95] By appealing to this cosmological principle of repetition ("circled"), Satan works to eliminate the need for a great maker. He subtly places the epithet "ethereal sons"—which seems to modify "self-raised, / By our own quickening power"—at the end of a parenthetical remark about "when" and how heaven came into being in a "birth mature." This displacement makes it seem as though the "ethereal sons" share a "birth mature" with their "native heaven," even if, as Satan has just argued, they know "none before us," they "know no time when [they] were not as now"—and therefore, by extension, cannot know that they are in fact native ethereal sons of heaven. But despite this speech's fancy footwork, its message is clear. Since he did not undergo infancy, since his memory seems coterminous with his first moment of awareness, and since he did not apprehend a maker at the moment his gaze snapped into focus, Satan escapes the force of Augustine's prime evidence for creatureliness only to articulate the Augustinian model for the origins of sin: the attempt to "forsake the foundation upon which the mind should rest, and to become and remain, as it were, one's own foundation."[96]

Because Adam's account follows in the conversation as a response to Raphael's tale of Satan's rebellion, we are meant to contrast Satan's rejection of a "maker [who] gave thee being" (5.858) with Adam's recognition, just after waking, that he came to be "Not of [him]self" but "by some great maker" (8.278). As we have seen, Adam's speech is a careful account of what it was like to awaken mature, with a full complement of bodily and mental capacities ready for immediate actualization. By contrast, Satan's speech never once discusses what it was like to suddenly pop into existence. Although the phrase "our own quickening power" suggests that this power is felt, Satan never describes what being "self-begot" was like. He simply moves from observation ("We know no time when we were not as now") to an ontology of natural and immanent sufficiency ("self-begot, self-raised / By our own quickening power"). Satan's claims rely on an implied conscious experience that he does not describe. Milton begins Adam's speech with a subtle reworking of the impossibility highlighted by Satan. Instead of Satan's suggestion that no one can recall being created—"Remembrest thou / Thy making, while the maker gave thee being?"—Adam's speech switches from this truly impossible scene of witnessing to one that is only very difficult for his neonatally mature memory to reconstruct: "For man to tell how human life began / Is hard; for who himself beginning knew?" (8.250–51).

Milton presents here a sophisticated grammar of beginning. Adam could have asked: "For who *his own* beginning knew?" The possessive pronoun *his* in this hypothetical sentence positions *beginning* as a gerund that invokes a state of being, the origin or very beginning of the *he* under consideration. Had Milton used this phrase, Adam would have echoed Satan's "Remembrest thou / Thy making," a phrase in which *making* is a gerund indicating an act. Instead, Adam's question as it appears in *Paradise Lost*— "For who himself beginning knew?"—uses *himself*, a direct object to which *beginning* is attached as a participle that modifies *himself* and stresses process. While Satan's "Thy making" gives us a possessive pronoun claiming ownership over a gerund (a verb transformed into a noun, an action removed from process), Adam's "himself beginning" flips this grammatical logic, presenting instead a pronominal object modified by a participle (a verb that maintains its connection with becoming). Adam could not have known his *beginning* (a gerund marking the moment when he first began to exist) because it is at that moment that he first gains being and so is not yet capable of awareness; he is not quite yet *there*. Despite the difficulty of the task, he can, however, know "himself *beginning*" (a participle marking the process of coming into personhood and awareness) because his being has, to borrow Satan's phrase, already been given. If Satan appeals to the impossibility of preexistence to set up ontological conclusions, Adam explores the process of beginning in order to conjure the origins not of "human life" in the sense of human *being* but of "human life" as the scene of *conscious experience*—

the movement of consciousness as it slips between various phenomenological modalities in the first-person field of "unexperienced thought."

In Milton's view, the human encounter with the world is itself enough
to validate the existence of a "great maker" in "goodness and in power pre-
eminent." Unlike Adam and Eve, Satan does not appeal to his first impressions, because such description would invalidate his claims. This is why
Milton is so careful to describe the birth of human thought as a structure
of self-finding. Adam's "I found me" and Eve's "I . . . found my self" already
contain the implicit, felt knowledge that the self is not self-given, that it
is "laid" or "reposed" by something other than the self. For Adam and Eve
in these initial moments, the term *self* cannot properly be used as a prefix
("self-begot, self-raised," in Satan's parlance), but only as something the
awareness of which is necessarily delayed. The *then* in Adam's "Myself I
then perused" (8.267) is significant, because it stresses that Adam comes to
himself belatedly. Yet this experiential structure of belated self-finding does
not, by itself, guarantee a "great maker." After all, Satan's claim is not that
he himself made himself—that he somehow preceded himself—but rather
that he came into existence as part of an emergent, natural process, that his
"quickening power" is one with that of his "native heaven," both of which
sprang "mature" into being in the same "fatal course."

C. S. Lewis captures the naturalness of this process when he suggests that
Satan thinks he "sprouted from the soil like a vegetable," a phrase intended
to dismiss Satan's claim as ridiculous but the power of which William Empson recuperates in his assertion that Milton was "attracted by the idea that
Nature somehow works of her own accord."[97] On this generous reading, expanded and deepened by Rogers, Satan can legitimately claim that the angels
are "self-begot, self-raised / By our own quickening power," because he posits
a completely rational explanation for their generation, one in which his being
is immanent in nature, isomorphic with a self-organizing matter that generates new forms on its own, without the need of any transcendent, divine
intervention. The superiority of Adam's account over Satan's becomes much
more difficult to maintain if the relationship between them is framed not as a
choice between "I made myself" and "I was made by a maker" but rather as a
choice between "I am an immanent part of self-organizing nature" and "I was
made by a maker." But this is precisely the choice that Milton wants readers
to make, and he provides the experience of Adam's and Eve's first impressions
as the most important evidence for any claim on behalf of a "great maker."

Satan's argumentative strategy uses a lack of knowledge ("We know
no time when we were not as now; / Know none before us") to establish
positive claims ("self-begot, self-raised / By our own quickening power").

Adam's "story" insists, as we have seen, on a similar lack: he "Knew not" "who [he] was, or where, or from what cause" (8.270–71). But whereas Satan roots his ontological assertions dialectically in the absence of knowledge, Adam's apprehension of a "maker" emerges from the positive evidence afforded by the givenness of consciousness at the heart of his initial, neonatally mature self-finding. In other words, Adam gets behind the intellectual knowledge on which Satan relies, back to the self-knowledge conveyed by a self-feeling that eludes propositional capture: he feels that he is happier than he knows. Adam's intuition of a "great maker" is correlated with feeling. To return once more to his first speech act, when Adam asks the other creatures, "[H]ow came I thus, how here?" his answer is immediate:

> Not of myself; by some great maker then,
> In goodness and in power pre-eminent;
> Tell me, how may I know him, how adore,
> From whom I have that thus I move and live,
> And feel that I am happier than I know. (8.278–82)

Adam's syntax suggests that his acknowledgement of "some great maker" is conditioned by the feeling in which he finds himself, by the *pathos* of the sentient flesh into which he awakens.[98] Since the feeling Adam encounters is complete happiness and joy, he knows his maker must be "pre-eminent" in "goodness." Milton thus takes the famous opening of Calvin's *Institutio* and echoes its logic. Claiming that human wisdom consists of "the knowledge of God and of ourselves," Calvin argues: "No one can look upon himself without immediately turning his thought to the contemplation of God, in whom he 'lives and moves.' For, quite clearly, the mighty gifts with which we are endowed are hardly from ourselves."[99] Milton's Adam follows this line of thought, since after he has "surveyed" himself, he turns to the God from and in whom he "move[s] and live[s]." For Calvin, the reason that we, who live in the postlapsarian wake of the "miserable ruin, into which the rebellion of the first man cast us," are compelled to turn to God is that each of us is "stung by the conscience [*conscientia*] of his own unhappiness." All fallen humans are directed unfailingly to God by the "feeling [*sensu*] of our own ignorance, vanity, poverty, infirmity, and—what is more—depravity and corruption."[100] Dwelling in paradise, Milton's prelapsarian Adam feels his way toward a maker preeminent in goodness through the "unexperienced thought" of his own happiness, a feeling of vital fullness.

Milton made the first impressions of Adam and Eve as ordinary as possible in order to encourage readerly recognition. In giving his own account

of the experience of human nature—a type of being that is thoroughly embodied and possesses an *appetitus societatis* as its driving impulse—Milton
endows the "new and strange" perspective of neonatal maturity with such
familiarity because he wants readers to check their own thoughts against
those described by Adam and Eve. This invitation militates against those
who would erect strict boundaries between pre- and postlapsarian human
life. Milton holds that the belated self-finding that structures Adam's and
Eve's narratives attends all of us constantly, smuggled into everyday life
through a self-feeling that constitutes a primitive self-knowing and provides the basis for any and every act we consciously attempt or accomplish.
In Milton's view, when anyone undergoes the felt bodily rhythms and in-
stincts of sentient life, follows the movements of reason, or apprehends the
beauty of creation, they gain access to the only argument for the existence
of a "great maker" in "goodness and power pre-eminent" that one would
ever need. If this theological purpose drove Milton to imagine the birth of
human consciousness, the primal scenes he conjured into concrete poetic
form would, as we will see in the rest of this book, give rise to radical and
unexpected ways of reimagining human life.

PART 2

Traherne and the Consciousness of Birth

CHAPTER THREE

From Creation to Birth

HOW TO DO THINGS WITH MILTON

Milton invented a literary technique for dramatizing the landscape of human thought: a first-person perspective afforded to human beings that are new and at the same time able to actualize all of their capacities from the first moment of their existence. By allowing Adam and Eve to narrate their experiences of neonatal maturity, Milton developed a proto-phenomenological poetic decorum that responded mimetically to the consciousness of self and world. Although many critics have attended to Traherne's exploration of the prelapsarian perspective, his reliance on Milton's *Paradise Lost* has gone all but unrecognized.[1] Such a critical lacuna is surprising, for even if Traherne—who perhaps suffered from the "anxiety of influence"—does not articulate his debt to Milton explicitly, he nevertheless repeatedly refracts and reframes the language and themes of *Paradise Lost*.[2] This lacuna can be explained in two ways: first, many of the relevant Traherne manuscripts have only recently been edited; second, Milton's use of neonatal maturity has gone unnoticed, unexplored, and untheorized. Familiarity with these scenes has left their originality hiding in plain sight. As one of Milton's earliest readers, however, Traherne recognized the remarkableness of Milton's accomplishment. Appropriating Adam's and Eve's ability to remember beginnings, Traherne projects an exploration of consciousness into his own natality and transports Milton's imagined perspective back into his own set of philosophical, anthropological, and theological assumptions. The originary experiences described by Traherne thus differ from those expressed by Milton. These differences arise from their views on human nature. Milton believes that the ego is thoroughly embodied, that bodily pressures and constraints actively shape all human thought. By contrast, Traherne, like Descartes, holds that the ego is best understood as an entity that is in principle separable from the body. When Traherne read *Paradise Lost*, he was inspired to develop a parallel system of thought antithetical to many of the ideas Milton held most dear.

Milton's Eve recalls how, newly awakened, she "went / With unexperienced thought, and laid me down / On the green bank, to look into the clear / Smooth lake, that to me seemed another sky" (4.456–59). Traherne's "Shadows in the Water," a lyric exploring how childhood experience informs adult spirituality, reworks Eve's innocent error as a "sweet Mistake":[3]

> In unexperienc'd Infancy
> Many a sweet Mistake doth ly:
> Mistake tho false, intending tru;
> A *Seeming* somewhat more than *View*;
>> That doth instruct the Mind
>> In Things that ly behind,
>> And many Secrets to us show
>> Which afterwards we come to know.
>
> Thus I by the Water's brink
> Another World beneath me did think. (6:168–69, 1–10)

Whereas Eve's "unexperienced thought" leads to her confusion between creature and reflection, Traherne's "unexperienc'd Infancy" leads him to "think" another world exists in puddles.

Framing himself as Eve, Traherne highlights the ancient association between inexperience and error, distilled, as we have seen, in the versions of Polus's dictum provided by Plato in the *Gorgias* ("it is experience [*empeiria*] that causes our times to march along the way of craft [*techne*], whereas inexperience [*apeiria*] causes them to march along the way of chance [*tuche*]" [794; 448c]) and by Aristotle in the *Metaphysics* ("experience [*empeiria*] made art [*techne*] . . . but inexperience [*apeiria*] luck [*tuche*]" [2:1552; 981a]). Traherne acknowledges that inexperience leads to mistakes, but they are "sweet mistake[s]." These mistakes open up a "*Seeming* somewhat more than view," a rich but absolute simplicity. Recognizing the full implications of what, in chapter 1, I described as the positive features of inexperience legible in Eve's watery encounter—a full receptivity to what is disclosed—Traherne suggests that "unexperienc'd Infancy" manifests the richness of phenomenality, a "*Seeming*" in excess of what is actually seen. When approached without experience, the world presents "somewhat more" appearance than what actually exists. These appearances "instruct the Mind,"

Traherne claims, revealing many "Secrets" that we come to know only afterward. "A seeming somewhat more than view": this is a stance toward the world that does not reduce what appears to material existence.[4] A reflection appears to exist as an autonomous entity, and "unexperienced thought" sees it as such. In this poem, Traherne conveys how parts of *Paradise Lost* were, almost immediately, read in exactly the way I outlined in chapter 1; namely, as meditations on the relationship between thought and experience.

This reframing of Eve's neonatally mature thought is only the most obvious example of how Traherne appropriates *Paradise Lost*. He returns to Adam's originary experiences obsessively, and his detailed accounts of humankind's first thoughts reformulate Milton's language. In *Commentaries of Heaven*, Traherne dedicates a section of an entry on "Adam" to the pleasures felt by the first man in his text *Commentaries of Heaven*, an unfinished, alphabetically ordered account of "All Things" that trails off, more than nine hundred printed pages after an initial entry on "Abhorrence," with a meditation on "Bastard."[5] The *Commentaries* was rescued from obscurity and a garbage fire in 1967, and has only recently become available in an edited form. In this truly remarkable text, Traherne meditates on the moment Adam awakens in paradise, and lavishes attention on the varied cognitive powers that enable his first encounter with the world:

> When Adam first awaked out of his Dust, and saw so Glorious a Brightness on evry Side, His Soul being a pure and Clear Mirror representing the Beauties of the Universe in their Divinity, his first Divertisement was a Rapture and Extasie inspired by his Sence of the Magnificence of the World. For the first Object making the first Impression, and his Soul being Right, he did rightly apprehend and resent that same on a suddain therfore being surprized with so much Beauty, Wideness, State and Splendor he was Ravished, and all at once seeing from whence, and by whom, and to what he was raised, his first Thought was a Mixture of Reverence Admiration Gratitude and Joy attending the World he conceived in his Mind. Which being of as much worth the Second Moment as it was the first, would continue forever. (2:217)

Traherne's interest in originary experience is flagged by the repeated adjective *first*. When Adam "first awaked" he experienced his "first Divertisement," which is brought about by the "first Object making the first Impression" and leads to "his first Thought." This concatenation of "first" events marks the joints in a typology of mental processes. Since Adam's "Second

Moment" will be "as it was in the first," every one of these "first" events is crammed into Adam's "first" waking moment. Traherne thus provides a microanalysis of Adam's first thought. The opening sentence of this account provides a summary of what happens: Adam awakens "out of his Dust"— out of his own body—and finds himself environed by light and the beauty of his milieu, both of which strike him with a "Sence of the Magnificence of the World," which, in turn, inspires an ecstatic reaction that amounts to his "first Divertisement," a diverting from the dust of the body toward the glorious world. This turning outward is captured by the terms "Rapture" and "Ecstasy," both of which imply a surpassing of the earlier mirror image: Adam's soul does not just reflect the world; it is "raised" up into it.

Having given an epitome of Adam's first moment, Traherne begins to unpack the coordinated psychological events that subtend this exposure to phenomenality. Adam's soul is "Right," incapable of distortion. The "first Object" this perfect soul encounters—the world in its environing totality— makes a "first Impression" on Adam's soul and he instantly ("on a suddain") apprehends the world while, at the same time, he "resent[s]" (that is, feels in a profound way) the richness of its appearance.[6] The world impresses itself on Adam and he is able to "apprehend" it rightly both in the sense that he experiences it for what it is and in the sense that he responds appropriately by resenting, by being "Ravished" and "surprized with so much Beauty, Wideness, State and Splendor." Still in the same first moment—an "all at once" coterminous with the previous "on a suddain"—Adam sees "from whence, and by whom, and to what he was raised": he perceives that he has been brought by God from nothing into an Edenic state.[7] Adam's first moment is thus structured by multiple modes of relation—impression, right apprehension, affective response, and intellectual judgment—all firing simultaneously. These forms of experience combine to make up Adam's "first Thought," which is a "Mixture of Reverence Admiration Gratitude and Joy attending the World he conceived in his Mind." Adam conceives the world "in his Mind," but this representation of an external environment is only part of a "first Thought" that is an irreducible "Mixture" of perception, affection, and intellection.

Verbal echoes suggest that Milton's Edenic awakenings inform this account. Traherne's examination of what happened "When Adam first awaked" invokes Milton's Eve, who remembers "when from sleep / I first awaked" (4.449–50). Note too how Traherne's Adam "did rightly apprehend and resent [the world] on a suddain," a phrase that references Milton's Adam's "sudden apprehension" when he names the other creatures in *Paradise Lost*: "I named them, as they passed, and understood / Their nature, with such knowledge God endued / My sudden apprehension" (8.352–54). But if such allusions reveal the tight bond between Traherne's project and *Paradise Lost*, they also bear the marks of a departure from Milton's account of Adamic awakening. As I argued in chapters 1 and 2, Milton works to bring his readers into Adam's and Eve's lived experience by making them as recognizable as possible. By contrast, Traherne endows Adam with immediately active cognitive superpowers. In *Commentaries of Heaven*, Adam is said "all at once" to see "from whence, and by whom, and to what he was raised." Traherne mimics Milton's concatenating prepositional phrases—Eve's "wondering where / And what I was, whence thither brought, and how" (4.451–52) and Adam's "But who I was, or where, or from what cause, / Knew not" (8.270–71)—to produce a very different picture of Adam's initial cognitive abilities. In these passages from *Paradise Lost* neither Adam nor Eve knows what they are, from whence they have come, or how they have come to be. Even at the initial moment of their existence—when they are as close to their source as they could possibly be—Milton's Adam and Eve are cut off from what is required for full self-knowledge. By contrast, in the very first moment of his existence, Traherne's Adam knows "all at once" "from whence, and by whom, and to what he was raised." Like the Adams imagined by Andreini and South, which we encountered in chapter 2, Traherne's Adam easily "sees" his origin, cause, and essence.[8]

Adam's originary experience is a privileged site of inquiry for Traherne. He addresses this moment again in the recently discovered and edited *Inducements to Retirednes*, a text in which he raises the legitimacy of his Edenic speculations. In *Inducements*, Traherne once again focuses on Adam's first thought in the moment he first awakened: "When he first waked out of his Dust, and saw so Magnificent a Frame, as that of Nature is, to entertain Him; his first Thought was a Mixture of Amazement, Wonder, Joy and Reverence to see Him self Exalted by the Deitie to such a Great Dominion in a World so Glorious." Just as the Adam in *Commentaries of Heaven* gleans immediate knowledge of self and God, so here Adam "had such a measure of Intuitiv Knowledge that He Knew Him self, and Knew there was a God whom He felt within Him: And that the World was made for his Sake, and that Him self was Lord and Possessor of it" (1:29). Here Adam's "first Thought" is a combination of amazed reaction and intuitive understanding. But what makes this passage significant is Traherne's description of how such knowledge is possible. How can speculations about Adam's "first Thought" possess any legitimacy whatsoever? Traherne acknowledges the skepticism with which his discussions of Edenic awareness might be met: "When we undertake to Disclose Adams first Imagination, we *seem Arrogant*: yet unless He were Defective in the first Instant, we can certainly tell" (1:29). Although it may seem like an exercise in hubris to claim knowledge of Adam's first thoughts, Traherne's project is based on what we can "certainly tell"—and for two reasons, both of which are based on the assumption that Adam was not "Defective in the first Instant."

The first justification is methodological: "The Rules are so Certain wherby we Discern Adams Thought, that they will Discover even [God's thought], if we Apply them to Him" (1:30). If one wants to ascertain the quality of a given person's thought, one must determine three things: first, the "Principles" from which action flows; second, the "Interests" that shape that action; and third, the "Object" toward which that action is directed (1:30). Unless Adam was "Abominable in the first Instant of his Creation" and therefore "Negligent and Ingrateful," his "Principles" should be thoroughly "Righteous." Traherne explains why he dwells on Adam's "first Instant": it is the only moment when Adam *must* conform to God's intentions. The first instant leaves no room to fall away from God. Adam's first thought is a lived disclosure of his nature, which is nothing less than God's intent. Since Adam's "Principles" are "Righteous," his interest in his first object (the world) must be likewise pure: "Tis certain," Traherne writes, "that Adam when his Eys were first Opened was taken with a Surprize, to see a World so New, so Divine and Glorious" (1:31).

Traherne's method establishes as fact that when Adam's eyes first opened, he was surprised by the novelty of the world's appearance. But the details that follow are far from certain, being placed under the probability of a conditional "if" clause: "And if [Adam's] Conscience did intimat and feel a Deitie, that was the Donor of it," Traherne continues, "and his Understanding see the Whole Magnificence of so Great a Gift; that he was Ravished at the Greatness of Gods Eternal Gratitude"—that is, God's grace (1:31).[9] To the degree that Adam is analogous to all of his descendants, he would certainly be surprised when he awakened into creation. But to the degree that Adam's cognitive capacities are radically different from all postlapsarian human life, it is impossible to be certain that Adam possessed an "Intuitive Knowledge" that enabled him to know "there was a God whom He felt within him." *If* he did feel a deity and understand the magnitude of the gift he had been given, surely Adam would have been "Ravished." But since such "Intuitive Knowledge" is so foreign to fallen humanity, it is impossible for us to truly occupy Adam's radically different state of mind, no matter what method we employ.

The conditionality of this account may reflect Traherne's discussions with a contemporary reader, an amanuensis whose marginal comments frequently appear in the manuscript (held at the Lambeth Palace Library) in which *Inducements* is contained. Written in what is known as Script B, which is distinct from Traherne's handwriting (Script A), these comments are interpretive and critical.[10] Alongside Traherne's introduction of "The Rules . . . wherby we Discern Adams Thought" there appears a condemnatory note written in Script B:

> This is not soe pertinent and profitable as it is daingerous, and Inconvenient and seemingly Arrogant if not Impious: bec[ause]: none can (strictly speaking) know the heart, and Thoughts of Man but God Alone and therefore impossible to know Adams: and the probable Guesses we may make by our owne sentiments. yet most uncertaine must thos conclusions be which of Necessity must arise out of the various Apprehensions of Men of soe different Conditions as we are now by Corruption from Adam in Innocency for tho[ugh]: we are restored by penitence to a Better Condition yet noe wher doe we find that we are Restored to that Knowledg he had in his Innocence much less to such a Knowledge as to know the Thoughts of him or any Man: or is it of any Necessity we should: since [it] would puf us up rather than Edefy. (1:30, n. 46)

These criticisms rest on an assumption about the accessibility of human interiority that gets at the kernel of Traherne's understanding of the ego. The thoughts of man are directly available to only two beings: God and the individual to whom those thoughts occur. There is a mine-ness at the core of whatever crosses the field of first-person thought, an irreducible privacy well captured in Shakespeare's *Othello* when Iago informs Othello that he could not "know [my] thoughts" even if "my heart were in your hand."[11] This mine-ness is central to Traherne's own understanding of the ego and its cognitive and affective life. Since even the thoughts of those we know best (spouses, children, lovers, friends) remain unknowable in any unmediated way, the same must hold a fortiori for Adam—someone whom we have never met, who lived in the distant past, and whose way of being was surely very different from our own. We may make "probable Guesses" about Adam's first thoughts but they must remain "impossible to know." After all, according to the writer of Script B, Adam lived in an "Innocency" very different from the "Corruption" of fallen humanity, and no matter how much postlapsarian human beings are restored to a "Better Condition," we will never be "Restored to that Knowledge [Adam] had in his Innocence much less to such a Knowledge as to know the thoughts of him or any Man." This marginal comment insists that the condition for

whatever "Probable Guesses" we might make about Adam's first thoughts
must be based on "our owne sentiments." The "sentiments" available to
Adam's fallen descendants are the only way we have of grasping Edenic
experience, but they are also precisely what separate us from Adam. We
may share broadly human sentiments with Adam, but they are, necessarily,
"various Apprehensions of Men of different Conditions." Our own first-
person experience simultaneously binds us to and divides us from Adam.
This double movement is registered in another marginal comment written
in Script B, which remarks on Traherne's claim that "When we undertake
to Disclose Adams first Imagination, we *seem Arrogant*: yet unless He were
Defective in the first Instant, we can certainly tell." Underlining *seem Arrogant*," the amanuensis adds, "It would appear Arrogant and were indeed
soe: if we should pretend a minuite, Exact, knowledge of Adams Imaginations: but by our owne Souls we can [feel] his Sentiments soe farre as we can
make True Apprehensions of him and of all those Objects present unto him
in such an Instantaneous manner as they were" (1:29, n. 44). According to
this early reader, we cannot "pretend a minute, Exact, knowledge of Adams
Imaginations"—we cannot, that is, perform a precise microanalysis of the
sort that Traherne elaborates in *Commentaries of Heaven*. Such an under-
taking would be arrogant. But the amanuensis concedes that we can nevertheless get close to Adam's first thoughts "in such an Instantaneous manner as they were." We can be accurate so long as we avoid excessive detail.
Insofar as we share a common humanity, we can feel Adam's "sentiments"
in "our owne Souls" and "make True Apprehensions of him and of all those
Objects present unto him." In other words, if we remain sufficiently general, we can apprehend what it is like to be Adam.

Perhaps Traherne internalized this position through conversations with
his amanuensis or perhaps he simply reached a similar set of ideas by following the development of his own thought, but his final account of Adam's
originary experience in *Inducements* aligns with these critiques. This passage suggests that Traherne uses Adam to think through the still-inchoate
concept of consciousness: "Tis certain that Adam when his Eys were first
Opened was taken with a Surprize, to see a World so New, so Divine and
Glorious. And if his Conscience did intimat and feel a Deitie, that was the
Donor of it; and his Understanding see the Whole Magnificence of so Great
a Gift; that he was Ravished at the Greatness of Gods Eternal Gratitude"
(1:31). The surprise with which Adam is, in his first moment, "taken"
should be understood as a feeling "akin to astonishment and wonder,
caused by an unexpected occurrence or circumstance."[12] The unexpected
gift of the world elicits wonder in a theological sense (God's works should

cause wonder, admiration, and praise) and a philosophical sense (Aristotle's *Metaphysics* claims that all philosophy begins when people wonder "at the obvious difficulties" [2.1554; 982b]). The movement from the certainty of Adam's wonder to the conditionality of the claim that he felt "a Deitie" in his "first Instant" marks a shift from what the amanuensis calls "True Apprehensions" to the sphere of "probable Guesses." The term that marks this shift is "Conscience," which is the condition both for Adam's ability to "see a World so New" and for the possibility of divine feeling. "Conscience" is not conditional. What is uncertain is whether conscience immediately feels a deity, a concession that indexes the debate, discussed in chapter 2, over the innate idea of God. If Adam possessed an innate idea of God—what Calvin describes as a "sense of divinity"—then that idea would drive him to "intimat and feel" the existence of God, who is the "donor" of all creation; he would understand the world as a divine gift and be "Ravished" by the greatness of God's grace.[13] If, however, Adam did not possess such an innate idea and needed—much like the Adam of *Paradise Lost*—to determine the fact of God's existence through observation and reasoning, then he would wonder at the existence of the world but not be ravished by an explicit knowledge of God's grace.

What does Traherne mean by "Conscience"? There is no simple answer, for, as we have seen throughout this book, the seventeenth-century meanings of *conscience* and *consciousness* were deeply entangled. Across his corpus, Traherne uses *conscience* in both evaluative and in more nonevaluative senses. He draws on such commonplace evaluative phrases as the "Convictions and Stings of Conscience" (3:155), refers to those who have "a good conscience" (2:152), and believes that in a difficult situation "your Conscience will quickly tell you what you have to do" (3:135). Traherne also employs *conscience* in a Ciceronian sense when he claims that the "Conscience" thinks it "should be Infinitely Beloved" (1:331) or when he writes about God's relationship to "the very inward Conscience of his Perfect Beauty" (3:226). In the lines from the *Inducements* quoted above, Traherne uses the term in a more nonevaluative way, framing *conscience* as something approximating *consciousness*. In this discussion of Adam's first waking moment, "Conscience" is not a faculty for making moral decisions. After all, if Adam was not "Abominable in the first Instant of his Creation," he could not "think any other Way, but he must swerv from the Principles of a Righteous Nature" (1:31). "Conscience" indexes, on the one hand, the possibility that Adam may have immediately intimated and felt God's existence and, on the other hand, the awareness that this God is the "Donor" of "Conscience" itself. The fuzziness of the neuter pronoun in the phrase "Donor of it" is integral to Traherne's point. God is the "Donor" of everything, and if *it* applies straightforwardly to the "World so New," the pronoun also syntactically folds its immediate antecedent ("Conscience") into the newly apprehended world. According to Traherne, then, Adam's first moment may have included a three-fold act, simultaneously achieved: first, a certain feeling of wonder at the existence of the world; second, a possible intuition of God's existence; and third, a possible corollary awareness that the "Conscience" that feels God's existence is itself a gift given by God. Traherne links Adamic awakening with the birth of *consciousness* as a concept impossible to disentangle from the language of *conscience*.

TRAHERNE'S DESCARTES

Like Milton, Traherne does not articulate a fully elaborated theory of consciousness. Also like Milton, when Traherne imagines the experience of Adamic awakening, he draws on the resources available from the broad discussion of human mindedness that was taking place in and across multiple spheres of discourse in seventeenth-century England. Despite these similarities, however, Traherne's understanding of mindedness diverges significantly from Milton's. One factor responsible for this divergence is the extent to which the philosophy of Descartes influenced Traherne. Given the presence of Descartes's ideas in Traherne's writing, it is surprising that next to nothing has been written about this influence.[14] Consider the idea that, as Traherne puts it in the *Centuries*, the "Infinite is the first Thing which is naturally Known" (5:82, bk. 2, sec. 81), a formulation that draws on Descartes's argument in the *Meditationes* that the "perception of the infinite . . . is in some way prior to [the] perception of the finite" (CSM 2:31). For Descartes, the infinite is a necessary background against which any understanding of finitude—of doubt, of desire, of lack—becomes possible, and Traherne shares this intuition. As this connection suggests, Traherne read Descartes with care. He acknowledges as much in *Kingdom of God*, a physico-theological treatise written in the early 1670s, where he lists Descartes among the most important "Modern Divines and Philosophers" (1:377).

It was Descartes's treatment of thought that most interested Traherne, who composed three poems entitled "Thoughts." In the first of these, Traherne claims that thought is that through which God's "Joys accessible are found / To you, and those Things enter which Surround / The Soul" (6:63, 34–36). Without thoughts, those "Living Things within," human experience would be impossible: "Where had all Joy and Glory been / Had ye not made the Soul

those Things to know. / Which Seated in it make the fairest Shew?" (6:63, 37–
39). Thought takes the "Things" that "Surround the Soul" and makes them
"shew" themselves "within." It is the precondition for appearance:

> What were the Skie,
> What were the Sun, or Stars, did ye not lie
> In me! and represent them there
> Where els they never could appear!
> Yea what were Bliss without such Thoughts to me,
> What were my Life, what were the Deitie? (6:63, 47–52)

The "Things" of the external world only "appear" insofar as they are "represent[ed]" in the "there" of thought, which exists "In me" and is manifest
"to me." Highlighting this internality through line breaks before the preposition "In" and after the demonstrative adverb "there," Traherne insists that
thought discloses everything that appears: "Life," the world, "the Deitie."
    The influence of Descartes becomes palpable when Traherne describes
those "brisk Divine and Living things, / Ye great exemplars, and ye Heavenly
Springs / Which I within me see" (6:62, 1–3). What exactly passes "within
me"? In "Thoughts III," Traherne answers in simple terms: "Thoughts are
the Things / That us affect" (6:69, 21–22), a capacious category that includes
within it the powers of will ("Thoughts are the Springs of all our Actions
here" [6:69, 7]); the free play of the imagination ("So Changeable, Capacious, Easy, free, / That what it self doth please a Thought may be" [6:69,
35–36]); the depths of memory ("Old Objects I / Far distant do even now
descrie / Which by your [thought's] help are present here" [6:62, 18–20]); the
passions, ranging from "Grief, Anger, [and] Hate" to "fear, and Love," and
"Joy"; and all of the varied objects of "Sence" to which we respond with
pleasure to their "Hony" and with pain at their "Stings" (6:62, 19–26). This
expansive list of what "I see within me" evokes Descartes's definition of
thought. Recall that in the *Principia* (1644), he defines thought as what "we
are conscious [*consciis*] of as happening within us, in so far as we have consciousness [*conscientia*] of it" (CSM 1:195; AT 8:7).[15] In the text that forms
the basis for this definition—a reply to Marin Mersenne's objections, published in 1641 alongside the *Meditationes*—Descartes claims that thought
"include[s] everything that is within us in such a way that we are immediately conscious [*conscii*] of it. Thus all the operations of the will, the intellect, the imagination, and the senses are thoughts" (CSM 2:113; AT 7:160).
    As Traherne may have understood, Descartes's claim that sensations
"are thoughts" works to undo the hierarchy of mental operations he had

inherited from earlier philosophers. Recall that in *De anima* Aristotle provides two arguments dedicated to explaining why "thinking" must be distinguished from "perceiving." First, although "perception of the special
objects of sense is always free from error," because thought is based upon
imagination and judgment it introduces wiggle room: one can "think falsely
as well as truly" (1:680; 427b). Second, unlike perception, which always
accompanies animal life, thought exists only "where there is discourse of
reason" (1:680; 427b). The condition for true or false statements, Aristotle's *thought* is an elevated mental activity that requires rationality and can
also be overpowered by sensation. By contrast, for Descartes, there is no
ontological distinction between the intellect and the senses: they are simply different modes of thought. No longer a mental activity arranged on a
vertical axis moving from sensation up to intellect, in Descartes's hands,
thought becomes, as I argued in the introduction, the rubric under which
all other mental activities—will, imagination, memory, passion, and even
sensation—are organized along a horizontal axis. As its defining feature,
conscientia is what enables thought to become the basic feature of all mental life.

In "Thoughts I," Traherne animates this Cartesian understanding of
thought and even invokes Descartes's technical distinctions while simultaneously diverging from Descartes by focusing on overwhelmingly positive
emotional states: "The Thought, or Joy Conceived is / The inward Fabrick of my Standing Bliss. / It is the Substance of my Mind / Transformed,
and with its Objects lind" (6:64, 60–63). As that which represents what is
outside the mind, thought brings the world to the ego and thereby makes
"Joy" possible. Insofar as thought transforms the mind by lining it with
its representational "Objects," it is "the Substance of my Mind." This is
a very Cartesian claim, for Descartes too aligns thought with mind and
substance. In Aristotle's *Categories*, a substance, or *ousia*, is simply an individual thing—a given person, say, Socrates—considered as a whole (1:4; 2a).
A substance is "that which is neither said of a subject nor in a subject," an
"individual thing" about which statements are predicated (say, Socrates is
a man) and in which accidents inhere ("colour is in body and therefore also
in an individual body" [1:4–5; 2a14, 2a–2b]). Descartes reworks scholastic
interpretations of this Aristotelian idea by refining it—a substance is, he
claims in the *Principia*, a thing "which exists in such a way as to depend
on no other thing for its existence" (CSM 1:210)—and then extending it, so
that individual bodies and individual minds each become substances. For
Descartes, substances are things in their own right; they are that through
which attributes and modes exist. An attribute is the "one principal prop-

erty which constitutes [the] nature and essence" of a given substance, that "to which all its other properties are referred" (CSM 1:210). The attribute of bodies is extension, and each mode of "corporeal substance"—shape, size, and motion, among others—refers back to extension. The attribute of minds is thought, and each mode of "thinking substance"—sensation, imagination, will, and so on—refers back to thought (CSM 1:210). If substances are things in their own right, modes are not. A mode is dependent on substance and shaped by that substance's attribute.

For Descartes, an attribute is the "one principal property which constitutes [the] nature and essence" of a substance. This claim has important consequences. As Marleen Rozemond has argued, Descartes holds that "the principal attribute constitutes the entire substance."[16] He often suggests that attribute and substance are interchangeable:

> Thought and extension can be regarded as constituting the natures of intelligent substance and corporeal substance; they must then be considered as nothing else but thinking substance itself and extended substance itself—that is, as mind and body. . . . Indeed, it is much easier for us to have an understanding of extended substance or thinking substance than it is for us to understand substance on its own, leaving out the fact that it thinks or is extended. For we have some difficulty in abstracting the notion of substance from the notions of thought and extension, since the distinction between these notions and the notion of substance itself is merely a conceptual distinction. A concept is not any more distinct because we include less in it. (CSM 1:215)

Descartes understands a given substance as isomorphic with its attribute. The mind is a "thinking substance" and the body is an "extended substance." There is a conceptual distinction between the substance of mind and the attribute of thought. But given that the essence of mind *is* thought, Descartes insists that one can understand thought as a substance in its own right.[17] Traherne's claim that thought is "the Substance of My Mind" is derived from this Cartesian background.

The notion that thought could be a substance was a topic important to the English reception of Descartes. In *Divine Dialogues* (1668), Henry More makes the connection between thought and substance central to his examination of the "so-much-admired Philosopher Renatus Des-Cartes."[18] The character Cuphophron is an "excessive Admirer" of Descartes's "Wisedom" (5) who expounds the Cartesian notion that mind is its own substance distinct from bodily substance—"Cogitation is *ipso facto* exempted or prescinded from all Extension"—and a corollary to this view: that the mind or soul is "no-where" (151). Hylobares, his interlocutor, counters, arguing that the mind must be "some-where" because the mind is "in the Body," and even if the *"Representations"* of the mind "respect neither Time nor Place," as *"Modes"* of a "Substance, they cannot but be conceived to be in that Substance." Since all substances are characterized by "essential Amplitude"—that is, extension—and the "Mode of a thing is inseparate from the Thing itself," cogitation or thought is nothing other than the mode of a given body. Cuphophron counters by refusing to allow "that there is a Substance of the Minde or Soul distinct from *Cogitation*." In his view, *"Cogitation* it self is the very Substance of the Soul, and therefore the Soul is as much no-where as if it had no substance at all." Hylobares refuses this idea because he cannot countenance the idea that thought is the substance of the mind; it is a "manifest falsehood" to claim that the *"very Operation* is the Substance." Rather, thought is an "operation" or activity of the mind. For Hylobares, it is ludicrous to contend that this activity is the substance of the mind. After all, thought is constantly "in flux and succession" and is not a "permanent thing," as a substance should be (152–54). But the notion that thought or "Cogitation is the Substance of the Mind" is precisely the position that Descartes's understanding of the relationship between substance and attributes forced upon his English readers. Thomas Baker's *Reflections Upon Learning* (1700) singles out Descartes for making "Cogitation to be the substance of the mind," while Edward Howard's *Remarks on the New Philosophy of Descartes* (1700) argues that the notion of "incorporeal substance" is a contradiction in terms by working through the implications of Descartes's "Thinking Substance of the Mind."[19] If the idea that thought might be the "Substance of the Mind" was a feature of Descartes's philosophy with which his earliest English readers struggled, it was a notion that Traherne embraced. He returns to this idea again in one of his greatest lyric poems, "My Spirit," which begins, as discussed in chapter 4, with an in-depth description of the originary experience unveiled when the act of thought first becomes "the Substance of My Mind" (6:26, 5).

Paradise Lost inspired Traherne's accounts of Adam and Eve waking up, but his reliance on Descartes also caused him to depart from Milton's anthropological and epistemological assumptions. Recall the degree to which Traherne focuses on Adam's soul or mind. In the *Commentaries of Heaven*, for instance, he discusses how, when Adam "first awaked out of his Dust," he was able to attend to "the World he conceived *in his Mind*" (2:217; emphasis mine). The stress here falls on the soul or mind and the world that it discloses within itself. The syntax of Adamic awakening, which is repeated in *Inducements*, suggests that Traherne sees Adam's essence as distinct from body. Traherne's "when he first waked out of his Dust" (1:29) is at odds with the view articulated by Milton's Adam, who is hailed by Raphael in a way that aligns living man *with* dust: God "formed thee, Adam, thee O man / Dust of the ground" (7.524–25). Traherne holds that human nature is a spiritual substance; his depictions of originary experience are grounded in and shaped by this conviction. For Milton, by contrast, human beings are, as we saw in chapter 2, defined by their embodiment; every human thought is structured by the body. Milton's Adam would not describe the world as Traherne does, as something "conceived in [my] Mind." This preposition *in* highlights the degree to which Traherne adopts Descartes's understanding of thought, since for Descartes *thought* is whatever happens "within" a given individual's mind. When Traherne rewrote *Paradise Lost* in *Commentaries of Heaven*, he focused on mind over body. By doing so, he developed his belief that although, as he puts it in *Seeds of Eternity*—a treatise on the soul that he sees as an improvement over Aristotle's "drie and Empty" *De anima* (1:237)—the body is not "the impediment and prison of the mind," it is nevertheless true that "the Body is but the Case of the Soul," the "glorious Instrument and Companion of the soul." (1:240). Such commitments underpin Traherne's rerouting of Milton's mimesis of neonatal maturity away from the primacy of embodiment in *Paradise Lost*.

Traherne was not alone in seeing the Cartesian potential coiled within Milton's depictions of originary experience. "Adam / in Eden was the father of Descartes," writes Wallace Stevens with wry humor about a connection that many late seventeenth-century thinkers made.[20] Consider the poet John Dryden, who was given permission by an aging Milton to "tag" the lines of *Paradise Lost* in an opera, *State of Innocence* (1667).[21] Nowhere is the freedom Dryden takes more evident than in the speech Adam gives upon awakening.[22] Described by the stage directions as "newly created," Adam speaks:

What am I? or from whence? For that I am
I know, because I think; but whence I came,
Or how this Frame of mine began to be,
What other Being can disclose to me?
I move, I see; I speak, discourse, and know,
Though now I am, I was not always so.
Then that from which I was, must be before:
Whom, as my Spring of Being, I adore.[23]

Dryden's Adam immediately grasps the implications of the Cartesian *cogito*, ascertaining the epistemic certainty of his being from the fact that he thinks. Thought guarantees existence and the speaking *I* seems, even in this first moment, separable from "this Frame of mine"; body is little more than a case for mind. If Milton's Adam adopts a slower, more tentative movement toward knowledge both of self and of God—in *Paradise Lost*, Adam "knew" not "himself beginning" (8.251); he "Knew not" "who [he] was, or where, or from what cause" (8.270–71); he can only desire to "know" his maker (8.280); and he feels that he is happier than he knows (8.282)—Dryden's Adam rushes into an elevated mode of self-apprehension: "that I am / I know, because I think." This Cartesian awakening has more in common with Traherne's unpublished texts than it does with *Paradise Lost*.

REFORMING THE EGO

In "Thoughts I," when Traherne claims that "Thought" is the "Substance of my Mind," he indexes the Cartesian horizon on which his work exists. Similarly, when he describes thought as that "Which I within me see," the placement of thought in the space "within"—between "I" and "me"—stresses another, related aspect of Descartes's influence: the identification of ego with thought. The internal rhyme between "me" and "see" only further emphasizes the extent to which the ego is a metaphorical "eye" apprehending all that is thought "within me." Traherne blurs ego into thought so that the "Substance of my Mind" becomes isomorphic with the ego itself, a move indebted to Descartes, who, as we have seen, argues that his essence consists of thought.

In the *Discours*, Descartes records his discovery that even when he was attempting to "think everything false, it was necessary that I, who was thinking this, was something [*moy, qui le pensois, fusse quelque chose*]," for the claim *je pense, donc je suis* is a truth that even the most virulent skepticism cannot undermine. This observation leads to an examination of "what I was [*ce que j'estois*]" that is motivated by the fact that Descartes can doubt his bodily existence but cannot, without contradiction, think that "I did not exist." "From this I knew," Descartes writes, that "I was a substance whose whole essence or nature is simply to think [*j'estois une substance dont toute l'essence ou la nature n'est que de penser*]" (CSM 1:127; AT 6:33). The fact of thinking enables Descartes to reduce his own essence to thought. In the *Meditationes*, he modifies these claims, concluding only that "this proposition, *I am, I exist* [*ego sum, ego existo*], is necessarily true whenever [*quamdiu*] it is put forward by me or conceived in my mind"

(CSM 2:17; AT 7:25). As Jean-Luc Marion argues, if in the *Discours* the "ego achieves its existence by conceiving a proposition that links existence and thought by an objectifiable formulation," in the *Meditationes* this occurs only when the ego is "actually thinking its existence as thought" in a "performative formulation" that must be "repeated from present time to present time."[24] Proof of existence is dependent on the act of thought.

Having established that he exists, the meditator then expresses confusion about the exact status of the ego in a Latin sentence difficult to translate into idiomatic English: *Nondum verò satis intelligo, quisnam sim ego ille, qui jam necessario sum* ("But I do not yet satisfactorily understand who I am, as that *I* who I now necessarily am" [CSM 2:17; AT 7:25]).[25] This grammar-exploding sentence sits at the heart of a tension between *quis* (who) and *quid* (what) that structures the Second Meditation.[26] Descartes uses the demonstrative *ille*, which denotes that which is not close to one (as opposed to *hic*), in order to identify *that* ego—a "what" over there, which is also, precisely, *qui jam necessario sum*, "who" I necessarily am here and now. Given that the meditator does not yet understand this ego, he must bracket "what" [*quid*] he "formerly" thought he was: a man, a body, a soul with nutritive and sensitive faculties, and so on. He cannot make any such assumptions about his quiddity because, as he claims, "I would not perhaps imprudently assume something else [*quid aliud*] in place of me [*in locum mei*] and thus err" (CSM 2:17; AT 7:25).[27] Not wanting to put *quid aliud* (another thing) *in locum mei*, the meditator rules out every *quid* he once believed himself to be. The only thing of which he is certain is that "thought" alone "is inseparable from me": "I am, I exist—that is certain. But for how long? For as long as I am thinking. For it could be that were I totally to cease from thinking, I should totally cease to exist." All that the meditator can say is that "I am, then, in the strict sense, only a thing that thinks [*res cogitans*]" (CSM 2:18; AT 7:27). Although the meditator knows "I exist" as a *res cogitans*, he is still unclear about *quis sim ego ille quem novi*, about *who* precisely I am as "that *I* [*ego ille*] whom I know" (CSM 2:18; AT 7:27).[28]

The answer to this problem rests on Descartes's expansive understanding of thought: "But what [*quid*] then am I? A thing that thinks. What [*quid*] is that? A thing that doubts, understands, affirms, denies, is willing, is unwilling, and also imagines and has sensory perceptions" (CSM 2:19; AT 7:28). A *res cogitans* is conscious of thought in all of its modes, and it is the presence of thought to the ego that constitutes what we might call the "whatness" of the who: "The fact that it is I who am doubting, who am understanding, who am willing [*Nam quod ego sim qui dubitem, qui intelligam, qui velim*] is so evident that I see no way of making it any clearer"

(CSM 2:19, translation modified; AT 7:29). Shorn of any pretensions to a quiddity beyond the manifestation of thought—"I certainly *seem* to see, to hear, and to be warmed," and these appearances "cannot be false"—the meditator begins to grasp that he consists only of thought: *Ex quibus equidem aliquanto melius incipio nosse quisnam sim*, from these things I am beginning to have a rather better understanding of "who I am" (CSM 2:19–20, translation modified; AT 7:29).

Quid or *quis*, *what* or *who*: these pronouns prompt two very different questions. What am I? This question can be answered in multiple ways. I am a human being, a man, a husband, a father, and so on. Who am I? This question can only be answered in one way: I am myself. In the *Meditationes*, Descartes attempts to think his whatness in terms of what Heidegger calls "whoness."[29] Descartes's most celebrated phrase—*je pense, donc je suis*—captures in slogan form a slow shift that had been underway in European culture at least since the theories of mindedness propounded by Augustine in late antiquity and that had been deepened by the theories of cognition advanced by such thinkers as Olivi in the Middle Ages, a movement in which all that is most important about being human comes to be rooted in the ego and its perspective on itself and the world.[30] In his iconic phrase, Descartes flips the commonsensical order of things. It seems obvious that one's being should ground one's thought—"I am a minded being, therefore I am able to think"—but Descartes reverses this intuitive order so that one's thought comes to ground one's being: "I think, therefore I am."[31] Since the conscious immediacy of the thought that grounds one's being in "I think, therefore I am" is inextricable from the "I" that thinks it, this means that one's being (*what* one is) is available through the ego (*who* one is).

Like Descartes, Traherne provides an account of *what* one is (a human being) in terms of *who* one is (a thinking ego with sensory impressions, affective states, memories, anticipations, experiences, and so on).[32] In the *Select Meditations* (an early work written sometime after 1662), Traherne reflects on the centrality of the first-person pronoun to his philosophical and theological project.[33] This text offers insight into the development of Traherne's thought because it manifests a more tentative mood, a writer still finding his voice. If such later works as the *Centuries* (probably written in the early 1670s) betray no qualms about Traherne's commitment to the first-personal quality of all knowledge, in the *Select Meditations* Traherne has not yet fully digested the implications of this approach.[34] He knows that he needs to theorize the ego, but he still feels the need to defend his peculiar use of the first person.

On 30 December 1657, Traherne became the rector of Saint Mary's Church in Credenhill, just outside Hereford, where he was raised. Traherne's love of conversation must have rubbed some the wrong way. This social strain is implicit in his acknowledgment that "too much openness and proneness to Speak are my Diseas," an admission that leads him to lament reactions to his use of the first person:

> Here I am censured For Speaking in the Singular number, and saying I. . . .
>   There it shall be our Glory and the Joy of all to Acknowledge, I. I am the Lords, and He is mine. Every one shall Speak in the First Person. . . . Can the Friend of GOD, and the Heir of all Things in Heaven and Earth Forbear to say, I. [W]e must attend the Reverence Due unto our Persons. (5:334; bk. 3, sec. 65)

"Here" in Credenhill or anywhere else on earth, Traherne claims, "I am censured" for "saying I," for expressing what "I am" in the only possible way. Overexposure has rendered "Nauseating and weary" even "those Things of which there Can be never Enough." It should be impossible to get "Enough" of something so wondrous as the ego—the fact that there is such a thing as the first-person perspective—but people are lulled by overfamiliarity into an unappreciative relationship with the property that makes them *them*. Those who censure Traherne have lost the amazement they should feel whenever they encounter anyone—themselves or another person—capable of "Speaking in the Singular number." Unfortunately, it is "Here" the case that "by Exposing Himselfe" a man "becometh cheap and Common." Yet Traherne continues to celebrate the "First Person" perspective, for "There" (a future heavenly state) "it shall be our Glory and the Joy of all to Acknowledge, I," and "Every one shall speak in the First Person." Traherne aims to peel back habit-induced weariness and apprehend the power of the ego here and now. "We must," in the present moment, "attend the Reverence Due unto our Persons."[35]

In *Select Meditations*, Traherne begins to articulate how his insistence on the first person is rooted in a conviction about the relationship between self and world. The ego is, in Traherne's view, the "Heir of all things in Heaven and Earth," and this claim prefigures three facts that condition the field of phenomenal thought, the appearance of all the somethings that show up for someone. First, the end or purpose of the world consists in being enjoyed, for without someone to enjoy it the world would be nothing but a jumble of unperceived, dead matter. Second, it follows that the world

exists for the sake of the living beings that enjoy it. And third, the world is
possessed by and belongs to those enjoyers. To capture this dynamic, Traherne transforms the term *enjoyer*—a word used only sparingly by earlier
English writers—into a term of art. From the late sixteenth century onward, *enjoyer*—"one who enjoys"—was used in a quasi-legal sense to refer
to goods or a societal position possessed by someone (the "enjoyer of the
Crowne"), to a happy sensual state (an "Enjoyer of his pleasures"), or to
a deep spiritual satisfaction that outstrips the pleasures of the world (the
"godly man" is able to "enjoy the sweetest delights and comforts of the
soule," so that he becomes a true "enjoyer of God").[36] So far as I know, however, no English writer prior to Traherne leant the agentive nominal *enjoyer*
such explanatory power and ontological force.

An important term in Augustine's *De doctrina Christiana* (begun c. 396,
completed 427), *enjoyment* and its cognates played a central role in the
Christian tradition. In Augustine's view, the various entities presented to
the human mind are grasped through either enjoyment (*frui*) or use (*uti*).
"To enjoy something is to cling to it with love for its own sake," Augustine
writes, but to "use something, however, is to employ it in obtaining that
which you love, provided it is worthy of love."[37] Any given thing can either
be enjoyed for "for its own sake" or used as a means to obtain something
that might be enjoyed. In *De trinitate*, Augustine explains that modulations
of the will (*voluntas*) make such inflections possible:

> For to use is to take up something into the power of the will, but to en-
> joy it is to use with joy, not of hope, but of the actual thing. Therefore,
> everyone who enjoys, uses, for he takes up something into the power of
> the will and finds pleasure in it as an end. But not everyone who uses,
> enjoys, if he has sought after that which he takes up into the power of
> the will, not on account of the thing itself, but on account of something
> else. (58; 10.11.17).

The will can determine if a person will enjoy a given thing in the present
with "joy" on "account of the thing itself" or with an eye to the future and
"hope" on "account of something else." For Augustine, enjoyment entails
use, at least insofar as the former finds "pleasure in [a given thing] as an
end." By contrast, use does not entail enjoyment.

Traherne's treatment of enjoyment is indebted to but also departs from
Augustine.[38] For Traherne, every ego is an "Enjoyer" of the world. In *Inducements to Retirednes*, Traherne states that God is "the Giver" of creation,
while "Man" is the preeminent created "Enjoyer" (1.34). In *Commentaries*

of Heaven, he argues that this privilege places human beings in a special position vis-à-vis the world: "Enjoying all we are made Higher than all, as much as the Enjoyer is above the Things Enjoyed" (2:59). Capable of enjoying "all"—everything that is created—human beings are "above" the "all" that they enjoy precisely because they are capable of such enjoyment. In *A Sober View of Doctor Twisse* (probably written around 1663)—a theological treatise that adopts an Arminian position against the hardline Calvinism of William Twisse—Traherne provides a theological justification for this view.[39] God's infinite love is the cause of creation. "For nothing but Love could move God to give a Beginning and Being to Creatures, since Hatred cannot frame an object from which it naturally flies," Traherne argues, before claiming that God's love is the origin and condition for all enjoyment: "And love only enjoys the Goodness and Beauty of what it Effecteth, and so is the End of its own Productions. Nor can any thing be Enjoyed, but by love alone" (1:59). In Traherne's view, the "End" is "higher" than the "Means," and the "End" of all creation is that "it might be Enjoyed": "To what purpose should Heaven and Earth be made, were there no Ey to see them, no Understanding to Contemplat the Goodness of God in making them; no Living Creature to Enjoy them?" (1:60). When he claims that created things would be "altogether useless" without a creature made to "enjoy" them, he works with Augustine's sense that one uses something in order to obtain later enjoyment and that enjoyment entails use.

But if God's love is the cause of creation, it is nevertheless true that creation is not, strictly speaking, made for God's enjoyment. God "cannot enjoy [the creatures] in him self, but only by Love"—that is, only insofar as His love binds him to His creatures. After all, God does not need anything "in him self." God only "needs" the sun, the sea, the land, and the air "for our sakes," and it is only "in us" that He "enjoys" what He has made: "Were there no Creature therefore made to enjoy them [all other created things] they would be altogether useless. And being well examined they [all created things] serve every Creature as much as if they served one alone. In whose Enjoyment God enjoyeth them. So that our Act of Enjoying is the End for which the World was made, and that by which we imitate God who rejoyceth in all his Works. . . . Enjoying Him in them, and pleasing Him by Enjoying them" (1:60). Created things are useful insofar as they are enjoyed. As enjoyers of all things, human beings facilitate God's enjoyment of creation through their own "Act of Enjoying"—the act through which we enjoy God "in" his creation, please God by virtue of our enjoyment, and, at the same time, "imitate God." It is thus no exaggeration to claim that some version of Augustine's enjoyment is central to Traherne's theological vision.

But Traherne refuses the normative framework within which Augustine mobilizes the distinction between *uti* and *frui*. *Res ergo aliae sunt quibus fruendum est, aliae quibus utendum*, writes Augustine in *De doctrina*: "Some things are to be enjoyed, others to be used." Augustine uses the passive paraphrastic (*fruendum est*) to articulate a powerful sense of obligation; one must be careful to enjoy the right things and not the wrong things. Such judgments can be tricky, since all human beings are "placed in the midst of both kinds of things" (those that should be enjoyed, those that should be used). It is all too easy to "wish to enjoy those things which should be used," and thus to be "retarded in obtaining those things which are to be enjoyed, or even prevented altogether, shackled by an inferior love" (9; 1.3). To make this mistake—to enjoy something that should be used—is to succumb to a "perverse sweetness." In this "mortal life, wandering from God, if we wish to return to our native country [that is, heaven] where we can be blessed, we should use this world and not enjoy it . . . so that by means of corporal and temporal things we may comprehend the eternal and spiritual" (10; 1.4). Although the world may be beautiful, it is not, in and of itself, worthy of our enjoyment. The world should be used so that we can orient ourselves toward the "things which are to be enjoyed"; namely, "the Father, the Son, and the Holy Spirit" (10; 1.5).

Traherne rejects this view out of hand, claiming that the world must be enjoyed. Our most important, divinely mandated work is to enjoy the world. This is what is at stake in Traherne's use of the suffix *-er*, which transforms action (I enjoy) into agent (I am an enjoyer): we must fully appreciate the "World which we are Born to Enjoy," and this activity of enjoyment defines what it is to be a creature. In Traherne's view, one should not use the world so as to enjoy God. Rather, "to Enjoy the World, is to Conceive the H. Ghos[t], and to see his Lov; Which is the Mind of the Father." The world manifests God's goodness, and since it is "made to be Enjoyed," there is "Nothing [that] can please or serv [God] more than the Soul that Enjoys it. For that Soul doth accomplish the End of [God's] desire in Creating it" (5:9, bk. 1, sec. 10). Traherne revises Augustine's *frui*: all creatures "are to be" enjoyed in and for themselves.

Traherne's claim that the ego is first and foremost an enjoyer breaks with received tradition even more radically. Although "Man" is the preeminent example, Traherne departs from Descartes's well-known convictions about human exceptionalism and holds that *each and every living being* is both an ego and an "Enjoyer." Traherne's understanding of the ego—each *I* is an "Heir of all things," a pole of phenomenality set over against the disclosure of a world made to be enjoyed and possessed—extends from angels to insects. Ants cannot use language to "Speak in the First Person" (5:334, bk. 3, sec. 65), but they are nevertheless little egos capable of enjoying the world. Each ant is above the world it enjoys. "The Ant is a more Glorious Creature then the Sun," Traherne states in the *Kingdom of God*, "for [ants] Know themselves, and are Sensible of the Light, and of the Comfort of their lives: But the Sun Knoweth not any thing. . . . That which can see, is more Glorious, and perfect then that which can Shine: That which can feel is far more sublime and venerable than that which can Warm" (1:411–12). Even the most insignificant living being is able to apprehend self and world. Their role as "Enjoyer[s]" elevates them above the "things Enjoyed": the "Heavens are Inferior to the least life in the World," for although the stars are glorious, this brilliance "is nothing to them, they have no interest and all their Existence is lost to themselves" (1:411). Creation is meaningless without creatures to behold and, by implication, to enjoy it: "All Worlds [are] but a Silent Wilderness, without som living Thing" (5:74, bk. 2, sec. 62).

For Traherne, the ego is simply that which enjoys the world, and the principle that enables enjoyment is nothing other than life itself, the "final cause" or "end" of which is that "the Glory of the univers might be usefull, and Enjoyed."[40] The defining feature of life is thus the capacity to apprehend what appears, which is inherent in all thinking minds. Life is "founded in perception, for whatsoever is able to Apprehend, liveth"; its very "Essence and Quidditie" lies in the "power to perceiv" (1:409). To be an "Enjoyer" is to be a form of life whose experience is structured as though the world was created for one's own enjoyment. Drawing on the recent discoveries of such natural philosophers as Robert Hooke and Henry Power, Traherne references phenomena revealed by the "Help of the Microscope" in order to test his belief that the world is created for any "Enjoyer," no matter how small (1:421).[41] He asks readers to imagine that the only living being in existence was "one of those Curious and High Stomachd Flies . . . whose Burnisht, and Resplendant Bodies are like Orient Gold, or Polisht Steel; whose Wings Are So Strong, and whose Head so Crownd with an Imperial Tuff, which we often see Enthroned upon a Leaf, having a pavement of living Emrauld beneath its feet, there contemplating the World" (1:422). Traherne adopts this fly's perspective. Like every single life form, the "contemplating" fly can mingle ecstatically with the world: "Having a life far greater then his body, [the fly] can feel a Remote object. He is able to exceed him self, and to be present there, where his Body is not. In spirit he is evry where and filles the World with sense, and Power" (1:423). Moving up the linguistic animacy hierarchy from the pronoun *it* ("its feet") to the pronoun *he* ("In spirit he is every where"), Traherne stresses that, like all living perceivers, the fly is an

I.[42] Imagining that this Adamic fly was the only living being in existence, Traherne argues that enjoyment is the end for which all things were created:

> That very Flie being made alone the Spectator, the Enjoyer of the Universe had been a little, but Sensible, King of Heaven and Earth. . . . [A]ll the labours of the Heavens terminate in him, He being the only Sensible that was made to Enjoy them. The very Heavens had been, but a Canopie to that Insect, and the Earth its footstool; the Sun, and Moon, and Stars its Attendants, the seas, and Springs, and Rivers its Refreshments, and all the Trees, and Fruits, and Flowers its Repasts, and Pleasures. There being none other living Creature . . . but he, as he had been the Centre; So he had been the End of the Material World. (1:422)

If the fly were the sole "Enjoyer of the Universe," all things would have existed for its pleasure and its use. It would be "the End of the Material World," that for which the world was made—an ego that is "Heir of All Things," able to enjoy and possess them.

Whether insect, animal, human, or angel, each ego is heir to the world, because each first-person "Enjoyer" apprehends and possesses the world. "All things were made to be yours," Traherne instructs readers of the *Centuries*, and God has made the world "infinitely Easy to enjoy, by making every Thing ours, and us able so Easily to Prize them. Evry thing is ours" (5:10–11, bk. 1, sec. 12–14). This possession is not literal but phenomenological. The manifestation of everything in the world—the stars, the sky, the oceans, the earth, and all the creatures in it—gives the full range of phenomenal appearance to every living being capable of apprehending the world into which it is born: "By the very Right of your Sences you Enjoy the World" (5:13, bk. 1, sec. 21). The simple and irreducible mine-ness of first-person experience—the fact that I cannot "See in any ones eye, as well as Mine" (1:484)—becomes, in Traherne's hands, the key to understanding how and why the world appears as it does. This position can sound solipsistic—"That all the World is yours, your very Senses and the Inclinations of your Mind declare" (5:11, bk. 1, sec. 18), or, stronger yet, "I alone am the End of the World" (5:11, bk. 1, sec. 15)—but is in fact profoundly intersubjective. If the world belongs to me, and I am that for which the world was made, it also belongs to and is made for "innumerable millions." Each and "every one" of the "innumerable" teeming, wriggling, leaping, flying, speaking, singing, thinking creatures is "the sole and single End of all Things" (5:72, bk. 2, sec. 55). All living creatures exist as egos. And all egos are, first and foremost, enjoyers.

NESCIUS UNDE

Enjoyment is a mode of thought, and all egos are enjoyers insofar as they think. Yet although Traherne holds that each living thing is an *I* and that the basic structure of self-world relations obtains for all life forms, he nevertheless insists on a strong distinction between human beings and other enjoyers. The difference between the human ego and that of other creatures is the extent of ecstatic projection. After exalting the fly's lived experience and exploring animal rationality in the *Kingdom of God*, Traherne addresses the limitations of nonhuman life, which is "confined within Narrow Bounds" and "guided but to feeble Ends." For animals, apprehension "is terminated within the compass of the Material World," locked within the "Concernments of their Bodies, and Minds, for the Present" and "Shut up within the Compass of their lives" (1:424). Nonhuman creatures ecstatically apprehend a world limited to the present moment, to the immediate pressures of self-preservation: embracing pleasure, fleeing pain.[43] By contrast, human beings are able to see the "secret Properties, uses and Relations of Evry being, which are retired from the Light and obscurely buried from evry Ey." Perceiving the intelligible within the sensible, human beings are "acquainted with Infinit distant things" to such an extent that "to live like a Man indeed, is to be guided by infinit, and Eternal Motives, to reason upon Sublime, and Everlasting grounds, and to be Illimited in Thoughts, and Considerations" (1:424–25). Human thought apprehends a world that is radically open, inexhaustible. Thought itself is a property shared by every living being, each of which must "of Necessity" have "an Abilitie to conceiv, or think" since "without that there is no Living" (1:409). But if animal thought is confined to sensation and limited forms of reasoning, "Shut up within the Compass of their Lives," human thought expands without limits—spatially beyond the limits of the cosmos, temporally back to "the first Original" or forward to "the last End of Things" (1:424).

The mystery on which Traherne dwells is that the thoughts a given thinker sees "within" himself are also what enable him to "exceed himself." As he puts the point in "Thoughts I," his "Invisible, yet Infinite" thoughts are "pent within my Brest, / Yet rove at large from East to West" (6:62, 10–12). Although human thought appears within a given body, it travels where bodies cannot go:

The Ey's confind, the Body's pent
In narrow Room: Lims are of small Extent.
    But Thoughts are always free.

And as they're best,
    So can they even in the Brest,
    Rove ore the World with Libertie:
    Can Enter Ages, Present be
In any Kingdom, into Bosoms see.
    Thoughts, Thoughts can come to Things, and view,
    They know no Bar, Denial, Limit, Wall:
    But have a Liberty to look on all. (6:64, 66–78)

Thought transcends bodily limitations. Through the modality of imagination, it reaches out to encompass the entire world and the entire extent of the past and the future.

Traherne returns obsessively to this idea, marveling at the fact that every human being exists within a body that is riveted to a spatiotemporal location but is, through the medium of thought, able to move swiftly across time and space. Human beings can imagine creation one moment and the *novissimum* the next, perceptually explore their own bodies one moment and then picture the furthest reaches of the cosmos the next. This idea is not new to Traherne; it was a commonplace. But Traherne is most taken with the formulation provided in the *Asclepius*, then attributed to Hermes Trismegistus, whom he quotes in a number of texts: "I am in Heaven, in the Earth, in the Water[,] in the Air, in the Living Creatures, in the plants, in the Womb, evry where." The lesson Traherne draws from this expansive list is that when one thinks about something, one is "Spiritualy present" with that thing (1:463).[44] Put otherwise, by claiming that he could be "in the Womb," Trismegistus "understood himself to be where his Thought was" (1:464). *Ekstasis* is the defining property of the human ego. Human thoughts always project one outside of oneself: the ego exists beside or beyond itself because it exists where and when it is carried by its thoughts. This capacity for *ekstasis* is what distinguishes the human ego from that of other creatures. The ability to contemplate origins is central to this distinction. In *Seeds of Eternity*, Traherne reiterates many familiar markers separating "Man" from other creatures: language ("his tongue can utter Words"), manual dexterity (the "infinite liberty and volubility" of human fingers), verticality ("Erect stature"), and invention ("he can make all that he can invent, Letters[,] Guns," and so on [1:241]). But the essential difference between human beings and the other creatures is that the latter are unable to "penetrate" into "hidden Qualities and virtues with their understanding" and, most importantly, that "they cannot look into the original or End of things" (1:242).

For Traherne, "man is an inquisitive and restless Creature, and Knowing that there is an Original and End he is not contented to see the surface or Colour of things, to taste their Qualities or smell their Odors, or take in the apparent Brightness or Beauty, but feeleth an Instinct strongly moving him to know from whence this Creature came, and whither it tendeth" (1:243). Human beings want to know where things come from, why they were made, and what will happen to them. To gloss this thought with the Aristotelian phrase that was surely on Traherne's mind: "All men by nature desire to know" (2:1552; 980a). When a man sees the "Glory of the univers," he is "apt to be delighted with what he beholds," but he is not satisfied: "In the midst of all the Splendor of Heaven and Earth [he] immediately inquires, (tho perhaps for no more at first then bare curiosity) Whether it began, and what was the original of so Divine a Being, and to what End and purpose it was created? What was before it? and what will be after it?" (1:243–44). Human apprehension is geared both to enjoy the world and to explore what lies behind it, to expand into the depths of time and space and examine the inexhaustible fecundity laid open when rationality is mingled with perception. To apprehend the world as a human being is to feel a latent pull tugging one back toward origins and forward toward ends: "The nature of man must of necessity enquire, bec[ause] it feels it self most eminently concerned in the Original and End of that Creation" (1:244). I want to bracket Traherne's concern with ends and focus here on the implications of the suggestion that to be human is to "feel" entangled with origins, for this felt compulsion to project away from the here and now back toward an origin sits in profound tension with the understanding of the first-person perspective I have examined in this chapter.

Traherne holds that the Delphic *nosce te ipsum* is an imperative directing us to gain knowledge of the soul. As the condition of possibility subtending the first-person perspective, the soul is what supports the human ego as it opens onto both itself and the world. Since the "nature of man must of necessity enquire," it should come as no surprise that "the Soul naturaly desires to see the Lineaments of its own face." Can such a desire be fulfilled? Traherne answers this question affirmatively in *Seeds of Eternity*. Since the soul's "Objects are within us," we have a privileged access to these objects, and can apprehend them in a manner that is "plain and easy." The *scientia animae* is, in fact, the "most certain of all Sciences, becaus we *feel* the Things it declares, and may by Experience, prove all it revealeth" (1:233). Since we stand in a relation of self-affection to our own inner life, knowledge of the soul is "plain and easy" to come by, for we cannot help but feel what happens within us. But does the feeling of one's own life constitute knowledge? In *Kingdom of God*, Traherne answers this question negatively, claiming that the very immediacy of our inner lives is an impediment to knowledge: our life "is Common, and allwayes neer, but too near us to be well considered, and too Mysterious to be understood. Becaus it is Invisible, becaus it is Spiritual, becaus it is a Pure Immaterial Power, an Interior Endowment, . . . we perceiv it not, we weigh it not, we know it not: We cannot tell what to fasten on, in the contemplation of it" (1:417). We may "*feel*" the things "declare[d]" by our own souls, but that does not mean that we have the distance requisite to properly "perceiv" those declarations. It may in fact be the case that our souls are "too near us to be well considered," let alone understood.

Although human beings are able to know a great many things—from the chemical processes undergirding minute physical changes to the speed at which the earth orbits the sun—we are unable to fully grasp ourselves. This situation arises partly because we cannot "weigh" or gain knowledge of ourselves through empirical investigation. But it is also partly because, as we have seen throughout this book, in the seventeenth century proper understanding was thought to require a grasp of causes and of origins. To be sure, "Man" can follow the "Instinct strongly moving him to know from whence [he] came." As we will see in chapter 4, embryology teaches how living beings develop and are born, while theology teaches when and how soul is fused with body *in utero*. But, according to Traherne, human beings are not the sorts of creatures one can know in an objective way. Human beings are first and foremost egos, known only from the inside. At bottom, each of us is an *I*, an enjoyer that possesses itself and the world through its own lived, felt experiences. And this means that we can never gain full understanding of our egos because we are denied access to the origins of that ego.

In making this point, Traherne follows and deepens an argument from *De trinitate*, in which Augustine claims both that self-knowledge must be derived from introspection and that this project is rendered impossible by the fact that we have, all of us, forgotten our first moments. Human beings can *infer* knowledge about infancy, Augustine claims: "We can," for instance, "infer how strongly [an infant] is attracted towards those sensible things that are from without from this one fact alone: the greediness with which it looks at a light." In fact, we can, without difficulty, make inferences or educated guesses about what transpires in the "mind of an infant that is still so small and plunged in so great an ignorance of things that the mind of a man that knows something shudders at the darkness of the infant's mind." But this sort of knowledge is different in kind from that which derives from actual knowledge of oneself. If, as Augustine states, "the mind knows nothing so well as that which is present to itself, and nothing is more present to the mind than it is to itself," then the knowledge of infancy gained by observing others can never be included among those things that the mind knows best (143; 14.5.7). When searching for genuine knowledge about the sorts of beings that we are, we should "pass over this age [infancy], which cannot be questioned about what goes on within it, and which we ourselves have forgotten to a great extent. Suffice it for us to be only certain that if a man is capable of thinking about the nature of his own mind, and of discovering what is true about it, he will not find it any-where else than with him himself" (144; 14.5.8). In Augustine's view, then, knowledge of what we are cannot come from a consideration of infancy, for three, interrelated reasons: first, any account of what we are needs to begin with the mind; second, any understanding of the mind can only be found in the mind, "with him himself"; and third, we no longer have any access to "what goes on within" [quid in se agatur] the infants we once were (144; 14.5.8). Augustine explores infant experience only to stress its unavailability.

Traherne articulates this claim even more forcefully: "Nescius unde [ignorant of his origin] is the proper Motto or Character of Man. A flaming Candle can as well tell whence it received its Light, almost, as a man" (3:170). If, as Traherne insists over and over again, the human soul or mind is an outward-radiating light, an ego that illuminates both itself and the sen-sible and intelligible world, then this ego is "almost" as ignorant as a candle when it comes to the source of its light. Each human ego is an I that "feels it self most eminently concerned in [its own] Original," that feels compelled to inquire into an origin that must nevertheless remain unknown (1:244). Nescius unde: in Traherne's view, we are ignorant of the ego's origins but must nevertheless strive toward that origin. The possibility for such striv-ing is registered in the "almost" that separates human from candle. In what remains of this chapter, I unpack the meaning of this "almost" by examin-ing how Traherne uses the capacity of imaginative thought, in its unlimited richness, to "be present there, with Adam in Paradice" at the moment he first awakens in order to bring readers as close as possible to the first spark of human consciousness (1:465).

Adam provides Traherne with a way to imagine the details of a moment that the limitations of the human condition prevent him from knowing directly. If "Nescius unde is the proper Motto or Character of Man," it is nevertheless the case that "this Ignorance of his Original he owes not to Na-ture, but the Corruption therof" (3:170). That is to say, the ignorance of ori-gins is not innate to human nature but a product of disobedience. When still untouched by "Corruption," Adam had complete knowledge of his "Original." Perhaps this is why Traherne's detailed accounts of Adam's cognitive abilities in *Commentaries of Heaven* and *Inducements to Retirednes* never once grammatically enter the first-person perspective. Traherne's expansive use of the *I* never extends to Adam's voice. Given Traherne's investment in both Adamic awakening and the human ego, it is striking that he does not adopt Milton's strategy and use the first-person *I* to articulate Edenic experience. This distancing effect is the fundamental claim of the poem with which Traherne concludes his entry on "Adam" in *Commentaries on Heaven*. The untitled poem examines the difference between the glorious appearance of Adam's body and the inaccessible nature of his inner life. Much like Du Bartas, Tasso, and the other Hexameral poets discussed in chapter 2, Traherne can describe nothing more than Adam's surfaces:

> Amazing sight! a Pile of Dust appeard,
> A Beauteous Angel, out of Nothing reard!
> How faire and Comly doth it shine, how Bright,
> How full of Vigor and Celestial light! (2:225, 1–4)

The appearance of Adam's body, reared from nothing, is celebrated in the first half of the poem. So beautiful that it shines, this body is "admird" by the Sun, remains so pure that it sparks the air's envy, and makes the stars dance for joy. But the body's mode of appearance is not what truly deserves the poet's praise. This distinction belongs to "What it is that within this Glorious Case / Lies hid" (2:225, 15–16). It is Adam's invisible interiority that most impresses Traherne: "I Admire / What kind of Creature tis that dwells within / That Animats and Beautifies the Skin" (2:225–26, 18–20). Adam's soul—a hidden principle of life made visible only insofar as it manifests itself on the surface of his body—is what Traherne deems the "Wonder of the World." This sentiment bears out Traherne's commitment to interiority, reiterated throughout his corpus but perhaps most forcefully in *Seeds of Eternity*: "True Humanitie is not the Knowledg of exterior Actions, but the interior endowments Qualities and Inclinations of the Soul. . . . Men in the World are like a Gallery of Pictures till they are seen within" (1:236).

But despite this elevation of the inner over the outer and despite, as we saw in the first section of this chapter, Traherne's explicit appropriation of Milton's scenes of Edenic awakening, the poem on Adam in *Commentaries of Heaven* refuses to see "within" Adam's interiority, which "Lies hid" behind the "Glorious Case" of the body. This distancing effect is also at work in Traherne's account of Adamic awakening. If Milton's Adam describes

the birth of human consciousness from the first-person perspective, Traherne accounts for this moment in clinical, theoretical terms: he lays out
the combination of objects, impressions, apprehensions, and mental vision
that powered the human mind in its very first moment. Traherne uses this
scene of primal awakening to shed light on idealized cognitive processes,
but Adam is not a vehicle for phenomenological description. Traherne's
"When Adam first awaked" (2:217) excludes readers in a way that Milton's
"When from sleep / I first awaked" does not (4.449–50, emphasis added).

To be sure, Traherne is fascinated by Edenic experience, and he frames
his larger project as an attempt to rethink the meaning of that experience
for fallen human beings. Near the end of the *Centuries*, Traherne refers to
his ambitions from an external vantage point, framing his endeavors as actions accomplished by a third-person *he*:[45]

> It was [his] delight to meditate [on] the Principles of Upright Nature:
> and to see how things stood in Paradise before they were Muddied and
> Blended and Confounded. For now they are lost and buried in Ruines.
> Nothing appearing but fragments, that are worthless shreds and parcels
> of them. To see the Intire Piece ravisheth the Angels. It was his Desire
> to recover them and to Exhibit them again to the Eys of Men. Above all
> things he desired to see those Principles which a Stranger in this World
> would covet to behold upon his first appearance. And that is what prin-
> ciples those were, by which the Inhabitants of this World, are to live
> Blessedly and to Enjoy the same. (5:163, bk. 4, sec. 54)

Traherne's greatest ambition is to "see" prelapsarian human experience, to
"recover" this experience and "Exhibit" it for the benefit of others. The way to
recapture this long-lost way of living is to apprehend the "Principles"—that is,
the "original or initial state[s]" or the "natural or innate disposition[s]"[46]—
"which a Stranger in this World would covet to behold upon his first appearance." "Appearance" here performs a playful double movement, suggesting that the "first appearance" of the world is bound up to Adam's "first
appearance" in the world. Strikingly, the "Principles" that "were" central to
Adam's experience in the past "are" still the principles by which "the In-
habitants of this World" should live and through which they should "enjoy"
the world.

When fallen human beings realize that we, like Adam, are enjoyers of
the world, our own first-person perspective can serve as the precondition
for seeing the world as though it were Eden. After all, Adam also encountered the world as an ego. Since we all occupy this position in the center

of the world (conceived as a phenomenological structure of transcendence), conscious thought and its necessary mine-ness are what grant us access to paradise. To encourage a correct apprehension of the relationship between self and world, Traherne asks readers of the *Centuries* to perform a spiritual exercise in which they imagine themselves to be Adam: "If you desire Directions on how to Enjoy [the world], Place yourself in it as if no one were Created besides your self." Imagining oneself as Adam enables one to capture the "first Thing which GOD bestows to every Infant, by the very Right of his nativity" (5:50, bk. 2, sec. 2). The descendants of Adam and Eve have forgotten what the "first Thing" bestowed to every infant actually was, for our view of the world has been dulled by habit. "Were we to see [the world] only once, the first Appearance would amaze us," Traherne writes, "But being daily seen, we observe it not" (5:57, bk. 2, sec. 21). No one is struck dumb by the environing air, by the feeling of the ground beneath their feet, by the sheer fact of appearance, by the ability to apprehend meaning in things (to see the rock *as* a rock, the tree *as* a tree). "When you enter into [the world], it is an illimited feild of Varietie and Beauty: where you may lose your self in the Multitude of Wonders and Delights": Traherne's central aim is to establish a decorum adequate to this "illimited feild," to rekindle the pleasurable shock of novelty (5:12, bk. 1, sec. 18).

To recapture the all-but-forgotten joy of our exposure to the simplest phenomena, Traherne wants readers to think themselves toward an Adamic perspective: "Place yourself therefore in the midst of the World as if you were alone: and Meditat upon all the Services which it doth unto you" (5:52, bk. 2, sec. 7). This practice guides attention toward the air that makes breath possible, the atmospheric warmth that sustains life, the surface of the earth that facilitates movement and enables the possibility for rest. When one pays attention to both the "Appearance" of and the services provided by the world, "Why," Traherne asks, "should you not render Thanks to God for them all? you are the Adam; or the Eve that Enjoy them" (5:54, bk. 2, sec. 12). We maintain the same relationship to the world that Adam and Eve once did, and we are capable of enjoying it just as much. But we must first lose the deadening weight of habit and recover our status as enjoyers. Imagining ourselves in Eden is one of the ways this recovery is enabled: "Everything is ours that serves us in its place. . . . And therefore in the Beginning, was it made Manifest to be mine, because Adam alone was made to Enjoy it. By making One, and not a Multitud, God evidently Shewed One alone to be the End of the World, and evry one its Enjoyer[,] for every one may Enjoy it as much as He" (5:11, bk. 1, sec. 14). God made Adam alone and therefore each *I* is the "End of the World," capable of enjoying it just "as much" as Adam did. Edenic solitude is proof that the world is "mine," and if one could remember this fact, then one could occupy an Adamic perspective and properly understand one's nature and place: "Adam and the World are both mine" (5:11, bk. 1, sec. 15).

When Traherne claims that Adam is "mine," he suggests that his mode of apprehending and enjoying the world is homologous to that experienced by Adam prior to the fall. When habitual attitudes are bracketed and Traherne encounters the world as if for the first time, he experiences something approaching life in Eden. Although Milton's accounts of neonatal maturity may have inspired this attitude, Traherne nevertheless refuses to imagine Adam's experience from the inside. To be sure, he attempts to see the world as Adam did; yet Traherne's corpus never invokes an Adamic *I* akin to that employed by Milton. In Traherne's work, Adamic experience is always positioned as a possibility for human life here and now. In other words, Traherne's attachment to Eden is consistently aspirational, never fully recuperative. He registers a difference between Adam and the first-person pronoun, and he sometimes marks this distance with a wistful consideration of what he would have done had he lived in Eden: "Had I been alive in Adams steed," he writes in the *Centuries*, "how should I have Admired the glory of the world! What a Confluence of Thoughts and Wonders and Joys and Thanksgivings would hav replenished me in the sight of so *Magnificent a Theater* . . . raised out of Nothing and Created for me and for me alone" (5:31, bk. 1, sec. 65). For Traherne, there is no going back; he can only try his best to put himself in Adam's shoes. He is primarily interested in how we can regain paradise in this life, not in Milton's project of imagining the lived experiences of Adam and Eve.

Seen from the vantage point of this book's central concerns, the absence of a fully Edenic *I* means that Traherne cannot use Adam or Eve as a way of imagining originary experience from the inside, of capturing what it is like to be radically new. Instead, Traherne transplants perhaps the central feature of Milton's neonatal maturity—the ability to remember one's own emergence into consciousness—back onto his own life. Traherne claims to remember neonatal experience and, in fact, his memories of neonatal life are what enable his aspiration to inhabit the world as Adam did. His self-proclaimed ability to remember his own first encounter with the world is the key condition enabling his attempt to reoccupy Adam's point of view.

Indeed, Traherne repeatedly suggests that his neonatal memories allow him to see the world as though it were Eden. "Those Acts which Adam in his Innocence / Performed, carry all the Excellence" (6:24, 7–8), he writes in "Silence," dwelling on how the "first and only Work [Adam] had to do / Was in himself to feel his Bliss, to view / His Sacred Treasures, to admire [and] rejoyce" (6:24–25, 21–23). Note the stress on Adam's originary experience here, how Traherne focuses on the "first" things that enter Adam's consciousness: a feeling of bliss and an admiration of the world into which he has just awakened. How does Traherne know what it was like to be Adam? The answer to this question lies in the poet's own originary experiences, which are identical to those enjoyed in Eden: "And this at first was mine; These were / My Exercises of the Highest Sphere, / To see, Approve, take Pleasure and rejoyce" (6:25, 27–29). Traherne repeatedly describes his own neonatal experiences as homologous with those available in Eden. When, in "Fullnesse," he describes the "first . . . Thought" of his new life, he argues that "My Bliss / Consists in this"; namely, the ability to continue thinking that thought today (6:30, 1–13). At the same time, his choice of diction suggests that his own "first" act discloses the initial Adamic "Work" described in "Silence": "in himself to feel his Bliss." The claim that "My Bliss / Consists in this" ability to recapture neonatal modes of thought aligns Traherne's infancy with Eden, since, as he writes in another poem, "All Blisse / Consists in this, / To do as Adam did" (6:65, 1–3). The phrase "Bliss / Consists in this," which Traherne repeats in at least three separate poems, binds neonatal and Adamic experience. In "Eden," Traherne equates his own originary experience with that of Adam. "Only what Adam in his first Estate / Did I behold" (6:8, 34–35), Traherne writes, "Those Things which first his Eden did adorn, / My Infancy / Did Crown" (6:8, 41–45). When, in "The Salutation," Traherne describes the moment "From Dust I rise, / And out of Nothing now awake" (6:4, 30–31), the relationship between this passage and his account of Adamic awakening in *Commentaries of Heaven*—the moment "When Adam first awaked out of his Dust"—could not be clearer. When his ego was born, Traherne claims, he entered "this Eden so Divine and fair, / So Wide and Bright" (6:4, 41–42). This Eden begins in the womb, the space in which the "ancient Light of Eden did convey / Into my Soul: I was an Adam there, / A little Adam in a Sphere / Of joys!" (6:10, 55–58).

When Traherne claims that his own originary experience resonates with that enjoyed by Adam, he suggests that Edenic experience remains possible in the fallen world, that human nature still chimes with the harmonies of paradise, and that his unique memories of prenatal and infant experience are the best way to gain access to one's true nature. To be sure, Traherne was not the first to connect Adam with childhood. Irenaeus, the patristic figure who most influenced Traherne's anthropological views, held that while in Eden Adam and Eve possessed the understanding of children;

God could have created "man perfect from the first," but Adam would have been unable to receive such perfection because he was "yet an infant."[47] If Adam was sometimes cast as an infant, writers also described infants as Adamic. In *Fire in the Bush* (1650), the political and religious radical Gerrard Winstanley urges readers to "Look upon a child that is new borne, or till he growes up to some few yeares: he is innocent, harmlesse, humble, patient, gentle, easie to be entreated, not envious. And this is *Adam*, or mankind in his Innocency."[48] But Winstanley is making observations from the outside—"Look upon a child"—while Traherne is adopting the perspective of infancy itself, discovering the experience of Adam through an exploration of what it is like to be an infant. Traherne transforms Milton's Adamic ego into his own neonatal *I*, the point of view that he attempts to recapture in much of his poetry.

THE BIRTH OF THE EGO

It is fair to say that Traherne was obsessed with what, in his poem "Ease," he calls the "first impressions, in our Earthly State" (6:34, 9). Across his corpus, he repeatedly describes "That Light, that Sight, that Thought, / Which in my Soul at first He wrought" (6:30, 2–3). These lines from "Fullnesse" suggest why this initial moment matters: the first thought is "wrought" by God; it provides a view of "all things." Since this is as close to God as living beings can come, our first thoughts are the best we can think. They are also close to those felt by Adam at the moment of his creation: of his time in the womb, Traherne writes in "The Preparative," "I was as free / As if there were nor Sin, nor Miserie" (6:12, 54–55). This is one reason why Traherne repeatedly imagines what it is like when the luminous glare of consciousness first appears to an embryonic mind. In an entry on "Babe" in *Commentaries of Heaven*, Traherne offers an account of a "helpless Infant" as a "little naked MAN, wrapt up in the Swaddling clothes of his own infirmities," a "stranger newly come into the World, as Great in his Hopes and Possibilities, as he is Small in the Appearance of his present Attainments" (3:437).

Although many of these ideas are commonplace, one stands out as original: that the experience of embryos should play an important role in how human life is understood. Describing what it is like to be a "stranger newly come into the World," Traherne writes, "The Beauty of the World is [the infant's] first Entertainment. The Light and Glory of it seems a Sphere into which he enters, out of the Obscuritie of an Eternal Abyss, which is called *Nothing*. Before he was conceived he was not" (3:437). The first phenomenon

encountered is the beauty, light, and glory of the world. Emerging from the
"Obscuritie of an Eternal Abyss," the neonatal being enters existence as the
center of a sphere of phenomenality, an ego around which the light of an
inchoate conscious awareness shines, rushing to meet the world. The infant
did not exist before "he was conceived" but begins at the moment of entry
into the world when "he" awakens from "*Nothing.*" Human life begins
with the advent of consciousness, which occurs sometime after conception while the infant is still "shut up in the Narrow Closet of his Mothers
Womb" (3:438).

Since the world is the babe's "first Entertainment" and since Traherne
uses such terms as "Infant," it is tempting to read this movement into what
"seems a Sphere" of light as the datable, public event of birth.[49] After all,
infancy was often understood as "the first age of man, which is from the
first year till the seventh."[50] But the term, etymologically derived from the
Latin *infans* (without speech), also designated any stage of pre-rational existence.[51] For instance, a seventeenth-century anatomical treatise claims that
the "Infant also liveth in the Wombe farre otherwise then hee liveth after
he is borne."[52] Traherne understands the terms *infant* and *babe* in this way.
In *Commentaries of Heaven*, he describes infant experience from beginning
to end: "His Life is the first Thing of which he is sensible, he is in his own
eys a Sphere of Light filling the World with Apprehension. The Great and
Glorious Presence of the World, and all the New Appearances and Varie-
ties in it, are the Objects of his Wonder and Meditation. Their Beauty and
Glory is first exhibited to his Ey, and known by Nature. But when he begins
to Speak, he ceases to be a Babe, and is infected with the Corruptions and
Customs of Men" (3:438). To experience infancy is to encounter a nature
that has not been shaped by understandings of culture. It is a state of being extending from one's first sensation until one "begins to Speak," when
one leaves nature and enters the sphere of "Fancy and Humane Invention"
(3:438). If infancy ends with language acquisition, it begins with the ego's
appearance—when the new being feels its own life as "a Sphere of Light
filling the World with Apprehension." By "world," Traherne means a structure of transcendence generated in and by thought, the phenomenal disclosure of what exists. For Traherne, the world appears simultaneously with
the birth of the infant's ego in the womb.[53]

Consider a passage from *Centuries* in which Traherne reflects on what
he describes as his unusual ability to recall his first impressions:

Those Pure and Virgin Apprehensions I had from the Womb, and that
Divine Light wherewith I was born, are the Best unto this Day, wherein

I can see the Universe. By the Gift of GOD they attended me into the
World, and by his Special favor I remember them till now. Verily they
seem the Greatest Gifts His Wisdom could bestow[,] for without them
all other Gifts had been Dead and Vain. They are unattainable by Books,
and therefore I will teach them by Experience. . . . Adam in Paradice had
not more sweet and Curious Apprehensions of the World, then I when
I was a child. All appeared New, and Strange, at the first, inexpressibly
rare, and Delightful, and Beautiful. I was a little Stranger which at my
Entrance into the World was Saluted and Surrounded with innumerable
Joys. (5:93, bk. 3, sec. 1–2)

Aware that his claims are unique, even outrageous, Traherne insists that he
remembers his time in the womb and the "Light wherewith [he] was born"
only by God's "Special favor," through revelation. He is also certain that this
divine "favor" has not been given to previous writers, for the "Pure and Virgin Apprehensions" he recalls are "unattainable by Books." Since Traherne
cannot appeal to previous authorities, he has no choice but to teach his readers "by Experience." He stretches the beginnings of thought back into prenatal existence, to the "Apprehensions" he "had from the Womb." The preposition *from* here indicates not "separation" but a "starting-point in time."[54]
The "Divine Light wherewith I was born" is a prenatal phenomenon.

Traherne sees the beginning of consciousness as a birth in utero prior
to the public birth that ushers infants into the world. This obsession with
beginnings brings Traherne into a charged conceptual field in which the
need to assert a break in the order of causation—the beginning begins *here*,
at this point—necessitates a bracketing of all relations of finite dependence:
the familiar phenomenal order in which one thing follows another. What
matters is God, the existence of a source capable of guaranteeing beginning
as such: "That Light, that Sight, that Thought, / Which in my Soul at first
He wrought." A thought counts as "first" because it stems not from a finite
cause but from an infinite source. Here lies one of the main reasons behind
Traherne's decision to take up Milton's depiction of Adamic awakening as a
model for his own entrance into mindedness: in *Paradise Lost*, God created
Adam's initial frame of mind; his first thoughts are God-given. Divine intent and human actualization are, in that initial moment, coterminous. It is
this proximity of creator and conscious life that Traherne seeks to discover
in his own embryonic past.

This is why, when Traherne recalls the birth of his own consciousness
in utero, he erases the womb in all but name. Bracketing all finite forms
of dependence so as to emphasize his ultimate dependence on an infinite

divine source, Traherne circumvents and, at the same time, emphasizes early modern epistemological worries about the "secrets of women";[55] he transforms the mother's body into a phenomenal backdrop fit for the initial flickering light of a newly conscious prenatal mind. Claiming that "I in my Mothers Womb was born" (6:4, 38) and then describing what it was like for thought to begin within the body of another person he does not yet know exists, Traherne represents the beginnings of thought as a birth that has stripped away the actual conditions of birth, the complete dependence on other finite beings that structures the entrance of new life into the world. This fantasy of sovereign infancy is of course not inevitable, and twentieth-century thought has been sometimes occupied with articulating precisely the opposite view—namely, that human beings realize themselves "initially through others," as Mikhail Bakhtin puts it.[56] Perhaps the psychoanalyst D. W. Winnicott best expresses this view when he asserts that "there is no such thing as an infant" in order to stress the necessity of motherly care.[57] Winnicott's statement reads like a corrective to Traherne's insistence on being "an infant"—alone with his thoughts and God's presence.

Traherne stresses his dependence on God at the expense of his mother and the other creatures that sustained his life. In doing so, he elaborates a popular seventeenth-century argument. In the *First Treatise*, Locke refutes those who would claim that the act of begetting grants fathers *"Power over the Lives of their Children"* by reminding his readers that it is in fact *"God, who is the Author and Giver of Life"*: "How can he be thought to give Life to another, that knows not wherein his own life consists?" (178, 1.52). This line of thought is based on an Augustinian tradition. Consider the description of infancy in the *Confessiones*, addressed to God: "The consolations of your mercies upheld me, as I have learned from the parents of my flesh, him from whom and her in whom you formed me in time." Although mother and father are involved in the process, it is ultimately God who "form[s]" and even feeds the infant, a point Augustine makes when he claims that "my mother or my nurses" did not make "any decision to fill their breasts," for it was God who "through them gave me food" (6; 1.6.7). Traherne's account of originary experience likewise places all forms of finite dependence—mother, father, family, community—under erasure.[58] Finite dependence implies a *before* that excludes true beginning, since, if one is, from the beginning, fully dependent on another finite being, one is not the beginning. Although Traherne is far from the only writer to bracket finite dependence in order to think through the relation between an infant and his or her infinite creator, he is, so far as I know, the first writer to dramatize this relation from within, to imagine the newly awakened mind of an embryo experiencing itself as though it were alone.

Giving voice to the voiceless *infans*, Traherne translates into a personal register what had, for centuries, remained under the auspices of abstract personification. Consider John Lydgate's *Dance of Death* (c. 1426). "Litel Enfaunt that were but late borne / Schape yn this worlde to have no pleasaunce / Thow moste with other that gone here to forne be lad yn haste," says Lydgate's personification of Death to a personified "Enfaunt," who responds:

> A a a a worde I can not speke
> I am so yonge I was bore yisterdai
> Dethe is so hasti on me to be wreke
> And list no lenger to make no delai
> I cam but now and now I go my wai
> Of me no more no tale shal be told.[59]

Lydgate presents an impossible entry into speech that is both premature and delayed by the repeated sound *a a a* that morphs into language proper only when its fourth iteration becomes the indefinite article *a* that modifies the noun *worde*. We are told that this "worde" cannot be spoken at the very moment it is uttered. Lydgate here flags the impossibility of an enterprise that works only because this child is a type, a personification of infancy. Like Milton, who transforms Hesiod's third-person mythic Athena into a first-person allegorical Sin and then rewrites this ancient legacy in the verisimilar lives of Adam and Eve, Traherne personalizes personifications. He mimetically depicts the origins of his own personhood while eschewing allegorical abstraction. "This is no personification," Traherne seems to say, "I am relating my own experience."

In "The Salutation," the poem with which the collection of manuscript poems in the Dobell Folio begins, Traherne celebrates the moment this light first appears. He marvels at what preceded this birth:

> When silent I,
>   So many thousand thousand yeers,
> Beneath the Dust did in a Chaos lie,
>   How could I Smiles or Tears,
> Or Lips or Hands or Eys or Ears perceive?
> Welcom ye Treasures which I now receiv. (6:3, 9–14)

In this lyric "now," the "Treasures" of the body—lips, hands, eyes, ears, and the world that they make available—are received by a newly created ego. Although the world into which this ego emerges, so "Wide and Bright," existed "Long time before / I in my Mothers Womb was born" (6:4, 37–42), the ego itself lay in a "Chaos" (6:3, 11). Separating the subject of this stanza's first sentence (the first-person pronoun) from its attendant verb (the passive "lie") by two line breaks and "many thousand thousand yeers," Traherne performs the non-existence of an ego preceded by "silen[ce]." Prior to its creation ex nihilo, the ego cannot even "perceive" until the moment when "From Dust I rise, / And out of Nothing now awake" (6:4, 30–31). Much like the scene imagined in *Commentaries of Heaven*, here the human ego enters "out of the Obscuritie of an Eternal Abyss, which is called *Nothing*," into the light of the world—all while still in the womb.

When Traherne claims that his ego emerges ex nihilo, he stakes out a position in an ancient debate about human learning. If, as Plato points out in the *Meno*, one cannot find what one is looking for unless one can recognize what one finds, then all knowing requires preknowing; learning is recollecting. This position is elaborated as Plato's doctrine of *anamnesis* or recollection, which relies on the soul's preexistence: "As the soul is immortal, has been born often, and has seen all things here and in the underworld, there is nothing which it has not learned; so it is in no way surprising that it can recollect the things it knew before, both about virtue and other things" (880; 81c–d). In the *Meno*, *Phaedo*, and *Phaedrus*, Plato argues in different ways for the soul's preexistence, for this explains human learning and knowing.[60] Aristotle dismisses this view. In the *Posterior Analytics*, *Metaphysics*, and other works, he agrees that "all intellectual learning come[s] about from already existing knowledge," but he eliminates preexistence (1:114; 71a). To know anything, one needs to possess "primitive, immediate, principles." But it is "absurd" to hold, as Plato does, that "we have pieces of knowledge more precise than demonstration and yet this escapes notice." It is equally "impossible" for these principles to "come about in us when we are ignorant" of them (1:165; 99b). Aristotle claims that the acquisition of new knowledge must be "notice[d]," and this position rules out *anamnesis*—according to which "pieces of knowledge" lie within unnoticed—as well as the notion that one could learn something new and remain "ignorant" of that fact. As we saw in chapter 1, Aristotle holds that all knowledge derives out of the movement from sensation, through memory, to experience, toward understanding. But the inventive method was not intended to explain how individuals learn as they grow up. Aristotle focused on how we obtain complex concepts and scientific knowledge.[61]

The same holds true for the doctrine now associated with Aristotle's theory of learning and infant cognition alike: the notion that humans begin as blank slates. The source for this idea is Aristotle's *De anima*: "Thought is in a sense potentially whatever is thinkable, though actually it is nothing until it has thought[.] What it thinks must be in it just as characters may be said to be on a writing-table on which as yet nothing actually stands written: this is exactly what happens with thought" (1:683; 429b–430a). For Aristotle, "thinking is like perceiving" insofar as "thought must be related to what is thinkable, as sense is to what is sensible." But although thought and sense both receive "the form of an object" such that "thought must be related to what is thinkable, as sense is to what is sensible," the reach of thought is much wider than that of perception (1:683; 429a). Since thinking "is held to be in part imagination, in part judgment" (1:680; 427b), it is less strongly tethered to the world than perception is; many more things are thinkable than are sensible. One does not, for instance, sense rightness or wrongness, the abstract principles in geometrical reasoning, or the mythical creatures of Homeric poetry. The purview of thought is wider than sense— so wide, in fact, that Aristotle claims, in terms that must have appealed to Traherne: "everything is a possible object of thought" (1:682; 429a).

A corollary of this position is that thought possesses "no nature of its own, other than that of having a certain capacity." Since thought has the capacity to become "everything," that "in the soul which is called thought (by thought I mean that whereby the soul thinks and judges) is, before it thinks, not actually any real thing" (1:682; 429a). There is no thought until one imagines a frog or a triangle, until one judges the correctness of something— until, that is, one *actually thinks*. Every thought begins as a blank slate. For Aristotle, this condition is not limited to infant minds. Indeed, Aristotle defends his claim that "thinking" is "distinct from perceiving" by stating that the former is possessed by a smaller subset of animals than the latter: "thought is found only where there is discourse of reason" (1:680; 427b). Only adult human beings and, perhaps, some other animals are able to think. Young children, who do not yet possess "discourse of reason," cannot, in the strict sense of the term, think.

Later Hellenistic thinkers imposed these epistemological terms onto infancy.[62] Take, for example, the philosopher Aëtius, who, in *De placita philosophorum* (second century CE), braids blank-slate imagery together with the movement from perception to understanding outlined in the *Posterior Analytics*. Attributed to Plutarch in the seventeenth century, Aëtius's text was translated by Philemon Holland in his edition of Plutarch's *Morals*:

The Stoicks are of opinion and say, that when a man is engendred, hee hath the principall part of his soulle, which is the understanding, like for all the world until a parchment or paper ready to be written in; and therein he doth register and record every several Notion and cogitation of his: for those who have perceived any thing by sense, (as for example sake, have seene a white thing) when the same is gone out of their eye, reteine it still in memorie: now after they have collected together many semblable memories of the same kinde, then they say, they have experience; for experience is nothing else but an heape or multitude of like sorts.[63]

Continuing this story to the development of rationality at around seven years, Aëtius moves from a soul that begins as a "piece of white Paper," through the "inscription" of the senses, memory, and experience, toward rational understanding. The transformation of Aristotle's empty "writing-table" (attributed to nonnaturalized adult thought) into the "piece of white Paper" characteristic of infant minds thus has a long history. Centuries prior to Locke's famous supposition that "the Mind [is], as we say, white Paper, void of all Characters" (104, 2.1.2), this idea had already been expressed by Avicenna, Aquinas, and other medieval thinkers.

Many seventeenth-century English writers nevertheless attributed the blank slate of infancy to Aristotle.[64] In lectures delivered at Cambridge in 1645 and published posthumously in 1652 as An Elegant and Learned Discourse on the Light of Nature, the philosopher Nathaniel Culverwell upheld the idea that human beings begin as blank slates. Aristotle "did not," Culverwell writes, "antedate his own knowledge, nor remember the several postures of his soul, and the famous exploits of his mind before he was borne; but plainly profest that his understanding came naked into the world. He shews you an abrasa tabula [blank tablet], a virgin-soul espousing it self to the body, in a most entire, affectionate, and conjugal union [that enables a newly born creature to] set open the windows of sense to welcome and entertain the first dawnings, the early glimmerings of morning light." Infants begin as blank slates, with "virgin souls" that emerge "naked into the world." It is through the "windows of sense" that the "early glimmerings of morning light" shine. Only once "outward objects" have "made some impression" on the infant's mind is the "Candle of knowledge lighted."[65]

Culverwell asks his readers to examine their own experience: "Do but analyse your own thoughts, do but consult with your own breasts, tell us whence it was that the light first sprang in on you." He then asks a series of questions calculated to dissolve Platonic "connate ideas":

Had you such notions as these when you first peept into being? at the first opening of the soul's eye? in the first *exordium* of infancy? had you these connate *Species* in the cradle? and were they rockt asleep with you? or did you then meditate upon these principles? *Totum est majus partae, & Nihil potest esse & non esse simul* [The whole is greater than the part, and Nothing can be and not be at the same time]. Ne'er tell us that you wanted organical dispositions, for you plainly have recourse to sensitive powers, and must needs subscribe to this, that all knowledge comes flourishing in at these lattices. Why else should not your Candle enlighten you before? Who was it that chained up, and fettered your common notions? Who was it that restrained and imprisoned your connate *Ideas*?[66]

Culverwell defends the *abrasa tabula* thesis through the authority of experience. Since no one can remember having such notions as *Totum est majus partae* when "light first sprang in" on them, one should not take arguments about innate ideas seriously. But upon reflection, Culverwell's polemic takes on a sheen of self-refutation, for human beings cannot recall anything about when they "first peept into being." If this lack of memory undercuts innate ideas, it likewise refuses any easy affirmation of an *abrasa tabula*. The experience that would support Culverwell's account of human awareness is impossible, lost to the opacity of infancy.

Traherne knew the Platonic and the Aristotelian traditions.[67] He also mentions Culverwell's *Discourse* in his notebooks.[68] Like Culverwell, Traherne holds that each human ego begins as an *abrasa tabula*. Contrary to the assumptions of most critics, Traherne's deepest intellectual impulses were, at least in this respect, Aristotelian.[69] In the *Select Meditations*, he claims that human "compr[e]hension" is a "Rasa Tabula Prepared in Him For the Drawing afterward of all the Pictures in Gods kingdom" (5:355, bk. 4, sec. 1). Traherne articulates this idea on numerous occasions, most famously in the opening sentence of the *Centuries* where, in an explicit gesture to the Aristotelian notion that "everything is a possible object of thought," Traherne claims: "An Empty Book is like an Infants Soul, in which any Thing may be Written. It is Capable of all Things, but containeth Nothing" (5:7, bk. 1, sec. 1). In the entry on "Babe" in *Commentaries of Heaven*, Traherne deepens this point by arguing that before the infant "was conceived he was not, and yet all the Matter of his Body was in the Universe before: Some think his Soul was too: but he received both by the Gift of his Creator." Although the matter out of which the infant's body was created existed "in the Universe before," the same cannot be said for the "Workmanship of his Body" or for the soul itself. Traherne rejects the views of Platonists and others committed to the soul's preexistence—those who think that, like matter, the infant's "soul" existed in the universe prior to its creation (3:437). Refusing *anamnesis*, Traherne stresses the originary human *encounter*, the first moment of one's initial Edenic "appearance" in the world.

By claiming to remember his own apprehensions in utero, Traherne likewise upends the negative certainty that had underpinned Culverwell's argument. When he read Culverwell's request to recall "whence it was that the light first sprang in on you," Traherne may have taken this request seriously. He may have written a poem in response. "The Preparative" is such a poem, a work in which Traherne conjures the instant of animation when his ego first emerged:

> My Body being Dead, my Lims unknown;   2
>   Before I skild to prize
>   Those living Stars mine Eys,
> Before my Tongue or Cheeks were to me shewn,   5
>   Before I knew my Hands were mine,
> Or that my Sinews did my Members joyn,
>   When neither Nostril, Foot, nor Ear
> As yet was seen, or felt, or did appear;
>   I was within   10
> A House I knew not, newly clothd with Skin. (6:11; 2–11)

The opening line captures a body shuddering into animation. "My Body being Dead": the present participle "being" binds the lack of animation expressed in the adjective "Dead" with the liveliness already implied in the use of the first-person possessive adjective "My." Departing from this moment, when the speaker's limbs remain "unknown," the stanza loops forward in time to the period when the speaking ego will have "skild to prize . . . mine Eys" or known "my Hands were mine." Only after the speaker has worked through this negative catalogue of "before" clauses does he return to the moment of animation when the embryonic body comes to life and the ego appears: "I was within / A House I knew not, newly clothd with Skin." Traherne's line arrangement creates a house for the ego on the page, with lines 9 and 11 expanding into an iambic pentameter that wraps, as a dwelling space, around the dimeter of line 10: "I was within." Although the "House" performed by line length could be read as the mother's womb, given the connection between this reference to nescience and the "Lims unknown" of the initial line, it is likely that "House" refers primarily to the speaker's body while also suggesting the environing womb.

When Traherne describes this new ego as "within" the "House" of the body, as "clothd with skin," he suggests that the ego emerges within a body. No Platonic preexistence here: the poem dramatizes the initial emergence of a blank slate. But as the line break separating "within" from "House" suggests, Traherne frames the ego as separate from the body, at least insofar as this primordial moment of self-awareness includes no consciousness of that body: the speaker's limbs were "unknown," and he finds himself "within / A House I knew not."[70] Without any knowledge of his own embodiment and before his body has even "appear[ed]" to him, it is *as if* the speaker were a disembodied soul: "Then was my Soul my only All to me," the poem continues, "A Living Endless Ey . . . Whose Power, whose Act, whose Essence was to see" (6:11, 14–16). What does this *I* that is an "Ey" see? Nothing less than "every Thing." Traherne brings into poetic form an idea he also articulates in the *Commentaries of Heaven*: "The first Thing which the Body feeleth is it self; and the Soul is by Nature the first Object of its own Apprehension[,] for by feeling it self it feeleth all other Things" (3:179). If, as Aristotle puts it, thought has "no nature of its own, other than that of having a certain capacity" and "everything is a possible object of thought" (1:682; 429a), then Traherne intensifies this point when he claims that at the moment the soul of an embryo engages in its first act of thought, that thought will, as he frames it in "My Sprit," be a thought of "all Things." (6:26, 10). This totalizing claim is at the heart of Traherne's account of originary experience, and it is his insistence on the singularity of this "first" experience that draws him back to the uterine birth of the ego: it is *only* in this initial moment of existence that the thought of "all Things" is actualized. But if such claims seem outlandish to modern eyes, for seventeenth-century readers the strangeness of Traherne's description would have begun, as we will see in chapter 4, with something most twenty-first-century readers will take for granted: the very notion that fetal sensation exists.

CHAPTER FOUR

In Utero

THE INVENTION OF PRENATAL SENSATION

In the beginning, there was nothing. While in the womb, human infants possess the capacity or potential to sense, remember, imagine, think, and reason, but they do not actualize these capacities. This means that, until birth, prenatal life exists without an inkling of consciousness, in the absence of even the most minimal forms of mental presence. So goes the sum of European embryological wisdom running from antiquity to the seventeenth century. Even Platonists held that the fetal body begins to sense only at the moment of birth.[1] And poets followed the lead of this embryological consensus. Traherne, however, rejects this broad consensus when he describes his originary experiences and the moment his ego was born within the womb. Although many poets imagined life in the womb, no one before Traherne attempted to express *what it is like* to be an embryo. Many poets depicted embryological development, but they imagined this process from the outside, as a series of surfaces, deprived of even the minimal perspective on the world afforded by basic sensation. Previous scholarship has failed to notice Traherne's startling novelty on this front because, surprisingly, no earlier critic has situated Traherne's work in an embryological or even, to my knowledge, a thoroughgoing philosophical context.[2] Drawing on the history of embryology and ancient debates about knowledge acquisition, in this chapter I demonstrate how Traherne's claims for embryonic consciousness extended the steps taken by a few previous thinkers and broke entirely with a tradition running from Hippocrates through Aristotle, Galen, and other ancient authorities up to seventeenth-century anatomists like Hyronymus Fabricius of Aquapendente.

Today, the existence of fetal sensation is taken for granted. Much of the current scientific research into the topic focuses on pain and is centered on the abortion debate, meant to address religious and legal questions of person-hood. But in seventeenth-century England, such contexts did not exist: abor-tion did not so dominate the cultural and political scene that considerations of fetal consciousness were pulled automatically into its orbit.[3] In the ab-sence of such political motivation, questions about fetal sensation remained speculative, and Traherne wrote at the cutting edge of such speculation. This chapter explores how Traherne's poetic endeavors drew on two contemporary lines of inquiry that questioned the experiential absence assigned to prenatal life: first, the natural philosophy of William Harvey, whose *Exercitationes de generatione animalium* (1651) revolutionized embryology and theorized an understudied form of minimal feeling open even to embryos; and second, the philosophy of René Descartes, which propelled the new, nonevaluative con-cept of *conscientia* back into the womb. Bringing these arguments together for the first time and showing how Traherne synthesized these spheres of in-quiry, this chapter tracks the development of a poetic phenomenology of pre-natal human life, a new way of imagining the birth of human consciousness.[4]

    In this section, I begin by sketching the outlines of a history of fe-tal sensation by showing how traditional embryological views shaped sixteenth- and seventeenth-century English poems about prenatal life.[5] I start with John Donne's depiction of prenatal development, using his poetry to sketch the basics of the long embryological tradition. Written in 1601, the unfinished Ovidian epic *Metempsychosis* concludes with a depiction of prenatal development in Eve's womb.[6] The poem's narrative describes the transmigrations of a Pythagorean soul through a variety of bodies be-fore it enters its first and only human host, the embryo of Themech, who would, according to Rabbinic tradition, marry her brother Cain.[7] Here the story stops, perched on a historical and ontological cusp—in Eve's womb, just outside of Paradise, just as the soul becomes fully human:

> Adam and Eve had mingled bloods, and now
> Like chemics' equal fires, her temperate womb
> Had stewed and formed it: and part did become
> A spongy liver, that did richly allow,
> Like a free conduit, on a high hill's brow,
> Life-keeping moisture unto every part,
> Part hardened itself to a thicker heart,
> Whose busy furnaces life's spirits do impart.
>
> Another part became the well of sense,
> The tender well-armed feeling brain, from whence,

Those sinewy strings which do our bodies tie,
Are raveled out, and fast there by one end,
Did this soul limbs, these limbs a soul attend,
And now they joined: keeping some quality
Of every past shape, she knew treachery,
Rapine, deceit, and lust, and ills enow
To be a woman. Themech she is now.[8]

Tracing the development of an embryo from the mingling of parental materials, through the gradual development of the organs requisite for life and
sense (liver, heart, brain), to the articulation of the fetal body (when nerves
bind limbs to brain), Donne concludes his poem with the fetus's entrance
into humanity. This moment is signaled grammatically in the misogynist
shift from *it* (Eve's womb "stewed and formed it") to *she* ("Themech she is
now").

These stanzas are structured by gradualist theories of embryological
animation first propounded by Aristotle and then elaborated by Galen and
Aquinas.[9] Pre-Aristotelian thinkers held that the embryo became animate
either at conception or at birth.[10] Working within the parameters of his theory of the soul, Aristotle claimed that the embryo slowly acquires the capacities it will actualize later in life. In *De anima*, he categorizes life forms
according to the capacities they possess. The capacities of plants (nourishment, growth, reproduction) also appear in animals (which can sense and
move themselves) and human beings (for whom reason is reserved).[11] The
higher levels of being subsume the capacities of the lower; a human soul
possesses vegetal, sensitive, and rational capacities.

Working within this framework, writers from antiquity to the seventeenth century saw embryological development as the unfolding of these
capacities alongside bodily growth. In *De generatione animalium*—which
is, alongside the Hippocratic *On the Seed* and *On the Nature of the Child*,
the foundational text in European embryology—Aristotle outlines how this
unfolding occurs. When its life begins, the "embryo of an animal [has] every bit as much life as a plant" (1:1142; 736a).[12] As the embryo develops
it acquires "the sensitive soul in virtue of which an animal is an animal"
(1:1143; 736b), before acquiring—mysteriously, "from outside" (1:1143;
736b)—the "share in reason" possessed "by those animals that participate
in this principle" (1:1143; 736b). Since, in Aristotle's view, the "soul is the
substance of a particular body" (1:1146; 738b), the soul's capacities develop
alongside the organization of the body, with the heart serving as the animal
body's "first principle" (1:1146; 738b). Subsequent thinkers argued with as-

pects of this story. Galen held that the first principle of the body was not the heart but the liver.[13] Despite such differences, however, Aristotle's gradualist theory remained, for centuries, the dominant explanatory model.

In *Metempsychosis*, Donne uses the strategic repetition of *now* to organize his account of embryological development according to this Aristotelian model. He begins with the nutritive soul, which emerges in the passage's first "now" ("now . . . [Eve's] temperate womb / Had stewed and formed it") and is responsible for the body's growth: the development of the "spongy liver," which produces "life-keeping moisture"; the heart, which disperses "life's spirits"; and the brain, which lays down the bodily conditions for sensation. The brain is figured as the "well" or spring from which "sense" emerges, a material source of feeling that generates the "sinewy strings" that connect brain to limbs in a "tender" web. In the "now" when this process is complete and limbs are knit to brain ("now they joined"), the embryo becomes an animal soul ready for the leap into rational ensoulment. This transformation is the final action of the poem's narrative, accomplished with the sequence's third "now" ("Themech she is now"). But although Donne follows the pattern set out in *De generatione*, he differs in the details. He flags his allegiance to Galen when he makes the "spongie liver" the principle part of the animal's bodily development. He also emphasizes the role of the body. Signaled in the repetition of "part" and in contrast with Aristotle or Aquinas, Donne's stress on the body minimizes the importance of the soul. Although implicit in Donne's use of "now," the "soul" does not appear until nerves have connected brain and limbs.

In addition to its biting satirical tone, this stress on the body also separates *Metempsychosis* from the poem that may have inspired Donne's account of prenatal development: Statius's embryological lecture in Dante's *Purgatorio* (c. 1320). Asked to explain how souls in purgatory grow thin, Statius describes how, after active and passive principles mingle at conception, a new human being develops:

> The active force, having now become a soul—
> like a plant's but differing in this: it is still
> on the way, while the plant has come to shore—
> next functions, moving now and feeling [*move e sente*],
> like a sea-sponge [*come spungo marino*], and from that goes on, producing
> organs for the faculties of which it is the seed.[14]

When the developing soul transitions from "plant" to "animal," Dante aligns the embryo's newfound capacities for movement and feeling with

those of a sea-sponge. Statius continues, noting that the pilgrim does "not
see as yet" "how from animal it turns to human [*fante*]." Using the word
fante ("one who speaks") to designate the potential for *logos* that resides in
a tiny being that remains *infans*, without speech, Dante describes the development of rational capacities:

> once the brain's articulation
> in the embryo arrives at its perfection,
> the First Mover turns to it, rejoicing
>   in such handiwork of nature, and breathes
> into it a spirit, new and full of power,
> which then draws into its substance
> all it there finds active and becomes a single soul [*alma sola*]
> that lives, and feels, and reflects upon itself [*vive e sente e sé in sé
>   rigira*]. (560–61; 25.62–75)

After the brain's "articulation," God "breathes" the rational soul into the
perfected body. Contained becomes container as the "new" and powerful
spirit draws the embryo "into its substance," which becomes the ground for
a "single soul that lives, and feels, and reflects upon itself."

Dante references the body—the "brain's articulation" and, earlier, "mingled" parental blood (560–61; 25.46)—but he focuses on the soul's development, following its trajectory from when it is "a soul, / like a plant's" until
it "becomes a single soul." Dante states that rational capacities are introduced when God "breathes / into" the embryo. In Aristotle's view, rationality
comes "from outside" (1.1143; 736b), and for Christians this external source
could only be God. The position favored by Dante, known as infusionism,
held that although the nutritive and sensitive souls develop as the embryo's
body grows, God creates the rational, properly human soul ex nihilo and then
infuses it into the fetal body. Infusionism was opposed to the view known as
traducianism (from *ex traduce*), which held that the rational soul was trans-
mitted from parent to child, just like the nutritive and sensitive souls.[15]

If, like Traherne, Dante maintains the infusionist position, Donne
leaves things up in the air.[16] Elsewhere, Donne insists that when it comes to
the soul, "It is the going out, more than the coming in, that concerns us."[17]
Donne remains undecided; both options are theoretically fraught. As he explains in a letter to Henry Goodyer written around 1607, those who "ad-
here" to the traducian position "can never excite necessarily and certainly a
natural immortality in the soul if the soul result out of matter," while those
who "follow the opinion of an infusion from God" can "very hardly defend

the doctrine of original sin," for that sin is ostensibly inherited from our parents and, ultimately, from Adam and Eve.[18] Caught on the horns of this theological dilemma, in *Metempsychosis* Donne minimizes the language of soul and employs a misogynistic version of Pythagorean transmigration in order to avoid the question of hominization: "keeping some quality / Of every past shape, she knew treachery, / Rapine, deceit, and lust, and ills enow / To be a woman. Themech she is now."[19]

This strategy also avoids the question of fetal experience—a move in keeping with embryological discourse. In *De anima*, Aristotle defines the soul as "an actuality of the first kind of a natural body that is potentially alive" (1.656; 412a). Without a soul, any natural body possesses only the capacity for life; it exists in "first potentiality." Once endowed with soul, the body moves into what Aristotle calls "second potentiality" or "actuality of this first kind": a state in which the ensouled body can perform but has not yet performed that for which it was made, the performance of which would constitute "second actuality" (1.656–57; 412a–b). In *De generatione animalium*, Aristotle claims that at first the embryo has "the nutritive soul potentially, but not actually, until . . . it absorbs nourishment and performs the function of the nutritive soul. For at first all such embryos seem to live the life of a plant" (1:1143; 736b). The creature acquires a sensitive and then a rational soul, but these are "possessed potentially before they are possessed in actuality" (1:1143; 736b). In *De foetuum formatione*, Galen hammers this point home: "It is not necessary for the fetus to see, hear, taste, or smell, nor must it use its feet or hands; similarly, it needs no sense of touch, and no imagination, thought, or memory."[20] The fetus's sensitive and rational capacities remain unused until after birth. This view was championed by one of the greatest embryologists of the early seventeenth century, Hyronymus Fabricius.[21] A professor of anatomy at the University of Padua, Fabricius argued forcefully against fetal sensation in *De formato foetu* (1600):

> Growth, then, which is accomplished through nutrition, is the action of the fetus as long as it is borne in the uterus, and although the fetus is indeed an animal, still it is not governed as an animal as long as it is shut up in the uterus, but as a plant. Now, according to Aristotle, the reason is that in the fetus, the vegetal operations are active, the animal merely potential. It therefore neither sees, hears, smells, nor tastes, and much less does it imagine, remember, or reason; and to summarize, it neither feels nor moves. "For a fetus is not made an animal and a man at one and the same time," says Aristotle, and in the same way, with equal reason, it is not made plant and animal at the same time.[22]

Because the same being cannot be an animal and a plant "at the same time," and since the fetus actualizes only "vegetal operations," it therefore feels nothing.[23]

If Dante's description of a soul that, after divine infusion, "lives, and feels, and reflects upon itself" is an orthodox account of un-actualized embryonic capacities, it nevertheless seems to invite speculation about what it might be like for such a being to feel and reflect.[24] Donne eliminates the possibility for such speculation. Themech actualizes only her vegetative capacities, a point Donne stresses by connecting the language of embryonic development with the poem's earlier account of a mandrake root growing within the earth: the embryo has a "spongy liver" and develops as "sinewy strings" connect brain with limbs, while the mandrake's "spongy confines" absorb water and the "ends" of its "arms" "digest / Into ten lesser strings."[25] Although the "sinewy strings" that emerge from the brain, that "well of sense," are the material underpinning for whatever Themech *will* feel, at this point the nerves convey as much feeling as tendrils sprouting from a mandrake's roots. Although the sponge would become central to theories of fetal sensation, as noted later in this chapter, in Donne's poem the repeated term "spongy" seems to be used only to conjure texture. Fully human, Themech remains a vegetable insofar as she feels nothing. This insistence on Themech's vegetal state is surprising, given the degree to which Donne takes readers inside the felt lives of other creatures. Recall Donne's description of a baby sparrow on "whose raw arms stiff feathers now begin, / As children's teeth through gums, do break with pain"—an account that, in John Carey's words, invites readers "inside the sparrow's skin" and asks "us to feel what it would be like to have a body all gums."[26] When Donne arrives at his first human character, however, he rescinds this invitation and offers instead a silence in accord with the embryological consensus.

When other English poets imagined life in utero, they adopted similar strategies. Consider the translation of Psalm 139 written in the late 1590s by Mary Sidney Herbert, the countess of Pembroke. Although Pembroke usually hews close to the Hebrew text, she inserts lines about development in utero, expanding on the address to God in Psalm 139:13–15: "For it was you who formed my inward parts; you knit me together in my mother's womb. . . . My frame was not hidden from you, when I was being made in secret, intricately woven in the depths of the earth. Your eyes beheld my unformed substance."[27] The Psalmist's embryonic being was "not hidden" from God because it was God who "formed" his "inward parts" and beheld him even when his "substance" was "unformed." Pembroke amplifies this asymmetry between knower and known, stressing the extent to which experience is absent from embryonic development:

> Each inmost piece in me is thine:
> While yet I in my mother dwelt,
> All that me clad
> From thee I had. . . .

> Thou, how my back was beam-wise laid,
> And raft'ring of my ribs, dost know:
> Know'st every point
> Of bone and joint,
> How to this whole these parts did grow,
> In brave embroid'ry fair arrayed,
> Though wrought in shop both dark and low.[28]

The switch from present tense ("Each inmost piece in me is thine") to past tense ("While yet I in my mother dwelt") establishes a distinction between presence and absence. The poet "dwelt" "in [her] mother," but she was not really present during this period of dwelling. After all, she does not know how her back was "laid," how her ribs were "raft[ered]," or how her "parts did grow." This knowledge is reserved for God, who can see what takes place within that "shop both dark and low." Although the mother knows a baby grows within her, she cannot access this process directly. And although the developing embryo and fetus is, in a way, present (in bodily terms) for its own generation, at the same time, it is as if the fetus were not really there—for the person it will become will remember no traces of her time in the womb. Only God is truly present as human life emerges slowly into being; at first, we are hidden even from ourselves.

The same idea is conveyed in "A Thanksgiving for our Being," a poem published in the poet and politician John Davies's *Muse's Sacrifice* (1612). Davies is less interested in embryological development than he is in the fact that God helped him survive his time in the womb: "For my *Conception*, to *Nativitie* / thou kepst me safe (thogh strait kept) in the womb, / My Mothers *Bowels* might have strangled me, / but that thy *Mercies* hand still made me room!"[29] In addition to the physical dangers of the womb, Davies was also, he insists, exposed to the risk that the "longings of my Mothers appetite" might rise up and—in a psychosomatic event commonly thought to be a leading cause of both miscarriages and birth defects—"diffuse me in the elements": "when I was an *Embrio*, but a *thought* / might have redrown'd me in *Not-beings Pit*." But the speaker passed through all these dangers, "Wherein I felt (ere I could feel or see) / the blessings of thy tender Providence."[30] The speaker "felt" God's "tender Providence"—that is, he was "acted upon, influenced, affected by [or] subjected to" that providence—before he could "feel" or possess "bodily sensation."[31] Davies's use of the verb *feel* raises the possibility of embryonic sensation only to dismiss it. In *Nosce te ipsum* (1599), Davies suggests the reasons for this choice when he writes that the soul has three "*Essential powers*": namely, "The *quickening* power, the *power of Sense*, and *Reason*." Not until an infant is born does it begin to sense:

> The first life in the mothers wombe is spent,
> Where she [the soul] her *nursing power* doth onely use;
> Where when she finds defect of nourishment,
> Sh'expels her body, and this world she views.
> This we call *Birth*, but if the child could speake,
> He *death* would call it, and of nature plaine,
> That she would thrust him out naked, and weake,
> And in his passage pinch him with such paine.
> Yet out he comes, and in this world is plac't
> Where all his *Senses* in perfection bee,
> Where he finds flowers to smell, and fruits to tast,
> And sounds to heare, and sundry formes to see.[32]

In the womb, the fetus "doth onely use" the "nursing" or "quickening" powers of the vegetal soul. The human senses do not achieve "perfection" (the maturity requisite for use) until after birth, when they are exposed to objects that elicit their powers, the "flowers," "fruits," "sounds," and "forms" that the infant "finds." When Davies entertains the notion of prenatal sensation ("Wherein I felt"), the embryological tradition pushes such speculations to the side (all this occurred "Ere I could feel").

Sir Thomas Browne exemplifies this dynamic. A physician and essayist, Browne read widely in the embryological tradition and often wrote about life in the womb. In *Hydriotaphia* (1658), he muses about our ignorance of the afterlife by imagining how a "dialogue between two Infants in the womb concerning the state of this world, might handsomely illustrate our ignorance of the next, whereof methinks we yet discourse in *Platoes* denne, and are but *Embryon* philosophers."[33] But even though adults can be likened to "*Embryon* philosophers" and the notion of a "dialogue between two Infants in the womb" is a useful fiction, Browne is certain that there is no sensation in utero. In *Religio Medici* (1643), he dwells on the beginnings of human life: "Some Divines count *Adam* 30 years old at his creation, because they suppose him created in the perfect age and stature of man; and surely wee are all out of the Computation of our age, and every man is some moneths elder that hee bethinks him; for we live, move, have a being, and are subject to the actions of the elements, and the malice of diseases in that other world, the truest Microcosme, the wombe of our mother." Unlike Adam, who came into being the moment he appeared on the earth, subsequent human lives are nurtured for months in secret. Although it is conventional to forget these months when calculating one's age, Browne insists on counting the period in which, following Paul's famous words in Acts 17:28, "we live, move, [and] have a being" in the womb. But this does not mean that we are conscious during this period: "In that obscure world and wombe of our mother . . . our selves being yet not without life, sense, and reason; though for the manifestation of its actions it awaits the opportunity of objects; and seems to live there but in its roote and soule of vegetation."[34] As conceptualized by Browne, the fetus possesses the capacities for "sense, and reason" but it cannot actualize them for want of "opportunity."

Fabricius was perhaps the strongest proponent of this view; the forcefulness of his formulations led some students and colleagues to question this stance. In *De formato foetu* (1600), when Fabricius claims that the fetus "neither feels nor moves," he acknowledges possible objections. Preemptively responding to an interlocutor who might hold that the "movements of the fetus" suggest sensation—perhaps the many mothers or midwives who may have informed him about how fetuses seem to respond to such stimuli as voices or prodding fingers—Fabricius argues that such motions are "very rare in the fetus." Those who think these "occur frequently" confuse fetal activity with "the movement and gurgitation of the fluids in which the fetus floats, which give the pregnant woman a feeling of local motion." And even "if the fetus should move at times, it is due to its vigor, which calls into operation faculties and actions present *in potentia*." Fetal movements are caused not by any purposive motion, but rather by the "vigor" of the fetus's life force, which summons otherwise dormant capacities into bursts of agentless activity. Fabricius's commitment to the embryological consensus forces him into awkward corners. A marginal gloss in *De formato foetu* concedes that "There is some doubt about the sense of touch in the fetus," but he only briefly entertains this possibility: "There will perhaps be some doubt about the sense of touch, whether or not the fetus feels the fluids which are sometimes acrid, irritating, or tumifacient. Galen thinks it does not, because there is no sensation unless sensory changes reach the brain and the principal faculties, . . . but such change cannot be perceived in the fetus because these faculties are *in potentia* and cannot be summoned into activity unless stimuli are first received by the senses."[35] Although it seems as though the fetus should feel the "fluids" that environ it, Fabricius follows Galen in holding that for sensation to exist, the "sensory changes" registered on, say, the skin must "reach the brain and the principal faculties." But such a scenario is impossible, for those "faculties" exist only as capacities and are unable to "perceive" such change. Since there are no proper objects of sensation in the womb, the faculty of sensation cannot be actualized in utero.

But it remains unclear why Fabricius does not consider amniotic fluid to be an object of sensation. After all, as Fabricius himself notes, the fluids are "sometimes acrid, irritating, or tumifacient." There is no obvious reason why such changes in the fetus's environment should not qualify as objects of sensation. Two of Fabricius's associates at Padua latched onto such cracks in the edifice of *De formato foetu* and argued for fetal sensation. Giulio Casseri (known as Placentinus) began his career as Fabricius's assistant in Padua and then came to eclipse his master, earning Fabricius's resentment.[36] In *Pentaestheseion* (1609), a treatise on the senses, Placentinus argues against Fabricius and claims that fetal experience is structured by the "absolute necessity of the sense of Touching." Although Placentinus is no longer well known, he was influential in seventeenth-century England because Helkiah Crooke, the physician to King James I, translated the introduction to *Pentaestheseion* in his popular *Microcosmographia* (1615), the first extensive English-language work on anatomy.[37] In Crooke's translation, Placentinus writes that when "the infant in the wombe yet liveth only a vegetative life, he is first of all endued with the sense of touching; whereby he is cherished, nourished, and increased, and is at length perfected; for so long as he is in the prison of the womb, he neither seeth, nor heareth, nor smelleth, nor tasteth anything, but yet hath absolute necessity of the sense of Touching, that he may be able to avoid imminent dangers."[38] The "infant in the womb" lives a vegetative life, but is, in the absence of all other forms of sense, "endued with the sense of touching" so that he can avoid "imminent dangers," presumably dangers like those Davies imagines when he claims, "My Mothers *Bowels* might have strangled me."[39]

Following Aristotle's claim that "a fetus is not made an animal and a man at one and the same time," Fabricius argues that the fetus "is not made plant and animal at the same time."[40] Against this logic, Placentinus argues that the infant *is* "plant and animal at the same time." This move is motivated by conceptual concerns. Only a few lines later, Placentinus quotes Aristotle's *De anima*: "The loss of [touch] alone must bring about the death of an animal. For as on the one hand nothing which is not an animal can have this sense, so on the other it is the only one which is indispensably necessary to what is an animal." Claiming that "plants . . . have no sensation" and that "Without touch, there can be no other sense," in *De anima* Aristotle divides plants from animals based on the absence or presence of touch (1:692; 435b). Placentinus summarizes Aristotle's position as *tactum animalis essentiam constituere* ("touch constitutes the essence of an animal").[41] If the fetus is, as Fabricius insists, an animal, and if tactility constitutes the essence of animal life, then, Placentinus suggests, it is a contradiction to claim that the fetus cannot feel.

The anatomist and physician William Harvey may have met Placentinus when he studied medicine in Padua from 1599 to 1602.[42] Those years coincided with the publication of *De formato foetu* in 1600 by Fabricius, with whom Harvey took classes and who remained an influence throughout Harvey's career.[43] In *Exercitationes de generatione animalium* (1651), Harvey sought to perfect the embryological tradition he inherited—"Aristotle is my general, Fabricius my guide"—but he also took up the problem of fetal sensation.[44] While Placentinus's arguments were conceptually driven, Harvey's were based on experimental research. He discovered empirical proof for prenatal sensation and, in so doing, solved a contradiction latent in Placentinus's account. In *Pentaestheseion*, Placentinus unpacks what he sees as a problem with the view that the fetus possesses animal capacities but lives the life of a plant: if fetuses are animals and the sense of touch is what distinguishes animals from all other things, then even though a given fetus "liveth only a vegetative life," it must actualize the sense of touch. When Harvey broached the topic of fetal sensation, he solved a new contradiction introduced by Placentinus: the fetus lives the life of a plant but actualizes the capacity to touch.

Harvey's inquiry began, he informs his readers, when, "casting my mind over perfected [that is, sexually mature] animals, reviewing the stages by which they were begun and grew to adults, [I realized] that I should follow the road backwards, as it were from the finish to the starting pits, so that finally, when I could go no further back, I might be fairly sure that I had arrived at the first beginnings." By studying the absolute beginning of animal life, Harvey hoped to see with his own eyes the "primordial matter" and "effective principle" from which "the capacity for formation and growth proceeds," for, if isolated in its original state, the stuff of animal life would "appear the clearer by stripping off and suppressing the accretions, being as it were stripped naked" (17). Using chicken eggs and deer embryos, Harvey's method of repeated dissections unearths what he considers to be the "first beginnings" of life, which had "never been observed by anyone till now" (89): a tiny spot in the middle of the egg that appears the first day after fertilization, slowly dilates "like the pupil of an eye," and constitutes the "rudiments of the foetus" (92). This spot marks the actualization of the vegetative capacities present in the unfertilized egg. On the fourth day, the "foetus passes from the life of a plant to that of an animal," a transition marked by a "capering bloody point" that oscillates between "diastole" and "systole" (96). In Harvey's view, the *punctum saliens*—the initial, tiny trace of an embryonic heart—actualizes animal capacities from its first appearance. Since the "operations" of the soul are "expressed in its actions" and the tiny "bloody point" moves, "we may justly say that it has put on the nature of an animal" (99).

If motion is present in the chicken fetus from the fourth day after fertilization, so is sensation: "upon every touch, be it never so gentle, you will see this *punctum* to be diverse ways disturbed, or as it were provoked (exactly as sensitive bodies are wont to give indications of their sensation by their movements), and it is so over-excited by an oft repeated touch that it becomes confused in the rhythm and order of its pulsation." Since the *punctum saliens* provides "diverse indications of sensation," there is, Harvey concludes, "no question but that this *punctum* lives just like an animal and has movement and sensation." But Harvey cannot quite commit himself to the idea that the *punctum* is fully an animal, for he deduces the presence of animal sensation in this tiny life form "in the same way we conclude that sensation is present in the plant we call sensitive and in zoophytes, because when they are touched, they contract themselves as if they took it unkindly" (99–100). Such zoophytes as sponges straddle the line between plant and animal; like plants, their life depends on their attachment to a given surface, but like animals they have at least some degree of sensation.[45] Harvey figures the advent of actualized animal capacities in terms of what were often called "plant-animals." To be sure, Harvey is not the first to think of fetal life in these terms. Recall Dante, who, in *Purgatorio*, describes the fetus as "moving now and feeling, / like a sea-sponge [*spungo marino*]" (558–59; 25.55–56), a common zoophyte. But if Dante describes developing *capacities*, Harvey locates the beginnings of animal *acts* in a four-day-old body without organs: "Sensation and movement begin clearly to shine forth before any particle of the body is formed." If one gently pricks the "first rudiment of the body" with a pin, Harvey writes, "it will, like a worm or grub, obscurely move and contract and twist itself, which is plain evidence that it has sensation" (296).

This responsiveness increases as the fetus grows, as its body and limbs are articulated, as its sensory organs develop. But a conceptual problem continues to nag at Harvey. As Fabricius, following Galen, had argued, "There is no sensation unless sensory changes reach the brain and the principal faculties. . . . but such change cannot be perceived in the fetus because these faculties are *in potentia*."[46] Harvey claims that animal faculties are present *in actu*, but long before the organ requisite for sensation has even begun to develop; the embryo moves itself and responds to stimuli before it has a brain, when there is nothing but clear liquid in its fragile skull. Harvey's discoveries force him to redefine sensation. The brain coordinates sensation, for it is the organ that enables us both to perceive what our eyes, ears, or flesh sense and, at the same time, to perceive that we perceive.[47] Since the embryo moves and responds to stimuli while the brain is nothing but liquid, "we must," Harvey writes, "conclude that there is a certain sense of touch that is not referred to the sensorium commune or communicated to the brain in any way, and [that] therefore, in that kind of sense we do not perceive our sensation. . . . We must believe in the existence of this kind of sensation which we therefore distinguish from animal sensation" (298). Harvey's exhaustive research into epigenetic development led him to the discovery of "a kind of sensation . . . without the perception of that sensation."

For Harvey, "touch as a natural action differs from the animal sense of touch and constitutes a different species of touch, so that the latter is communicated to the common sensorium or the brain, but the former not at all." Harvey threads the needle between the vegetable and the animal, and in this way he resolves the tension between vegetal soul and the action of touch that we saw in Placentinus's treatment of fetal sensation: "This kind of sensation," Harvey writes of his discovery, "I have observed to exist in zoophytes or plant-animals, such as the sensitive plant, sponges and the like" (298). Fetuses thus live the life of a plant-animal, the life of a sponge. The figure Harvey uses to illuminate the animal soul is thus as close to a plant as an animal can come.

Placed in this context, Traherne's claims about the privilege of prenatal experience are jarring, for they run against the grain of an established way of thinking. Indeed, they ignore one of the basic tenets of early modern embryology—at least as it existed prior to Placentinus and Harvey. To a seventeenth-century reader, the strangeness of Traherne's alien originary experiences would have begun with the idea that the embryo was able to sense anything at all.

WHAT IS IT LIKE TO BE A SPONGE?

If Harvey fractured the embryological consensus and opened up the possibility of a sense without the perception of sensation, Traherne took this hint and ran with it. Harvey completed the experiments for *Exercitationes de generatione animalium* between 1642 and 1646, while at Merton College, Oxford. Serving as physician to Charles I when Oxford was the base for royalist operations during the civil war, Harvey conducted a rigorous program of research. As Robert Frank has shown, Harvey cultivated a circle of colleagues with whom he frequently discussed embryology.[48] Published in 1651, *Generatione animalium* was read intensively at Oxford from 1652 to 1656, during which time Traherne was a student at Brasenose College. Well-read in natural philosophy, Traherne was fascinated by anatomy, which he praises in "The Person":

> The Naked Things
> Are most Sublime, and Brightest Shew,
> When they alone are seen . . .
>   They best are Blazond when we see
>   The Anatomie,
> Survey the Skin, cut up the flesh, the Veins
>   Unfold: The Glory there remains.
> The Muscles, Fibres, Arteries and Bones
> Are better far then Crowns and precious Stones.[49] (6:39–40; 19–34)

Traherne admired Harvey's profession, and he references the anatomist's work on the circulatory system, first published in *De motu cordis et sanguinis* (1628). In *Kingdom of God*, Traherne uses Harvey's discovery to understand the analogy between human body and world: "For as by the Systole, and Diastole of the Heart all the Pulses of the Body beat, and by the circulation of the blood (lately found out) all Life and Motion is maintained: This in the Microcosm is answered with an Universal Circulation in the Macrocosm: the Sun being as it were the Heart of the Univers, drinking in the Blood, and sending it forth Continualy to all the Parts impregnated with motion and Refined, for the Conservation of the whole" (1:350). This physico-theological text, discovered with the Lambeth Palace Manuscript in 1997, confirms what earlier critics had long suspected: namely, that Traherne's reading of Harvey stands behind the lyric "Circulation": "All things to Circulations owe / Themselvs; by which alone / They do exist" (6:46, 32–34).[50] Given Traherne's fascination with embryonic life, his interest in scientific discovery, his references to Harvey, and the timing of his education at Oxford, we have every reason to believe that he read *Generatione animalium*.

In fact, Traherne explicitly references Harvey's "sense without sensation" in "The Improvment," a poem that begins with an elevation of memory over *poiesis*: "Tis more to recollect, then make" (6:17, 2). This poem— a thing made—will, Traherne suggests, be concerned with what surpasses mere making, the memories that guarantee the truth of its making. This is why, after describing a set of rarified originary experiences—"How vast and Infinit / Our *Pleasure*, how Transcendent, how Compleat / If we the *Goodness* of our God possess, / And all *His Joy* be in our *Blessedness*!" (6:19, 67–70)—Traherne corrects himself and returns to a more accurate vein of "recollect[ion]" (6:17, 2):

> But Oh! The vigor of mine Infant Sence
> Drives me too far: I had not yet the Eye
> The Apprehension, or Intelligence
> Of Things so very Great Divine and High.
> > But all things were *Eternal* unto me,
> > And *mine*, and *Pleasing* which mine Ey did see.
>
> That was enough at first: Eternitie,
> Infinitie, and Lov were Silent Joys;
> Power, Wisdom, Goodness and Felicitie;
> All these which now our Care and Sin destroys,
> > By Instinct *virtualy* were well discernd,
> > And by their *Representatives* were learned. (6:19; 79–91)

Driven "too far" by the "vigor" of what he remembers his "Infant Sence" to be, Traherne exaggerates. As an "Infant," he did not actually "possess" the "Goodness of our God," for he did not yet have "the Eye," the adult "Apprehension, or Intelligence" requisite for such possession.[51] Instead, he encountered a phenomenal field in which "all things were *Eternal*" and "Eternitie, / Infinitie, and Lov were Silent Joys."

This sounds equally unbelievable and may not register as much of a correction. But despite the elevated language, Traherne's claims are straightforward. In the *Centuries*, the experience of eternity plays a central role in Traherne's account of what it was like to be an infant: "The Corn was Orient and Immortal Wheat, which never should be reaped, nor was ever Sown. I thought it had stood from everlasting to Everlasting." Likewise, the "Aged" people seemed as "Immortal" as the "Boys and Girls Tumbling in the street": the infant Traherne "knew not that they were Born or should Die." This absence of knowledge about the finite temporality of all created things means that "all things abided Eternaly as they were in their Proper Places" and "Eternity was Manifest in the Light of the Day" (5:93–94; bk. 3, sec. 3). If "All Time was Eternity," this is not the result of some extraordinary event. Rather, Traherne's description of his encounter with eternity stems from the seriousness with which he approaches the experience of infancy, how he strives to capture the radical difference encoded in the very notion that "What is it like to be an infant?" is a meaningful question. This also holds true of how he treats infinity. When, in "The Preparative," Traherne describes what it was like to exist "within / A house I knew not, newly clothd in skin" (6:11, 10–11), he claims that he was a "Living Endless Ey / Just bounded with the Skie," that he was "an inward *Sphere of Light*, / Or an Interminable Orb of *Sight*, / An Endless and a Living Day / A *vital Sun* that round about did ray / All Life and Sense" (6:11, 14–21).[52] In the womb, Traherne insists, there is no differentiation. The embryo does not apprehend a difference between self and world. Since the self-other dyad that will structure later experience is not yet in place, the embryo's experience is one of unity, an expansiveness signaled by such words as "endless," "wider," and "interminable." This lack of differentiation explains why, in "The Improvment," Traherne claims that he encountered "Infinitie" "at my Birth." In the *Centuries*, he admits as much:

> yet Infinitie is the first Thing which is naturally Known. Bounds and Limits are Discerned only in a Secondary manner. Suppose a Man were Born Deaf and Blind. By the very feeling of His Soul He apprehends infinite about Him, infinit Space, infinit Darkness. He thinks not of Wall and Limits till He feels them and is stopt by them. That things are finite we therefore learn by our Sences, but Infinity we know and feel by our Souls: and feel it so Naturaly, as if it were the very Essence and Being of the Soul. (5:82, bk. 2, sec. 81)

We learn to sense finitude, but we feel the infinite immediately both because it is intertwined with the very essence of our souls and because our initial experiences are oceanic, without "Bounds and limits."

This is the state described in "The Improvment," in which "Eternity, / Infinity, and Lov were Silent Joys": not yet able to sense "that things are finite," without any exposure to differentiation or distinction, and absent any understanding of how things begin and end, "at first," Traherne feels eternity and infinity as all-encompassing joys. But he "discern[s]" these "Joys" by "Instinct *virtualy*," a phrase that reveals the extent of Traherne's learning by combining scholastic terminology with new philosophical ideas.[53] In his commentary on Aristotle's *Posterior Analytics* (c. 1268), Aquinas elaborates on Aristotle's refutation of Meno's paradox ("either a man learns nothing or he learns what he already knew") by rehearsing the difference between what is "known *in potentia* or virtually [*virtute*]" and "proper actual knowing":

> What is generated does not exist fully before generation, but in one way exists and, in another way, does not exist. It is being *in potentia*, not being in act. And this is what generation is, to bring from potency into act. What someone learns is not completely known before that, as Plato held. Neither is it completely unknown. . . . But it was known *in potentia* or virtually [*virtute*] in the foreknown principles, while unknown in act in terms of the knowledge proper. And to learn is to bring knowing from the potential or virtual or universal [*potentiali seu virtuali aut universali*], into proper actual knowing.[54]

To actually know something is, according to Aquinas, "to know [*cognoscere*] it perfectly," to "perfectly apprehend [*apprehendere*] its truth." By contrast, to know something "only virtually [*virtute*] . . . is to know only in a way and accidentally."[55] Traherne makes this distinction when he claims that as an infant he "had not yet" the "Apprehension, or Intelligence / Of Things so very Great Divine and High," but he remained able to "*virtualy*" discern eternity and infinity.

Such "Joys" are "discerned" virtually through "Instinct." The term *instinct* was used in a wide number of contexts, but Traherne seems to have in mind the definition offered by his older contemporary Edward Herbert, who in *De veritate* defined instinct as *the* fundamental way in which things are known. Instinct is "an immediate emanation of the mind, co-extensive with the dictates of nature," a faculty that brings such notions as "the good, bad, beautiful, pleasing," and other things that "tend towards the preservation of the individual" into "conformity" with a given being "independent of discursive or rational thought" (123). This form of apprehension fulfills "itself irrationally" and "occupies the first position among [human] faculties," while "discursive reason" occupies the "last" (122). Herbert's natural instinct aligns with Aquinas's understanding of the virtual insofar as instinct knows, as it were, without actually knowing: "Natural instinct anticipates reason in perceiving the beauty of the proportions of a house built according to architectural principles; for reason teaches its conclusions by laborious consideration of the proportions, first severally and then the whole." This sort of ability—to determine easily, immediately, and without the aid of reason what is or is not beautiful—exists within the purview of instinct, which Herbert sees as necessary for the preservation of all creatures: "Thus this faculty promotes self-preservation in the elements, the zoophytes, and even the embryo" (139). Like the zoophytes, "even" embryos can, in Traherne's words, discern "By Instinct *virtualy*" such notions as eternity and infinity.

When he attempts to explain this idea in "The Improvment," Traherne turns to the sponge, the zoophyte favored in the embryological accounts of Dante and Harvey:

> As Spunges gather Moisture from the Earth
>   (Which seemeth Drie,) in which they buried are;
> As Air infecteth Salt; so at my Birth
> All these [infinity, eternity, and so on] were unperceivd, yet did appear:
>   Not by Reflexion, and Distinctly known,
>   But, by their Efficacy, all mine own. (6:20, 93–98)

This scene takes place "at my Birth"—the moment when the ego first appears, which is, in Traherne's radical redefinition, the moment when "I in my Mothers Womb was born" (6:4, 38). At first, Traherne's reference to sponges invokes experiments that demonstrate how a sponge buried in the earth absorbs liquid even though the ground seems dry. Through a catachrestic wrenching of the bodily into the spiritual, Traherne claims that just as sponges "gather Moisture" from the driest ground and just as salt is "infecte[d]" by the moisture present in a given body of air, so "at [the] Birth" of his ego such "Joys" as eternity and infinity were simply absorbed from his milieu. The comparison hinges on Traherne's spiritualization of ancient ideas about fetal nourishment. In *Directory for Midwives* (1651), the physician Nicholas Culpeper recorded the view of the philosopher Alcmaeon, who thought that while in the womb "the Infant drew in his Nourishment by his whol Body; because it is rare and Spongy, as a sponge sucks in water on every side and so he thought it sucked Blood, not only from the Mothers

Veins, but also from her Womb."[56] Traherne's embryo is far more refined;
it absorbs eternity and infinity.

But the sponge also carries with it other embryological associations. Recall Dante's "sea-sponge," which marks how the embryo acquires the capacities associated with the animal soul ("moving now and feeling [*sente*]"
[558–59; 25.55]). This capacity for animal *sente* is different from the capacity for human *sente* that emerges after the moment of divine infusion when,
Dante writes, the embryo becomes "a single soul / that lives, and feels,
and reflects upon itself [*vive e sente e sé in sé rigira*]" (560–61; 25.74–75).
Traherne takes up this distinction and shifts its conceptual register from
potentiality to actuality. At the moment of his "birth," Traherne claims, he
did not encounter eternity or infinity "by Reflexion." The mode of thought
with which Traherne's life began in utero was not the reflexivity captured
by Dante's *sé in sé rigira*, but rather a more basic form of openness to what
is given, what I have called minimal mental presence. Infinity and eternity
were not "Distinctly known" but rather "discerned" by "Instinct *virtualy*"
(6:19, 90); they were "unperceived, yet did appear" (6:20, 96). Traherne imagines that his first thoughts consisted of an "appear[ance]" without perception. This phrasing echoes Harvey's "sensation . . . without the perception
of that sensation"—a mode of primitive sensory activity that the physician associates with sponges. The sponge that appears at the beginning of
Traherne's stanza thus subtly prepares for the notion of "Joys" that were
"unperceivd, yet did appear." If Dante uses the sponge to invoke the advent
of unactualized capacities for feeling and moving, Harvey takes it up as an
analogue for embryonic sensation—the fetus feels as a zoophyte feels, without a perception of that feeling. This absence of perception means that even
if Harvey's novel form of sensation is actualized in utero, it exists either
before or beyond phenomenality. Traherne takes the question lurking in
Harvey's text—"What is it like to be a sponge?"—and provides a phenomenological answer. Harvey holds that "sense without the perception of sensation" explains the responsiveness of living tissue. By claiming that what
goes "unperceivd" could somehow "appear," Traherne transplants Harvey's
physiological account into the register of first-person experience.

Traherne was not the only English writer to make use of Harvey's novel
idea. The physician and natural philosopher Walter Charleton, a writer with
whose works Traherne was familiar, advanced the idea in his *Natural History of Nutrition, Life, and Voluntary Motion* (1659).[57] Charleton translated
all of Harvey's Latin prose on the "Sensation without Sense" into English.[58]
Transplanted from its embryological origins into a text on the basics of
"animal oeconomy," Harvey's idea offers Charleton a way of explaining the

obscure features of living bodies. After describing how bodily tissue contracts itself in response to stimuli, Charleton adopts the voice of a puzzled
reader putting on "the cloudy aspect of dissatisfaction" and asks, "Doth not
this Irritation and spontaneous Contraction of Membranous and Nervous
parts, when they are molested, imply a certain sense in them, distinct from
the sense of Feeling or Touching, and independent upon the Common sense
or Brain? For whatever is any ways moved by it self, in avoidance or resistance to what is offensive to it; must be endowed with a sense, whereby
to discern that offensiveness. . . . But we are not conscious to ourselves
of any such sense within us."[59] After framing Harvey's paradox as a sense
of which "we are not conscious," Charleton launches into his translation,
using Harvey's embryological work to illustrate a phenomenon central to
animal life as such. Francis Glisson performs a similar move when he uses
Harvey's embryological findings to support his theory—initially published
in *Tractatus de natura substantiae energetica* (1672)—that all living bodily
tissue is irritable.[60] Harvey's idea also appears in John Davies's translation
of Marin Cureau de la Chambre's *The Art How to Know Men* (1665), which
argues, "Before the formation of the Heart and Brain, there is motion and
sentiment in the Embryo."[61]

Although other writers were fascinated by Harvey's simultaneous actualization and defamiliarization of embryonic sensation, Traherne is alone in
seizing on the phenomenological implications of this idea. In "The Improvment," he claims that even if the "Joys" of infinity and eternity go "unperceivd," they nevertheless "appear." What might he mean? In Traherne's
view, infinity and eternity appear to the newborn ego, "Not by Reflexion
and Distinctly known, / But, by their Efficacy, *all mine own*" (6:20, 97–98).
This sense of mineness implies both the presence of the ego "at my Birth"
and the organizational structure of the phenomenal world. Traherne states
as much earlier in "The Improvment":

> But neither Goodness, Wisdom, Power, nor Love,
> Nor Happiness it self in things could be,
> Did not they *all in one fair Order* move,
> And jointly by their Service End in *me*.
>   Had he not made an *Ey* to be the Sphere
>   Of all Things, none of these would e're appear. (6:17, 23–28)

In order for what gives value to human life—goodness, happiness, love, and
so on—to "be" "in things," those "things"—the "Fabrick" of the "World,"
the "*Starry* Sphere," the "*fruitFull* Ground," and "all [God's] Works in their

varietie" (6:17, 4–20)—must obey two conditions. First, the created world must "*all in one fair Order* move"; it must be organized so that human life can flourish. And second, all creatures must "jointly by their Service End in *me*." They must, that is, "appear" to "*me*," the metaphorical "*Ey*," or *I*, who, as a pole of phenomenality, is the precondition for appearance itself. As Joan Webber noted long ago, Traherne's favorite pun involves the substitution of *eye* for *I*.[62] In "The Improvment," Traherne employs "*Ey*" as a synecdoche for the ego, so that the final lines of this stanza mean that nothing would "e're appear" visually without the organ of the eye, nor would anything appear at all without the ego, which is the "Sphere / Of all things." The poem's concluding stanza returns to the memories generated by the "vigor of mine Infant Sence" (6:19, 79) in order to describe the moment of "my Birth" (6:20, 95), when the ego and the world it co-constitutes first came into being.

Although "The Improvment" suggests that Traherne had read Harvey's embryology, he offers a radically different vision of life in utero. In *Generatione animalium*, Harvey's topic is embryonic tactility: "touch as a natural action [that] differs from the animal sense of touch and constitutes a different species of touch" (298). By contrast, Traherne describes completely luminous embryonic *sight*: he was a "Living Endless Ey, / Just bounded with the Skie / Whose Power, whose Act, whose Essence was to see" (6:11, 14–16). Traherne emphasizes this difference by reworking Placentinus's account of embryonic touch. Recall that in Crooke's translation, Placentinus claims that "for so long as [the fetus] is in the prison of the womb, he neither seeth, nor heareth, nor smelleth, nor tasteth anything, but yet hath absolute necessity of the sense of Touching."[63] Traherne adopts the structure of this negative list, but argues instead for the "absolute necessity" of sight. Expanding on the claim that, while in the womb, he was a "Meditating Inward Ey" (6:12, 30), in "The Preparative" Traherne writes,

> For *Sight* inherits Beauty, *Hearing* Sounds,
> The *Nostril* Sweet Perfumes,
> All *Tastes* have hidden Rooms
> Within the *Tongue*; and *Feeling Feeling* Wounds
> With Pleasure and Delight, but I
> Forgot the rest, and was all Sight or Ey. (6:12, 35–40)

This sensory catalogue refuses the basic status of the "*Feeling*" that wounds "*Feeling*" with "Pleasure and Delight." Forgetting hearing, smell, taste, and touch, in the beginning Traherne was, he claims, "all Sight or Ey." This move from feeling to vision expands the purview of neonatal sensation, moving from a limited form of perception toward the field of phenomenality indexed by Descartes's new use of *conscientia*.

In the introduction, we saw the extent to which Descartes imagined the possibility of neonatal thought. In chapter 3, I unpacked much of the logic behind this evocation of originary experience: first, thought is the defining attribute of all mental life; second, thought is the essence of the human ego; third, since it is the essence of the ego, thought is always operative within an existing ego; and fourth, thought is always available to first-person scrutiny through its defining feature, *conscientia*. This constellation of arguments pushed Descartes's critics relentlessly toward prenatal existence as a means of rebutting the philosopher's arguments. For example, while attacking the idea that the ego always thinks, Gassendi shares a similar worry as that discussed by Arnauld in the introduction when he wonders "whether you think that you were infused into the body, or one of its parts, while still in the womb or at birth." Portraying Descartes's position as ridiculous, Gassendi continues, "I do not want to press the point too insistently and ask whether you remember what you thought about in the womb or in the first few days or months or even years after you were born; nor, if you answer that you have forgotten, shall I ask why this is so. I do suggest, however, that you should bear in mind how obscure, meager and virtually non-existent your thought must have been during those early periods of your life" (CSM 2:184). Human minds probably begin in the womb or at least in early childhood, Gassendi argues, but it is lunacy to insist, against all evidence, that prenatal life is defined in terms of constant thought. Descartes's reply is simple and straightforward: since the mind is "implanted in the body" while the child is in the womb, since the ego must think, and since all thought requires *conscientia* in order to be thought, fetuses are conscious of their thought. But while in utero, infants are conscious only of the passive mode of thought that Descartes calls sensation.

Descartes clearly lays out this position in August 1641, when, in a passage that I quoted in part in the introduction, he responds to Hyperaspistes:

> I had reason to assert that the human soul, wherever it be, even in the mother's womb, is always thinking. What more certain or evident reason could be wished for than the one I gave? I proved that the nature or essence of the soul consists in the fact that it is thinking, just as the essence of the body consists in the fact that it is extended. Now nothing can ever be deprived of its own essence; so it seems to me that someone who denies that his soul was thinking during those periods when he

does not remember having noticed it was thinking deserves no more attention than if he were to deny that his body was extended during those periods when he did not notice that it had extension. This does not mean, however, that I believe that the mind of an infant meditates on metaphysics in its mother's womb; not at all. We know by experience that our minds are so closely joined to our bodies as to be almost always acted upon by them; and although when thriving in an adult and healthy body the mind enjoys some liberty to think other things than those presented by the senses, we know there is not the same liberty in those who are sick or asleep or very young; and the younger they are, the less liberty they have. So if one may conjecture on such an unexplored topic, it seems most reasonable to think that a mind newly united to an infant's body is wholly occupied in perceiving in a confused way or feeling the ideas of pain, pleasure, heat, cold and other similar ideas which arise from its union and, as it were, intermingling with the body. (CSM 3:189–90)

Tackling the "unexplored topic" of thought in utero, Descartes maintains that fetuses perform the act of thought, but only in the mode of sensation. They are conscious only of such "ideas" as pain and pleasure. While in the womb, the fetus possesses "in itself the ideas of God, of itself and all such truths as are called self-evident," but it does so only "in the same way as adult human beings have these ideas when they are not attending to them" (CSM 3:190). Taken together, Descartes's inclusion of sensation within thought and his claim that he is a *res cogitans* both push him to break with the long embryological consensus and to argue that thought (in the modality of sensation) is actualized in the womb. Higher-order thought is relegated to the sphere of potentiality—a given fetus has the capacity to think ideas "of God" and "of itself" but does not actualize these thoughts. Yet thought itself begins to work the moment mind first appears.

Traherne takes up this Cartesian scene in almost all of his depictions of originary experience, but nowhere with more subtlety than in the opening stanza of "My Spirit":

> My Naked Simple Life was I: 2
>   That Act so Strongly Shind
> Upon the Earth, the Sea, the Skie,
> It was the Substance of My Mind;   5
>   The Sence it self was I.
> I felt no Dross nor Matter in my Soul,

No Brims nor Borders, such as in a Bowl
We see, My Essence was Capacitie.
      That felt all Things,   10
      The Thought that Springs
Therefrom's it self. It hath no other Wings
   To spread abroad, nor Eys to see,
      Nor Hands Distinct to feel,
        Nor Knees to Kneel: 15
But being Simple like the Deitie
   In its own Centre is a Sphere
   Not shut up here, but evry where. (6:26–27, 2–18)

The topic of this stanza is the nature of the "Thought" that "Springs" into being at the moment when, as Traherne puts it in "The Salutation," the infant ego from "Nothing now awake[s]." The Cartesian phrase "Substance of My Mind"—used, as we saw in chapter 3, in "Thoughts I" to define thought itself—appears in "My Spirit" as a way of summarizing the act that "so Strongly Shind" from the speaker's ego. The act that is the "Substance" of the speaker's "Mind" is *thought*, the act captured in the image of "the Thought that Springs" into actuality from the capacity to feel. Descartes held that thought was the first act produced by any given person, and that this was true in two ways: thought is the "first" act because it is the most important, but it is also "first" chronologically. Thought is the originary act performed by any human being. When an embryo develops in the womb, at first it is only nature that acts as it weaves the body together. But as Descartes points out in his response to Arnauld, at the very moment the mind is "implanted in the body" the act of thinking begins (CSM 2:171). Since thought includes sensation within its orbit, the first proper act of a new human being is to sense. Traherne's "My Spirit" defamiliarizes this initial act.

    The poem begins with a sentence that registers embodied life transforming into conscious thought: "My Naked Simple Life was I," a line the syntax of which suggests an ego emerging from nonconscious bodily life. The sentence that occupies the next three lines introduces this new ego's first act, the thought that makes up the newly implanted mind's "Substance." This first thought is an experience of a "Naked Simple Life" suddenly aware of itself. In the *Commentaries of Heaven*, Traherne claims that when an infant wakes, "His Life is the first Thing of which he is sensible, he is in his own eys a Sphere of Light filling the World with Apprehension" (3:438). Since this life is the only thing of which the infant is conscious, it seems to "his own eys"—that is, from the infant's own perspective—that this subjective life fills the entire world "with Apprehension." The oceanic dimensions of this originary felt vitality are captured in the lyric "Wonder," in which Traherne claims of his initial waking moments that "I felt a Vigour in my Sence / That was all SPIRIT. I within did flow / With Seas of Life" (6:5, 23–25). The "Vigour" here is "in" Traherne's "Sence," which intransitively relishes its own self-affection. "My Spirit" marks how this initial thought feels as though it were ecstatically connected to a world retrospectively described in terms of the features the fetus will only come to know later in its life—"That Act so strongly Shind / Upon the Earth, the Sea, the Skie"—but here encompassed within the expanding "Sphere" of its own phenomenality.

The rest of this stanza provides a vision of this initial moment, when thought is active but remains all but unrecognizable. Now that the "I" has become "Sence it self," now that a primitive act of thought has been initiated, the "I" no longer needs to be passively subordinated, but can become the syntactical subject of a sentence: "I felt no Dross nor Matter in my Soul, / No Brims nor Borders, such as in a Bowl / We see, My Essence was Capacitie. / That felt all Things." Traherne's "essence was capacity" in a manner more capacious than the bowls "we" fully grown human beings see. If, as Traherne writes in the *Centuries*, "Bounds and limits are Discerned only in a secondary manner," one's first thought must be that of infinity. The speaker's essential capacity—its infinite, passive receptivity—enables him to encounter "no Brims nor Borders," but to feel "all Things." The essence of Traherne's embryonic ego is thus a felt passive capacity for receptivity that shapes the act of thought. Given that thought here is exhausted by the modalities of sense or feeling, it is fair to say that the act of thought here is itself passive. Traherne thus uses the word *capacity* very cleverly in this stanza, both in the sense of a radical, passive receptivity and in the sense of an active power or ability.

The thought that springs from this state of essential capacity, the thought that enables the feeling of "all Things" is, Traherne tells us, "it self." It is self-generated, a sort of self-affection. This thought does not, that is, come from elsewhere, which is what Traherne means when he claims that it has "no other Wings": it does not come from some Platonic preexistence, the period when souls had wings described in Plato's *Phaedrus*. At the same time, this thought is not mediated through bodily organs, for it cannot yet draw on the resources of the fully organized body, and it cannot rely on eyes to see or hands to feel. But it is not, for all that, a disembodied thought. After all, Traherne claims that he was the "Sence it self," able to feel "all Things." Embodied enough to have sense and to feel but still lacking limbs and sense organs, Traherne's thought exists in its *own* center. And because this thought is not differentiated from the surrounding world, it feels as though it were "evry where."

Traherne articulates this claim more fully in an entry on "Apprehension" in *Commentaries of Heaven*: "The first Thing which the Body feeleth is it self; and the Soul is by Nature the first Object of its own Apprehension[,] for by feeling it self it feeleth all other Things" (3:179). Although many critics have aligned this drift toward the thought of "all Things" with various forms of Platonism, Traherne is in fact quoting Aristotle's definition of thought in *De anima*: since thought is "potentially whatever is thinkable" (1:683; 429b), and "since everything is a possible object of thought," then "it follows that it can have no nature of its own, other than that of having a certain capacity" (1:682; 429a). In "My Spirit," Traherne glosses this passage when he claims, "My Essence was Capacitie. / That felt all Things." His essence is thought, and thought is nothing but the capacity to be affected by "all Things." Traherne elaborates on this idea in an entry on "Assimilation" in *Commentaries of Heaven*:

> The soul is an Abilitie [that is, a capacity] of becoming All Things. It is an Empty Chaos of Faculties and Powers, that can no where be imagined or conceived to exist, till it does actualy contemplat som Object. It is not what it is till it consider it self: For it is a Capacitie infinit . . . [but] till it reflect on it self, it self is not aware of the Power which it is. The Soul being so meer a Capacitie of resembling, that till it think on its Power to contain all, it is not like it self: but when it does the Image of infinit Space may be seen within it. (3:261)

What Traherne describes over and over in his accounts of originary experience is the moment in which the soul comes into contact with itself and thereby encounters everything else. Such "feeling it self" is the "first" thought an embryonic being thinks.

To return to the poem with which this chapter opened, in "Fullnesse" Traherne claims, "That Light, that Sight, that Thought / Which in my Soul at first He wrought, / Is sure the only Act to which I may / Ascent to this Day." Since the "first" thought is an act "wrought" by God, it is close to perfect, "A Spiritual World Standing within, / An Univers enclosd in Skin" (6:30, 2–9). But if this thought remains the "best" that Traherne can remember "to this Day," it is not perfect, for, as he stresses in "The Improvment," it is discerned "By Instinct *virtualy*," a felt thought that approximates but cannot attain God's actual knowledge. This divine knowledge is reserved, he tells readers of "Thoughts III," for a later moment:

The Best of Thoughts is yet a thing unknown,
But when tis Perfect it is like his [God's] Own:
Intelligible, Endless, yet a Sphere
Substantial too: In which all Things appear.
All worlds, all Excellences, Sences, Graces,
Joys, Pleasures, Creatures, and the Angels Faces. (6:70, 67–72)

The perfect thought of "all Things" is not attainable here on earth, but Traherne's memory of his first thought brings him as close to such perfection as humanly possible.

In "My Spirit," he struggles to make this idea believable. When he claims that the "Substance of My Mind" was an act of thought and that his ego was coterminous with the "Sence it self," it strikes me that the expansiveness of a feeling without "Brims or Borders"—a feeling of "all Things"—can exist for Traherne only because the "I" does not yet exist in any recognizable form. I was once "the Sence it self": this claim could be read as a reframing of Harvey's insights about perceptionless embryonic sense. Animating Dante's sentient sponge from within, Traherne puts himself in the truly impossible position of mimetically representing what it was like to exist prior to the development of the brain, prior to the material conditions for the coordination of raw sensation into a higher-level, synthetic perception. In other words, Traherne aims to describe conscious thought before the advent of the bodily conditions that would, for Harvey, make such thought possible. Harvey provides the embryological correlative to having one's "essence [be] capacity." Undifferentiated from his surroundings, Traherne's embryonic self is truly expansive—a living, pulsing sensorium abiding in the utter absence of any perceiver. This is the first human thought, Traherne's version of the act of sensation imagined by Descartes.

Traherne articulates this mimetic fiction of originary experience through verse, which provides formal resources for capturing that which escapes propositional utterance. In Traherne's hands, verse expands the possibilities of meaning creation so that the impossible becomes articulable, amenable to mimesis. I will point out just two examples. First, note how Traherne describes his originary experience in the womb: "I felt no Dross nor Matter in my Soul, / No Brims nor Borders, such as in a Bowl / We see, My Essence was Capacitie." We—the adult poet and his readers—are cut off from undifferentiated feeling, a gap performed by the line break, which divides us even from the bowl used as an example to illustrate what prenatal feeling is *not*. Second, notice how Traherne uses rhyme. He employs an internal rhyme— "We see," "Capacitie"—that separates mature perception from a felt state in which essence is capacity even as it acknowledges that the only way to imagine such a state is through adult perception. This rhyme is repeated in the "nor Eyes to see" of line 13 and the "simple like the Deitie" of line 16. The rhyming of line 9's "Capacitie" with "nor Eyes to see" in line 13 performs the difference between vision and pure capacity by revealing that human essence can be capacity only when such organs as eyes have yet to develop. In line 16, Traherne links the fact that his thought was "Simple like the Deitie" back to the claim that his "Essence was Capacitie," a rhyme that acoustically performs the comparison made in line 16, even if the intervention of "see" in line 13 reinforces the differences separating the simplicity of an essential capacity from the simplicity of divinity. Traherne produces this impossible experience by using the resources of verse.

WAYS INTO LANGUAGE

In *Commentaries of Heaven*, as we have seen, Traherne argues that a human being exists as a "Babe" from the moment he first becomes "sensible" of "His Life" until he becomes an active speaker of language: "But when he begins to Speak, he ceases to be a Babe, and is infected with the Corruptions and Customs of Men" (3:438). If infancy is a state of innocence, that innocence is broken when a child learns to speak. The entrance into language repeats Adam's fall. Everyone is "Naturaly Born" into a pure "Enjoyment" of the world, Traherne argues in *Centuries*. From the moment they are "first born"—when conscious thought initially flares into existence—children apprehend "only those Things . . . which did [appear] to Adam in Paradice, in the same Light, and in the same Colors." Their experience does not include within its purview "Ambitions, Trades, Luxuries, inordinat Affections, [or the] Causal and Accidental Riches invented since the fall." (5:96, bk. 3, sec. 5).

Prior to speech and their introduction into the intergenerational and historical matrix of norms and values that precede their existence, children are struck full of wonder at the sky, the water, the earth, and their fellow creatures. However, once children are contaminated by the fact of human culture and its histories, the "first Light" of infancy, with its "Primitive and Innocent Clarity," is "totaly Ecclypsed." Traherne explains how this loss takes place:

> If you ask me how it was Ecclypsed? Truly by the Customs and maners of Men, which like Contrary Winds blew it out: by an innumerable company of Objects, rude vulgar and Worthless Things that like so many

loads of Earth and Dung did over whelm and Bury it: by the Impetuous
Torrent of Wrong Desires in all others whom I saw or knew that carried
me away and alienated me from it: by a Whole Sea of other Matters and
Concernments that Covered and Drowned it: finaly by the Evil Influence
of a Bad Education that did not foster and cherish it. All Mens thoughts
and Words were about other Matters; They all prized New Things which
I did not dream of. I was a stranger and unacquainted with them; I was
little and reverenced their Authority; I was weak, and easily guided by
their Example: Ambitious also, and Desirous to approve my self unto
them. And finding no one Syllable in any mans Mouth of these Things,
by Degrees they vanishd, My Thoughts, (as indeed what is more fleeting
then a Thought) were blotted out[,] and at last all the Celestial Great and
Stable Treasures to which I was born, as wholly forgotten, as if they had
never been. (5:96–97, bk. 3, sec. 7)

If Traherne fancies himself blessed, later in life, to re-remember his initial
period of existence, most people are not so lucky. The process of encultura-
tion and education—both of which are enabled by language acquisition—
erases our infant "Thoughts," the glory of our initial existence. It is the
intense impressionability of the human mind that facilitates both the ecstatic wonder at our initial exposure to the givenness of things and also our
later refashioning in the likeness of our culture. "Thoughts are the most
Present things to Thoughts, and of the most Powerfull Influence," writes
Traherne: "Souls to Souls are like Apples to Apples, one being rotten rots
another. When I began to Speak and goe[,] Nothing began to be present to
me, but what was present in their Thoughts. Nor was any thing present to
me any other way, then it was so to them" (5:98, bk. 3, sec. 10). Language
shapes thought. Since the essence of language is to be repeated and shared
by many speakers, those who speak a given language share a structure of
what might be called *mutual presencing* with their fellow speakers. Having
entered language, the young Traherne's world—what shows up as present to
him—becomes limited to "what was present" in the thoughts of the many
people who make up his community. Born innocent, each human being
falls, dragged down, in Traherne's Pelagian phrasing, not so much by "our
Parents Loyns, so much as our Parents lives." If all of "our Corruption [is]
Derived from Adam," the medium connecting our sin to his Fall is not nature but nurture (5:97, bk. 3, sec. 8).

As I have argued throughout this book, one key context for Traherne's
thought is Augustine's theology. Rejecting the Augustinian notion of original sin and its deployment by such Reformation thinkers as Luther and

Calvin, Traherne presents a semi-Pelagian view of human nature. More precisely, the claim that all of us are innocent until we have acquired language is pitched very carefully against Augustine's own account of learning to speak.[64] In the *Confessiones*, Augustine argues that all human beings are vitiated and fallen from the moment they first exist. Writing of the "sin of infancy," he recalls having "personally watched and studied a jealous baby. He could not yet speak and, pale with jealousy and bitterness, glared at his brother sharing his mother's milk" (9; 1.7.11). Prior to the acquisition of language, infants are full of terrible urges and behaviors. They manifest desires for power, for dominance, for pleasure—and language is merely an extension of this desire. "Little by little I began to be aware where I was and wanted to manifest my wishes to those who could fulfill them as I could not," writes Augustine:

> For my desires were internal; adults were external to me and had no means of entering my soul. So I threw my limbs about and uttered sounds, signs resembling my wishes, the small number of signs of which I was capable but such signs as lay in my power to use: for there was no real resemblance. When I did not get my way, either because I was not understood or lest it was harmful to me, I used to be indignant at my seniors for their disobedience, and with free people who were not slaves to my interests; and I would revenge myself upon them by weeping. (7; 1.6.8)

The urge to communicate begins as a violent desire to impose one's will on others. If these initial efforts are frustrated because there is "no real resemblance" between a flailing limb and the toy too far away to reach, the acquisition of speech enables the fine tuning of the resemblance between the expression of desire and the desired object. "By groans and various sounds and various movements of parts of my body I would endeavor to express the intentions of my heart to persuade people to bow to my will," Augustine claims, reconstructing his own past through the observations he has made as an adult: "I gradually gathered the meaning of words . . . and already I learnt to articulate my wishes by training my mouth to use these signs. In this way I communicated the signs of my wishes to those around me" (11; 1.8.13). For Augustine, the entrance into language marks the refinement of a structure of desire and intentional expression that exists almost immediately after birth, long before the first word is spoken.[65] The flow of desire and violence moves from inside out, as an always already fallen inner life becomes increasingly adept at manifesting its will. In this model, a vitiated infant nature develops into the vitiated world of nurture.

For Traherne, by contrast, language is an external force that slowly enters into and gradually shapes the soul of each infant. While, in Augustine's view, the infant, a being predicated on lack, flails about to fill the emptiness within, in Traherne's view, from the moment of its birth into conscious thought, the embryo is radically full, overwhelmed by the inexhaustible givenness of the created world. As the infant grows older, this fecundity of experiential wonder is gradually erased until "the Heavens and the Sun and Stars they disappeared, and were no more unto me then the bare Walls," and the "Strange Riches of Mans Invention quite overcame the Riches of Nature" (5:98; bk. 3, sec. 10). Language is both the villain and the hero of Traherne's theology. On the one hand, speech is what drags each human being into an irrevocably fallen state. On the other hand, speech is what enables Traherne to share a mimesis of human life as it existed before the acquisition of language. If the prose of *Centuries* lays out the narrative of this Fall, Traherne aims to transform language into a cure, a mechanism that places readers back in the scene of unfallen glory that they themselves lived through but can no longer remember.

As an example of this double movement, consider the lyric "Dumnesse," in which Traherne insists that human beings are "Speechless made at first" (6:22, 6) so that they can take sustenance from their inner life before they are exposed to the world:

This, my Dear friends, this was my Blessed Case;
For nothing spoke to me but the fair Face
Of Heav'n and Earth, before my self could speak,
I then my Bliss did, when my Silence, break.
My Non-Intelligence of Human Words
Ten thousand Pleasures unto me affords;
For while I knew not what they to me said,
Before their Souls were into mine conveyd . . .
Before my Thoughts were levend with theirs, before
There any Mixture was; the Holy Door,
Or Gate of Souls was closd, and mine being One
Within it self to me alone was Known.
Then did I dwell within a World of Light,
Distinct and Seperat from all Mens Sight,
Where I did feel strange Thoughts, and such Things see
That were, or seemd, only reveald to Me,
There I saw all the World Enjoyd by one;
There I was in the World my Self alone. (6:22, 18–37)

Before his "Thoughts were levend" with the ideas of other people, conveyed through newly understood speech, the infant Traherne "did feel strange Thoughts" unfamiliar to adult conscious life because they were not structured by the collective organizing power of language and were therefore "only reveal to Me." Prior to his "Intelligence of Human Words," Traherne lived without the "Mixture" of culture, which infects the purity of one's own nature with the "infected Mind[s]" of others. When he broke his silence and learned to speak, he simultaneously destroyed his state of unadulterated bliss. The condition of pure consciousness that Traherne describes can only exist prior to the acquisition of language.

But this condition must nevertheless be expressed in and through language, a fact that Traherne emphasizes throughout the poem, which is staged as a discussion. In addition to opening with the address to "my Dear friends," the poem also engages in playful questions: "No Work / But one was found; and that did in me lurk. / D'ye ask me What? It was with Cleerer Eys / To see all Creatures full of Deities; / Especially Ones self" (6:23, 38–42). This direct address—"D'ye ask me What?"—to a set of interlocutors ("Dear friends") draws attention to the fact that the poem is a work made of "Human Words," the very medium of shared culture through which Traherne's fall from innocence took place. What is more, the opening lines of "Dumnesse" establish the poem as the continuation of an ongoing conversation, both staged and intertextual: "Sure Man was born to Meditat on Things" (6:22, 2). The opening interjection "Sure" implies that the poem begins from a place of agreement with a set of interlocutors, but it also places "Dumnesse" in conversation with Henry Vaughan, who begins three poems from the *Silex Scintillans* volumes (1650, 1655) with the interjection "Sure."[66] Born and raised in close proximity to one another, there is much that Vaughan and Traherne share—most notably an interest in early childhood experience.[67] But Traherne's use of "Sure" seeks to establish distance from the vision of early human life (just after the postlapsarian expulsion from Paradise) articulated in Vaughan's "Corruption":

> Sure, it was so. Man in those early days
>   Was not all stone, and earth,
> He shined a little, and by those weak rays
>   Had some glimpse of his birth. (196, 1–4)

Although the human beings imagined by Vaughan "sighed for *Eden*" and longed for *"those bright days"* prior to the Fall (196, 19–20), "Man" nevertheless shone "a little" and had "some glimpse of his birth." Expelled from

Eden, there remained some compensation in "those early days": "still *Paradise* lay / In some green shade, or fountain" (196, 23–24). Unlike "now"—when "man is sunk below / The centre" and "thick darkness lies / And hatcheth o'er thy people" (196, 35–38)—back then, some of Eden's light still lingered.

Traherne transforms Vaughan's hedging and qualifications—"Sure . . . Man in those early days . . . Had some glimpse of his birth"—into confident assertions:

> Sure Man was born to Meditat on Things,
> And to Contemplat the Eternal Springs
> Of God and Nature, Glory, Bliss and Pleasure;
> That Life and Love might be his Heavnly Treasure:
> And therfore Speechless made at first, that he
> Might in himself profoundly Busied be:
> And not vent out, before he hath ta'ne in
> Those Antidots that guard his Soul from Sin. (6:22, 2–9)

The topic is still man in his "early days," but instead of ancient people who possess "some glimpse" of their "birth" in Eden, Traherne offers a vision of man at the moment he is "born," by relating a mimetic account of what his own experience of birth was like. Traherne's confidence contrasts starkly with Vaughan's caution. "I cannot reach it," Vaughan writes of infancy in "Childhood," "and my striving eye / Dazzles at it, as at eternity" (288, 1–2). If, despite years of "study," Vaughan can only see its "edges" and "bordering light" but not its "centre and mid-day" (288, 39–42), Traherne positions himself in the well-lit "centre" of what Vaughan cannot so much as enter.[68] While Vaughan's "Man" only "shined a little," Traherne's "Man" dwells "within a World of Light" (6:22, 32).

Building atop the assumption that human beings were "born to Meditat on Things," in "Dumnesse" Traherne confidently moves toward the conclusion that they must "therfore" have been born without language so that they can take God, nature, glory, bliss, and pleasure in before they begin to "vent out" into the world. Since speech is the mechanism that enables one to actively reach out and make the world one's own—instead of simply receiving the world for what it is—speech must necessarily come later in one's development. In the beginning of human life, there were no words. Traherne's claim to recall his originary experience corrects Augustine's anthropological views by shedding light on the important period that the writer of the *Confessiones* claims is "lost in the darkness of my forgetfulness" (10; 1.7.12). Augustine's claims about infant experience are derived from the *observation* of children. Traherne's evidence is supposedly stronger, rooted in what he claims to be the legitimacy of a remembered account of *what it was like* to be an infant. Whereas, for Augustine, language acquisition marks an extension of an always already present desire to "vent out" into and then exert mastery over the world, for Traherne, preverbal experience is instead exhausted in an absolute passivity: "My Essence was Capacitie," as he claims in "My Spirit." Prior to his entrance into language, Traherne writes in "Dumnesse," everything came "with Voices and Instructions"—"evry Stone, and evry Star [possessed] a Tongue"—but from the moment Traherne "gained a Tongue, there Power began to die" (6:23, 62–69). Language interrupts the passive receptivity to the world that enables the pure enjoyment of infant experience. The moment that Traherne "gained a Tongue," he entered the constant push and pull of Augustinian lack and desire, for this structure is learned, acquired from the "other Noises" that are produced by a fallen human culture: "having once inspird me with a Sence / Of forrein Vanities," these acquired noises are then amplified within the self until they acquire the strength to "march out thence / In troops that Cover and despoyl my Coasts, / Being tho Invisible, most Hurtfull Hosts" (6:23–24, 70–79). Language "Cover[s]" the natural world with inherited cultural categories, invisibly draping the contours of everything with the "Nois" and corruption of both intersubjective community and historically realized ways of knowing. In Traherne's view, once one has learned to speak, it becomes all but impossible to return to the state of passivity in which the world appears unsullied by the categories of culture. This is why it is only by "the Gift of GOD"—by the power of revelation—that Traherne is able to "remember" his originary experience "till now" (5:93; bk. 3, sec. 1).

If Traherne's view of language acquisition revises the Augustinian narrative of human development, it is also at odds with the vision articulated by Milton. Far from a corrupting medium that leads individual human beings into the clutches of a fallen culture, language is, in Milton's eyes, a vibrant force for good that opens the possibility of understanding and communication. Consider once more the opening lines of "At a Vacation Exercise in the College," which describes in positive terms the process described in Traherne's "Dumnesse":

> Hail native language, that by sinews weak
> Didst move my first endeavouring tongue to speak,
> And mad'st imperfect words with childish trips,

Half unpronounced, slide through my infant lips,
Driving dumb silence from the portal door,
Where he had mutely sat two years before. (*Shorter Poems*, 79, 1–6)

Milton describes how speech emerges from "dumb silence" when an active "endeavouring tongue" is passively moved by a preexisting language. For Traherne, it was a good thing that the "Holy Door, / Or Gate of Souls was closed" prior to the acquisition of language, but for Milton the "Driving [of] dumb silence from the portal door" marks the entry of eloquence, the end of a "silence" that is "dumb" both because it exists without speech and because, in the absence of language, it remains unintelligent. This celebration of language is reflected in *Paradise Lost*, which employs the inset, first-person, retrospective narratives inherited from the epic tradition as a platform for Adam and Eve to describe a form of unfallen life in which language is inextricable from and necessarily coterminous with human existence. In postlapsarian life, human beings are born with the capacity to *learn* one or more languages, a process that takes years. In Milton's Paradise, Adam and Eve are created with the capacity to speak; there is no learning involved, no intergenerational inheritance of strategies for naming and ordering. Preverbal human life in *Paradise Lost* exists only in the brief period prior to the moments when Adam and Eve actualize their ready-made capacity to speak. Their language is a pure and unfallen medium of communication, used with ease to name and address the world's many creatures: "to speak I tried, and forthwith spake," recalls Adam of his first utterance, delivered only moments after he awakens, "My tongue obeyed and readily could name / Whate'er I saw" (8.271–73).

The difference between Milton's and Traherne's understanding of language is partly attributable to the degree of harmony they envision between originary experience and its context. Milton's Adam and Eve awaken in an unfallen world without the faintest hint of corruption, while in infancy Traherne experiences his own unfallen existence within the broader context of fallen human culture; as the medium enabling all manner of vitiated norms, relations, and institutions, language must, in Traherne's view, carry depravity within it. In conveying the beginnings of human consciousness, then, each writer was faced with a different mimetic problem. Milton needed to find a verbal decorum adequate to the depiction of paradisal originary experience, the inner life of unfallen beings that have not sinned and are not yet mortal. Traherne was forced to invent a mode of writing capable of describing in words a pure infant experience completely untouched by language.

THE DIFFERENCE VERSE MAKES

Traherne's obsessive treatment of originary experience is a critical tool for working out the sorts of thinking that his use of verse makes possible. For Traherne, in order to live a fulfilling life, one must see everything as though one were a stranger in the world, a newcomer untouched by corrupting customs and therefore able to apprehend the beauty and wonder of things as they really are. To truly see oneself and one's place in the world, one must see things as a fetus or an infant. Only then can one live a life of felicity. Since Traherne articulated nearly identical versions of this idea in both prose and verse, his corpus provides an unusual point of entry to consider the sort of thinking made possible in and through verse. To what extent does verse form inflect the power and efficacy of a given thought?

To ask such questions of Traherne is to return with new eyes to an older moment in the history of criticism. In recent decades, the discoveries of multiple new Traherne texts—*Commentaries of Heaven*, *Kingdom of God*, *A Sober View*, *Seeds of Eternity*, and so on—has changed the course of Traherne criticism. The best recent scholarship has drawn on these newly discovered and now finally edited manuscripts to place Traherne in his historical moment, to demonstrate that he was not just the proto-Romantic that the poetry and prose discovered at the end of the nineteenth century suggested he was. Most recent criticism has thus focused primarily on Traherne's *ideas* and their relationship to theological and political contexts.

By contrast, earlier critics—relying mainly on the poetry in the Dobell Folio and the prose of the *Centuries*—were driven by questions about how the verse should be valued in relation to the prose. For instance, in her 1936 study of religious poetry, Helen C. White claimed that although Traherne "may be the most original" of the seventeenth-century poets commonly classed as "metaphysical," and "in a good many ways as a man and a thinker, [he is] the most interesting," when viewed "simply as a poet" Traherne is "almost certainly to be put below" Donne, Herbert, Crashaw, and Vaughan.[69] The reason assigned for this judgment is the prosiness of Traherne's verse, the fact that he does not do with verse form what critics expect great poets to do. Writing in 1911, little more than a decade after the original rediscovery of Traherne, F. E. Hutchinson claimed that the poet "achieved more unquestionable success with his prose than with his verse" because "as a poet Traherne has not mastered his technique" and his "poems are often diffuse."[70] In T. S. Eliot's 1930 judgment, Traherne was "more mystic than poet," for he "has not the richness and variety of imagery which poetry needs; and in his prose the matter and expression are much better adapted to each other."[71]

Where Traherne's prose succeeds, his verse fails. And the problem, according to these early critics, is that his verse seems to be modeled on prose. This was the 1945 judgment of Douglas Bush: "The *Centuries of Meditation* are generally ranked above the poems, since it is the poet who is chiefly given to prosaic stumbling and incoherent diffuseness, but the two portions of his work are as like in substance and manner as prose and verse can be. Both prose and verse are all 'News,' a series of mainly lyrical variations on Traherne's one great theme." For Bush, the problem with Traherne's verse is that it is "given to prosaic stumbling." Traherne's explicit avoidance of "curling metaphors" do not, in Bush's view, enable the poet to "roll all his sweetness up into a ball."[72] His verse is too linear, too diffuse, too like prose. Indeed, Bush sees Traherne's poetry and prose "as like in substance and manner" as "can be." I want to tarry with the residual difference registered in this "can be" by returning to Bush's insight while bracketing the question of value. Focusing on the depiction of embryonic consciousness in "The Salutation," I isolate the forms of thinking that even Traherne, with his ostensibly prosy style, reserves for verse.

As we have seen, descriptions of prenatal and infant experience are everywhere in Traherne's prose. Recall the opening of the spiritual autobiography in the *Centuries*:

> Those Pure and Virgin Apprehensions I had from the Womb, and that Divine Light wherewith I was born, are the Best unto this Day, wherein I can see the Universe. By the gift of GOD they attended me into the World, and by his Special favor I remember them till now. . . . Certainly Adam in Paradise had not more sweet and curious Apprehensions of the World, then I when I was a child. All appeared New, and Strange, at the first, inexpressibly rare, and Delightfull, and Beautifull. I was a little Stranger which at my entrance into the world was saluted and surrounded by innumerable Joys. (5:93, bk.3, sec.1–2)

Despite the radical nature of Traherne's claims—the rejection of the precursors we have examined in part 2 of this book—his prose is confident. Steady in its presentation of temporal order, it is written in the present, a "now" in which Traherne "remember[s]" his time in the womb and the first days after his birth, the recollected apprehensions of which remain the best way to see the world "unto this day." When Traherne was a child, he possessed Adamic "apprehensions of the world" that he can recall "now" in the moment of writing: "All things were spotless and pure and glorious; yea, and infinitely mine." Without any understanding of mortality or of change in time, to Traherne it was as if "all things abided Eternaly as they were in their Proper Places" (5:94, bk. 3, sec. 3). Writing from an adult perspective in which mortality and temporality are all-too-familiar existential facts but from which the radically different perspective of infancy remains available through memory, Traherne inscribes in his prose the difference between now and then. But at the same time, he insists that readers should "pray for" the apprehensions that he remembers and is now attempting to teach through experience. The point of the autobiographical retelling of infant memories is to teach readers how to see the world one knows as an adult as though it were the world of infancy, when everything was "new, strange, and inexpressibly delightful." The prose insists on the separation of the present from the past even as it works to show readers how to see the present through the past.

Traherne's verse dwells at length on the originary scene when consciousness first blossoms into existence. Consider "The Salutation" once more:

These little Limmes,
These Eys and Hands which here I find,
These rosie Cheeks wherwith my Life begins,
Where have ye been? Behind
What Curtain were ye from me hid so long!
Where was? In what Abyss, my Speaking Tongue?

When silent I,
So many thousand thousand years,
Beneath the Dust did in a Chaos lie,
How could I Smiles or Tears,
Or Lips or Hands or Eys or Ears perceive?
Welcom ye Treasures which I now receiv.

. . .

From Dust I rise,
And out of Nothing now awake,
These Brighter Regions which salute mine Eys,
A Gift from GOD I take.
The Earth, the Seas, the Light, the Day, the Skies,
The Sun and Stars are mine; if those I prize.

Long time before
I in my Mothers Womb was born,
A GOD preparing did this Glorious Store,
The World for me adorne.

Into this Eden so Divine and fair,
So Wide and Bright, I come his Son and Heir.

A Stranger here
Strange Things doth meet, strange Glories see;
Strange Treasures lodg'd in this fair World appear,
Strange all, and New to me.
But that they mine should be, who nothing was,
That Strangest is of all, yet brought to pass. (6:3–4, 2–49)

This poem articulates many of the ideas expressed in the *Centuries*. In the prose work, Traherne was a "little Stranger" at his "Entrance into the World," when "all appeared New and Strange," while in "The Salutation," Traherne is a "Stranger" who sees how "Strange Treasures lodg'd in this fair World appear, / Strange all, and New to me." In the *Centuries*, Traherne recalls "Those Pure and Virgin Apprehensions I had from the Womb, and that Divine Light wherewith I was born," while in verse he focuses on the moment when "I in my Mothers Womb was born."

If prose and verse are almost isomorphic, the starkest difference between the two does not, I argue, lie only in the most obvious formal features of the verse: line breaks and rhymes. To be sure, these features are important for Traherne, but in many ways the verse remains quite prosaic. Consider this version of the third stanza rewritten without line breaks: "I that so long Was Nothing from Eternitie did little think such Joys as Ear or Tongue to Celebrate or See: Such Sounds to hear, such Hands to feel, [or] such Feet Beneath the Skies, on such a Ground to meet" (6:3, 16–21). The sentence reads a little oddly as prose. It would, for instance, sound smoother to modern ears if the infinitive verbs—"to hear," "to feel," "to meet," and so on—preceded instead of followed their accompanying noun phrases: "to feel such Hands" sounds more intuitive than "such Hands to feel." But on the whole what critics have described as the "diffuseness" of the verse makes it quite similar to Traherne's prose.

So what, if anything, truly differentiates these two forms of writing? Was verse a distinctive medium through which Traherne thought? The feature that most distinguishes the account of originary experience provided in "The Salutation" from that provided in the *Centuries* is exactly what enables Traherne to *think* in and through poetic form: namely, the presentation of time made possible in verse. "The Salutation" repeats the memories described in the *Centuries*, but the poem deliberately and consistently eschews the conventions of temporal linearity that structure the prose, and, for that matter, the recollected "stories" told in the inspiration for Traherne's approach: *Paradise Lost*. In the *Centuries*, Traherne recalls a memory in the present so that he can "teach" readers "by Experience" how to see the world in terms of his remembered "Virgin Apprehensions." By contrast, Traherne's verse collapses past into present, thereby *performing* the goal toward which the prose must labor. This strategy is visible in the demonstrative pronouns with which Traherne begins each text. In the *Centuries*, he invokes *"Those* Pure and Virgin apprehensions I had from the womb," while in the opening lines of "The Salutation" he focuses on *"These* little Limmes, / *These* Eys and Hands which here I find." As the deictic *here* and the present tense of the initial verb (*find*) make obvious, the pronoun *those* refers, in the words of Benjamin Norton's 1735 *New English Dictionary*, to "persons or things at a distance from one," while *these* refers to "things near to one."[73]

By pointing out that this poem is written in the present tense and refers to a here and a now, I am saying something more than, "Look! This poem is written in what critics call 'the lyric present.'" Jonathan Culler has recently argued that the use of the present tense in lyric poetry stresses that the events invoked in such poems "happen now, in time, but in an iterable *now* of lyric enunciation, rather than in a now of linear time."[74] The present of the lyric is, for Culler, a "'floating now,'" which is "repeated each time the poem is read" in the "present of enunciation."[75] Surely this is true of Traherne's poem and many others. But in "The Salutation" Traherne uses this common feature of lyric poetry to think the beginnings of thought, the *now* in which both ego and world first emerge, the moment in utero when "Life begins," and it becomes possible to "find" and "perceive" the soul, the flesh of the body, and their relationship to a surrounding milieu. Traherne attempts to articulate the present moment in which presence itself first becomes possible. He wants to put into words the exact *now* in which the "Speaking Tongue" first emerged from the abyss of nothingness and acquired the potential for speech. Here, he says, is where poetry begins.

Given Traherne's idiosyncratic personal mythology, remembered access to this "now" belongs to him and him alone. But given his desire to teach readers how to see the world here and now by retelling his experience, "The Salutation" also expresses an invitation to imagine what it would be like to be present at the birth of consciousness, when absolutely everything was "new and strange." Drawn, as we saw in chapter 3, from the meditations on *ekstasis* in Trismegistus's *Asclepius*, Traherne's own theory of thought holds that such an imaginative feat is possible. Human thought always projects one outside of oneself: the ego exists beside or beyond itself because it exists where and when it is carried by its thoughts. Even if his readers cannot remember the moment when phenomenality first appeared, they can project themselves into that moment through the ecstatic powers of thought. They can occupy the position of the lyric *I*, and use the poem to think their way inside the here and now when "I in my Mothers Womb was born."

As the past tense of this line suggests, "The Salutation" uses what Culler calls the lyric present in order to perform the conflation of infant and adult perspectives that the prose explicitly aims to elicit but does not itself enact. Traherne does not want his readers to be infants; he wants adult readers to see the world *as if* they were infants. "The Salutation" brings readers into the now when consciousness was born, but it also tries to bring this "past present" of infancy into the adult world. Consider stanza 5 once more:

> From Dust I rise,
> And out of Nothing now awake,
> These Brighter Regions which salute mine Eys,
> A Gift from GOD I take.
> The Earth, the Seas, the Light, the Day, the Skies,
> The Sun and Stars are mine; if those I prize.

The "now" of the second line situates the time of the poem at the moment when "From Dust I rise / And out of Nothing now awake," when the light of first-person consciousness first appears out of the "Dust" of the body and what Traherne considers the essential nothingness of inanimate creation. But the conditional "if those I prize" with which the stanza concludes subtly reframes this *now*: it becomes not simply the now of originary awakening and of the poem's enunciation but also the now in which the reader might actually value the earth, seas, light, and so on as her own, as a God-given gift that can be taken and enjoyed. The conditional "if" does not apply to the embryo but to the adult author and reader, both of whom make choices and have a say in the matter.

The acknowledgment of the adult present encoded in this "if" shapes the reader's entry into stanza 6:

> Long time before
> I in my Mothers Womb was born,
> A GOD preparing did this Glorious Store,
> The World for me adorne.
> Into this Eden so Divine and fair,
> So Wide and Bright, I come his Son and Heir.

The stanza opens with a temporal in-between. At first it seems as though the "Long time before" stretches from the adult present at the end of stanza 5 back to the moment in the past when "I in my Mothers Womb was born." To be sure, the third line qualifies this sense, for Traherne claims that God was "preparing" and "adorn[ing]" the "World" a "Long time" before "I . . . was born." Yet the past tense of "was born" nevertheless distinguishes this birth from the full present of the fifth stanza's "now awake." Thus when the stanza closes with the claim that "Into this Eden so Divine and fair, / So Wide and Bright, I come his Son and Heir," the present tense "I come" is double: it refers to the emergence into the world initiated at the moment his unfallen ego was born in utero and to the acknowledgment in the fallen, adult present that the speaker will try to see the world for what it still is (an "Eden so Divine and fair"). Although the verse may be prosy, as many earlier critics have argued, it remains a vehicle for thought capable of mobilizing grammatical and stylistic conventions in ways that enable Traherne to perform the thought he struggles to describe in prose. For Traherne, the point of what Culler calls "the lyric present" is the extent to which it enables the performance of a radically defamiliarized presence. If Milton uses the conventions of epic narrative to invite readers to identify with a mimetic representation of Adam and Eve at the birth of human consciousness, Traherne draws on the affordances of lyric poetry to mimetically perform the Edenic consciousness of birth here in the fallen adult world.

PART 3

Locke and the Life of Consciousness

CHAPTER FIVE

Natality and Empiricism

PRINCIPIO

John Locke's *Essay Concerning Human Understanding* is a landmark in the history of modern epistemology. Many of its arguments about human mindedness remain influential today. Yet although this text and especially Locke's formulation of the tabula rasa as the image for infant human mindedness are familiar to many philosophers, intellectual historians, and literary critics, the importance of originary experience in Locke's book has gone all but unremarked. This lack of critical attention is surprising, since, as we will see, the *Essay* is grounded on the embryonic consciousness of fetuses and infants. In this chapter, I draw out the implications of a tension that emerges from Locke's treatment of originary experience. On the one hand, insofar as the *Essay* is dedicated to determining the "original" of human understanding, Locke needs to trace the source of human ideas back to the very beginning, where and when they first emerged. On the other hand, insofar as the *Essay* argues that all ideas are derived from experience, Locke cannot make positive claims about embryonic thought. His method requires access to a state that is blocked by his own method. To solve this problem, the *Essay* draws on the resources of poetry, deploying a set of minimally mimetic fictions—figures that exist in time and space, among particulars, but are nevertheless general, types or everymen—that support his epistemological agenda.[1]

I am not the first reader to see these issues as central to Locke's *Essay*. Just as the importance of neonatal maturity to Milton's *Paradise Lost* was discovered by Traherne, so the role played by originary experience in the *Essay* was first noted by Thomas Gray, a poet who elaborated on Locke's treatment of both embryonic consciousness and poetic thinking. Late in 1740, Gray set out to describe the primal scene of originary experience conjured so many times throughout Traherne's corpus: the advent of sensation in the womb. First published in 1775 as part of William Mason's *Memoirs of the Life and Writings of Mr Gray*, this unfinished poem, abandoned by Gray in 1742 and entitled *De principiis cogitandi*, celebrates Locke's epistemology in verse. Locke is, in Gray's estimation, the "great priest of truth" who has disclosed "the unseen causes of things." Gray aims merely to "mark [Locke's] faint footprints and to follow, albeit with hesitant tread."[2] If his treatment of the "primordial origins . . . of the human individual" has struck some critics as "extraordinary,"[3] from the vantage point of the archive unearthed in this book, *De principiis cogitandi* is not a historical anomaly but part of a discourse many decades in the making: the effort to intertwine consciousness with natality that we have seen in the works of Milton and Traherne, but also in the writings of Culverwell, Harvey, Descartes, and others. Locke's *Essay* takes up, reworks, and popularizes this heritage, positioning the experience of natality as the bedrock for a philosophical system. Gray's poem performs what the *Essay* suggests but cannot—because of its intellectual commitments—fully endorse. Usually translated as "On the Principles of Thinking," *De principiis cogitandi* might also be rendered as "On the Beginnings of Thinking." Gray's poem fuses empiricism and natality in an effort to generate a philosophically grounded mimetic account of what it is like for the conscious life of a human being to begin.

According to Gray, *De principiis cogitandi* was a "metaphysical poem."[4] What might it mean to turn Locke's philosophy into a poem? Mason provided a straightforward answer by arguing that Gray attempted "to make the same use of Mr. Locke's Essay on the Human Understanding, which Lucretius did of the Dogmas of Epicurus."[5] In other words, by recognizing Locke's importance and responding to the vogue for Lucretius that preoccupied many English intellectuals in the first half of the eighteenth century, Gray versified Locke with honeyed words, making the philosopher's doctrines sweeter, more appealing.[6] Although this answer is straightforward enough, it does not account for why Gray would think that a "metaphysical poem" is, as he put it in a 1641 letter to his friend Richard West, a "contradiction in terms."[7] After all, Lucretius's *De rerum natura* might, along with many other verse treatises, be described as a "metaphysical poem"; seen from one perspective, there was ample historical precedent for Gray's endeavor.

When placed in the intellectual and literary context that I have elaborated in *Coming To*, it should not come as a surprise that the contradiction Gray sees in the conjunction of metaphysics and poetry springs from the line of early modern Aristotelian thought inherited by such writers as Milton and Traherne. In the *Poetics*, Aristotle claims that Empedocles's verse treatises should not be considered poetry because, as Renaissance thinkers like Philip Sidney would also insist, verse, meter, rhyme, and other features of the formal language sometimes considered to be isomorphic poetry are not, in fact, integral to poetry.[8] As we have seen in the introduction and throughout this book, many early modern writers took mimesis to be the *differentia* that distinguishes poetry from other forms of discourse. Since metaphysics is directed toward the most general of concepts, and mimetic poetry exists on the horizon of particularity, a "metaphysical poem" is indeed a "contradiction in terms." This is what makes Gray's endeavor so difficult: in order to turn Locke's philosophy into a poem, he needed to blend concept with mimesis, to find the universal not merely in the patterns of a given unity of human actions (to summarize Aristotle's claim in the *Poetics*) but also in the lived existence of the human species. Locke's treatise aspires to explain human understanding in general, as it should work for all human beings. Can one provide a mimetic account of species being? This is the question to which Gray's "contradictory" and unfinished poem attempts to respond.[9] His answer clarifies the extent to which originary experience and mimesis are entangled in Locke's *Essay*. *De principiis cogitandi* discloses the poetic foundations of Locke's philosophy both by crystallizing the originary experience upon which it is built and by representing Locke's narrative of epistemological development in explicitly mimetic terms, thereby spotlighting the role played by mimesis in the *Essay*.

Gray's poem interweaves its own beginning with the beginning of human mindedness. This stress on beginnings is evident in the poem's opening lines, to an absurd degree:

Unde Animus scire incipiat: quibus incohet orsa
Principiis seriem rerum, tenuemque catenam
Mnemosyne: Ratio unde rudi sub pectore tardum
Augeat imperium; et primum mortalibus aegris
Ira, Dolor, Metus, et Curae nascantur inanes,
Hinc canere aggredior. (1.1–6)

[From what origins the Mind begins to have knowledge; from what beginnings the Muse of Memory arises and sets in order the sequence of events and her slender chain; whence Reason spreads its slow mastery in the savage breast; and whence anger, grief, fear and insubstantial cares are first born to wretched mortals; it is from these matters that I begin my song.] (328–29, translation modified)

Incipio and *principium* jostle in the first two lines of Gray's poem as beginnings from whence [*unde*] knowledge, memory, and such passions as
anger and grief are "first born" [*primum . . . nascantur*]. The first two lines
alone feature *incipio, incohet, ordior,* and *principium,* all of which carry
meanings related to beginning. Through this proliferation of beginnings,
Gray attempts to articulate the cognitive origins that underpin his ability to
write such a poem. In lines addressed to West, Gray asks for patience: "Do
not despise the simple poem nor the poet; for these beginnings [*primordia*],
though small, will give rise to no trivial activities" (329, 1.16–19).[10] Perhaps
tipping his hat to the opening lines of *Paradise Lost,* Gray conflates poem
and subject: the *primordia* to which he refers are both the first lines of the
poem and, at the same time, the first beginnings through which any and all
phenomena emerge—the "origin" [*origine*] of the arts, wisdom, virtue, and
even the "Muse herself" (329, 1.20–31). In the beginning of his poem, Gray's
topic is conceptual, general. Concerned with how the "Mind" acquires
knowledge, how "Memory" first works, how "Reason" becomes operative,
and how passions "are first born," Gray begins in the sphere of abstraction.

This emphasis on the general begins to soften as Gray's story shifts from
abstract concepts to the body within which they are found in a particular-
ized form. Like Locke, Gray is concerned not with an abstract conception of
understanding but with how understanding emerges in the life of individual
human beings, a process that begins with the initial flickering of sensitivity in the embryonic body. Every phenomenon springs from the primordial
flesh and nerves by means of which a sentient body is stitched together in
utero. "In the beginning [*Principio*]," Gray intones at the outset of an account of human generation pitched in the explanatory register of Genesis
itself, "when all-creating Nature confirmed the great covenant and ordered
divine souls to grow in sluggish bodies," she wanted to ensure that the soul
did not "exercise its special powers in isolation, lest it despise the jointed
limbs of the mass to which it was bound, forgetful of their weight and conscious [*conscia*] only of its celestial flame" (329, 1.32–38). The soul is never
conscious of its own powers in isolation. Consciousness emerges only
through the soul's attachment to body. This is why Nature "arrange[s] that
the fibres of the nerves should tremble in every part in innumerable ducts;
and, distributing them throughout the body, she interwove the branches
everywhere, a sensitive network [*sensile textum*]" (329, 1.39–41). Human
beings are, from the very beginning, thoroughly sensitive, susceptible, like
the *punctum saliens* we saw Harvey theorize in chapter 4, to the slight-
est sensations, all of which "hurry emulously to present themselves to the
mind [*menti*]" (329, 1.62–63).

Touch is the most basic sensation; it takes "the leading part [*Primas tactus agit partes*] and first [*primus*] lays open the dark route for the tiny throng [of sensations]" (329, 1.64) distributed throughout the embryo's body—from "the marrow and the vitals" to the "outermost web of the skin" (330, 1.68), coextensive with bodily life both spatially and temporally:

Necdum etiam matris puer eluctatus ab alvo
Multiplices solvit tunicas, et vincula rupit;
Sopitus molli somno, tepidoque liquore
Circumfusus adhuc: tactus tamen aura lacessit
Iamdudum levior sensus, animamque reclusit. (1.70–74)

[Even before the child has struggled from the mother's womb and broken through his many layers of covering and burst his bonds; while he is still drugged with soft sleep and surrounded in warm fluid, a slight breath has already stimulated his sense of touch and released his soul.] (330, translation modified)

In the opening lines of the poem, Gray thus moves from a consideration of mind in general, through an account of how human bodies first become sensitive, to a focus on an individual male child [*puer*] in the womb, a singular being whose senses have just begun to be "stimulated." This *puer* will remain the protagonist for the rest of the poem. As I have argued throughout *Coming To*, human beginnings encourage the union of concept and mimesis. Gray's poem weaves a consideration of human understanding in general into the slow development of a particular child from originary experience in the womb, through his birth and exposure to the world, toward the acquisition of knowledge. As his conscious life begins, surrounded [*circumfusus*] by amniotic fluid, the fetus's soul is awakened by the sense of touch. Playing on the etymological connections between *anima* as soul and *anima* as breath, Gray claims that a slight *aura* or breath—coterminous with touch—unlocks the *anima* from a state of complete slumber. This is the moment when the sensitivity of living tissue—recall chapter 4's discussion of Dante's *spungo marino* and Harvey's zoophytes—is nudged into the sphere of human thought, into what Gray later calls the "field of awareness" [*Notitiae campus*] (331, 1.169). Gray imagines the moment when a fetus becomes conscious. He brings readers into the scene of first impressions explored by Milton and Traherne.

What is the content of a human being's first thought? By this point in the book, Gray's answer should be familiar. Recall Descartes's response to

Hyperaspistes: "It seems most reasonable to think that a mind newly united to an infant's body is wholly occupied in perceiving in a confused way or feeling the ideas of pain, pleasure, heat, cold, and other similar ideas which arise from its union and, as it were, intermingling with the body" (CSM 3:190). But even as Descartes holds that the only form of *conscientia* available to an embryonic mind is the pleasures and pains of the body in relation to an ambient milieu, he also argues that the mind is endowed with innate ideas, stamped with indelible characters that exist even if they cannot be consciously accessed. As soon as the fetus acquires mind, "it has in itself," Descartes argues, "the ideas of God, of itself and of all such truths as are called self-evident, in the same way as adult human beings have these ideas when they are not attending to them; . . . I have no doubt that were it released from the prison of the body, it would find them within itself" (CSM 3:190). All humans possess ideas they have not yet actively thought. Even if a given adult is not, at this very moment, pondering the idea of God, he nevertheless possesses that idea *in potentia*, within his mental reservoir. The same holds for fetuses. The ideas are *there*, but they cannot be accessed because the mind of the fetus is too closely bound to the pleasures, pains, and needs of the body. If the mind were "released" from the body, it would, "no doubt," apprehend these ideas. Descartes's conditional "were it released" flags the major difference between his account and the story told in Gray's poem.

In *De principiis cogitandi*, "all-creating Nature" ordered that souls "grow [*inolescere*] in sluggish bodies" (329, 1.32–33). The human soul is not "implanted" as Descartes and many others argued; instead it *grows*. The verb *inolesco* has a rich heritage. Virgil uses it in the *Georgics* when describing how the practice of grafting requires the gardener to "insert a bud" into an "alien tree" and then "teach it go grow [*inolescere*] into the sappy bark"; in the *Aeneid* Anchises informs Aeneas how the "plagues of the body" remain with the soul even after death, for these taints are "long ingrained," and the body and soul have, during life on earth, "grown [*inolescere*] together" in a wondrous manner.[11] If Virgil's *Aeneid* captures the aftereffects of the mutual ingrowing of body and soul, Gray follows Dante's *Purgatorio* in accounting for the beginning of this temporary union by stressing the extent to which Nature cultivates the growth of soul into body. Precisely in order to prevent the "release" of the soul that Descartes imagines, Gray's Nature distributes the sensitivity of the soul "throughout the body" in "innumerable," "trembling" fibers. From the initial moment of generation, soul is immanent to body. Indeed, when the *puer* awakens into his own mindedness, this process is initiated, as we have just seen, by touch; the sense that "releases" or "lays open" [*reclusit*] consciousness is also the sense most basic to bodily life.

Gray's commitment to Locke leads him to isolate touch as the bodily sense that ushers originary experience into being. As *De principiis cogitandi* continues, Gray sketches the basic elements of Locke's epistemological theory. All ideas enter the mind by way of sensory exposure to the outside world or through the perception of one's own mental operations: "The mind stirs up by some inner sense images of its own functions and consciously examines its own features [*Sic sensu interno rerum simulacra suarum / Mens ciet, et proprios observat conscia vultus*]" (331, 152–53). Gray even adopts scenes from Locke's *Essay*. For instance, Gray's "for the first time [*primum*], the bright face of light is revealed, . . . it is then that the newborn eyes first [*primum*] drink in the sunlight unknown before" recalls Locke's description of newborn children in the *Essay*: "And how covetous the Mind is, to be furnished with all such *Ideas*, as we have no pain accompanying them, may be a little guess'd, by what is observable in Children new-born, who always turn their Eyes to that part, from whence the Light comes, lay them how you please" (145, 2.9.7). Gray tracks Locke's argument dutifully. But by beginning with the *principium* of human thought, *De principiis cogitandi* reveals an aspect of the *Essay* that remains under-analyzed and is still all but invisible despite what I argue is its vital importance to Locke's thought. Locke pursues a project of "metaphysical deflationism," as Kathryn Tabb puts it, that admits only "experience" as a source of knowledge.[12] As Gray's poem suggests, however, Locke's appeal to experience is subtended by the originary experience to which this book is dedicated, an experience that is impossible for normal human beings to access. To render his account of such an experience probable, Locke relies implicitly on the resources of mimesis, situating his epistemology within a skeleton narrative that traces the development of an imagined individual from the acquisition of his first ideas toward intellectual maturity. As Gray's poem suggests, Locke deploys a minimal form of mimesis.

Locke is far from the first philosopher to write in this way. For my purposes, Montaigne serves as an illustrative antecedent, for he is a writer who blends an examination of absolute particularity with far-reaching generality. *C'est moy que je peins*, "it is myself that I portray" (2; 26), he declares in "Au lecteur," the prefatory note to a book that discusses its author's singular dietary, sexual, medical, affective, and intellectual proclivities. Montaigne "offers to the view one [man] in particular," as he puts it in "Du repentir," but this depiction of a singular human life approaches the generality of the concept *human being* for "Every man bears the entire form of the human

condition" [*Chaque homme porte la forme entire de l'humaine condition*].
In portraying his own "universal being" [*mon estre universel*], Montaigne
writes simultaneously about every human being (611; 845, 3.2, translation
modified). In "De la force de l'imagination," he suggests that this blend-
ing of the general and the particular is indebted to Aristotle's conception
of poetry as a discourse that straddles the contingent particularity of history and the universality of philosophical abstraction: "There are authors
whose end is to tell what has happened. Mine, if I could attain it, would be
to talk about what can happen [*ce qui peut advenir*]" (75; 108, 1.20). This
nearly verbatim quotation from Aristotle's *Poetics*—"the poet's function is
to describe, not the thing that has happened, but a kind of thing that might
happen, i.e., what is possible as being probable or necessary" (2:2322–23;
1451a)—positions Montaigne's philosophical project in the realm of *poiesis*.
Montaigne welds particular to general by exercising the poet's ability to
sound the limits of the probable in order to articulate what "can happen."

Locke performs something approximating an inversion of Montaigne's
approach. Instead of finding the contours of the general human condition
amid the welter and noise of a particular life as it is mimetically represented,
Locke articulates the general features of human intellectual development
by crafting an account of a posited human being stripped of all particularity
except for his status as an individual. This mimetic approach to epistemology is necessitated by the seriousness with which Locke treats the concept
of consciousness. Since consciousness is nothing other than the appearance
of all the various somethings that might appear to someone—since, that
is, particularity is baked into the very concept—Locke needs to ground his
philosophy of mind in a form of writing that is at least minimally mimetic.
In order to understand human mindedness as it is organized around and
through consciousness, Locke's *Essay* draws on the resources of poetry both
insofar as it depends on a fiction of originary experience that is impossible
to verify experientially and because it depicts this fiction in terms of a representation of, to borrow Aristotle's words, "a kind of thing that might happen, i.e. what is possible as being probable or necessary" (2.2322–23; 1451a).
Locke's discomfort with this aspect of his thinking shapes his argument.

By claiming that Locke's philosophy exploits the resources of poetry, I
am not arguing that Locke is a poet like Milton and Traherne. These latter
writers use verse to craft vivid mimetic representations, scenes of human
life that convey what Milton calls the "simple, sensuous, and passionate"
nature of existence in a fictional but probable phenomenal world.[13] When
he borrows from poetry, then, Locke uses only the lever of fiction calibrated
through minimal mimesis. Since the abstract fictions at play in many of

Locke's famous thought experiments do not conform to the standards of mimesis in question in this book, I set aside most of them in this chapter. Instead, I focus on how Locke organizes his epistemology around a narrative of intellectual development that traces the growth of a human mind onward from a necessarily fictional—albeit highly probable—originary experience.[14] This narrative is minimally mimetic both because it follows the life trajectory of a posited individual human being and because Locke's commitment to experience and consciousness as the bedrock of his epistemology means that he needs to embed this individual human life within all of the particulars that show up to human beings living in the world. The child is, in effect, a type. Because Locke's narrative is a general account of human intellectual development as such, it cannot be fully particular. But at the same time, since his empiricist commitments entail that all knowledge is ultimately grounded in particular sensations, his account cannot be fully general. The particular ideas (of objects, feelings, and so on) that make up the intellectual world of Locke's posited human individual are never depicted vividly as *there*, in the way that, say, Milton describes the trees of Eden. Rather, they come and go as so many exempla—replicable insofar as they are particular instances of a given thing (*"Whiteness, Hardness, Sweetness, Thinking, Motion, Man, Elephant, Army, Drunkenness, and others"* [104, 2.1.1] to borrow the list of words expressive of ideas that Locke provides in the opening of book 2 in the *Essay*), but nevertheless necessary insofar as they are required by the particularity that defines how the phenomenal world appears.[15] Like the poet of Aristotle's *Poetics*, Locke straddles a middle ground between the abstract universal and the phenomenal particular.

HUMAN NATALITY AND ADAMIC BEGINNINGS

The first appearance of consciousness is ground zero for Locke's account of human understanding, his inquiry "into the *Original* of those *Ideas*, Notions, or whatever else you please to call them, which a Man observes, and is conscious to himself he has in his Mind" (44, 1.1.3). An *idea* is the "Object" of thought, the phenomenon that appears whenever "a Man thinks" (47, 1.1.8). If David Hume would later disambiguate impressions from ideas, Locke, like Descartes before him, claims that any object of thought— whether it be perceived, felt, intuited, remembered, imagined, and so on— counts as an idea.[16] Locke's *Essay* attempts to think the *principium* of human thought. He aims to do so through what he calls a "Historical, plain method" that provides a genetic account of human knowledge, what I have been calling a minimally mimetic narrative about the "Ways, whereby our

Understandings come to attain those Notions of Things we have" (44,
1.1.2).[17] In telling this story, Locke must begin with the simplest and earliest ideas possessed by human beings and show how these "Originals" lead
to the most complex ideas. Locke must begin his *historia* at the beginning.

When the first edition of the *Essay* was published in 1689, beginnings
were something about which Locke had been thinking for decades and
across a variety of discourses. In the first draft of the *Essay*, written in 1671,
Locke affirms that beginnings entail a positive existence: "Beginning is the
first Instance of being or Existing & is not by any body conceived to be a
bare negation, but something positive."[18] This idea was important enough
that Locke preserved it through all of the published editions of the *Essay*
from 1689 onward. Locke holds a nominalist theory of individuation in
which it is the existence of a given thing that individuates it from other
things, and he fleshes out the relationship between this theory and his understanding of beginnings in his investigation of "Identity and Diversity,"
which was added to the *Essay* in the second edition of 1694. There he writes
that the *"principium Individuationis"* is nothing other than "Existence it
self, which determines a Being of any sort to a particular time and place
incommunicable to two Beings of the same kind." Locke takes up an atom
as an example of this principle. So long as a given atom exists, it is, at any
given "instant" of that existence "the same with it self," it is "what it is,
and nothing else" (330, 2.27.3). This theorization clarifies Locke's claim,
made in the first edition of the *Essay*, that beginning is "the first instant of
Being" belonging to a given existing thing (217, 2.17.14).

If Locke started to write about the "Original" of human thought in
1671, he turned his attention to the beginning of human politics as early
as 1679, when he began drafting what would become the *Two Treatises of
Government*, a text grounded in an examination of the claims made about
Adam's Edenic existence by Robert Filmer in *Patriarcha* (probably written
in the 1630s and early 1640s, but first published in 1680).[19] The *Essay* and
the *Two Treatises* were both published in 1689, and Locke worked on these
texts simultaneously in the decade leading up to their publication. It should
be no surprise, then, that the consideration of beginnings in each text co-
alesces around natality. Locke's treatments of epistemological and political
beginnings are mutually illuminating; the account of Adam provided in the
Two Treatises sheds light on Locke's understanding of originary experience
in the *Essay*.

Filmer's *Patriarcha* argues against the views of political contract laid
out by republican and Monarchomach theorists in the late sixteenth and
early seventeenth centuries.[20] Milton was a vocal proponent of the views

with which Filmer took issue. "No man who knows ought can be so stupid to deny that all men naturally were born free," writes Milton in defense of regicide in *The Tenure of Kings and Magistrates* (1649), summarizing a popular view.[21] If humans are "born free," they must consent to be ruled through a collective voluntary act that can also be collectively rescinded. The power of rulers is "nothing else, but what is only derivative, transferr'd, and committed to them in trust from the People"[22] Following in the footsteps of Hadrian Saravia and other apologists for monarchy, Filmer wrote *Patriarcha* against the view that "mankind is naturally endowed and born with freedom from all subjection."[23] This argument marks part of an attempt to determine "from whom" human rights and liberties "first came" (4). The answer to this question is Adam. Created by God as the "first" man, Adam was the initial "patriarch," and, as such, held "power" over his children, who in turn inherited that power "over their own children, but still with subordination to the first parent, who is lord paramount over his children's children to all generations" (6–7). In Filmer's view, order and stability depend on the maintenance and affirmation of this patriarchal lineage, which is subtended by the idea that, as Filmer clarifies in *The Anarchy*, since the "subjection of children to parents is natural, there can be no natural freedom." Human beings are not "born free," and they are similarly unfree when it comes to political order, which was established through and is still maintained in light of God's creation of Adam (142).

In the *Two Treatises*, Locke latches onto this connection between natality and political order. According to Locke, Filmer's "System" rests on two claims: first, "*all Government is absolute Monarchy*," an idea founded on the second—"*no Man is Born free*" (142, 1.1.2). To refute this "system," Locke must convince readers that human beings are in fact "born free," that freedom is a constitutive part of human nature. He must, that is, return to the fact on which the argument of *Patriarcha* is built, which is nothing other than Adam's createdness: "*Adam* being the only Man Created, and all ever since Being Begotten, no body has been born free" (176; 1.6.50). Only by establishing the nature of the relationship between Adam's creation and the natality of all subsequent human infants can Locke refute Filmer's attempt to "perswade all Men, that they are Slaves, and ought to be so" (141; 1.1.1.).[24]

Locke advances a number of arguments against Filmer's views—there is no reason for thinking, as Filmer does, that the notion of natural freedom denies the fact of Adam's createdness; in Genesis, God gives Adam sovereignty over animals and plants, not other human beings; and so on—but the one on which I focus uses natality to undermine the idea that human beings are born into a form of subjection stretching back to Adam's children. In the

First Treatise, Locke rejects Filmer's claim that Adam and all subsequent fathers are "sovereign" over their children by virtue of their fatherhood. This claim is ridiculous on a number of grounds, Locke argues, not least because mothers (including Eve) are equal "if not the greater" partners in the generation of children. Locke, whose interest in embryology and midwifery is well documented, knew much about how the child exists "a long time in [the mother's] own Body," where it is "fashion'd" and receives from her the "Materials and Principles of its Constitution."[25] Since it is "hard to imagine" that the "rational Soul should presently Inhabit the yet unformed Embrio, as soon as the Father has done his part in the Act of Generation," if the child owes anything to its parents, "it must certainly owe most to the Mother" (180, 1.6.55).

But Filmer's patriarchal obsession is problematic for an even more fundamental reason that forces Locke to think through the state of knowledge with regard to the beginnings of human life. Filmer argues that children are subject to their fathers because it is fathers who give their children *"Life and Being."* The problem with this position, Locke claims, is that its advocates fail to "remember God," who is the true giver of life:

> To give Life to that which has yet no being, is to frame and make a living Creature, fashion the parts, and mould and suit them to their uses, and having proportions' and fitted them together, to put into them a living Soul. . . . But is there any one so bold, that dares thus far Arrogate to himself the Incomprehensible Works of the Almighty? Who alone did at first, and continues still to make a living Soul, He alone can breathe the Breath of Life. If any one thinks himself an Artist at this, let him number up the parts of his Childs Body which he hath made, tell me their Uses and Operations, and when the living and rational Soul began to inhabit this curious Structure, when Sense began, and how this Engine which he has framed Thinks and Reasons. (179, 1.6.53)

If a given father is going to claim that the mere fact of his fatherhood grants him sovereignty over his child, he should be able to provide a detailed account of how he made the child that he now insists is subject to his power. But this is impossible. Fathers cannot breathe the breath of life, nor can they know anything about the moment "when Sense began"—the moment that is, as we will see, so fundamental to Locke's *Essay*. Locke's meditations on the originary experience of infants in the *Essay* color his ideas about political obligation in the *First Treatise*, which draws on the inaccessibility of "when Sense began" in order to refute Filmer's views.

In the *Second Treatise*, Locke further undermines his adversary by focusing on the distinction between Adam's creation and the birth of his descendants. This difference rests on what I have been calling neonatal maturity, an existential state that has implications both political (Adam's immediate maturity means that he can take care of himself, in the absence of human community) and epistemological (Adam is able to actualize his mental capacities in the "first Instant of his being," and is thus conscious of the moment "when" his own "Sense began"): "*Adam* was created a perfect Man, his Body and Mind in full possession of their Strength and Reason, and so was capable from the first Instant of his being to provide for his own Support and Preservation, and govern his Actions according to the Dictates of the Law of Reason which God had implanted in him. From him the World is peopled with his Descendants, who are all born Infants, weak and helpless, without Knowledge or Understanding" (305, 2.6.56). All subsequent human lives begin in the "imperfect state" of infancy and childhood, but Adam was "created a perfect Man" (306, 2.6.58).

While Locke seems to claim more for Adam's prelapsarian perfection than the perfection of any mature adult, as the text unfolds it becomes clear that *perfect* here means *mature* in the sense put forward by Harvey in *Generatione animalium*: "an animal is called 'perfect' [*perfectum*] when it has the power to beget its like," when it has passed all of the biological milestones of adulthood (17).[26] Adam was neonatally mature from the "first Instant of his Being," his body in "full possession" of its strength, his mind already rational. Since this account of Adam's neonatally mature powers is similar to that sketched by Milton and picked up by Traherne, it is possible that Locke was inspired by the depiction of Adam's first moments in *Paradise Lost*. Locke owned a copy of the English epic, and he praised its author as one of the greatest modern Latinists. As his journal from 1667 attests, Locke was also a close reader of Milton's account of Edenic marriage in the *Doctrine and Discipline of Divorce*.[27] Whether or not Locke was inspired by Milton's account of Edenic neonatal maturity, he adopts a similar view on Adam's epistemological capacities.

Locke asserts that infants enter the world "without Knowledge or Understanding"—and therefore require parents to help them—but never once claims that Adam possesses "Knowledge" from the "first Instant of his being." Adam is instead created with a "Mind" in "full possession" of "Reason," with "the Dictates of the Law of Reason . . . implanted in him" by God. This means that Adam could use his reason *ab initio*; it does not mean that he entered the world full to the brim with knowledge. Like Milton, Locke positions himself against Edenic superpowers. After all, Locke

is certain that the reason "implanted" in Adam by God is identical to that
into which each healthy human child eventually grows:

> The Law that was to govern *Adam*, was the same that was to govern all
> his Posterity, the *Law of Reason*. But his Off-spring having another way
> of entrance into the World, different from him, by a natural Birth, that
> produced them ignorant and without the use of *Reason*, they were not
> presently *under that Law*: for no Body can be under a Law, which is not
> promulgated to him; and this Law being promulgated or made known by
> *Reason* only, he that is not come to the Use of his *Reason*, cannot be said
> to be *under this Law*; and *Adam*'s Children being not presently as soon
> as born, *under this Law of Reason* were not presently *free*. (305, 2.6.57).

Adam's descendants, who enter the world not through creation but by way
of "natural Birth," cannot use their reason right away. Since children are
not "under" the law of reason until they have reached a certain age, their
parents are "bound" to help "govern" their actions "till Reason shall take
its place." In Locke's view, "*the end of Law* is not to abolish or restrain, but
to preserve and enlarge Freedom" (306, 2.6.57), and this means that only
those capable of living according to the "*Law of Reason*" are able to be free
in actu. If Adam was created immediately "free" because he possessed this
law from his "first Instant," all subsequent humans are "born free" insofar
as they enter the world with the *capacity* for reason, with the potential to
be free later in life, once they have reached an appropriate age and should
they follow the dictates of rationality. Human beings "naturally," as Locke
puts it in *Some Thoughts Concerning Education* (1693, 1695), "even from
our cradles, love liberty" and want to "have our freedom," but are not capable of properly actualizing the capacity suggested by this love until we
"grow up to the use of reason."[28] Infants are not, as Filmer argues, "subject"
to their fathers (or, in Locke's correction, their parents). Parents are instead
"bound" to help their offspring actualize the capacity for rationality and
free action with which they are born.

Locke undermines Filmer's argument by leveling the differences between Adam and his descendants. Epistemologically speaking, Adam's only
advantage is the ability to actualize his rational capacities when he comes
into being. As noted above, Locke insists that the "*Law of Reason*" implanted in Adam is "the same" as the law into which each human child
grows; by the time most humans reach adulthood, they live according to a
law of reason identical to that possessed by Adam. In this way, Locke's position resembles Milton's: Adam was neonatally mature but fully human,

more or less just like us. This interpretation is confirmed by a thought experiment Locke advances in the *Essay*. Inquiring into the origin of the relationship between mixed ideas and words, Locke asks the reader to "suppose *Adam* in the State of a grown Man, with a good Understanding, but
in a strange Country, with all Things new, and unknown about him; and
no other Faculties, to attain the Knowledge of them, but what one of this
Age has now" (466, 3.6.44). Like the Adam of *Paradise Lost*—who, as I argued in chapter 1, comes into the world neonatally mature but without any
knowledge of the world around him—Locke posits an Adam in possession
of a "good Understanding" but lacking any knowledge of the world ("all
Things" are "new" and "unknown"). This Adam is capable of "attain[ing]
the Knowledge" of these things, but he can do so only by using the mental
"Faculties" that the mature human beings of Locke's "Age" possess.

As we saw in chapter 2, by suggesting that Adam and Eve enter the
world as blank slates—with both neonatally mature minds and a complete
lack of experience—Milton flirted with Socinus's Edenic epistemology.
Jonathan Edwards, the principal of Jesus College at Oxford, accused Locke
of harboring precisely such sympathies.[29] Responding to Locke's anony-
mously published *Reasonableness of Christianity* (1695) in *Socinianism
Unmasked* (1696), Edwards claims that Locke's treatise denies the force
of the Apostle's Creed because this creed was not "*Socinianized, all over
Socinianized.*"[30] Later outing Locke as the author of *Reasonableness* in
The Socinian Creed (1697)—an exposition of "English Socinians" and their
regrettable influence—Edwards discusses Socinus's view that "there is no
proof of a God from any innate apprehensions of his being and nature."[31]
Citing the *Essay*, Edwards then attempts to position Locke's denial of innate ideas as Socinian:

> It may be observed that he [Locke] began first to deny the *Natural No-
> tions and Principles* that Mens Minds furnish them with: and this was
> an Introduction to his late enterprize [the Socinian version of Christian-
> ity presented in *Reasonableness*]. He by no means allows of *Connate
> Ideas*, those Treasuries of all Natural Knowledge. It is remarkable that
> he that is so much against the *Scholastick Way*, and *Systems*, yet main-
> tains the Old Maxim of the *Schools*, that the Understanding is a mere
> Blank, with nothing written in it. Where it might be noted further that
> herein he exactly agrees with *Socinus*, whose words I quoted before.[32]

If Locke dislikes scholastic thought, why, Edwards wonders, does the *Essay*
maintain the idea that the mind is a tabula rasa? The only plausible answer

is that Locke wants to smuggle Socinian views into his epistemology in order to pave the way for his Socinian view of Christianity. Although Edwards does not tie what he sees as Locke's Socinian epistemology with the depictions of Adam in the *Essay* and *Two Treatises*, had he done so, he would have found more grist for his mill. As we saw in chapter 2, Edwards was disgusted by Socinus's view that Adam was "born a frail, mortal Creature, having only the bare faculties of understanding and will, but without the accomplishments of either, being neither endued with wisdom nor holiness: a pure *rasa Tabula*."[33]

Locke's depiction of Adam as a blank beginner suggests that Edwards's wrath was not misdirected, for Locke was drawn, both in the *Essay* and in the *Two Treatises*, to the connection between Adam's neonatal maturity and the natality of his descendants. If human infants begin as blank slates, without any innate knowledge, the same holds true for Adam. From an epistemological standpoint, then, the true difference between Adam and his heirs lies in the presence or absence of memories stretching back to the "first Instant" of one's being. If Adam's neonatal maturity enables him to actualize memory immediately, human infants find themselves "weak and helpless," in an "imperfect state." Even later in life, when one is able to actualize the requisite mental capacities, one is unable to learn anything about "when Sense began." As Locke insists in the *First Treatise*, this moment *should* be inaccessible; only God can know anything about its details. And yet, as Gray's reading of Locke in *De principiis cogitandi* suggests, this moment—truly accessible only to Adam and Eve—is vital to Locke's epistemology. His philosophical commitments demand access to originary experience, for if he is to provide a genetic account of how we came to know what we now know, then Locke needs to pinpoint when and how this process began. But he also knows that this originary experience is unavailable through any empirically derived account. Although Locke does not want to argue "from the thoughts of Infants, which are unknown to us," he is nevertheless committed to the notion that we can say something meaningful about the beginnings of human thought in the minds of fetuses, infants, and young children: "'There is certainly a time, when Children begin to think," (62, 1.2.25), and it is the nature of this moment on which the *Essay* stands or falls.

Locke considers the view that the mind "brings" innate characters "into the World with it" (48, 1.2.1) to be nonsense because the mind must, he holds, be able to perceive everything that is within it: "No Proposition can be said to be in the Mind, which it never yet knew, which it was never yet conscious of" (50, 1.2.5). Adopting the argument we saw Culverwell make in chapter 3, Locke claims that anything that can be properly said to exist within the human mind must, at least in principle, be able to rise into consciousness in the moment it is said to exist. "If therefore these two Propositions, *Whatsoever is, is;* and *It is impossible for the same thing to be, and not to be,* are by Nature imprinted, Children cannot be ignorant of them," Locke writes, reducing the argument for innate ideas to absurdity: "Infants, and all that have Souls must necessarily have them in their Understandings, know the Truth of them, and assent to it" (51, 1.2.5). At stake in Locke's denial of innate ideas is the character and content of originary experience. Any truths that are innate—such maxims as *the whole is greater than the part*—must, Locke argues, exist as "innate thoughts," for it is impossible that a truth could exist in the mind without appearing through thought: "If there be any *innate Truths*, they *must necessarily be the first of any thought on;* the first that appear there [in the mind]" (63, 1.2.26). But it is ridiculous that children "join these general abstract Speculations with their sucking Bottles, and their Rattles" (63, 1.2.25). The argument for innate ideas rests on the premise that such ideas exist *in potentia* in the minds of fetuses, infants, and young children, woven into the structure of the mind. Locke denies this premise. All ideas that exist in the mind must, in principle, be able to be actualized immediately; one cannot truly possess an idea that one cannot, here and now, call to mind.

What was at stake in Locke's focus on the first actualized thought experienced by human beings? The answer is as simple as it is expansive: everything. As we have seen throughout this book, from antiquity onward, many thinkers attempted to access human nature through an examination of what they imagined "first impressions" to be. From Cicero through Grotius, the posited contents of *prima naturae* were examined in order to exclude the multiple familial and cultural inheritances passed down through nurture and to isolate what might be given to each new human life by nature itself. Locke addresses this problem directly. Human beings are, he argues, from the beginning—even while still nursing—"instructed" about the beliefs central to the culture into which they are born.[34] When they are older and begin to "reflect on their own Minds, they cannot find anything more ancient there, than those Opinions, which were taught to them, before their Memory began to keep a Register of their Actions." Since they cannot recall having first learned such facts as, say, *God exists* from another human being, they "make no scruple to *conclude, That those Propositions, of whose knowledge they can find in themselves no original, were certainly the impress of God and Nature upon their Minds; and not taught to them by any one else*" (82, 1.3.23). Human beings tend to project the products of culture back onto nature. Since no one can remember having learned the most basic truths, it is easy to assume that they have always been there. But this is false. Human nature must, in the first instance, be separated from culture. If such separation is not properly conceived, we will fail to understand what we are and how we have come to know what we think we know. And if we are mistaken about what grounds our knowledge, if we mistakenly believe that our cherished truths derive from innate ideas, then both our knowledge and our truths are precarious, built on shifting sand.

In the absence of innate ideas, all human knowledge emerges from impressions made through the senses, which "furnish the yet empty Cabinet" of the mind. Of course, the "Knowledge of some Truths" is, Locke confesses, "very early in the mind," but even the earliest ideas are always "acquired" (55, 1.2.15). To be sure, human beings do not enter the world as *complete* blank slates. But if we enter the world with "Inclinations" and "natural tendencies" that guide us, the mind is devoid of any ideas that might lead to *theoretical understanding*:

> Nature, I confess, has put into Man a desire of Happiness, and an aversion to Misery: These indeed are innate practical Principles, which (as practical Principles ought) do continue constantly to operate and influence all our Actions, without ceasing: These may be observ'd in all Persons and all Ages, steady and universal; but these are Inclinations of the Appetite to good, not Impressions of truth on the Understanding. I deny not, that there are natural tendencies imprinted on the Minds of Men; and that, from the very first instances of Sense and Perception, there are some things, that are grateful, and others unwelcome to them; some things that they incline to, and others that they fly: But this makes nothing for innate Characters on the Mind, which are to be the Principles of Knowledge, regulating our Practice. (67, 1.3.3)

From the "very first instances of Sense and Perception," every living being desires pleasure and shuns pain. Hardwired into the very makeup of the human organism, this fact exerts a determining influence on each and every life. But this inbuilt propensity for attraction and repulsion does not generate ideas that lead to understanding. Taking the old chestnut that each creature's drive for self-preservation is modulated through pleasure and pain—an idea we saw Cicero articulate in chapter 2—Locke recasts the meaning of the term "Impressions." If, for the Epicureans and Stoics, *prima naturae* are whatever is found within a given organism at the beginning of its life, Locke is after the first "Impressions of Truth on the Understanding." Although some degree of pleasure and pain surely accompanies all sensation and, in this sense, these qualities are "steady and universal," they are not, for all that, epistemically efficacious. Pleasure and pain determine action but are not foundational for knowledge. Locke's attempt to determine the "Original . . . of humane Knowledge" leads him back to the moment of originary experience when knowledge, properly speaking, can be said to begin. This is one impulse from which Locke's theory of consciousness emerges.

LOCKE'S CONSCIOUSNESS IN CONTEXT

In the second book of the *Essay*, Locke offers a definition of consciousness that builds on and rejects Descartes's philosophical commitments. For Descartes, thought encompasses all mental activity, from the most primitive form of sensation—what I have been calling minimal mental presence—to the most abstract speculation. *Conscientia* is a necessary feature of all thought; Descartes employs the term to index the various somethings that appear to someone. Since all human beings are, at least in part, *res cogitantes* defined by the activity of thinking, they are, insofar as they are minded creatures, always thinking. As we have seen, it was the combination of these two arguments that led Descartes to the idea that fetuses actualize their capacity to think while still in the womb. Locke unpacks Descartes's understanding of how consciousness relates to thought while, at the same time, rejecting both the premise that minds always think and the metaphysics of substance that subtends this premise.

Locke is certain that we think. "In every Act of Sensation, Reasoning, or Thinking," he writes in the *Essay*, "we are conscious to our selves of our own Being; and, in this Matter, come not short of the highest degree of *Certainty*" (619, 4.9.3). But he famously refuses to commit to an account of what it is that thinks. Although it is "the more probable Opinion" that consciousness is "annexed to, and the Affection of" an "immaterial Substance," Locke nevertheless sees no contradiction in the idea of thinking matter (345, 2.27.25). Bracketing such issues, Locke focuses only on what happens when one thinks, on what shows up. Like Descartes, Locke holds a capacious understanding of what falls under the rubric of *thought*. In a chapter on "the Modes of Thinking," he elaborates a typology similar to that sketched by Descartes. Ranging from sensation through remembrance, recollection, contemplation, reverie, attention, intention, dreaming, reasoning, judging, volition, and knowledge, Locke's list of the "modes of thinking" covers the breadth of mental happenings (226–27, 2.19). Perception is the only mode "distinct from all other Modifications of *thinking*" because it alone is "annexed to any impression on the Body, made by an external Object" and is therefore able to "furnish" or supply the mind with the ideas "we call *Sensation*" (226, 2.19.1).

If the contours of thinking presented in the *Essay* resemble Descartes's definition of thought, Locke's rejection of the Cartesian substance eliminates the necessity behind the claim that the mind is always thinking—and, by extension, the logic that supports Descartes's claim that the fetus thinks while still in the womb. Locke argues instead from what he calls *experience*: "We know certainly by Experience, that we sometimes think, and thence draw this infallible Consequence, That there is something in us, that has a Power to think: But whether that Substance perpetually thinks, or no, we can be no farther assured, than Experience informs us" (108–9, 2.1.10). One does not think while in a dreamless sleep or swoon. The act of thought is always accompanied by consciousness: one "cannot think at any time waking or sleeping, without being sensible of it [thought]. Our being sensible of it is not necessary to any thing, but to our thoughts; and of them it is; and to them it will always be necessary, till we can think without being conscious of it" (109, 2.1.10). To think is to be "conscious" of what one thinks, and the link between thought and consciousness is "necessary." Locke reiterates this point a number of times. It is hard, Locke claims in the next paragraph, "to conceive, that any thing should think, and not be conscious of it" (110, 2.1.11).

But what exactly does he mean by *consciousness*? In recent decades, historians of philosophy have advanced different answers. Some scholars contend that Locke understands consciousness as isomorphic with perception, while others claim that he sees it as a higher-order thought akin to reflection.[35] In my view, Udo Thiel provides the best interpretation: "Thinking and other mental operations are not 'objects' that are somehow separate from consciousness; rather, they are characterized by an inherent reflexivity which Locke calls consciousness (rather than reflection). This reflexivity is part of their nature as mental states and operations."[36] Since, in Locke's parlance, *reflection* is the attentive perception of one's own mental operations—willing, understanding, and so on—this term marks a special set of the somethings that might appear to someone through consciousness. Reflection reveals one subset of things that might show up through consciousness, which is itself the minimal reflexivity immanent to any and all mental goings-on. Drawing on and refining this insight, Shelley Weinberg argues that Locke's consciousness is a nonformalized, nonevaluative, and self-referential form of awareness that is an immanent and necessary part of all mental activity. Whenever one perceives, understands, wills, remembers, or reflects, that act of thinking contains within it the consciousness that it is happening here, now, and for me.[37] Consciousness is nothing more or less than a necessary feature of all thought.

Locke clarifies this point when he uses consciousness to separate the act of thinking from a substance dualism that insists on constant thought:

> If they say, The Man thinks always, but is not always conscious of it; they may as well say, His Body is extended, without having parts. For 'tis altogether as intelligible to say, that a body is extended without parts, as that any thing *thinks without being conscious of it*, or perceiving, that it does so. They who talk thus, may, with as much reason, if it be necessary to their Hypothesis, say, That a Man is always hungry, but that he does not feel it: Whereas hunger consists in that very sensation, as thinking consists in being conscious that one thinks. If they say, That a Man is always conscious to himself of thinking; I ask, How they know it? Consciousness is the perception of what passes in a Man's own mind. Can another Man perceive, that I am conscious of any thing, when I perceive it not myself? No Man's Knowledge here, can go beyond his Experience. (115, 2.1.19)

Just as parts are necessary to extension, so consciousness is necessary to thinking. Consciousness is thus axiomatic to any discussion of what happens within one's "own mind." It is ludicrous to argue that one is hungry without taking account of the feeling of being hungry. On Locke's view, hunger "consists" precisely in the "sensation" of hunger. By extension, it is nonsensical to contend that one can think without being conscious of one's thought, for "thinking consists in being conscious that one thinks."

Locke remains consistent with Descartes, who advances the same argument: thought is what happens within us "in so far as we have *conscientia* of it" (CSM 1:195; AT 8:7). Descartes's followers, many of whom Locke read, made versions of this claim. Consider the definition advanced by Louis de La Forge in *Traitté de l'esprit de l'homme* (1666): "The essence of thought consists in this consciousness and this perception which the mind has of everything that takes place in it [*l'essence de la Pensée consistoit dans cette conscience & cette perception que l'Esprit a de tout ce qui se passe en luy*]."[38] Earlier, in a chapter entitled "Everything which thinks, Thinks Continuously as long as it Thinks," La Forge makes a more expansive claim:

I can define the nature of thought as that consciousness [*conscience*], awareness [*tesmoignage*], and inner feeling [*sentiment interieur*] by which the mind notices [*adverty*] everything it does or suffers and, in general, everything which takes place immediately in itself at the same time as it acts or is acted on. I say "immediately" to let you know that this testimony and inner feeling is not distinct from the action or passion and that the actions and passions themselves make the mind notice [*avertissent*] what is taking place in itself. Thus you will not confuse this inner feeling with the reflection that we sometimes make on our actions, which is not found in all our thoughts because it is only one type of thought.[39]

La Forge defines thought through an immanent and immediate *conscience* that is nonevaluative because it is "of everything" that appears either passively or actively in the mind. Consciousness is a *sentiment interieur* that reflexively phenomenalizes everything that appears. Locke's definition of consciousness as a necessary feature of thought is part of this Cartesian heritage.

Locke maintains the relationship between thought and consciousness as presented by Descartes, but, as we have already seen, he eliminates two important features of Cartesian thought: first, the notion that the essence of the mind is to think; and second, the position that the mind is always thinking. In making this argument, Locke drew on the work of Ralph Cudworth, a philosopher, theologian, philologist, and the Regius Professor of Hebrew and master of Christ's Church College at Cambridge University. Published in 1678, Cudworth's *True Intellectual System of the Universe* provided one of the earliest philosophical uses of *consciousness* in the English language. Cudworth helped generate the semantic milieu from which Locke's usage emerges. As I argued in the introduction, the use of *consciousness* in a nonevaluative sense increased dramatically in the 1670s, and much of this increase was due to Cudworth's text. Locke read Cudworth attentively. In 1682—the same year in which the earliest evidence of his friendship with Cudworth's daughter, the philosopher Damaris, appears—Locke's journal notes mention the *True Intellectual System*.[40] When Locke wrote the first drafts of the *Essay* in 1671, he used the word *consciousness* only once.[41] The term became absolutely central to the *Essay* only in the second edition of 1694, when, in the new chapter on "Identity and Diversity," Locke used it to tackle the problem of personal identity over time. But, as we have already seen, *consciousness* also played an important role in the first edition of 1689. In this first edition, Locke models his utilization of *consciousness* on Cudworth's *True Intellectual System*.

Cudworth deploys *consciousness* in order to isolate a form of life that is defined by the fact that it is "inconscious."[42] This is what he calls "plastic nature," the vital energy that subtends all living things and is evident in phenomena as diverse as plant life and the beating of human hearts. Although this plastic nature acts, it is not "clearly and expressly conscious of what it doth." In this way, it is unlike the activities of humans and even of animals, which are "generally conceived to be conscious." By contrast, the "plastic nature in the formation of plants and animals seems to have no animal fancy, no express *synaisthesis*, 'con-sense' or 'consciousness' of what it doth. . . . In a word, nature is a thing that hath no such self-perception or self-enjoyment in it, as animals have" (1:244, 3.37.15). If this idea draws on Plotinus, it also repeats the insights from Harvey's *Exercitationes de generatione animalium*, which we examined in chapter 4. When Cudworth claims that nature is "such a thing as doth not know, but only do," he summarizes a passage from Harvey's embryological text, which he quotes only a sentence later: "In the works of nature there is neither prudence nor understanding" (1:240–41, 3.37.12). Indeed, Cudworth is primarily interested in consciousness insofar as it helps him to isolate something like Harvey's sense without sensation. "There is some appearance of life and sympathy in certain vegetables and plants, which, however called sensitive-plants and plant animals, cannot well be supposed to have animal sense and fancy, or express consciousness in them" (1:247, 3.37.17), Cudworth claims, reiterating Harvey's view of zoophytes.

But if the isolation of a plastic nature that senses without producing sensation or "express consciousness" is Cudworth's most pressing task at this point in the *True Intellectual System*, he also aims to mobilize his intellectual framework against Descartes.[43] Cudworth claims that some "late philosophers" argue that there are only two types of action: first, the "local motion" of extended bodies; and second, "expressly conscious cogitation." Such philosophers exclude plastic nature. Cudworth resists this framework by arguing that the two basic types of being are not body and mind, but rather body and *life*—that is, "internal energy and self-activity."[44] If body is more or less straightforward, life must be further "subdivided" into two types of act: that "with express consciousness and synaisthesis, or such as is without it." According to Cudworth, the latter is the "plastic life of nature: so that there may be an action distinct from local motion, or a vital energy which is not accompanied with that fancy, or consciousness, that is in the energies of animal life; that is, there may be a simple internal energy or vital autokinesy, which is without that duplication that is included in the nature of *synaisthesis*, 'con-sense and consciousness,' which makes

a being to be present with itself, attentive to its own actions, or animadversive of them, to perceive itself or to suffer, and to have a fruition or
enjoyment of itself" (1:245, 3.37.16). For Cudworth, *consciousness* names a
form of reflexivity characterized by a "duplication" through which a being
becomes "present with itself." The prefix *con-* (present in both *consciousness* and *con-sense*) is what matters. If the intentional content of the mental act could be disparate and varied—it might involve being "attentive"
or "animadversive," having "fruition or enjoyment," or straightforwardly
"perceiv[ing]"—the "duplication" of an act that returns a subject back to
"itself" remains constant.

By framing "express consciousness" as a more elevated form of the same
"self-activity" that defines all life, Cudworth positions himself to attack
Descartes's conviction that minds are always thinking so long as they exist
as minds:

> That there may be some vital energy without clear and express *synais-
> thesis*, "con-sense" and "consciousness, animadversion, attention," or
> "self-perception," seems reasonable upon several accounts. For first,
> those philosophers themselves, who make the essence of the soul to
> consist in cogitation, and again, the essence of cogitation in clear and
> express consciousness, cannot render it any way probable that the souls
> of men in all profound sleeps, lethargies, and apoplexies, as also of em-
> bryos in the womb, from their very first arrival thither, are never so
> much as one moment without expressly conscious cogitations; which
> if they were, according to the principles of their philosophy, they must,
> ipso facto, cease to have any being. Now, if the souls of men and animals
> be at any time without consciousness and self-perception, then it must
> needs be granted that clear and express consciousness is not essential to
> life. (1:246–47, 3.37.17)

Cudworth aims to remove "express consciousness" from the essence of the
mind or soul. Through a series of examples, he shows that Descartes is
wrongheaded: no one is "always conscious of whatever they have in them";
we all do things "non-attendingly"; we have no "direct consciousness" of
the "knot" tying our souls to our bodies; we are not usually conscious of our
nictitations or respiration; and so on (1:247–48, 3.37.17). Since conscious
thought is simply a mode of life and life is the essence of living beings, human or otherwise, such beings will not "cease to have any being" should
they become "inconscious." Embryos "in the womb" might sometimes
possess consciousness—Cudworth does not rule out this possibility—but it

is highly unlikely that they would, "from their first arrival thither," not live through at least "one moment without expressly conscious cogitations."

Locke adopts the full sense of Cudworth's use of *consciousness* in his argument against Descartes in the *Essay*. If the Cartesians insist that "a Man is always conscious to himself of thinking" (115, 2.1.19), then how, Locke asks, do they know this? There is no doubt in Locke's mind that the "Soul of a waking Man is never without thought," but it is unlikely that a state of dreamless sleep involves any thought, "it being hard to conceive, that any thing should think, and not be conscious of it" (109–10, 2.1.11). Against the Cartesian *res cogitans*, Locke insists that it is "the Man" that thinks (110, 2.1.10). In the chapter on "Identity and Diversity," Locke claims that by "Man" he means "an Animal of such a certain Form." Against those who claim that humanity consists in a certain relation to rationality, Locke places a "dull irrational *Man*" against a "very intelligent rational *Parrot*." Surely, he insists, no one would say that the parrot is more of a human being (333, 2.27.8). In an argument indebted to Cudworth, Locke claims that Descartes's doctrine of constant thought ignores the form of life—the living body of the *homo totus*—that conditions the workings of the mind. Conscious thought is ultimately rooted not in the mind but in the life of a human being.

This argument marks Locke's attempt to solve what he sees as an absurd consequence of the Cartesian position. If the mind thinks while the body is sleeping, then it is conscious of whatever happens within it during sleep. But if this is the case, then

> it is certain, that *Socrates* asleep, and *Socrates* awake, is not the same Person; but his Soul when he sleeps, and *Socrates* the Man consisting of Body and Soul when he is waking, are two Persons: Since waking *Socrates*, has no Knowledge of, or Concernment for that Happiness, or Misery of his Soul, which it enjoys alone by it self whilst he sleeps, without perceiving any thing of it; no more than he has for the Happiness, or Misery of a Man in the *Indies*, whom he knows not. For if we take wholly away all Consciousness of our Actions and Sensations, especially of Pleasure and Pain, and the concernment that accompanies it, it will be hard to know wherein to place personal Identity. (110, 2.1.11)

If waking human life emerges from the union of soul and body, when a given human being falls asleep, the relationship between soul and body is loosened. Talking *to* the body of someone who is sleeping is quite different from talking *with* someone who is conscious. Building on this intuition, Locke argues that if the waking human being—"the Man"—is not conscious of the pleasures, pains, and concerns ostensibly experienced by the soul while it thinks during sleep, then the soul that thinks during sleep and the human being (the union of body and soul) that thinks while awake must constitute "two Persons." What the Cartesians see as the conscious thoughts of the soul during a dreamless sleep are as closely connected to the "Concernment" of the waking Man as "the Happiness, or Misery of a Man in the *Indies*."[45]

Here Locke adumbrates the position he advances later in the chapter on "Identity and Diversity"; namely, that "personal Identity" over time rests on "Consciousness of our Actions and Sensations." In Locke's presentation of the Cartesian view, "*Socrates* asleep" is not the same person as "*Socrates* awake" because the identity of persons is predicated on and constituted by an identity of conscious experience. If the identity of an inanimate body depends on a particular "Cohesion of Particles of Matter" at a given instant, the identity of a living being *qua* living being—an oak tree, a dog, a human being—depends on the "Organization of Parts in one coherent Body, partaking of one Common Life." Although the matter of living beings is in constant flux—entering, moving through, and exiting a given body according to the rhythms of what we now call metabolism—that matter is "vitally united" to the living body in a "like continued Organization" (330–31, 2.27.4). The identity of a given "Man" consists in "nothing but a participation of the same continued Life, by constantly fleeting Particles of Matter, in succession vitally united to the same organized Body" (331–32, 2.27.6). In addition to this form of identity, "Man" also possesses a "personal Identity"; the "Person" is one *aspect* of the life form "Man."[46]

By "Person," Locke means "a thinking intelligent Being, that has reason and reflection, and can consider it self as it self, the same thinking thing in different times and places; which it does only by that consciousness, which is inseparable from thinking, and it seems to me essential to it: It being impossible for any one to perceive, without perceiving, that he does perceive" (335, 2.27.9). Locke understands consciousness to be a minimally reflexive form of awareness that accompanies all mental acts. This reflexivity—the nonformalized mineness of a given act of perception, or will, or memory, or imagination, or even of explicit reflection—is the condition that binds the self to itself through what Cudworth describes as the "duplication" that makes a being to be "present with itself." Note that this "duplication" does not lead to the formalization of self-consciousness as such but marks the introduction of phenomenality or mental presence that distinguishes what is conscious from what is not conscious. This aspect of consciousness is the condition for personal identity over time: "For since consciousness always accompanies thinking, and 'tis that, that makes every one to be, what he calls *self*; and thereby distinguishes himself from all other thinking things, in this alone consists *personal Identity*, *i.e.* the sameness of rational Being: And as far as this consciousness can be extended backwards to any past Action or Thought, so far reaches the Identity of that *Person*" (335, 2.27.9). Right now, I am awake and thinking, conscious of many things ranging from perceptions (the weight of my fingers on the keyboard, the light coming through the window, the beginnings of hunger as it settles over my stomach) to many other mental acts (the will to write, the inability to fully understand a given topic, the anticipation of a meeting later in the afternoon). Part of this scene of conscious life involves the capacity to extend consciousness "backward" to past actions and thoughts (an argument I had yesterday, a day with a friend whom I have not seen since I was a child). My personal identity over time extends as far as I can stretch my consciousness "backward." I am responsible—in a forensic sense—for those actions and thoughts to which my consciousness can be extended.[47] My personhood consists in this.

Locke ascribes what Thiel calls a "constitutive function" to consciousness.[48] The "Person" is not a substance that is conscious. Rather, consciousness constitutes the person, which is a unity coextensive with the various thoughts and actions that consciousness is capable of summoning into presence. Locke's argument against the role played by consciousness in Descartes's philosophy is pitched against both Cartesian substance metaphysics and the picture of personal identity that it produces. Since one's person is constituted by consciousness, if the soul of Socrates is conscious during sleep (when the "Man" is unconscious), then, to employ Locke's example, Socrates must exist as two persons: the personal identity constituted by the conscious thought of the soul during sleep and the personal identity constituted by the union of body and soul during waking life. In light of this, it cannot be the case that the soul thinks. It is only "the Man," the human being, who thinks. If the life of a given human being is shaped by the flow of material particles into and out of the living body of "one Animal, whose *Identity* is preserved, in that change of Substances, by the unity of one continued Life," so the identity of a given person depends "only" on the fact that it is "the same consciousness that makes a Man be himself to himself" (336, 2.27.10). Consciousness is a property of human life, and personal identity is produced through that consciousness.

With this background in place, I want to return to the passage in which Locke first defines consciousness in the *Essay*: "To suppose the Soul to think, and the Man not to perceive it, is," Locke claims, for reasons I have laid out above, "to make two Persons in one Man." A "Man" is a living human being. It is for this reason that although Descartes and his followers argue that the "Soul always thinks," they never say that "a Man always thinks." In Locke's view, it is unreasonable to hold that the soul thinks but the human being does not. It is similarly unreasonable to hold that a human being thinks but is not conscious of that thought. Consciousness is necessary to thought just as parts are necessary to extension. Having argued against the view that the soul can think by itself, separate from the human being, Locke imagines his Cartesian interlocutor switching tactics:

> If they say, That a Man is always conscious to himself of thinking; I ask, How they know it? Consciousness is the perception of what passes in a Man's own mind. Can another Man perceive, that I am conscious of any thing, when I perceive it not myself? No Man's knowledge here, can go beyond his Experience. Wake a Man out of a sound sleep, and ask him, What he was that moment thinking on. If he himself be conscious of nothing he then thought on, he must be a notable Diviner of Thoughts, that can assure him, that he was thinking. (115; 2.1.19)

The force of Locke's definition of consciousness is that it is the awareness of what happens "in a *Man's* own mind," what shows up for a human animal. Thought exists in and for human beings. It is possible, even likely, that the soul is involved in the production of thought, but—for all of us at least—the act of thinking is necessarily something undertaken by a human being. This marks the limits of knowledge, for when it comes to consciousness and the matter of one's own thoughts, no Man can "go beyond his Experience." If, at first glance, Locke's explicit treatment of consciousness sounds similar to that of Descartes, his insistence that it is the "Man" that does the thinking is in fact a rebuttal of Descartes. By skirting the question of essence ("What is the thing that thinks?") and sticking to the question of access ("Who or what has access to thought?"), Locke locates consciousness in waking life: "It cannot be less than Revelation, that discovers to another, Thoughts in my mind, when I can find none there my self" (115, 2.1.19). Only the waking Man can access consciousness.

Why does Locke work so hard to ensure that consciousness is a property available only to human beings considered in holistic terms? The answer is grounded in Locke's account of how ideas come to exist in the human mind, which, it turns out, is the very point at which consciousness intersects with natality.

NEONATAL CONSCIOUSNESS

Drawing on the work of Arnold Davidson, I argued in the introduction that the emergence of the concept of consciousness in the seventeenth century entailed the development of a new "style of reasoning." As *conscientia* began to index a nonevaluative phenomenon (in addition to or alongside its ancient evaluative connotations), the word began to be linked with other nonevaluative terms in ways that generated a new "conceptual space."[49] Instead of being associated with good, bad, virtue, vice, and other such terms, *conscientia* or the slowly desynonymizing English *consciousness* began to be linked with terms like thought, ego, self, and experience. If the work of Descartes and his followers went a long way toward linking *conscientia* with ego and thought, Locke provides a vivid and influential example of a writer who extended this network to the semantic riches long associated with the term *experience*. Indeed, Locke provides a set of nesting definitions that perfectly encapsulate this emergent "style of reasoning." In the *Essay*, he defines thought in terms of consciousness, which is, in turn, located in the sphere of experience. The act of "thinking consists in being conscious that one thinks"; consciousness is the "Perception" of that thought (what "passes in Man's own mind"); and one's own "Experience" is the medium by means of which consciousness is available. "No man's knowledge here can go beyond his experience": the knowledge of consciousness (specified by "here") emerges if and only if one undergoes the "experience" of being conscious to which such knowledge corresponds. This yoking of consciousness, thought, ego, and experience both helps to ground a new "conceptual space" and completely governs Locke's epistemological principles. For Locke, as we have already seen, the appearance of thought is a given. But if one's present consciousness cannot be doubted, the process by which one came to acquire the ideas that populate one's consciousness remains opaque.

Following Aristotle, Aquinas, Culverwell, and many of the thinkers discussed in chapter 3, Locke turns to the *abrasa tabula* thesis, a move that has come to be synonymous with his own name: "Let us then suppose the mind to be, as we say, white Paper, void of all characters, without any ideas." Having ruled out innate ideas, Locke presents his version of "How" the mind comes "to be furnished": "Whence has [the mind] all the materials of Reason and Knowledge? To this I answer, in one word, From *Experience*: In That, all our Knowledge is founded; and from that it ultimately derives it self. Our Observation, employ'd either about *external, sensible Objects; or about internal Operations of our Minds, perceived and reflected on by our selves, is that, which supplies our Understandings with all the materials of our thinking.* These two are the Fountains of Knowledge, from whence all the *Ideas* we have, or can naturally have, do spring" (104, 2.1.2).

Everything in the mind comes from "*Experience,*" that on which "our Knowledge is founded" and from which our knowledge derives. The "*materials of our thinking*" are "furnished" by "*Experience,*" which is synonymous with "Observation," the power by means of which we perceive both "*external, sensible Objects*" and the "*internal Operations of our Minds.*" These two "Fountains" present what Étienne Balibar calls the "double origin" of human ideas: first, *sensation* or the perception of things in the world; and second, *reflection* or the perception of the mind's own operations.[50] Both of these "Fountains" are forms of perception. It is in this sense that they are indexed by the term "*Experience,*" which, for Locke, is something of which one is conscious. My analysis of Milton's "unexperienced thought" in chapter 1 captured the early stages (around 1667) of the conceptual drift that would bring experience into alignment with consciousness. When Locke published the first edition of the *Essay* in 1689, this new style of reasoning received an influential stamp of approval.[51]

This semantic conflation is evident in Locke's initial treatment of reflection, which is a form of perception based on sensation:

> The other Fountain, from which Experience furnisheth the Understanding with *Ideas*, is the *Perception of the Operations of our own Minds* within us, as it is employed about the *Ideas* it has got; which Operations, when the Soul comes to reflect on, and consider, do furnish the Understanding with another set of *Ideas*, which could not be had from things without: and such are, *Perception, Thinking, Doubting, Believing, Reasoning, Knowing, Willing*, and all the different actings of our own Minds; which we, being conscious of, and observing in our selves, do from these receive into our Understandings, as distinct *Ideas*, as we do from Bodies affecting our Senses. (105, 2.1.4)

Experience is that through which the mind is "furnish[ed]" with ideas: namely, the perception of "Bodies affecting our Senses" and the "*Perception of the Operations of our own Minds* within us" engaging the ideas received through sensation. The mind perceives, "reflect[s] on," and "consider[s]" these mental "Operations." It then obtains a series of ideas about its own "actings," ideas that are passively generated (the mind "receive[s]" them) because we are "conscious of" them "in our selves" just as we are conscious of "Bodies affecting our Senses." Experience thus consists in a relationship between one's own mind and something that the mind perceives (whether that be an external body or a mental operation). If "Consciousness is the perception of what passes in a Man's own mind," then experience is what comes about as a result of consciousness; it is what consciousness gives to the mind. This is why Locke uses "Observation" to clarify the meaning of both experience and consciousness.[52]

In the thought of an adult human being, considered synchronically, reflection and sensation each make important contributions to the pool of available ideas. But when examined diachronically in terms of individual development, there is a temporal gap between the advent of sensation and the moment reflection begins. When children first come into the world, they are "surrounded with Bodies, that perpetually and diversely affect them" so that a "variety of *Ideas*, whether care be taken about it or no, are imprinted on the Minds of Children." Even before the "Memory begins to keep a Register of Time and Order," when the "Eye is but open" it is impressed with colors and light, while sounds "force an entrance to the Mind" through the always open ears (106–7; 2.1.6). Simple ideas (color, sound, and so on) emerge through sensation easily, without effort or "care." But the ideas generated by reflection are not so readily acquired. It is only when a human being "turn[s] his Thoughts" toward the operations of the mind and "considers them *attentively*" that he begins to have ideas generated by reflection (107, 2.1.7). Since the work of introspective attention is difficult, it is "pretty late, before most Children get *Ideas* of the Operations of their own Minds." In fact, many people live their whole lives without acquiring such ideas with any clarity. Vague notions brought about by mental operations pass through the minds of children "continually," but because they are unable to consider these ideas "attentively"—attention being a difficult skill to master—they exist as "floating Visions," for they "make not deep Impressions enough, to leave in the Mind clear distinct lasting *Ideas*, till the Understanding turns inwards upon it self, *reflects* on its own *Operations*, and makes them the Object of its own Contemplation" (107, 2.1.8).[53] Only later in their mental development, when they are more in control of their powers of discernment and attention, do human beings begin to reflect on their own minds and derive ideas from this reflection. Prior to this stage, the "world of new things" is busy in the "constant solicitation of their senses, draw[ing] the mind constantly to them" (107, 2.1.8). Although the mental operations that condition this engagement with the world—perception and sensation foremost among them—no doubt exist, their workings appear to the child's mind as mere "floating Visions," too blurry to be acknowledged.

We are now in a position to appreciate how Locke's various intellectual commitments cohere in his discussion of embryonic "first thoughts."

Innate ideas do not exist. If such ideas did exist, they would exist as objects of thought. Since thoughts exist only *in actu*, any innate ideas, should they exist, must exist as actualized thoughts. Consciousness is a reflexive awareness sewn into the fabric of each and every thought. If innate ideas—say, *the whole is greater than the parts*—exist in the mind of a given infant, this infant must, necessarily, be conscious of that thought: "No Proposition can be said to be in the Mind, which it never yet knew, which it was never yet conscious of" (50, 1.2.5). Given how small children behave, this position is ridiculous—and it becomes even more so when applied to newborns or fetuses. One cannot make the position more acceptable by taking the Cartesian route and arguing that it is not the infant that thinks but rather the mind itself, for consciousness exists only in and for the human animal. If it is unreasonable to think that the fetus actualizes the thought of God's existence while still in the womb—a position that Descartes himself rejects in his correspondence with Hyperaspistes—then the force of Locke's rejection stems both from his insistence that thought is coterminous with its actualization and from his belief that consciousness is also operative in other animals. But Locke does not, for all that, return to the pre-Cartesian embryological consensus about the nonexistence of fetal thought that we examined in chapter 4. Thought does not preexist the generation of a given human being in the womb. But neither is thought constantly present from the moment the fetus becomes minded. Thought (and therefore consciousness) appears with the generation of "the Man" in utero, with the moment when a sentient body first thrills to contact with its environing world. Such thoughts may be few and far between for most fetuses, but they probably exist. Locke cannot follow Descartes and claim that the fetus is always sensing. He can, however, craft probable fictions about the moment experience begins, and he does so throughout the *Essay*, drawn back repeatedly to the *principium* of thought, the originary experience from which his entire epistemological theory must emerge.

In book 1 of the *Essay*, Locke occasionally touches on infant and prenatal experience in order to debunk innate ideas. Before he elaborates his own account of the "originals" of human knowledge in book 2, Locke gives readers an early hint of his position: "The Senses at first let in particular *Ideas*, and furnish the yet empty Cabinet: And the Mind by degrees growing familiar with some of them, they are lodged in the Memory, and Names got to them" (55, 1.2.15). Here Locke provides an epitome of his argument. The mind starts out as an "empty Cabinet," then becomes, "by degrees," familiar with ideas "let in" by the senses until it begins to lodge those ideas in memory. Eventually, when the capacity for "general Words and Reason" develops sufficiently, "Names" are added to these ideas. Locke isolates what he means by an idea, which is distinct from both memory and word. After all, "a Child knows certainly, before it can speak, the difference between the *Ideas* of Sweet and Bitter (*i.e.* That Sweet is not Bitter) as it knows afterwards (when it comes to speak) That Worm-wood and Sugar-plumbs, are not the same thing." But Locke can only argue for his conception of an idea by making a claim about what happens in the minds of children and infants. If "the Knowledge of some Truths" exists, Locke is forced to admit, "very early in the Mind," this knowledge is never innate but always acquired, for the earliest knowledge human beings acquire is generated by "external Things, with which Infants have earliest to do, and which make the most frequent Impressions on their Senses" (55, 1.2.15).

But Locke does not, for all that, want to "argue from the thoughts of Infants, which are unknown to us, and to conclude, from what passes in their Understandings, before they express it" (62, 1.2.25). After all, he is committed to arguments based on experience. If a newly awakened human being cannot express what he was conscious of in the moment before he was awakened, no philosopher can tell that human being that he was in fact conscious while he slept. The same argumentative principle must also hold in the case of the infant. One cannot legitimately "argue from the thoughts of Infants" both because they are "unknown to us" and because Locke's philosophical commitments demand that all knowledge be based on experience, which is, at least in principle, available "to us." At the same time, however, Locke's epistemological program depends on his ability to isolate the "Original" of knowledge, to determine when and how human thought begins. On the one hand, then, Locke needs to base his claims about the understanding on the access enabled by experience. On the other hand, he needs to make claims about how thought begins in the minds of infants. But if Locke finds himself in the quandary faced by so many of the thinkers examined in *Coming To*, his plight is more acute: unlike, say, Descartes or Harvey, Locke cannot appeal to a nonexperiential standard of proof (metaphysical claims about the essence of mind, the repeated trials and controlled conditions of natural philosophical experiments), and unlike Milton and Traherne, he cannot explicitly appeal to mimetic fictions in order to describe originary experience.

Locke's discomfort about this position is palpable: "Whether we can determine it or no, it matters not, there is certainly a time, when Children begin to think, and their Words and Actions do assure us, that they do so. When therefore they are capable of Thought, of Knowledge, of Assent, can it rationally be supposed, they can be ignorant of those Notions that

Nature has imprinted, were there any such?" (62, 1.2.25). The first sentence makes a claim about which everyone agrees. There "certainly" exists a moment "when Children begin to think." When they reach a certain age, their "Words and Actions" manifest the existence of thought. But even at this stage in their development—when they are capable of articulating what they know—children remain "ignorant" of the axioms many take to be innate. Locke's question proposes a dare: ask any four-year-old if the whole is greater than the parts and see for yourself whether or not this principle exists even in the mind of a child that is "capable of" thought, knowledge, and assent. But even if this point is granted, it is not enough. Someone like Traherne could (and would!) claim that the knowledge of, say, God's existence available to infant thought is in fact superior to what even an older child might possess; the latter is, after all, cut off from the primordial joys of originary experience by the fact of language acquisition, the evidence on which Locke relies.

In order to shore up his claims, then, Locke ventures into the zone of infant thought he wants to avoid. In book 1, he moves in this direction by philosophizing in the subjunctive:

> If we will attentively consider new born *Children*, we shall have little Reason, to think, that they bring many *Ideas* into the World with them. For, bating, perhaps, some faint *Ideas*, of Hunger, and Thirst, and Warmth, and some Pains, which they may *have* felt in the Womb, there is *not* the least appearance of any setled *Ideas* at all in them; especially of *Ideas, answering the Terms, which make up those universal Propositions*, that are esteemed innate Principles. One may perceive how, by degrees, afterwards, *Ideas* come into their Minds; and that they get no more, nor no other, than what Experience, and the Observation of things, that come in their way, furnish them with. (85, 1.4.2)

If one "may" perceive how ideas enter the minds of children as they grow older—a four-year-old who has never encountered a pineapple has no idea of a pineapple—the same standard does not apply to "new born Children." By "attentively consider[ing]" a newborn, one will find "little Reason" to think they are contemplating the idea of God or rehearsing the principle of noncontradiction. But Locke nevertheless holds that the birth of an infant into the world need not mark the beginning of thought. As an inheritor of the still-novel idea that prenatal sensation might exist, Locke was open to the possibility that ideas began to accumulate in the womb and that the "Original" of human thought derives from the contact between fetal body and uterine milieu. But note the hesitations in Locke's prose: infants are born empty-minded, except "perhaps" for "some" ideas—hunger, thirst, warmth, pain—that "may" have been "felt" in the womb. Since to have an idea, however faint, is to engage in the act of thinking, whatever the fetus might feel in the womb would, necessarily, be accompanied by consciousness, by minimal mental presence. At stake in this passage, then, is nothing less than a claim about when human consciousness begins. This makes Locke's series of qualifications and hesitations all the more remarkable. The hypothetical adverb "perhaps," the indeterminate adjective "some," and the auxiliary verb of possibility "may" together conspire to remove any certainty from this picture of cognitive life in the womb. At this point in the *Essay*, Locke is sure that there exist no innate human ideas, but his positive account—his description of the originary experience from which ideas first begin to furnish the mind—remains unclear.

In his first extended account of the fetus's inner life in book 2, Locke argues for the likelihood that we do not think all that much while in the womb. Anyone who considers newborns and how they spend most of their time sleeping (unless hungry or in pain) will "perhaps, find Reason to imagine, That a *Foetus in the Mother's Womb, differs not much from the State of a Vegetable*," a claim that nearly aligns the author of the *Essay* with the pre-Cartesian embryological consensus on the absence of fetal sensation. But then Locke pivots, for it is likely that the fetus "passes the greatest part of its time without Perception or Thought, doing very little, but sleep in a Place, where it needs not seek for Food, and is surrounded with Liquor, always equally soft, and near to the same Temper; where the Eyes have no Light, and the Ears, so shut up, are not very susceptible of Sounds; and where there is little or no variety, or change of Objects, to move the Senses" (117, 2.1.21). The situation in which the fetus finds itself does not often elicit its sensory attention. After all, the tiny creature has what it needs; it lives in a more or less unchanging environment. But Locke maintains the possibility that the fetus *does* perceive and think, for it probably "passes the greatest part of its time without Perception and Thought." The fetus might spend some of its time engaged in these mental activities.

Given the reticence with which Locke treats this topic, it is striking to observe the degree of certainty he has acquired when he returns to the topic in a chapter on "Perception" slightly later in book 2. In Locke's view, perception is "the first faculty of the Mind," a capacity the "bare naked" essence of which is "passive"; what the mind "perceives, it cannot avoid perceiving" (143, 2.9.1).[54] This passivity leads Locke to formulate a rule: any act of perception or sensation must necessarily be accompanied by the presence of an idea in the mind (144, 2.9.4).[55] Since fetuses seem sentient, it is probable that they are conscious: "Therefore I doubt not but *Children*, by the exercise of their Senses about Objects, that affect them *in the Womb*, *receive some few Ideas*, before they are born, as the unavoidable effects, either of the Bodies that environ them, or else of those Wants or Diseases they suffer; amongst which, (if one may conjecture concerning things not very capable of examination) I think the *Ideas* of Hunger and Warmth are two: which probably are some of the first that Children have, and which they scarce part with again" (144, 2.9.5). Everything about this passage points toward a belief in the existence of prenatal thought. Given the structure of perception, given the pure passivity of sentient flesh (which cannot help but receive impressions from the "Bodies that environ" it), prenatal sensation is "unavoidable." By extension, so is prenatal consciousness. This topic is "not very capable of examination" insofar as no one can completely fill in the content of fetal experience. It is "probably" the case that such experience is dominated by "*Ideas* of Hunger and Warmth"; without Adamic access to these memories, Locke cannot provide details. But he is nevertheless certain that fetuses "exercise" their senses and therefore "receive" ideas while still in the womb.

Note the differences between the treatment of this topic in books 1 and 2 of the *Essay*. In the former, Locke suggests that fetuses "may" "perhaps" sense while in the womb. In the latter, Locke "doubt[s] not" that such sensation exists, precisely because it is "unavoidable." Moreover, Locke transforms the notion that fetuses "may" have "some faint *Ideas*" into the more forceful claim that they "*receive some few Ideas*," a formulation that replaces qualitative fuzziness with a quantitative restriction: if the ideas are few, they exist as ideas in a fully unqualified sense; Locke has moved from the subjunctive to the indicative. What enables this transition from "perhaps" to "unavoidable"? How does Locke justify the move from "faint" to "few"? Since all knowledge must be based on experience, and since originary experience is irrecoverable, how does Locke buttress his claims about prenatal thought?

These questions are especially pressing, given all of the embryological happenings about which Locke, even in book 2, claims ignorance: "But whether the Soul be supposed to exist antecedent to, or coeval with, or some time after the first Rudiments of Organisation, or the beginnings of Life in the Body, I leave to be disputed by those, who have better thought of that matter" (108, 2.1.10). Locke brackets the traditional questions from theology or natural philosophy, focusing only on the epistemological problem. Those who insist on constant thought should "tell us, what those

Ideas are, that are in the Soul of a Child, before, or just at the union with the Body, before it hath received any by *Sensation.*" (113, 2.1.17). The when, where, and how of the union of body and soul is, as we have just seen, off the table—and so is the notion that there could be any ideas prior to the advent of sensation, which, it seems, takes place sometime just after the union of body and soul. "To ask, *at what time a Man has first any* Ideas," Locke writes, "is to ask, when he begins to perceive" (108, 2.1.9). Thought begins with perception, and that process starts while the fetus remains in the womb. About this Locke has no doubts. Given that Locke is not, as a general rule, certain about anything unmoored from experience, how is he so sure about the content of an impossible experience? The key to answering this question lies in how Locke develops a mode of philosophical *poiesis* at the edges of mimesis, a form of writing that is as alive to the givenness of revelation as it is to the abstractions of reason.

PHILOSOPHICAL *POIESIS*

During the transition from book 1 to book 2 of the *Essay,* Locke initiates an important transformation in his philosophical method: he ceases making a series of arguments that seek to undermine an existing claim—"that Men have native *Ideas,* and original Characters stamped upon their Minds, in their very first Being" (104, 2.1.1)—and begins to make claims about what actually happens in the psyche of infants and young children. In other words, the movement from book 1 to book 2 involves a slippage from reason to revelation, from philosophical abstraction toward a minimally mimetic philosophical *poiesis.* When arguing against the Cartesian claim that the soul always thinks, Locke states that it "is something beyond Philosophy; and it cannot be less than Revelation, that discovers to another, Thoughts in my mind, when I can find none there my self" (115, 2.1.19). The point here—made in a tone dripping disdain for religious enthusiasm—is that if a given human being cannot remember thinking while he was asleep, then the philosopher has no place informing that human being that he was in fact thinking. Experience is the only legitimate source for such claims, and experience in the sense in which Locke understands the term is nothing if not profoundly first-personal. To make claims about what happens within another human being while denying the privileged access accorded, through experience, to that human being about his or her own inner states is, Locke argues, to move beyond "Philosophy" and enter the terrain of "Revelation," the realm of prophets and poets. But this is precisely what Locke does in the early chapters of book 2: he makes claims about thoughts that are impossible to access. If the thoughts of a sleeping human being are off limits, the same must hold true *a fortiori* for prenatal thought. Locke engages the very mode of revelation that he condemns.

But he does not do so by following the dictates of reason in a space of philosophical abstraction. If Descartes's claims about the conscious life of fetuses were based on abstract principles and were justified in light of a chain of reasoning about the essence of the human mind, Locke's methodology explicitly eschews any such claims. Instead, Locke confines himself to the world of particulars, to the details of experience as it is lived, the various somethings that show up for someone. His entrance into the realm of fetal and infant experience at the beginning of book 2 relies on a combination of philosophy and poetry. Locke makes this explicit by advertising how everything that follows is built upon a fictional foundation: "Let us then suppose the Mind to be, as we say, white Paper, void of all Characters, without any *Ideas*; How comes it to be furnished? Whence comes it by that vast store, which the busy and boundless Fancy of Man has painted on it, with an almost endless variety? Whence has it all the materials of Reason and Knowledge? To this I answer, in one word, From *Experience*" (104, 2.1.2). Both question and answer are subtended by a foundational fiction. An inquiry into how the mind comes to be "furnished" with ideas only makes sense if the mind begins in a state of emptiness. Likewise, Locke is able to argue that *"Experience"* provides the faculties of "Fancy" and "Reason" with the ideas that fill the minds of adult human beings only by first positing that the mind is, in its originary state, empty. But although Locke has argued against the existence of innate ideas, the notion that the mind begins like "white Paper" remains a conceptual leap. Neither Locke nor any of his readers can remember this state of experiential emptiness.

Locke's discomfort with making this leap is perhaps registered in the shifting metaphors through which he articulates his view.[56] The mind begins in this passage as "white Paper"—a phrase that positions the "Characters" that will be written upon it as the *"Ideas"* that will come to be inscribed in the mind through experience—but then begins to shift, as though under the pressure generated by the need to articulate the contents of originary experience within an empiricist framework. Although seventeenth-century English used *to furnish* to mean "equip" and applied the language of furnishing to both paper and minds, when accompanied by the notion that "Fancy has painted" ideas on the mind, it is difficult to avoid the sense that Locke is metaphorizing the infant mind not only as "white Paper" but also as a room within a house.[57] After all, this is the metaphor he uses in book 1: "The Senses at first let in particular *Ideas*, and furnish the yet empty Cabinet" (55, 1.2.15).[58] This metaphorical fuzziness points to the difficulty Locke has in admitting his need to use a fiction as the basis for his entire epistemological project.

It is important to note that Locke is explicit about the fact that it is fiction that enables him to bridge this gap: "*Let us then suppose* the Mind to be, as we say, white Paper." To suppose is to assume "as a basis of argument" or to "put as an imaginary case."[59] In the seventeenth century, the phrase "let us suppose" was used to indicate the beginning of a thought experiment, an imaginary scenario. Although the phrase was in English usage from the early sixteenth century onward, it appeared with increasing frequency as the seventeenth century progressed. The conditionality of the phrase was often emphasized with parenthetical qualifications. Consider the polemical collective Smectymnuus's 1641 argument about scriptural interpretation: "But now let us suppose (which notwithstanding we will not grant) that the word *Angell* is taken individually for one particular person, . . . yet nevertheless there will nothing follow out of this acceptation."[60] The phrase was often used in this way to indicate that what follows must be entertained temporarily, without supporting evidence, merely for the sake of argument. The Jesuit Edward Knott clarifies this strategy in *Infidelity Unmasked* (1652)—"Let us suppose (not grant)," he writes a number of times—while others used slightly different formulations: "Let us suppose (but not believe)," says the 1664 English translation of the works of the chemist Jean Baptiste van Helmont, while the Presbyterian controversialist John Humfrey marks the provisional nature of a point with "Let us suppose (until it appears farther)."[61]

But the phrase was also charged through its association with the imagination. Consider this passage from the religious controversialist Thomas Pierce's *The Sinner Impleaded* (1656): "And therefore let's fancy to our selves, that the year of recompence is now at hand. . . . Let us suppose, and imagine (at least as strongly as we can) that the Sun is now growing black as a Sackcloth of Hair."[62] To suppose is to imagine, to pretend as if something that is not necessarily true were in fact true. This is how the phrase was used in Locke's circle. Responding to an early version of the *Essay* printed in France, William Molyneux challenged Locke with a famous thought experiment about a man, born blind, who acquires, through the sense of touch, the ideas of a cube and a globe. "Let us Suppose," Molyneux's experiment begins, that the blind man has "his Sight restored to Him." Could he, "by his Sight, and before he touch them, know which is the Globe and which is the Cube?"[63] Molyneux was responding to Locke, who argues against constant thought by way of a thought experiment:

Let us suppose then the Soul of Castor, whilst he is sleeping, retired from his Body, which is no impossible Supposition for the Men I have here to do with [the Cartesians]. . . . *Let us then, as I say, suppose* that the Soul of Castor separated, during his Sleep, from his Body, to think apart. *Let us suppose* too, that it chuses for its Scene of Thinking, the Body of another Man, v.g. Pollux, who is sleeping without a Soul: For if Castor's Soul can think whilst Castor is asleep, what Castor is never conscious of, 'tis no matter what Place it chuses to think in. (110–11, 2.1.12; my emphasis)

Locke's repeated use of the phrase here flags the thought experiment as a fiction that presupposes exactly the set of Cartesian assumptions against which he is arguing. The ridiculousness of the conclusion—two bodies sharing one soul—buttresses Locke's position. But if the fictionality indexed by "Let us suppose" reveals the falsity of Descartes's position, Locke's alternative likewise occupies an imagined space of supposition: "Let us suppose the Mind to be, as we say, white Paper." I want to pause for a moment with the difference between these two uses of "suppose." In general, when Locke advances a fictional thought experiment, he does so in order to argue that a given claim is *not* true. The prince and the cobbler, the day man and the night man, Castor and Pollux, and most of the many other memorable thought experiments in the *Essay* are directed negatively against positions Locke does not wish to affirm.[64] When supposing that the mind begins as "white Paper," however, Locke uses the resources of fiction not to deny the force of a given claim but to affirm the nature of originary experience.

In imagining the mind to begin as a "white Paper," Locke follows the strategy used by Milton, Traherne, and many of the other writers examined in this book: he deploys the power of fiction in order to return to an inaccessible beginning. But, as I argued in the introduction, the use of fiction does not, in itself, make a given act of writing poetic. Recall the philosophical fictions that were used repeatedly by philosophers attempting to isolate human nature by setting aside any and all forms of nurture. Consider Avicenna, who aims to elucidate the immaterial nature of the human "self" through a philosophical supposition. In order to grasp this truth, one must, Avicenna argues, "suppose" [*putare*] a man "created all at once [*subito*] and in a perfect state [*perfectus*]."[65] Or take Hobbes, who follows a similar strategy in *De cive*: "Consider men as if but even now sprung out of the earth, and suddenly [*subito*], like mushrooms, come to full maturity, without all kind of engagement with each other."[66] Since they are inaccessible, beginnings must be conjured through the imagination. Elsewhere in the *Essay*,

Locke follows a similar line of thought. As we have already seen, he asks readers to imagine an Adam very much like that portrayed by Milton: "Let us suppose *Adam* in the State of a grown Man" (466, 3.6.44), neonatally mature in the midst of a world about which he knows nothing.

Most of Locke's *Essay* emerges from exactly such a philosophical fiction. If book 1 is dedicated to the careful rebuttal of an existing idea, the remaining three books are elaborations of a philosophical view grounded in the explicit fictionality of a "Let us suppose." In the *Essay*, all of the many details about how knowledge acquisition works—how simple ideas emerge from experience and build one atop the other, lead to complex ideas, and interact with language—are supported by an explicitly fictional claim about how the mind begins as "white Paper." As he concludes his treatment of simple ideas, Locke summarizes his initial method:

> And thus I have given a short, and, I think, true *History of the first beginnings of Humane Knowledge*; whence the Mind has its first Objects, and by what steps it makes its Progress to the laying in, and storing up those *Ideas*, out of which is to be framed all the Knowledge it is capable of; wherein I must appeal to Experience and Observation, whether I am in the right: The best way to come to Truth, being to examine Things as really they are, and not to conclude they are, as we fancy our selves, or have been taught by others to imagine. (162, 2.11.15)

Although the spirit of this claim hews true to Locke's practice, he nevertheless obfuscates what would, if he noticed it, have struck him as an uncomfortable and recalcitrant fact at the heart of his method: the centrality of fiction within his own philosophical system. Since he cannot "appeal to Experience and Observation" in order to elucidate the content of the true "first Beginnings" of human knowledge, he needs to rely on the power of "fancy," to "imagine" his way inside an experience he can never access.

If Locke's account of how the understanding comes to be "furnished" with ideas is based on a fiction, it is also, I want to argue in conclusion, carried out by way of what I have been calling a form of minimal mimesis that blurs the universal with the particular. Just as Milton's Adam lives a singular life in which all of humanity is represented, so the epistemological history lived out by Locke's child represents the journey toward knowledge undertaken by each human being. "He that attentively considers the state of a *Child*, at his first coming into the World, will have little reason to think him stored with plenty of *Ideas*, that are to be the matter of his future Knowledge," writes Locke. " 'Tis by degrees he comes to be furnished with them" (106, 2.1.6). Locke invokes this singular child repeatedly throughout the early stages of his argument in book 2. Readers are instructed to "Follow a *Child* from its Birth, and observe the alterations that time makes" so that they can discover how

> as the Mind by the Senses becomes more and more to be furnished with *Ideas*, it comes to be more and more awake; thinks more, the more it has matter to think on. After some time, it begins to know the Objects, which, being most familiar with it, have made lasting Impressions. Thus it comes, by degrees, to know the Persons it daily converses with, and distinguish them from Strangers; which are Instances and Effects of its coming to retain and distinguish the *Ideas* the Senses convey to it: And so we may observe, how the Mind, *by degrees*, improves in these, and *advances* to the Exercise of those other Faculties of *Enlarging, Compounding*, and *Abstracting* its *Ideas*, and of reasoning about them, and reflecting upon all these; of which I shall have occasion to speak more hereafter. (117, 2.1.22)

Having begun by using fiction to establish the emptiness of originary experience, Locke uses the figure of "a *Child*" to organize his exploration of mental development over time. This passage provides a blueprint for what follows "hereafter" in the *Essay*, as Locke moves, chapter by chapter, along a line of epistemological development stretching from "Birth" through to "reasoning" and "reflecting" on the ideas first acquired by sense. Beginning with such "Simple Ideas" as "Solidity," the progression of chapters in book 2 is organized by the growth of a child's mind, moving from such processes as perception and retention toward more "Complex Ideas."

This "Historical, plain Method" (44, 1.1.2) follows the life of a child in a minimally mimetic way, but it also, at the same time, traces the epistemological trajectory of each and every one of us. After asking readers to consider "the state of a *Child*, at his first coming into the World," Locke turns almost immediately to a consideration of all human beings: "all that are born into the World being surrounded with Bodies, that perpetually and diversely affect them, a variety of *Ideas*, whether care be taken of it or no, are imprinted on the Minds of Children" (106, 2.1.6). For Locke, a child (a posited particular being) is almost always synonymous with children (a general class). Beginnings nudge particularity toward the general—we are all "born into the world" surrounded by other bodies—and if the details differ (we are "diversely affect[ed]" by the bodies that "perpetually" affect us), in Locke's view, the structure of exposure and engagement with the phenomenal world remains more or less the same for all human beings. Locke's child is, then, like Milton's Adam and Traherne's fetus or infant, a proxy for human species being, a mimetic figure exposed to the particulars of the phenomenal world in order to elevate it toward the universal. Subtended by fiction and minimally mimetic, Locke's *Essay* attempts to illuminate the concept of consciousness while maintaining a connection to the variety and particularity that must necessarily structure the appearance of all the somethings that might show up for someone.

Perhaps the student of Locke who understood this point most clearly was Étienne Bonnot de Condillac, who amplified Locke's brand of philosophical *poiesis* and brought the imaginative exercise underpinning the *Essay* out into the light. Citing "Locke's arguments" as opening the path that led away from the "prejudices" that shaped the *Essai sur l'origine des connaissances humaines* (1746) and led him to the new method displayed in the *Traité des sensations* (1754), Condillac begins this latter text with a dedication that summarizes the problem I have been examining throughout this book:

> We cannot recollect the ignorance in which we were born. It is a state which leaves no traces behind it. . . . Reflective memory which makes us conscious [*sensible*] of the passage of one cognition [*conaissance*] to another, cannot go back to beginnings [*premières*]: it supposes them, and this is the origin of our propensity to believe that our cognitions were born with us [*c'est là l'origine de ce penchant que nous avons à les croire nées avec nous*]. To say that we have learned to see, to hear, to taste, to smell, to touch appears a strange paradox. It seems that nature at the very instant that formed our senses must have given us the entire use of them; and since we have not now to learn their use we suppose we must from the first have used them without learning.[67]

Since our memories cannot "go back to beginnings," we cannot use experience to determine what our first experiences were like. This is why, in Condillac's view, a "new way of approach" is required.[68] "For this purpose," Condillac writes, "we imagined a statue constructed internally like ourselves, and animated by a mind which as yet had no ideas of any kind."[69] Throughout the *Traité*, which is not a short book, Condillac opens the senses of this statue slowly, one by one, in an extended imaginative exercise designed to reveal which senses and types of experience are responsible for particular ideas. He begins with the sense of smell, asking what ideas the statue would possess if only its olfactory receptors were stimulated, and then moves to taste, touch, and the other senses. The *Traité* provides a mimetic account of the various somethings that show up to a fictional statue waking up one sense at a time. The "first beginnings" of human knowledge are, Condillac openly admits, available to human reason only through the imagination. The reader must approach the statue of the *Traité* as they would Milton's Adam and Eve or Traherne's embryonic self: "He must enter into its life, begin where it begins."[70] This is the lesson that Locke taught Condillac but that he could not quite bring himself to fully articulate: only through the revelatory powers of the imagination can originary experience and, by extension, the foundations of human thought be known. As Locke—following Descartes, Milton, and Traherne—shows us in the *Essay*, the birth of consciousness as a concept was intimately and paradoxically grounded in the consciousness of birth.

CODA

The English word *concept* has been traced back to its roots in the Latin *conceptus*, a term that originally meant *fetus*. The figurative sense of *conceptus*—a mental representation gestating in the mind—was already used in antiquity, but it became a widespread term of art in the Middle Ages, when *conceptus* was deployed by the scholastics to index an internally developed and general object of thought. The bringing together inherent in *con-capere*, which was understood to determine the meaning of *conceptus*, signaled the collection and subsumption of the many particulars perceived through the senses into a single general mental object perceived through the intellect.[1] The generation of concepts was thus analogous to the embryological development of fetuses in the womb. Coiled within this etymological coincidence lies the core of the argument I have presented in *Coming To*.

I have argued that the emergence of the concept of consciousness brought with it important shifts in how mindedness and natality could be represented and understood. To use the terms proposed by Arnold Davidson that I laid out in the introduction, the emergence of consciousness opened up a new style of reasoning that changed the conceptual space within which human beginnings (whether they be created or gestated) could be thought. This conceptual space stabilized new sorts of statements subject to truth and falsity, which, in turn, led to new discursive practices and new opportunities for mimetic representation. When consciousness became established as a nonevaluative concept tying together the appearance of all the many somethings that might show up for someone, the question of originary experience—by definition inaccessible for most if not all human beings— became both philosophically important and aesthetically significant. Insofar as consciousness is a concept that acquires meaning on the horizon of

251

particularity, it is perhaps uniquely suited to mimetic representation, to the phenomenal fictions of an early modern poetics invested in the question of *what it is like* to be in a particular state, to think a particular thought, or to perform a particular act. In its seventeenth-century infancy, consciousness was a concept that sought to grasp what I have called mental presence, phenomenality itself. Milton and Traherne elucidated the concept of consciousness by pursuing a strategy of *phenomenalization* in which concepts are inhabited as they might be experienced, in which human mindedness is represented in its purest state, at the very moment consciousness first sparks into existence. My treatment of Locke and Condillac suggests that later philosophers followed suit, exploiting a line of thought previously developed by poets—the mimetic and imagined inhabitation of an experience that is impossible to access—in order to understand the beginnings of human mindedness, a topic tricky to elucidate according to the official methods and strictures of empiricism. By tracing the emergence of consciousness in seventeenth-century poetry and philosophy, we see how the relationship between concept and *conceptus* became unexpectedly important to early modern intellectual life, acquiring meaning through a metaphoric shuttling between (and sometimes disconcerting literalization of) the resemblances shared by embryonic development and mental activity.

As I have argued, poetry was a privileged discursive form through which consciousness—a new way of thinking about thinking—could be thought. In closing, I want to pause for a moment on a deeper connection between poetry and concepts. According to Aristotle and the thinkers indebted to him that were discussed in earlier chapters—Castelvetro, Sidney, Tasso, Milton, and Traherne, among others—a poem, or *poiema*, is a "thing made," emergent from *poiesis*, the activity of making something, of bringing something into being that did not exist before. The etymological connection between concept and fetus should recall for us the fact that concepts are, like poems, things that are made—a fact that, as I suggested in the introduction, is at the heart of the seemingly insurmountable difficulties nagging the scientific pursuit of an empirically verifiable account of a consciousness increasingly shorn of its historical and cultural properties, increasingly naturalized into an emergent property of brain states. Concepts are shared ways of thinking that are made in and then change over historical time, crafted by and for a human culture that uses them and makes sense of the world through them. This is not to say that concepts are fictions in any reductive sense. Rather, they are tools for demarcating, organizing, and simplifying the world such that human beings can attempt to understand it and live more easily within

it. When, in the mid-seventeenth century, the concept of consciousness began to change how a number of European writers approached the topic of
human mindedness, this did not mean that an older, benighted vision of
mental activity was slowly superseded by a lucid modern view. Concepts
abide: if affect has, in recent years, become a newly powerful way of con-
ceptualizing certain aspects of human life, it coexists along with emotion,
feeling, passion, and other more ancient concepts.[2] The concept of consciousness simply provided a new way of thinking through old problems,
one with affordances and limitations that enabled new questions ("What is
the originary experience shared by all human beings and how might it matter?") and established new problems ("What separates the conscious from
the nonconscious, and does it make sense to think of human life as divided
in this way?"). In the seventeenth century, different discourses responded
to this emergent nexus of possibilities and troubles in different ways. Poets
grappled with the inchoate concept of consciousness by making use of the resources of imagination and mimetic representation in ways that clarify how
subsequent philosophers approached the topic.

Originary experience has had a long, influential, and unstudied afterlife.
Taking up the torch lit by Milton and others, William Wordsworth wrote
"Ode: Intimations of Immortality from Recollections of Early Childhood,"
part of which almost reads as though it could have been penned by Traherne:

> There was a time when meadow, grove, and stream,
> The earth, and every common sight,
>> To me did seem
> Apparelled in celestial light,
> The glory and the freshness of a dream.[3]

The consciousness that accompanies infancy and early childhood reveals
the "glory" of what is "common," what is later covered over by habitual
acquaintance. Oscillating between the serious and the satirical, similar
meditations on originary, infant, and childhood experience run through the
modern European traditions of poetry and fiction, from Laurence Sterne
and Mary Shelley through Rainer Maria Rilke, Henry James, and Marcel
Proust, to Ian McEwan's recent *Nutshell*, which rewrites *Hamlet* from the
perspective of a fetus in the womb.[4] Philosophers have likewise taken up
the theme. From Gottfried Wilhelm Leibniz to Maurice Merleau-Ponty,
meditations on fetal and infant experience recur with startling frequency.[5]
In the twentieth century, psychoanalytically informed thinkers have taken

up and reworked the legacy of Sigmund Freud, with such writers as Otto Rank, Melanie Klein, Didier Anzieu, and Julia Kristeva basing their theories on the encounter between a fetus or infant and its environs.[6]

If embryonic originary experience has dominated the field, the figure of Adam awakening also continues to appear. Contemporary philosophers of mind like David Chalmers use Adam in Eden as a way of clarifying the nature of perceptual consciousness,[7] while earlier thinkers like the Spanish philosopher José Ortega y Gasset dwelled on Adam's first experiences: "When Adam appeared in paradise, like a new tree," he was "the first being who, living, felt his own life." Aware of himself and an environment stretching from the vegetation around him toward an ever-expanding horizon, Adam is, Ortega claims, "life pure and simple."[8] Perhaps most strikingly, in the late 1940s, when the French philosopher Pierre Hadot was an adolescent living in Rheims, he encountered what he would later call the "sentiment of the presence of the world." This newfound "awareness of existence" preoccupied the young Hadot because he felt it "might correspond to questions such as *What am I? Why am I here? What is this world I am in?*" Unable to express how he felt, Hadot wrote "a sort of monologue in which Adam discovers his body and the world around him." He translated his own "pure sentiment of existing" into the voice of Adam as he awakens in a long-lost paradise. Hadot grounded the beginning of his illustrious philosophical career in an explicitly imagined account of neonatal maturity.[9]

In these examples we can not only see the longevity of originary experience as a prompt for mimetic fictions and philosophical reflections alike. We can also glimpse how the limitations woven into the style of reasoning proper to a given concept at the moment of its emergence persist even as it changes over time. When Ortega responds to the question "Who is Adam?" with the answer "Anyone and no one in particular: life," he articulates the enduring power of a fantasy that roots the essence of human life—nature without nurture—in an implicitly male universality.[10] Ortega is part of a long lineage. As we have seen, when it comes to fictions of originary experience, early modern writers consistently elevated a masculine perspective. Recall the inequality of Adam and Eve in *Paradise Lost*, Gray's *puer* in *De principiis cogitandi*, or Locke's child as it develops in the *Essay*. Or consider Traherne's articulation of embryonic experience, which positions the mother's womb as a background for the emergent light of consciousness. Insofar as Traherne figures a male subject literally discovering himself against the environing confines of a female body that he conceives to be the world, his treatment of originary experience reveals in particularly vivid terms the gendered implications of modern philosophies of mindedness, the long project stretching from Descartes, through Immanuel Kant, to the phenomenology of Edmund Husserl, Martin Heidegger, and Merleau-Ponty. In this tradition, a lone thinker, subjectivity, consciousness, *Dasein*, or living body encounters itself and the world—never anything less than universal, always silently male.

But as my earlier invocation of Kristeva and Klein suggests, reflections on originary experience need not be cut according to this mold. I want to conclude by discussing a poem that conjures fetal originary experience as imagined from the outside—"To a Little Invisible Being Who is Expected Soon to Become Visible" (1825), by Anna Letitia Barbauld, which is written in the voice of an unnamed mother awaiting the arrival of her child. The poem begins by addressing this "Germ of new life, whose powers expanding slow / For many a moon their full perfection wait."[11] The "powers" or "faculties" of the fetus are not yet *perfectus*, or fully developed. These "powers" are, the speaker claims (adopting a view that courts what, in chapter 4, I described as the embryological consensus), "folded" in the fetus's "curious frame,— / Senses from objects locked, and mind from thought!" (5–6). The capacities that the fetus will actualize later in life are, at this early stage, "folded" in on themselves; the senses are unable to access their usual objects, and the mind is unable to open onto thought. But Barbauld has not foreclosed the possibility of phenomenality as had Donne, Davies, Pembroke, and many of the other poets we encountered earlier in this book. If the fetus's senses are "locked" "from objects," the tiny "infant bud of being" (12) might be caught in something approximating the self-affection that Traherne describes in so many of his poems, the link between consciousness and natality. Such an openness to phenomenality is suggested by the speaker's future-oriented invitation to the fetus:

And see, the genial season's warmth to share,
Fresh younglings shoot, and opening roses glow!
Swarms of new life exulting fill the air, —
Haste, infant bud of being, haste to blow! (9–12)

The speaker asks the fetus to "see" how the "opening" roses glow and, by implication, to take inspiration and "Haste" toward the opening of its own "bud." The "infant bud of being," turned in on itself, must "haste to blow," to open like the "roses" that now "glow" in the ambient world surrounding the poem's speaker. What matters here is openness to the world, a state of full relationality in which mother, infant, other life forms, and the world itself are interconnected in the fullness of a future that will arrive only once the child has "Launch[ed] on the living world, and spr[ung] to light" (30). In this poem, originary experience begins out in the light, with a mother thinking about and alongside a "Part of herself, yet to herself unknown," waiting for the "stranger guest" to arrive (22–23), to enter the phenomenal world in which the future of all things born and all things made will unfold.

ACKNOWLEDGMENTS

When it comes to work, I am a compulsive oversharer. These acknowledgments represent the flip side of this oversharing, a testament to the generosity of the people who supported me, guided me, or responded to me in one way or another—even when I was unreasonable in making a request or pursuing a path of inquiry. I am beyond grateful to have lived for so long among so many people who are open, curious, and kind. The excess of these acknowledgments emerges from my disposition and is prompted by my unusual journey into academia.

It is not an exaggeration to say that the eleven years I spent at the University of Toronto changed my life. I entered the university as a mature student through the Academic Bridging Program at Woodsworth College before completing a BA and then a PhD at Toronto. Given the rather dismal state of my previous academic history, there is no way that I could have gained admission to the university were it not for the existence of this program. And I could not have flourished as an undergraduate were it not for the patient and determined care of J. Barbara Rose, who guided me from the Bridging program through to graduate school. I owe a great debt to Vala Holmes, Tanuja Persaud, Barbara Track, and the many others in the Department of English, Woodsworth College, and the School of Graduate Studies who repeatedly engineered the scholarships I needed to pursue my studies. I am also grateful to all of the people involved in the Records of Early English Drama, Massey College, the Program in Book History and Print Culture, and the Center for Reformation and Renaissance Studies for helping me to navigate my way through the university.

Elizabeth D. Harvey was an immensely generous, savvy, and committed adviser and has remained a true mentor. She taught me how to construct an argument, showed me the extent to which writing simply *is* rewriting, made me think about the relationship between one's scholarship and one's wider life, and constantly surprised me with her willingness to engage my ideas and projects in a serious and collaborative way. Elizabeth's continued advice, excitement, intellectual kinship, and friendship have been vital to my growth as an intellectual and as a person. Alexandra Gillespie was an almost impossibly attentive reader; she remains my pedagogical role model. I continue to learn from Lynne Magnusson, Mary Nyquist, and Paul Stevens, all of whom have taught me about how to be a scholar, a critic, and a teacher. I benefited enormously from the gracious and unexpected mentorship of Jim Carscallen and Brian Stock, both of whom read my work and talked through my ideas when they had many better things to do. Jason Peters was the ideal interlocutor; his continued friendship is one of the things I value most about my time in Toronto. I am also grateful for the help and support of many others from Toronto, particularly Piers Brown, Rob Carson, Ted Chamberlin, David Galbraith, Ian Lancashire, Tom Laughlin, Deidre Lynch, Amyrose McCue Gill, John O'Connor, Simon Reader, John Reibetanz, Julia Reibetanz, William Robins, Virginia Lee Strain, and Evan Thompson. While at Toronto, I benefited from a year-long seminar at the Folger Shakespeare Library led by James Siemon and Keith Wrightson. I have grown as a scholar and critic through conversations and ongoing friendships with Liza Blake, Ryan Hackenbracht, Ivan Lupić, Debapriya Sarkar, and Kathryn Vomero Santos that began in that seminar.

I am thrilled to have landed at the Department of English at the University of Chicago, a place committed to intellectual conversation of the most intense and worthwhile sort. I could not have written this book anywhere else. My senior colleagues have been unfailingly generous and incisive. Joshua Scodel has been a model of what unpretentious, kind, collegial, and rigorous mentorship should look like. Josh read everything (many times) and this book is immeasurably better because of the care and intelligence he invested in my work, his willingness to share his immense learning, and his ability to critique while, at the same time, helping to instill confidence. Richard Strier read more drafts of this book's chapters than I can count—always with fresh excitement, even joy, and always with good advice and useful disagreement about my arguments and interpretations. My regular brunches with Richard have helped shape my approach to the field and to literary criticism, and I am thankful both for his mentorship and for his friendship. Always supportive and insightful, Ellen MacKay and Mark Miller read full, early drafts of the manuscript and provided transformational feedback. Bill Brown read early and late drafts of the introduction and the coda, and his comments were detailed and revelatory. I am also grateful to David Bevington, James Chandler, Michael Murrin, Frances Ferguson, and Lisa Ruddick, all of whom read parts of the manuscript in progress and helped me to achieve argumentative, methodological, and stylistic clarity. Lauren Berlant, Tim Campbell, Maud Ellmann, Elaine Hadley, Patrick Jagoda, Josephine McDonagh, Deborah Nelson, Sianne Ngai, Eric Slauter, and Ken Warren all gave advice or encouragement that remains important to me. I would also like to thank Lex Nalley Drlica, Laura Merchant, Angeline Dimambro, and the other staff members in the department who have helped me in numerous ways. Across the university, I have benefited from my collaborative work with Ada Palmer. Thomas Pavel has been a luminous interlocutor. I am grateful to David Finkelstein, Jean-Luc Marion, Raoul Moati, and Justin Steinberg for allowing me to audit their classes and to Marc Berman, James Evans, Willemien Otten, Boris Maslov, Larry Norman, Mark Payne, Rocco Rubini, Nathan Tarcov, Rosanna Warren, and Christopher Wild, among many others, for horizon-expanding conversations. It has been an honor to have taught so many brilliant students since arriving in Chicago. I would like to thank Beatrice Bradley, Ethan Della Rocca, and Michal Zechariah, all of whom read the manuscript for errors and made many excellent suggestions, as well as Sam Catlin, Ryan Campagna, Ben Jeffery, Sarah Kunjummen, Sarah-Gray Leslie, Jane Mikkelson, Jo Nixon, and Sophie Zhuang for the things they have taught me. I have benefited from the vibrant conversations that regularly take place at the Chicago Renaissance Seminar, the Chicago Renaissance Workshop, and the Early Modern Reading Group. Since 2016, the students in Behar House have helped to keep me young and have taught me much about how care and community must be at the heart of both teaching and intellectual life more broadly.

It was my great fortune to have arrived at Chicago at a moment when there was a large and expanding cohort of amazing junior faculty in the Department of English, a fact that has made my time in Chicago not only stimulating but also truly happy. For their willingness to read my writing, for the vigor with which they discuss my ideas and almost everything else, and, most importantly, for their friendship, I am extremely grateful to Edgar Garcia, Heather Keenleyside, Julie Orlemanski, Ben Saltzman, Zach Samalin, David Simon, and Chris Taylor, all of whom have spent many hours— over coffee or drinks, over lunch or dinner, in the hall or the quad, at the lake or the pool, or over email—thinking through the contours of this book with me. In different ways, they have all helped me to improve my arguments and deepen my sense of what I should know, what I am capable of thinking, and, most significantly, what it means to live a good life. This early stage of my career has also been made immeasurably better by the intelligence, conviviality, compassion, and overall wonderfulness of my colleagues Sophia Azeb, Adrienne Brown, Alexis Chema, Rachel Galvin, Sarah Johnson, Benjamin Morgan, John Muse, Noémie Ndiaye, Kaneesha Parsard, Tina Post, Richard So, Sarah Pierce Taylor, and Sonali Thakkar. I assume that my children are unusual in thinking that the word *colleague* is synonymous with the word *friend*. The Chicago Junior Faculty Writing Group was also an incredible source of inspiration and feedback. I am particularly grateful for conversations with Harris Feinsod and Megan Heffernan.

I am continually dazzled by the brilliance of my colleagues across the globe. My friend Ethan Guagliardo has been an attentive and repeated reader of this book at a variety of stages; his critiques and suggestions have helped me strengthen both my arguments and my readings. Joanna Picciotto has been an important inspiration, advocate, and reader of my work. Brian Cummings has been a scholarly model as well as a trans-Atlantic mentor and collaborator. Katie Kadue and Ross Lerner have been both good friends and wonderful readers of my work. For reading sections of this book and making helpful suggestions, I am grateful to Sharon Achinstein, Andrew Cutrofello, Jim Knapp, Gary Kuchar, Mary Nyquist, and Ayesha Ramachandran, who was also kind enough to share sections from her book in progress, *Lyric Thinking*, with me. Special thanks are due to Paul Stevens, Sebastian Sobecki, Kim Coles, Steve Fallon, Nigel Smith, Rhodri Lewis, Laura Knoppers, Russ Leo, and Paul Hecht. Their kind invitations enabled me to present material from my book manuscript in progress at, respectively, the Canada Milton Seminar at the University of Toronto, Groningen University, the Marshall Grossman Lecture at the University of Maryland, the Newberry Library Milton Seminar, the North Eastern Milton Seminar at Princeton University, the Early Modern English Literature Seminar at Oxford University, the Early Modern Seminar at the University of Notre Dame, the Medieval and Early Modern Colloquium at the University of California at Berkeley, the Intellectual Lives of Hugo Grotius conference at Princeton University, and Purdue University. I owe a great debt to these hosts for the invitations, for their generous individual responses to my work, and for facilitating discussions with faculty and students that repeatedly changed how I understood both my local arguments and my project as a whole. For helpful comments, probing questions, great advice, and stimulating conversations, I want to thank Bradin Cormack, Kathy Eden, Roland Greene, Achsah Guibbory, Jessie Hock, Wendy Beth Hyman, Maggie Kilgour, András Kiséry, Jesse Lander, Micha Lazarus, Russ Leo, Julia Reinhard Lupton, David Marno, Geoffrey Miller, Feisal Mohamed, Susannah Monta, Joe Moshenska,

Kathryn Murphy, Lodi Nauta, James Nohrnberg, Gerard Passannante, Annabel Patterson, Giulio Pertile, David Quint, Kelly Robertson, John Rogers, Michael Schoenfeldt, Regina Schwartz, Daniel Shore, Nigel Smith, Garrett Sullivan, Jason Rosenblatt, Ramie Targoff, Gordon Teskey, Joanne van der Woude, Jennifer Waldron, Christopher Warren, Lindsay Waters, Reginald Wilburn, and Esther Yu. I owe a special debt to Susan James, who was kind enough to let me audit a class on Spinoza that she taught at Chicago and who also read through and commented on early drafts of the introduction and chapter 4. The title for this book came from a lunch with Quentin Skinner, who, after listening to me describe my book, responded—immediately and with a clarity for which I am grateful—by saying: "Your title must be *Coming To*." Alan Thomas and Randolph Petilos at the University of Chicago Press did an incredible job of ushering this book through the publication process. I am grateful for their savvy advice and for their suggestions, all of which have made this a better book. I want to thank Nicholas Murray and Amy Sherman for the care they took in editing my manuscript and also the anonymous readers for the University of Chicago Press for really understanding my book.

I thank my parents, Sam and Helen Harrison, who instilled in me both the creative thinking and the disciplined approach to work without which I could not have written this book. Childhood conversations with my brother Jeff Harrison lie in the background to many of the questions pursued in this book. My extended family in Canada (especially John and Gail Root and John and Miriam Lekx) has supported me and inspired me at pivotal moments in my life. My extended family in the Netherlands (Ina and Bert Smit, Paulien Smit, Peter Machiel Lotgering, Derk Smit, and Anne Zdunek) have provided me with a home away from home and for that, among many other kindnesses, I am very grateful. David Leaney not only saved my life when I was young and very sick but also helped to nurture my curiosity. Ken Mavor believed in me in ways that have stuck with me for decades. Growing up, I was lucky to have a strong group of friends. Much of what is best about me I owe to my continued friendship with Ken Angeles, Phil Elder, and Brody Paul.

Christina Smit and our children, Livia and Elise, give me joy every day. Livia's intelligence and determination give me hope, and the many book covers she drew for me over the years really helped me to visualize the fact that this book could indeed be finished. Elise's good humor, hugs, and love of play are often the best part of my day. I was so sorry to disappoint both of them with the news that finishing my book did not mean I could just stop going to work. This book would not be possible without the love and support of Christina, my partner in all things, without whom I can no longer imagine my life. I met Christina in 2002, when I was still a clueless twentysomething living abroad. When we fell in love, we promised each other that if we stayed together, we would go back to school together. Two years, two attempts at immigration, and one impromptu wedding later, we enrolled together in university. Without Christina's love, intelligence, patience, care, wit, spontaneity, honesty, and fundamental goodness, there is no way that I could have written this book—much less gotten a job, finished a PhD, or even begun my BA. This book could not exist without Christina because without her the version of myself capable of writing this book would not have existed, let alone suspected he could do such a thing. For almost eighteen years, I have loved her more than anything and I am very proud of her and the life we have built together. This book is for her.

NOTES

INTRODUCTION

1. I borrow *minded* and *mindedness* from Jonathan Lear, "Leaving the World Alone," 385–86.

2. "[W]e do not believe in eternal concepts," as Friedrich Nietzsche puts it; "we view all concepts as having *become*" (Qtd. in Guido Mazzoni, *Theory of the Novel*, 358, n. 25).

3. The nonconscious has haunted consciousness from the beginning. See Geneviève Lewis, *Le problème de l'inconscient*. As we will see in chapter 5, the "inconscious" was the telos of the first English philosophy of consciousness. See Ralph Cudworth, *True Intellectual System*, 215.

4. See, e.g., Jacques Derrida, *Speech and Phenomena*.

5. This formulation is indebted to Joanna Picciotto, *Labors of Innocence in Early Modern England*, 1: "The question raised by objectivity is how innocence, traditionally understood to be a state of ignorance, ever came to be associated with epistemological privilege."

6. For histories of consciousness, see Lewis, *Le problème*; C. S. Lewis, *Studies in Words*, 181–217; Catherine Glyn Davies, *Conscience as Consciousness*; Udo Thiel, *Early Modern Subject*; Étienne Balibar, *Identity and Difference*; and Shelley Weinberg, *Consciousness in Locke*.

7. For Descartes, see Alison Simmons, "Cartesian Consciousness Reconsidered." For Cudworth, see Udo Thiel, "Cudworth and Theories of Consciousness." For Locke, see Balibar, *Identity*.

8. Previous scholars have studied the reception of consciousness by poets, the literary *responses* to conceptual innovation undertaken by the philosophers usually credited with inventing the concept. See Christopher Fox, *Locke and the Scriblerians*, and Jonathan Kramnick, *Actions and Objects*. Studies of Renaissance or early modern literature that was written prior to the emergence of consciousness as a concept—e.g., Charles Trinkaus, *Poet as Philosopher*—often treat consciousness as a stable, ahistorical concept, even if the studies themselves are deeply historical. To take a recent example, Giulio Pertile, *Feeling Faint*, begins with an introductory study of the term *consciousness* in the seventeenth century, grounded in an analysis of Descartes's *conscientia*, and then turns to chapters

that examine a back projection of this consciousness onto authors—Montaigne, Spenser, Shakespeare—who were certainly thinking about human mindedness in sophisticated ways but who did not have the concept of consciousness at their disposal. When treating the use of concepts in the past, it is easy to fall prey to what Arnold Davidson (*Emergence of Sexuality* 41), calls the "immediate application of concepts, as though concepts have no temporality," a practice "that allows, and often requires, us to draw misleading analogies and inferences that derive from a historically inappropriate and conceptually untenable perspective." So far as I know, I am the first critic to argue that literature *contributed* to the historical emergence of consciousness *qua* concept. For a complementary account of the relationship between consciousness and literature that stresses the disciplinary knowledge enabled by literary studies, see Kramnick, *Paper Minds*.

9. John Milton, *Paradise Lost*, 4.457. Subsequent quotations are cited parenthetically in the text by book and line numbers.

10. See Jacques Brunschwig, "The Cradle Argument."

11. Thomas Traherne, *The Works*, 6:4, line 38. Subsequent Traherne quotations are all taken from this edition and are cited parenthetically in the text by volume and page number (for most of Traherne's works); by volume, page, book, and section number (for the *Centuries of Meditation* and *Select Meditations*); and by volume, page, and line number (for any poetry that appears across the corpus).

12. Hannah Arendt, *Human Condition*, 8.

13. Arendt, *Human Condition*, 177. On natality in Arendt, see Peg Birmingham, *Hannah Arendt and Human Rights*; Miguel Vatter, "Natality and Biopolitics in Hannah Arendt"; Anne O'Byrne, *Natality and Finitude*; and Adriana Cavarero, "'A Child Has Been Born Unto Us.'"

14. See Arendt, *Human Condition*, 178: "Action as beginning corresponds to the fact of birth, [and] is the actualization of the human condition of natality."

15. Hannah Arendt, *Origins of Totalitarianism*, 479: "Beginning, before it becomes a historical event, is the supreme capacity of man; politically, it is identical with man's freedom. *Initium ut esset homo creatus est*—'that a beginning be made man was created' said Augustine. This beginning is guaranteed by each new birth; it is indeed every man."

16. See Rémi Brague, "Necessity of the Good," 50.

17. Arendt intended to publish the revised document but halted the project when the trial of Adolf Eichmann began. See Joanna Scott and Judith Stark, "Rediscovering *Love and Saint Augustine*."

18. Hannah Arendt, *Love and Saint Augustine*, 51.

19. Arendt, *Love*, 47; Augustine, *Confessions*, 193, translation modified; Augustine, *Confessiones*, 10.16.25. Subsequent quotations are cited parenthetically in the text, citing pages from the English and book, chapter, and section from the Latin.

20. Jean-Luc Marion, *Negative Certainties*, 190. So far as I know, the phenomenology of birth began in 1950s France. See Paul Ricoeur, *Freedom and Nature*, 433–43. Similar points about the opacity of birth have been made by Claude Romano, *Event and World*; and Emmanuel Falque, *Metamorphosis of Finitude*. See also Jean-Luc Marion, *Being Given*, 248–319; and Jean-Luc Marion, *In Excess*, 41–44.

21. I take the phrase "horizon of expectation" from Hans Georg Gadamer, *Truth and Method*.

22. Arendt, *Love*, 50–51.

23. From Arendt's earliest discussion of birth, this discursive transfer is evident in her return to Augustine's treatment of Adam's creation in *De civitate Dei* (427)—*Initium ut esset homo creatus est*, "That a beginning be made man was created"—in order to make the claim that human begins are "*initium*, newcomers and beginners by virtue of birth" (Arendt, *Human Condition*, 177). See also, Arendt, *Origins*, 479; and Arendt, *Love*, 55. On the gendered implications of this usage, see Cavarero, "'A Child Has Been Born'"

24. Jean-Luc Marion, *In the Self's Place*, 78, captures this dynamic: "*Memoria*, such as Saint Augustine develops it to its extreme, no longer concerns what was present to my mind in the past and could become so again in the future—in the literal sense, the *re*-presentable and re-*presentable*—but what in me remains inaccessible to me and un-controllable by me (what I forgot, my forgetting of what I forgot, and even my forgetting of this forgetting itself), and which, despite or *because* of this, governs me through and through." This claim is supported by the passage in the *Confessiones* in which Augus-tine's use of *conscientia* veers closest to modern usage: "*Et tibi quidem, domine, cuius oculis nuda est abyssus humanae conscientiae, quid occultum esset in me, etiamsi nollem confiteri tibi?*" [Indeed, Lord, to your eyes, the abyss of human *conscientia* is naked. What could be hidden within me, even if I were unwilling to confess it to you?] (179; 10.2.2). *Conscientia* indexes not only what is conscious, but what is open to God—everything that might be in the mind, even those things that might be hidden from Augustine himself.

25. For *memoria* as unconscious, see Etienne Gilson, *Christian Philosophy*, 299.

26. Arendt, *Love*, 46–47.

27. See Daniel Heller-Roazen, *Inner Touch*, 21–30. Heller-Roazen is right to take issue with the use of consciousness in Charles H. Kahn, "Sensation and Consciousness in Aristotle's Psychology." I would place Victor Caston, "Aristotle on Consciousness" in the same camp.

28. Cicero, *On Ends*, 456–57, translation modified (5.20). All subsequent quotations are cited parenthetically in the text according to page number for the English translation and chapter and section numbers for the facing-page Latin text.

29. See Joseph Needham, *A History of Embryology*; G. R. Dunstan, ed., *The Human Embryo*; Justin E. H. Smith, ed., *The Problem of Animal Generation*; Luc Brisson, Marie-Hélène Congourdeau, and Jean-Luc Solère, eds., *L'embryon*; Fabrizio Amerini, *Aquinas on the Beginning and End of Human Life*; and James Wilderbing, *Forms, Souls, and Embryos*.

30. For sensation *in utero*, see Alessandra Piontelli, *Development of Normal Fetal Movements*, 111–27. Although much work on fetal pain brackets issues generated by reproductive rights—see, e.g., Giuseppe Buonocore and Carlo V. Bellieni, *Neonatal Pain*—the specter of fetal suffering is often invoked to restrict abortion access. See American College of Obstetricians and Gynecologists, "ACOG Opposes U.S. Senate Effort to Limit Abortion Access": a bill proposed by the US Senate "ignores scientific evidence regard-ing fetal inability to experience pain at that gestational age." See also Royal College of Obstetricians and Gynecologists, *Fetal Awareness*.

31. For gender in early modern reproductive knowledge, see Mary E. Fissell, *Vernacular Bodies*; and Eve Keller, *Generating Bodies and Gendered Selves*.

32. See especially Katharine Park, *Secrets of Women*. It is worth noting that Jane Sharp's *Midwives Book*, the first text by an English midwife, was not published until 1671.

33. For the supposed dangers mothers posed to fetuses, see Fissell, *Vernacular Bodies*, 53–89.

34. Simmons, "Cartesian Consciousness," 1. Descartes did not invent consciousness; his was one voice among many. Nor is he the *wunderkammer* of error attacked by philosophers, critics, and undergraduates. This book's Descartes is a brilliant thinker whose remarks on embryonic thought carried unexpected importance for English contemporaries. For a dismantling of Descartes's dualism as usually understood, see Jean-Luc Marion, *On Descartes's Passive Thought*. For a rethinking of Descartes's "errors," see Harry G. Frankfurt, *Demons, Dreamers, and Madmen*.

35. René Descartes, *Philosophical Writings*, 1:195, translation modified; René Descartes, *Oeuvres*, 8:7. All subsequent quotations are cited parenthetically according to volume and page number: CSM 1:195 (for the English) and AT 8:7 (for the Latin or the French). I always indicate when I have modified the English translation, except when I quote *conscientia* and its variants (*conscia, conscii*, and so on). The translators of CSM render these words most often as "awareness," "aware," or another similar word. Since I think this translation distorts what Descartes is in fact doing with *conscientia* and also what his seventeenth-century English readers took him to be doing, I translate such words as "consciousness," "conscious," and so on, while always including the original Latin as part of the quotation. See also CSM 2:113, translation modified; AT 7:160: "*Thought.* I use this term to include everything that is within us in such a way that we are immediately conscious [*conscii*] of it."

36. As Marion, *Passive Thought*, 7, points out, the necessary modality of thought is apparent in the *Meditationes*: "I am a thing that thinks: that is, a thing that doubts, affirms, denies, understands a few things, is ignorant of many things, is willing, is unwilling, and also which imagines and senses" (CSM 2:24). The point is also made in a letter to Arnauld from 1648: "So by 'thought' I do not mean some universal which includes all modes of thinking, but a particular nature, which takes on those modes, just as extension is a nature which takes on all shapes" (CSM 3:357).

37. For Descartes's understanding of fetal mindedness, see Rebecca Wilkin, "Descartes, Individualism, and the Fetal Subject." For the *Meditationes* as dialogical and the centrality of the "Objections" and "Replies," see Jean-Luc Marion, *On the Ego and on God*, 30–41.

38. Voltaire, *Philosophical Letters*, 53, was wrong: "Our Descartes [maintained] that the soul makes its arrival in the body already provided with every possible metaphysical notion, knowing God, space, and infinity, as well as a whole range of abstract ideas, and filled, in other words, with splendid knowledge all of which it unfortunately forgets as it leaves its mother's womb."

39. Andrea Gadberry, "The Cupid and the Cogito," 745.

40. This is the definition advanced in Weinberg, *Consciousness*, 3.

41. On *conscientia*, see especially Henry Nettleship, *Contributions to Latin Lexicography*, 420–21. I have also consulted Charlton Lewis and Charles Short, *Latin Dictionary*.

42. Cicero, *Pro Cluentio*, 397 (159), translation modified.

43. Cicero, *De senectute*, 18–19 (3.9).

44. For Stoic *conscientia*, see G. Molenaar, "Seneca's Use of the Term 'Conscientia.'"

45. For the most extensive treatment of the topic in the Middle Ages, see Timothy C. Potts, *Conscience in Medieval Philosophy*.

46. See Davies, *Conscience*.

47. Louis de La Forge, *Treatise on the Human Mind*, 76, 54, translation modified; Louis de La Forge, *Traitté de l'esprit de l'homme*, 96, 57.

48. C. S. Lewis, *Studies in Words*, 183. Thanks to the Early English Books Online (EEBO) database, which includes most things printed between 1473 and 1700, I can narrate how this "desynonymisation" occurred. I have used the basic search functions available on Early English Books Online TCP, as well as the functions available through the Brigham Young EEBO corpus and the Early English Print website, run through Washington University at Saint Louis. For a different but related approach to the history of *conscience*, see Esther Yu, "Tears in Paradise."

49. William Perkins, *A Discourse of Conscience*, 2.

50. Graph 1 represents a decade-by-decade distribution across the seventeenth century of (1) all uses of consciousness recorded in the EEBO website and (2) each of the books or pamphlets that includes consciousness.

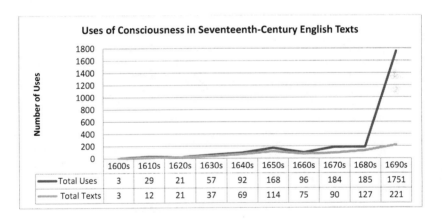

	1600s	1610s	1620s	1630s	1640s	1650s	1660s	1670s	1680s	1690s
Total Uses	3	29	21	57	92	168	96	184	185	1751
Total Texts	3	12	21	37	69	114	75	90	127	221

Uses of Consciousness in Seventeenth-Century English Texts

51. John Calvin, *Institutes of the Christian Religion*, 1:36 (bk. 1, chap. 1); Jean Calvin, *Institutio Christianae religionis*, 3:31.

52. William Struther, *True Happiness*, 36.

53. Robert Sanderson, *Ten Lectures on the Obligation of Humane Conscience*, 4; see also 5.

54. Joseph Hall, *Epistles*, 142.

55. René Descartes, *Six Metaphysical Meditations*, 123–24; AT 7:176.

56. Graph 2 represents decade-by-decade evaluative and nonevaluative uses of *consciousness*. It is based on my reading of each usage in context. This method is open to instance-by-instance dispute, but the trend is clear.

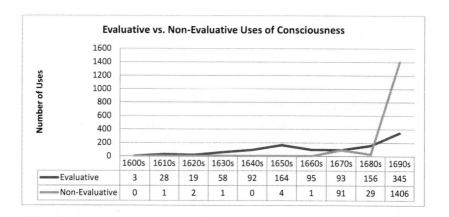

Evaluative vs. Non-Evaluative Uses of Consciousness

	1600s	1610s	1620s	1630s	1640s	1650s	1660s	1670s	1680s	1690s
Evaluative	3	28	19	58	92	164	95	93	156	345
Non-Evaluative	0	1	2	1	0	4	1	91	29	1406

57. Thomas Stanley, *History of Philosophy*, 60. For the claim that this is the first philosophical use of the English *consciousness*, see Thiel, *Early Modern Subject*, 12. For Stanley as intellectual, see Dmitri Levitin, *Ancient Wisdom in the Age of the New Science*, 38–53.

58. Cudworth, *True Intellectual System*, 1:245.

59. John Locke, *Essay Concerning Human Understanding*, 115 (2.1.19); 340 (2.27.16). All subsequent quotations from the *Essay* are cited parenthetically by page, book, chapter, and section numbers. For Locke and consciousness, see especially Galen Strawson, *Locke on Personal Identity*; Balibar, *Identity*; and Weinberg, *Consciousness*.

60. Richard Burthogge, *An Essay Upon Reason*, 8; Thomas Wilson, *Christian Dictionary*, 488.

61. This book's focus on the history of consciousness differentiates it from analogous histories of the self and the subject. For self, see Charles Taylor, *Sources of the Self*; Richard Sorabji, *Self*; and Vincent Carraud, *L'invention du moi*. For subject, see Alain de Libera, *Archéologie du sujet*, *L'invention du sujet moderne*, and "When Did the Modern Subject Emerge?"

62. The roots of this distinction are ancient, reaching back at least to Aristotle's *De interpretatione*, in which words, which are conventional, are distinguished from mental states, which are natural: "just as written marks are not the same for all men, neither are spoken sounds. But what these words are in the first place signs of—affections of the soul—are the same for all" (1:25, 16a). This distinction between word and thought has been debated endlessly. I have found Benjamin Straumann, "The Energy of Concepts," a recent and helpful approach.

63. This formulation is indebted to Quentin Skinner, *Visions of Politics*, 1:180, who studies "transformations in the applications of the terms by which our concepts are expressed." See also Heather Keenleyside, "Matter, Form, Idea."

64. Peter de Bolla, *Architecture of Concepts*, 40.

65. I draw here from Davidson, *Emergence of Sexuality*, 125–41. Lorraine Daston and Peter Galison, in *Objectivity*, show how Davidson's "styles of reasoning" coexist while developing over time.

66. Davidson, *Emergence of Sexuality*, 139.

67. Davidson, *Emergence of Sexuality*, 186.

68. Antoine Le Grand, *An Entire Body of Philosophy*, 10.

69. The term *mineness* is a translation of the German term *Jemeinigkeit*, explained in Martin Heidegger, *Being and Time*, 67–68: "That Being which is an *issue* for this entity in its very Being, in in each case mine. . . . Because Dasein has *in each case mineness* [*Jemeinigkeit*], one must always use a *personal* pronoun when one addresses it: 'I am,' 'you are.'"

70. Thomas Nagel, "What Is It Like to Be a Bat?"

71. For the insufficiency of "imitation" as an English translation of *mimesis*, see Stephen Halliwell, *Aesthetics of Mimesis*. As Halliwell explains (37–147), Plato's position vis-à-vis mimesis is more complex than the typical gloss of his views. Plato and the tradition he initiated "established," as Halliwells puts it (322), "the idea that artistic mimesis [is] tied to an anthropocentric perspective of the world, a perspective that views things at the level of physical description, of embodied life, of human actions, desires, and emotions."

72. Mazzoni, *Theory*, 29.

73. Mazzoni, *Theory*, 31.

74. Milton and Traherne are both, then, "theoretical poets," to borrow an insight from Gordon Teskey, *Delirious Milton*, 1–2: "Claiming no primary existence for itself, theory is the detached representation of what already is, rather than a part of what already is. In contrast, 'poetry,' which means 'production' or, as we would now say, 'creation,' is turned toward the future, a future in which it will itself be a presence and a power, whence the nearness of poetry to prophecy. To be a *theoretical poet*, therefore, is to look in both directions at once."

75. For early modern versions of this point, see, e.g., Kenelm Digby, *Two Treatises*, 364: "Before the production of Eve, the notion of a *man* was as fully taken up by Adam alone."

76. Gordon Teskey, *Poetry of John Milton*, 593, n. 2.

77. Aristotle, *Complete Works*, 2:2323 (1451b). All subsequent quotations are cited parenthetically by volume, page, and Bekker numbers (excluding line numbers).

78. For Aristotle's association of poetry and the universal, see Halliwell, *Aesthetics*, 164–71, 193–200; and Kathy Eden, *Poetry and Legal Fiction*, 49. For Reformation understandings of this Aristotelian connection to which Milton subscribed, see Russ Leo, *Tragedy as Philosophy*. For Milton's attempt to dwell in the "origins," prior to the advent of history, see Teskey, *Poetry*, 340–69.

79. Edmund Spenser, *The Faerie Queene*, 387 (3.10.60).

80. Philip Sidney, *Defence of Poesy*, 12. Drawing on Aristotle's *Poetics* (2:2316, 1447b), Sidney deepens this claim by arguing that verse is an "ornament and no cause of poetry, since there have been many most excellent poets that never versified, and now swarm many versifiers that need never answer to the name of poet."

81. Sidney, *Defence*, 34.

82. Sidney, *Defence*, 11.

83. Victoria Kahn, *Wayward Contracts*, and *Future of Illusion*.

84. Frédérique Aït-Touati, *Fictions of the Cosmos*.

85. Ayesha Ramachandran, *The Worldmakers*.

86. See Kahn, "Allegory, Poetic Theology, and Enlightenment Aesthetics."

87. For a parallel exploration of poetry as an aesthetic alternative to the protocols of knowledge production implicit in a nascent empiricism, see Rachel Eisendrath, *Poetry in a World of Things*.

88. Sidney, *Defence*, 10. See Micha Lazarus, "Sidney's Greek *Poetics*."

89. Halliwell, *Aesthetics*, 23.

90. Mazzoni, *Theory*, 46–47: "Stories never talk about dislocated human beings, about humankind-in-itself or about a general human type, as do the abstract discursive formations (philosophy, theology, natural sciences, the human sciences); and even when the character is an *everyman*, the generic subject is always treated as being located in place."

91. Halliwell, *Aesthetics*, 199.

92. As Guido Mazzoni, *Sulla poesia moderna*, 43–84, has argued, it was not until the late eighteenth century that "lyric poetry" came into being as a category reserved for the utterances of an individual subjectivity.

93. Sidney, *Defence*, 9.

94. Milton, *Of Education*, 403.

95. Milton, *Of Education*, 368–69.

96. Balachandra Rajan, "Simple, Sensuous and Passionate," 295–96.

97. Milton, *Reason of Church Government*, 817. Translating Aristotle's notion of epideictic rhetoric from the *Rhetoric*—speech that treats "excellence and vice, the noble and the base," the "objects of praise and blame" (2:2174, 1366a)—medieval and Renaissance criticism interpreted Virgil's *Aeneid* as a "poem of praise" and then adopted the opening line of Averroes's paraphrase of the *Poetics* as an adequate representation both of Aristotle's view and of poetry itself: "Every poem and all poetic discourse is blame or praise" (Qtd. in O. B. Hardison Jr., *Enduring Monument*, 34–35). Many humanists understood poetry in light of praise. See Hardison, *Enduring Monument*; and Brian Vickers, "Epideictic and Epic in the Renaissance."

98. See Ludovico Castelvetro, *Art of Poetry*, 70: "In epic poetry thought must not be kept hidden, for it is a principal part of the invention, and the hearers desire to know precisely what thoughts occupy the character's minds. Moreover, it is easier to reveal the thoughts of characters in narrative than in any other type of poetry, for the epic poet not only detects the secrets of the human mind, but penetrates to the abyss, and soaring above the heavens presumptuously scrutinizes the very bosom of God." Milton, *Of Education*, 405, commends Castelvetro and Tasso for teaching the "laws" of a "true *Epic* poem."

99. Torquato Tasso, *Discourses on the Heroic Poem*, 90.

100. Tasso, *Discourses*, 17.

101. For the relationship between poetry and philosophy framed in terms of revelation and reason, see Stanley Rosen, *The Quarrel Between Philosophy and Poetry*.

102. Thomas Hobbes, *Man and Citizen*, 205; *De cive*, 160 (8.1).

103. The library of Nathan Paget, which Milton used, contained several copies. For the catalogue, see Nathan Paget, *Bibliotecha Medica*, which lists a number of Avicenna's books, including one edition of *De anima*—(47) *Avicennae Logica, de Sufficientia, de Caelo & Mundo, de Anima & Animal, Metaphysc &c.*—and two *opera*: (1) *A Bohali Abynsceni vel Avicenae opera* and (12) *Avicennae Arabum Medicorum Principis Opera Omnia*. On Milton's use of the library, see Christopher Hill, *Milton and the English Revolution*, 492–95; and James Holly Hanford, "Dr. Paget's Library." English contemporaries read Avicenna, and members of Milton's intellectual circles were interested in Arabic thought. See Muhammad Sid-Ahmad, "Ibn Tufayl's Hayy and Milton's Adam." Even if Milton did not read the original, it is likely he would have encountered it as mediated by scholastic thinkers. See Dag Nikolaus Hasse, *Avicenna's "De Anima" in the Latin West*. See also Étienne Gilson, "Les sources gréco-arabes de l'augustinisme avicennisant."

104. Avicenna, *Avicenna Latinus*, 36 (1.1).

105. Avicenna, *Avicenna Latinus*, 36–37 (1.1).

106. The independence of soul is how both Gundissalinus and William of Auvergne introduce Avicenna's thought experiment: "That the soul is not a body, the philosophers prove by saying . . ." See Hasse, *Avicenna's "De Anima*," 89.

107. For the possible influence of Avicenna on Descartes, see Thérèse-Anne Druart, "The Soul and Body Problem"; and Ahmad Hasnawi, "La conscience de soi chez Avicenne et Descartes." For Digby as historian, see Levitin, *Ancient Wisdom*, 245–50.

108. Digby, *Two Treatises*, 416–17. In 1637, while living in Paris, Digby introduced Descartes to England by sending Hobbes a copy of the just-published *Discours de la méthode* with a letter claiming that if the French philosopher "were as accurate in his metaphysicall part as he is in his experience, he had carryed the palme from all men living." See Thomas Hobbes, *Correspondence*, 1:51.

109. Huygens, qtd. in Ramachandran, *Worldmakers*, 179. In Ramachandran's view, texts like Descartes's *Le monde* contend that the "world has an aesthetic order that can only be revealed through literary figuration," recasting "philosophy in terms of fiction and suggest[ing] that such fiction could pave the way to knowledge" (*Worldmakers*, 153–54).

110. Mary Shelley, *Frankenstein*, 105.

111. Throughout this book, my treatment of the relationship between poetry and thought has been shaped in a general but profound way by conversations with Ayesha Ramachandran and from unpublished writing from her book in progress, *Lyric Thinking: Poetry, Selfhood, Modernity*.

112. Although Louis Martz, *Paradise Within* provides a sustained comparative study, even Martz considers Milton and Traherne in isolation. In Martz's treatment, the main point of connection between these two poets is a shared commitment to the psychology propounded by Augustine in *De trinitate* and taken up by Bonaventure.

113. For Brookes's account of the discovery, see Traherne, *Works*, 6:321–24.

114. For the history of discovering Traherne's manuscripts, see Julia J. Smith, "Traherne and Historical Contingency." Under the editorship of Jan Ross, as of 2019, D. S. Brewer has published six of a projected eight volumes in the collected *Works of Thomas Traherne*. Under the editorship of Julia J. Smith, Oxford University Press will be

publishing a fully annotated edition of Traherne's collected works. The projected fourteen-volume *Oxford Traherne* is in preparation.

115. Jean Starobinksi, *Montaigne in Motion*, serves as a critical model.

116. This position shares much with that articulated by Richard Strier, "New Historicism."

117. Theodor Adorno, "On Lyric Poetry and Society," 46. Responding to William Empson's claim that "a profound enough criticism could extract an entire cultural history from a single lyric," Richard Strier, in "How Formalism Became a Dirty Word," argues that to follow through on Empson's sense that history is coiled up within poetry, one must share a "belief that one has to know the texture as well as the content of ideas to do intellectual or cultural history with true sensitivity, and [also] a corollary belief that this texture is most fully experienced at the level of verbal and stylistic detail, where tensions are manifested in texts in very subtle and unpredictable ways. The level of style and syntax is the true level of 'lived' experience" (212).

118. See, e.g., Reinhart Koselleck, *The Practice of Conceptual History*; Skinner, *Visions of Politics*, vol. 1; Davidson, *Emergence of Sexuality*; and Libera, *Archéologie*.

119. Markus Gabriel, *I Am Not A Brain*, 28. Although I borrow Gabriel's formulation here, my thinking has been most informed by Shigehisa Kuriyama, *The Expressiveness of the Body*.

120. This understanding of experience is indebted to Katharine Malabou, *Before Tomorrow*, 17, where Malabou equates experience with "adventure and surprise."

CHAPTER ONE

1. See especially Joshua Scodel, "Edenic Freedoms."

2. For an account of what Milton read, see William Poole, *Milton and the Making of "Paradise Lost."* For a catalogue, see Jackson Campbell Boswell, *Milton's Library.*

3. For how Milton used the literary tradition he inherited, see especially David Quint, *Inside "Paradise Lost."*

4. Augustine, *City of God*, 767; Augustine, *De civitate Dei*, 16.43.3. For works by Augustine other than the *Confessiones*, I take Augustine's Latin from J. P. Migne, ed., *Patralogia . . . Latina*, which I cite parenthetically by the book, chapter, and section numbers of a given Augustinian work after the page numbers of the various translations that I have used.

5. For how familiarity with the poem has obscured its radical features, see Ramachandran, *Worldmakers*, 202–8.

6. Patrick Hume, *Annotations on Milton's "Paradise Lost,"* 150. For Hume's place in English literary criticism, see Ants Oras, *Milton's Editors and Commentators*; and John Leonard, *Faithful Labourers*, 12–14.

7. For broad histories, see Gary Anderson, *The Genesis of Perfection*; John Flood, *Representations of Eve*; and Stephen Greenblatt, *The Rise and Fall of Adam and Eve*. For early modernity, see James Grantham Turner, *One Flesh*; Philip C. Almond, *Adam and Eve in Seventeenth-Century Thought*; William Poole, *Milton and the Idea of the Fall*; and Kathleen M. Crowther, *Adam and Eve in the Protestant Reformation*. For the visual arts,

see Diane Kelsey McColley, *A Gust for Paradise*. For Adam, Eve, and the development of the sciences, see Charles Webster, *The Great Instauration*, 465–83; Peter Harrison, *The Bible, Protestantism, and the Rise of Natural Science*, 205–49; Peter Harrison, *The Fall of Man and the Foundations of Science*; and Picciotto, *Labors*.

8. Petrarch, *Lyric Poems*, 326–27 (poem 181, 7–8). See also 550–51 (poem 354, 12–13).

9. For a different version of this view, see Timothy M. Harrison, "Adamic Awakening."

10. See Crooke, *Microcosmographia*, 264; Sharp, *Midwives Book*, 106–7. I thank Beatrice Bradley for directing me to the connection between "sweat" as amniotic fluid and Adam's "sweat" in the moments after his creation.

11. C. S. Lewis, *A Preface to "Paradise Lost,"* 118, claims, "No useful criticism of the Miltonic Adam is possible until the last trace of the *naïf*, simple, childlike Adam has been removed from our imaginations." Blaine Greteman, *Poetics and Politics of Youth*, 160–65, overstates his case when he argues that Adam and Eve were not created as "adult human beings" and that critics who understand Adam and Eve as having undergone a "birth mature" "misrepresent the universe of *Paradise Lost.*" Adam and Eve *were* born mature insofar as they were created with every bodily and mental capacity available for immediate actualization.

12. William Harvey, *Disputations Touching the Generation of Animals*, 17; John Locke, *Two Treatises*, 306 (Treatise 2, 58). I take Harvey's Latin from William Harvey, *Exercitationes de generatione animalium*, B2r.

13. On Milton's "Edenic life [as] radical growth and process," see Barbara Kiefer Lewalski, "Innocence and Experience in Milton's Eden," 88; and Scodel, "Edenic Freedoms," 158.

14. Adam's and Eve's stories use birth to depict creation, thereby deepening a line of thought Milton develops elsewhere. Addressing the Holy Spirit in the opening lines of *Paradise Lost*, he presents creation as birth—"thou from the first / Wast present, and with mighty wings outspread / Dovelike satst brooding on the vast abyss / And mad'st it pregnant" (1.19–22)—dramatizing an etymological connection made in *De doctrina Christiana*, 1:24–25: *natura natam se fatetur*, "nature declares that it was born." For cosmos as womb, see Louis Schwartz, *Milton and Maternal Mortality*, 245–60. For birth imagery, see Michael Lieb, *Dialectics of Creation*.

15. Although almost all Milton critics treat this theme in one way or another, Teskey, *Poetry*, 340–69, provides a particularly powerful conceptual exploration of this Miltonic preoccupation. See also David Quint, *Origin and Originality in Renaissance Literature*, 207–20; and Regina Schwartz, *Remembering and Repeating*, 1.

16. On Milton's verisimilar Eden, see David Carroll Simon, *Light without Heat*, 169–212.

17. Milton's choice of topic, as Basil Willey argues in *The Seventeenth Century Background*, 227–28, is deliberate, part of Milton's "dismissal" in *Paradise Lost* of the "fabled knights," "battles feigned," and "tinsel trappings" around which previous epic poetry had been organized (9.30–36). It is this "rejection," Willey contends, that drove Milton from his original plan to write a poem based on the Arthuriad and toward the presentation of Genesis, since Milton "felt all proper contact with biblical material to be, in a quite special sense, contact with Truth." Teskey (*Poetry*, 17) claims that the "largest problem facing the modern reader of Milton" is "Milton's insistence that the Bible is true, that it

is the one text that cannot be doubted, submitted to critical scrutiny, or examined in the light of the historical circumstances of its composition."

18. Hesiod, *Theogony and Works and Days*, 30 (924–26).

19. I stress that it only appears this way because in Hesiod (*Theogony*, 29), Athena is the product of Zeus's marriage with Metis: "But when [Metis] was about to give birth to the pale-eyed goddess Athene, he tricked her deceitfully with cunning words and put her away in his belly."

20. I consulted Homer, *Homeric Hymns*, 210 (Hymn 28, "To Athena," 4–7). This translation is taken from Armand D'Angour, *The Greeks and the New*, 138. See also George Chapman's translation *The Crowne of all Homers Workes*, 149: "his unbounded Brows, / Could not containe her; such impetuous Throw's / Her birth gave way to; that abrode she flew / And stood in Gold arm'd, in her Fathers view, / Shaking her sharpe Lance: all *Olympus* shooke / So terrible beneath her; that it tooke / Up, in amazes, all the Deities there."

21. Jean de Sponde, ed. and trans, *Homeri quae extant omnia*, 376.

22. Alex Preminger and T. V. F. Brogan, eds., *The Princeton Encyclopedia of Poetry and Poetics*, 902. See also Boris Mazlov, *Pindar and the Emergence of Literature*.

23. For the view that Sin and Death have more in common with ancient myth than with personification, see Gordon Teskey, *Allegory and Violence*, 42.

24. See Alastair Fowler, *Renaissance Realism.* Framed differently, Sin exposes the extent to which *Paradise Lost* is written in a register that Joanna Picciotto and other critics have described as "literal figuralism" or "figural realism." See Picciotto, "Circumstantial Particulars, Particular Individuals, and Defoe," 35.

25. Steven Knapp, *Personification and the Sublime*, 2.

26. Knapp, *Personification*, 138.

27. *Oxford English Dictionary* (*OED*), s.v. "pensive," adj. A.1, A.2.

28. Teskey, *Poetry*, 46.

29. The fullest discussion of gendered differences is Susannah B. Mintz, *Threshold Poetics*, 33–67.

30. *OED*, s.v. "I," pron. I.1; s.v. "me," pron. 4a; s.v. "myself," pron. II.5.

31. Thomas Browne, *Religio Medici*, 86.

32. Connecting Milton to Hobbes, Kahn, *Wayward Contracts*, 220–21, claims of Milton's Adam and Eve that, "*Pace* Hobbes, we do not construct ourselves and our obligations ex nihilo. Note that, in this contrast, Hobbes is the radical constructivist . . . while Milton insists on the ways in which we come into the world if not fully formed, at least already created."

33. *OED*, s.v. "find," v. I.7a–c; s.v. "find", v. I.4; s.v. "feel," v. II.6d.

34. Martin Heidegger, *Being and Time*, 55. The German is taken from *Sein und Zeit*, 119.

35. Theodore Kisiel, *The Genesis of Heidegger's "Being and Time,"* 300. Kisiel is quoting from a course on Aristotle that Heidegger delivered in the summer semester of 1924.

36. The term *Befindlichkeit* is used in Heidegger, *Sein und Zeit*, 172. I take this very exact translation from Christopher Smith, *The Hermeneutics of Original Argument*, 18. The term is notoriously difficult to translate; it has been rendered as variously as "state

of mind," "attunement," "affectedness," and "primordial affection." On this diversity of translations, see Ratcliffe, *Feelings of Being*, 47.

37. Of these lines, Lewis, *Preface*, 47, writes, "The syntax is so artificial that it is ambiguous . . . the very crumbling of consciousness is before us."

38. John Milton, *Masque Presented at Ludlow Castle*, 70 (l.1001).

39. Edmund Spenser, *Faerie Queene*, 40 (1.1.41); William Shakespeare, *Complete Pelican Shakespeare*, 1675 (*Antony and Cleopatra*, 2.7.105).

40. It is the difference between angelic softness and Hell's extremes that causes discomfort: angels "feel by turns the bitter change / Of fierce extremes, extremes by change more fierce, / From beds of raging fire to starve in ice / Their soft ethereal warmth" (2.598–601).

41. Joe Moshenska, *Feeling Pleasures*, 261.

42. On the history of being environed, see Leo Spitzer, *Essays in Historical Semantics*, 179–316.

43. Elizabeth D. Harvey, "*Samson Agonistes* and Milton's Sensible Ethics," 660, makes a similar observation about Milton's Samson: "We are made to *feel* rather than see the difference between sun and shade—a distinction that becomes a function of temperature rather than light."

44. See, e.g., Coffin, "Creation and the Self," 5–6: Adam's "first gesture"—eyes opened heavenward, an upward leap—"signals his rapport with heaven." See also Lieb, "Adam's Story," 25, 30: Adam springs up "immediately" and "immediately" beholds the sun. Froula, "When Eve Reads Milton," 330, claims that Adam "leap[s] upright to apostrophize a transcendent sky while Eve, supine, gazes into a 'sky' that is to Adam's as her knowledge is to his."

45. For Philo, see Harrison, *Fall of Man*, 23–25; and Flood, *Representations*, 17–19.

46. See Hugh MacCallum, *Milton and the Sons of God*, 132: in the beginning of Adam's account, "Tactile, thermal, and olfactory sensations dominate, and bring a fugitive awareness of self that gives way almost at once to wonder as he gazes awhile at the expanse of heaven above him." For early modern touch, see Elizabeth D. Harvey, "The 'Sense of All Senses.'"

47. *OED*, s.v. "quick," adj., n.1, and adv.

48. Robert Cawdrey, *Table Alphabetical*, F2v. Hume, *Annotations*, 234, glosses "quick instinctive motion" with *instinctus*, which he translates as "a natural Perswasion, and inward Motion."

49. In antiquity, *instinctus* denoted poetic inspiration and sexuality; it was tethered to the innate responses of animals in the writings of Aquinas, who claims that the sheep flees the wolf by means of a "*naturali[s] instinctu[s]*." See Aquinas, *Summa theologica*, 1.q.83.1.

50. By aligning Adam with vegetable life and with feeling in these opening lines, Milton may be gesturing toward vegetal feeling. For Aristotle on the claim that plants could feel, see Aristotle's *De plantis* in *Complete Works*, 2:1251 (815a). Michael C. Schoenfeldt, *Bodies and Selves*, 142, claims that it is "deeply significant" that "the first thing the first human does, even prior to consciousness, is sweat," but the term could also invoke a residue left behind after the act of creation or even amniotic fluid.

51. Milton associated animal life with sentience. In *Artis Logicae*, 466, he uses the ancient definition of the animal as *vivens sentiens* (a living, feeling thing). For Adam and animal life, see Scodel, "Edenic Freedoms," 155–58. For Adam and instinct, see Harrison, *Fall of Man*, 155–56.

52. Genesis 1:20–21 invokes the "moving creature that hath life" and "every living creature that moveth." Milton also draws on an Aristotelian tradition in which the identifying feature of life is self-movement: the ability of living bodies to perform such processes as digestion, growth, bodily locomotion, sensation, feeling, and thought. See, e.g., Aquinas, *Summa theologica* 1.q.18.1: in order to "distinguish living from lifeless things," one must determine the identifying feature of life, that by which "life is manifested first and remains last," and "an animal begins to live when it begins to move itself." See also Aquinas, *Summa contra gentiles*, 1.97.3. Early moderns also linked life and motion. See, e.g., Thomas Hobbes, *Leviathan:* life is "but a motion of the limbs, the beginning whereof is in some principle part within" (3).

53. Milton follows Augustine, *On the Trinity*, 14 (8.6.9): "For we also recognize, from a likeness to us the movements of bodies by which we perceive that others besides us live. Just as we move our body in living, so, we notice those bodies are moved." Subsequent quotations are cited parenthetically by page number (English) and book, chapter, and section numbers (Latin).

54. The fullest reading of these lines is Christopher Ricks, *Milton's Grand Style*, 81–82.

55. *OED*, s.v. "gaze," v. 1a.

56. *OED*, s.v. "peruse," v. II.3; s.v. "survey," v. 3.

57. My appeal to Aristotle complements Paul Stevens, *Imagination and the Presence of Shakespeare in "Paradise Lost,"* 65–66, who reads this passage as modeled on the ascent *per viam eminentiae.*

58. *OED*, s.v. "supple," adj. I: "Of a soft or yielding consistency."

59. My claim here chimes with Richard Strier, "Milton's Fetters," 25–48.

60. Olivi draws on an Augustinian tradition. In *De trinitate*, Augustine claims that nothing "is so present to the mind as the mind to itself" (52; 10.7.10), for the mind "knows itself for no other reason that that it is present to itself" (54; 10.9.12). Even when one is not explicitly thinking about oneself, one is, Augustine insists, always aware of oneself: "the mind always remembers itself, always understands itself, and always loves itself [*semperque se ipsam intellegere et amare*]" (146; 14.7.9).

61. Pierre Jean Olivi, *Quaestiones*, 146–47. On Olivi's *sensus experimentalis*, see François-Xavier Putallez, *La connaissance de soi*, 96.

62. There is no evidence that Milton read Olivi, but he knew the Augustinian tradition. Olivi cites a passage from Augustine's *De libero arbitrio* (c.395) in which Augustine claims that all animals are certain of their existence because they feel their lives: "It is not so clear whether this life, which feels that it senses material objects, also senses itself—except that everyone who considers the matter will realize that every living thing flees death. Since death is the opposite of life, it must be the case that life feels itself [*vita etiam seipsam sentiat*], because it flees from its opposite" (Augustine, *On Free Choice of the Will*, 37 [2.4]). Augustine's stress on vitality also structures his so-called *cogito* argument—see, e.g., *De beata vita* (c. 386): "You know therefore that you have *life,*

since nobody can *live except by life"* [*Scis ergo habere te vitam, si quidem vivere nemo nisi vita potest*] (qtd. in Marion, *In the Self's Place*, 59)—but the passage from *De libero arbitro* is where he most clearly expresses the idea that life *feels itself*. Milton could have drawn this idea from elsewhere. In *De rerum natura*, Lucretius claims, "We feel [*sentimus*] that vital sense [*vitalem sensum*] inheres in the whole body" (236–37; 3.634–35). But Adam's link between vital feeling and self-knowledge points to the Augustinian tradition.

63. Acts 17:25–28. I'm thankful to Richard Strier for helping me see the relevance of these verses.

64. Milton, *Areopagitica*, 508.

65. Aratus, *Phenomena*, 207 (1.5). For Milton's love of Aratus, see Poole, *Making*, 180, 219–20. Milton's annotated copy of the *Phenomena* survives, on which see Maurice Kelley and Samuel Atkins, "Milton's Annotations of Aratus."

66. Virgil, *Eclogues*, 42 (3.60). See Theodor Beza, ed. and trans., *Jesu Christi Domini nostri Novum Testamentum*, 533.

67. Edward Herbert, *De veritate*, 120. Subsequent quotations are cited parenthetically.

68. See especially Strier, "Milton's Fetters"; Turner, *One Flesh*; and Greenblatt, *Rise and Fall*.

69. Although no earlier scholars have treated experience in the way that I do in this chapter, many have discussed experience in *Paradise Lost*. See Lewalski, "Innocence and Experience"; Picciotto, *Labors*; Karen Edwards, *Milton and the Natural World*; and Debapriya Sarkar, "'Sad Experiment' in *Paradise Lost*." For inexperience in the early novel, see Stephanie Insley Hershinow, *Born Yesterday*, a book that also contains a brief discussion of the newness of Adam and Eve in *Paradise Lost* (19–20).

70. Cockeram, *English Dictionary*, s.v. "inexperience."

71. Gadamer, *Truth and Method*, 341, describes experience as "one of the most obscure [concepts] that we have." See also Martin Jay, *Songs of Experience*; and Frank Ankersmit, *Sublime Historical Experience*.

72. Cassin, ed., *Dictionary of Untranslatables*, 329.

73. Works that shaped my general sense of the topic are Charles B. Schmitt, "Experience and Experiment"; Peter Dear, *Discipline and Experience*; Ian MacLean, *Logic, Signs, and Nature*; Pamela H. Smith, *The Body of the Artisan*; Peter Harrison, "Experimental Religion and Experimental Science"; and Marco Sgarbi, *The Aristotelian Tradition and the Rise of British Empiricism*.

74. This is surprising, since nowadays *experience* is synonymous with *consciousness*, and a number of prominent thinkers insist the terms are "interchangeable." See Galen Strawson, *The Subject of Experience*, 3, and 3, n. 4. See also Alva Noë, *Out of Our Heads*, 8: "I use the term 'consciousness' to mean, roughly, experience. And I think of experience, broadly, as encompassing thinking, feeling, and the fact that a world 'shows up' for us in perception."

75. This formulation is indebted to the notion of an "observational mood" in Simon, *Light*.

76. My analysis of Milton's use of *conscientia* is indebted to Joshua Scodel, *Excess and the Mean*, 269–70.

77. John Milton, *Defensio secunda*, 70–71.

78. Scodel, *Excess*, 269, quoting Cicero, *De senectute* 3.9.

79. John Milton, *Pro se defensio*, 214–15.

80. John Milton, *Major Works*, 86 ("To Mr. Cyriack Skinner Upon his Blindness," 9–11).

81. Mary Nyquist, "The Genesis of Gendered Subjectivity," argues that Eve's story in book 4 precedes Adam's in book 8 so that readers can see how her subjectivity will supplement Adam's; we see her inner fitness before she is created at the end of book 8.

82. See especially Maggie Kilgour, *Milton and the Metamorphosis of Ovid*, 165–228; and Mandy Green, *Milton's Ovidian Eve*.

83. John Leonard, *Naming in Paradise*, 38–39.

84. Picciotto, *Labors*, shows the importance of Adam's naming of the animals in the period.

85. John Milton, *Tetrachordon*, 602.

86. Milton, *De doctrina*, 1:308–09. Subsequent quotations are cited parenthetically. Leonard, *Naming*, 1, brings these passages from *Tetrachordon* and *De doctrina* together.

87. See Strier, "Milton's Fetters."

88. Milton, *Tetrachordon*, 602.

89. Leonard, *Naming*, 12.

90. David Hume, *An Enquiry Concerning Human Understanding*, 17.

91. On the composition of Milton's *Logic*, see Barbara Lewalski, *The Life of John Milton*, 208; and Gordon Campbell and Thomas N. Corns, *John Milton*, 366–67.

92. For the "inventive" method, see Sgarbi, *Aristotelian Tradition*.

93. Walter Ong, *Ramus, Method, and the Decay of Dialogue*.

94. According to Sgarbi, *Aristotelian Tradition*, 24–25, Milton's *Artis logicae* was probably the "last important Ramist logic" printed in England.

95. Harris Fletcher, *The Intellectual Development of John Milton*, 2:145.

96. See Sgarbi, *Aristotelian Tradition*.

97. As Noël Sugimura, "*Matter of Glorious Trial*," 13, has argued, Milton's complaints about scholastic Aristotelianism are not a critique of the philosopher; Milton "labors to siphon off the dross of the Schools from Aristotle so that Aristotle himself is saved."

98. Milton, *Artis logicae*, 10–13. Subsequent quotations are cited parenthetically by page number.

99. George Downame, *Commentarii in P. Rami Regii*, 21–22.

100. Plato, *Complete Works*, 806 (*Gorgias* 462c). All subsequent quotations are cited parenthetically according to page number and Stephanus numbers.

101. If Milton inherits this mistake from Downame, he rewrites Downame's prose. See Downame, *Commentarii*, 22: "*Experientia enim artem fecit (id est, legitimi praecepti) ut rectè Polus (in Gorgia Platonis) inexperientia fortunam (id est fortuita praecepta).*"

102. See Pavel Gregorić and Filip Grgić, "Aristotle's Notion of Experience," 22–23. See also Dominic Scott, *Recollection and Experience*, 87–132.

103. For the importance of this text in the period, see Dear, *Discipline*, 22.

104. This understanding of *empeiria* is expressed in a parallel manner in the *Posterior Analytics*: "From perception there comes memory, as we call it, and from memory (when

it occurs often in connection with the same thing), experience; for memories that are many in number form a single experience" (1:165–66; 100a).

105. Downame, *Commentarii*, 21.

106. Sgarbi, *Aristotelian Tradition*, 156–57.

107. Robert Sanderson, *Logicae Artis Compendium*, 226–27; treated in Sgarbi, *Aristotelian Tradition*, 156.

108. Robert Burton, *Anatomy of Melancholy*, 3:415.

109. It is only after awakening from their first post-lapsarian nap that the couple discovers how their rash act has "opened" their eyes and "darkened" their minds: "innocence, that as a veil / Had shadowed them from knowing ill, was gone," and they are "naked left / To guilty shame" (9.1053–58). Adam and Eve now see, as Augustine puts it in *De civitate Dei*, "in the movements of their bodies a certain shameless novelty" (615; 14.17). The couple had always been aware of their nudity; Adam was, from the beginning, "transported" when he "beh[e]ld" or "touch[ed]" Eve's beauty (8.529–33). But their unfallen bodies had been covered with what Augustine terms "the garment of grace" (615; 14.17); cf. Giorgio Agamben, *Nudities*, 55–90. After the fall, this garment, which Milton equates with the "veil" of "innocence," is "gone."

110. See Turner, *One Flesh*.

111. Sarkar's smart and related account in "Sad Experiment" differs from my reading insofar as Sarkar focuses on natural philosophical discourse—a focus that brings *experiment* into a normative position in the foreground of the analysis. By contrast, my argument that Milton derived his understanding of *experience* from his training in and teaching of logic means that I subordinate *experiment* so that its meaning is determined by *experience*.

112. On this use of *experience*, see MacLean, *Logic*.

113. *Experientia* is derived from the verb *experior* ("to try," "to attempt," "to put to the test") and originally meant "trial" or "experiment." This sense of individual trial was overtaken by something like Aristotle's use of *empeiria*: "the knowledge gained by repeated trials" (Lewis and Short, s.v. "experientia"). For early modern natural philosophers, as Dear, *Discipline*, 125, points out, *experientia* was "usually constituted as statements of *how things happen* in nature, not as statements of how something *had happened* on a particular occasion." The conclusions of early modern natural philosophers were based not on *experiments* in the sense of discrete events, but on *experience*, a synthesis from the collected memories of "many instances." To be sure, the distinction between *experientia* and *experimentum* is murky. In classical Latin, the terms were nearly synonymous. In the Middle Ages, Aristotle's *empeiria* was translated both as *experientia* (in John Argyropoulos's fifteenth-century renderings) and as *experimentum* (in the *versio communis* of Aristotle's works). See Schmitt, "Experience." It took some time before *experimentum* came to mean a "particular procedure" whereby *experientia* was tested out or proven to be true, but, as Dear, *Discipline*, 56, argues, this process was well underway by the late sixteenth century. According to Schmitt, "Experience," 120, as early as *De motu* (c. 1590), Galileo distinguished between *experientia* (apprehended passively from repeated observations) and the precursor to *experiment*, the *periculum* (generated actively through a trial initiated by an agent): *experientia* is the observable result, which impinges passively on the investigator after an active and repeated performance of a *periculum*. This is what *experiment* will come to mean.

114. Lisa Jardine, *Francis Bacon*, 136. See also Murphy, "The Anxiety of Variety," 120–25.

115. In translating *logos* as "reason" instead of a "account," I follow Gregorić and Grgić, "Aristotle's Notion of Experience," 22–23. Scott, *Recollection*, 87–132, argues that Aristotle's experience is not about concept formation, but the generation of scientific principles. However, the framework within which Milton would have read this text—one mediated by the revival of Hellenistic theories about early concept formation in which human beings move from perception, through memory, to experience, and finally to reason—would have inflected how he understood the philosopher's account of *empeiria*.

116. The most thorough reading of these lines, Stevens, *Imagination*, 186, glosses "unexperienced thought" as "the kind of thinking where the evidence of the senses is unrestrained by the distinctions of judgment. Since 'thought,' according to Aristotelian psychology, 'is held to comprise imagination and judgment,' thought without judgment, what Eve calls 'unexperienc't thought,' means uninformed imagination." In my view Milton derived his understanding of *experience* and its absence not from Aristotle's definition of *thought*, which does not refer to experience, but from the discussions of *empeiria* in the *Metaphysics* and *Posterior Analytics*.

117. See Davidson, *Emergence of Sexuality*. See also my discussion of Davidson in the introduction.

CHAPTER TWO

1. Michel de Montaigne, *Complete Essays*, 838; *Essais*, 1141, 3.13). Subsequent quotations are cited parenthetically, according to page number for the English translation and then the page, book, and chapter numbers for the French.

2. Hume, *Annotations*, 150. For more on Hume, see chapter 1.

3. Guillaume de Salluste Du Bartas, *Divine Weekes and Workes*, 162.

4. J. Martin Evans, *"Paradise Lost" and the Genesis Tradition*.

5. I discuss Grotius's play in section 3. For Salandria and Vondel, see Watson Kirkconnell, *The Celestial Cycle*, 290–349 and 434–79. In general, medieval drama provided far less information about Adam's and Eve's inner lives. Consider the *Cardmaker's Play* in Anonymous, *York Plays*, 16, where Adam's most revealing speech is one of praise: "A Lord! Ful mekill is [th]y myght, / And [th]at is seene in ilke a side, / [For] nowe is here a joifull sighte, / To see this worlde so long and wide. / Many diverse thynges nowe here is, / Of Beestis and foules, both wilde and tame, / [yet] is non made to [th]i likenesse / But we allone."

6. Daniel C. Matt, trans., *Zohar*, 2:231. For Milton's possible acquaintance with the *Zohar*, see Denis Saurat, *Milton*, 231–47.

7. Moses Gaster, ed. and trans., *Chronicles of Jerahmeel*, 16–17.

8. Giambattista Andreini, *L'Adamo*, 230.

9. Victor Shklovsky, "Art as Technique," 12.

10. For Augustine's fallen anthropology in relation to Adam, see Harrison, *Fall of Man*, 52–88.

11. Picciotto, *Labors*, esp. 400–405, is central to my understanding of *Paradise Lost*, especially her refusal to take for granted the severity of the Fall. In Harrison, "Adamic

Awakening," I made a version of this argument. Recent work has extended this line of inquiry. See Sharon Achinstein, "Milton's Political Ontology of the Human"; and Simon, *Light*, 169–212.

12. The privileged role played by embodiment in Milton's thought has, of course, been discussed by many critics, with Kahn, *Wayward Contracts*, 196–222, providing the most sophisticated account to date. I aim both to show how the Edenic body shapes prelapsarian experience and to connect the phenomenological contours of Milton's thought to his views on human nature.

13. For Milton's mortalism, see George Williamson, "Milton and the Mortalist Heresy"; and William Kerrigan, "The Heretical Milton."

14. My treatment of the *subject* in this paragraph relies on three works by Libera, *Archéologie*; *L'invention*; and "Modern Subject."

15. Libera, *L'invention*, makes this connection.

16. I take these translations from Barbara Cassin, ed., *Dictionary of Untranslatables*, 1077. For a fuller discussion, see Libera, "Modern Subject," 208–9. An edited Latin text of the argument on which this scholarship is based—article 19 of Olivi's *Impugnatio quorundam articulorum Arnaldi Galliardi*—is available in Catherine König-Pralong, ed., *Pierre de Jean Olivi*, 453–62.

17. Hobbes's argument runs contrary to many assumptions about Descartes. The objection works because Descartes refuses to have a theory of the subject. See Libera, "Modern Subject," 198–201; and Michael Moriarty, *Early Modern French Thought*, 10–12.

18. Milton, *De doctrina*, 1:424–25.

19. Milton, "At a Vacation Exercise in the College," in *Milton: The Complete Shorter Poems*, ed. John Carey, 81–82, ll.74–82. Subsequently cited parenthetically in the text as *Shorter Poems*, with page and line number.

20. For a reading of this poem that focuses on substance, see Sugimura, *"Matter of Glorious Trial,"* 17–25.

21. J[ohn] B[ullokar], *English Expositor*, defines "repose" as "To lay upon."

22. For this detail, see Balibar, Cassin, and Libera, "Subject," in Cassin, *Dictionary of Untranslatables*, 1069.

23. Augustine, *On the Trinity*, 29; 9.4.5.

24. The angel's report was not that of an eyewitness, since, as we learn a few lines later, Raphael was "absent" on the sixth day (8.229). This absence anchors the legitimacy of Raphael's account not in angelic memory but in scriptural authority. Another way to understand the absence is that suggested by Coffin, "Creation," 5, who argues that Raphael's absence "makes room" for Adam's first-person account. But Raphael's account, no matter how full, could never remove the "room" necessitated by Adam's unique subject position.

25. For the issues behind Milton's treatment of scripture, see Evans, *Genesis Tradition*, 9–25. For the harmonization of Genesis, see Arnold Williams, *Common Expositor*, 67–70; and Nyquist, "Genesis," 102.

26. Consider Calvin's commentary, which claims of Genesis 2:7 that Moses "nowe expoundeth" that which "he had omitted before in the creation of man"; namely, "that his bodie was taken out of the earth" (*A Commentarie . . . upon the first booke of Moses called Genesis*, 57).

27. Calvin, *A Commentarie*, 57.

28. Guillaume de Salluste Du Bartas, *Divine Weekes and Workes*, 208; *Works of Guillaume de Salluste, sieur Du Bartas*, 1:6, 470–76.

29. Cf. Joseph Hall, qtd. in Williams, *Common Expositor*, 68: "Other creatures thou madst by a simple command; man, not without divine consultation: others at once; man thou didst first form, then inspire."

30. John Rogers, *The Matter of Revolution*, 125, claims that this episode is one of "the poem's scandalous expressions of creaturely self-generation." Placed in the context of the hexameral tradition, Milton's lion appears more orthodox. Like all other nonhuman creatures of the sixth day, it is, in the words of Genesis 1:24, part of the living menagerie that the "earth bring[s] forth."

31. See Scodel, "Edenic Freedoms."

32. Thomas Aquinas, *Summa theologica* 1.q.91.4.3. Andrew Willet summarizes Aquinas in *Hexapla in Genesin*, 32: "Adams bodie and soule were created in the same instant together."

33. Calvin, *Commentarie*, 58, lays out these "three degrees." Willet, *Hexapla*, 32, summarizes them succinctly: "Man's creation is set forth in three degrees: the forming of his bodie, the giving of his life, the endewing him with a reasonable soule created after God's image."

34. For the relevant background, see Stephen Fallon, *Milton Among the Philosophers*, 99–102.

35. Francis Brown, S. R. Driver, and Charles A. Briggs, *A Hebrew and English Lexicon of the Old Testament*, 659–60 (1 and 4). I am grateful to Jason Rosenblatt for help with the relationship between Milton's Latin and the Hebrew text.

36. Weber and Gryson, eds., *Biblia sacra*, 1787; Desiderius Erasmus, ed. and trans. *Novum testamentum omne*, 378.

37. Theodor Beza, ed. and trans., *Novum Testamentum*, RR.r i v. For the editions of scripture used in *De doctrina*, see John K. Hale and J. Donald Cullington, "Introduction," xlvii–li.

38. If Milton's position here is similar to that of Aquinas, it departs from that of Augustine. In *City of God*, 575 (13.24), Augustine states, "This man, then, who was formed from the dust of the earth . . . was made, as the apostle teaches, an animal body when he received a soul. He was 'made a living soul'; that is, this fashioned dust was made a living soul." Augustine rejects the claims of those who, like Milton, argue that when Adam was formed "he already had a soul: otherwise he would not have been called man. For man is not a body alone nor a soul alone; rather, he is composed of both soul and body." Augustine's sense of the passage is clear: Adam's "body," was formed by God "from the dust," and "the soul was given so that it might become a living body: that is, so that man might be made a living soul." Milton's *De doctrina* rejects this interpretation.

39. To be fair, most writers had difficulty understanding the divine breath. Here is Augustine's most involved attempt to work it out: "[The breath is] a thing which is not a body, nor God, nor life without sensation [*vita sine sensu*], which apparently exists in trees, nor life without a rational mind [*vita sine rationali mente*], but a life now inferior to that of the angels [*vita nunc minor quam Angelorum*], but destined to be one with

their life if in this world it lives according to the will of the Creator" (Augustine, *On Genesis*, 338 [*Genesi ad litteram* 7.21.30]).

40. Later in *De doctrina*, Milton cements this point. The passages most often cited as evidence that soul is separable from body "do indeed usually point out that nobler origin of the soul, coming out of God's mouth as he breathed; yet they no more prove the direct creation of individual souls than the texts now following show that each person's body is directly shaped by God in the womb" (1:307). Moreover, "not only did God infuse the breath of life into the other animate creatures, too, as above, but also, having infused it, he mixed it in matter so thoroughly that, no differently from the other forms, human form too would be propagated and produced from the power implanted in matter by God" (1:309).

41. Tremellius's Latin—quoted in Milton, *De doctrina Christiana*, 1:300—renders the *and* linking the formation of dust to the breath of life with an enclitic *que*—*sufflavitque in nares ipsius halitum vitae*—but the effect is the same as the English *and* or the Vulgate's *et*: "*formavit igitur Dominus Deus hominem de limo terrae, et inspiravit in faciem eius spiraculum vitae, et factus est homo in animam viventem.*"

42. I disagree with Fowler, who, in Milton, *Paradise Lost*, 422, nn. 524–28, draws on Willet's *Hexapla* to claim that Milton sides "with Chrysostom (soul created after body) against Origen (soul created earlier) and Thomas Aquinas (both together)."

43. Milton's position here resonates not only with his treatment of the topic in *De doctrina*, but also with the pithy assessment in *De augmentis scientiarum*, in Francis Bacon, *Philosophical Works*, 493: "It is not said that 'He made the body of man of the dust of the earth,' but that 'He made man'; that is the entire man, excepting only the breath of life."

44. For a summary of the prevailing view, which she wishes to complicate, see Victoria Kahn, "'The Duty to Love,'" 84. For a succinct historical account, see Jon Miller, *Spinoza and the Stoics*, 100–43. The fullest treatment of Milton's relation to notions of self-preservation is Christopher Warren, "When Self-Preservation Bids."

45. For a historical account of *prima naturae* in relation to Grotius, see René Brouwer, "Ancient Background of Grotius's Notion of Natural Law."

46. See Henk Nellen, *Hugo Grotius*.

47. Milton, *Tetrachordon*, 715.

48. For Milton's meeting with Grotius, see Campbell and Corns, *John Milton*, 106–7.

49. Christian Gellinek, "The Principal Literary Sources to John Milton's *Paradise Lost*."

50. The first sustained case for the influence of *Adamus exul* on *Paradise Lost* was made by William Lauder, *Essay on Milton's Use and Imitation of the Moderns*. The unfortunate result of this inquiry was a sharp repudiation of Lauder's claims, which were based on fabricated evidence: Lauder interpolated lines and phrases from Hogg's Latin translation of *Paradise Lost* into his quotations from *Adamus exul* in order to make it seem as though Milton were translating Grotius. For the most sustained comparison of the two works, see Carey Herbert Conley, "Milton's Indebtedness to his Contemporaries in '*Paradise Lost*,'" 35–86. See also Evans, *"Paradise Lost" and the Genesis Tradition*, 210–16; and Poole, *Milton and the Idea of the Fall*, 101–7.

51. Hugo Grotius, *Commentary on the Law of Prize and Booty*, 21. Subsequent quotations are cited parenthetically.

52. Richard Tuck, "Grotius, Carneades, and Hobbes."

53. Grotius, *Rights of War and Peace*, 1:180 (*De jure belli ac pacis*, 1.2.1). Subsequent quotations are cited parenthetically according to volume and page numbers for the English and book, chapter, and section numbers for the Latin.

54. Benjamin Straumann, *Roman Law in the State of Nature*, 83–102.

55. See Brunschwig, "Cradle Argument."

56. Richard Tuck, "Introduction," xxiii.

57. Hans W. Blom, "Sociability and Hugo Grotius."

58. For Stoicism in *Adamus exul*, see Arthur Eyffinger, "The Fourth Man."

59. Grotius, *Adamus exul*, in Kirkconnell, *Celestial Cycle*, 156–57. Subsequent quotations from *Adamus exul* are cited parenthetically according to page number.

60. Qtd. in Alastair Minnis, *From Eden to Eternity*, 143–44.

61. Du Bartas, *Divine Weekes and Workes*, 256.

62. Augustine, *On Genesis*, 231 (*De genesi ad litteram* 3.16.25); qtd. in Minnis, *From Eden to Eternity*, 144.

63. For how Milton includes the fear of death within Eden but—through an adherence to an Augustinian notion of fear only emerging through sin and punishment—minimizes its role in order to stress his own commitment to freedom, see Scodel, "Edenic Freedoms," 176–81.

64. For learning by warning and learning by experience in Milton's Eden, see chapter 1.

65. See Cicero, *De finibus*, 215–98 (bk. 3).

66. See Cicero, *De finibus*, 77–214 (bk. 2).

67. Achinstein, "Milton's Political Ontology," 596.

68. See Nyquist, "Genesis."

69. Robert South, *A Sermon Preached at the Cathedral Church of St. Paul*, 11–14. Subsequent quotations are cited parenthetically.

70. Qtd. in Lewalski, *Life*, 413.

71. [Faustus Socinus, Valentin Smalcius, Hieronim Moskorzewski, and Johannes Völker], *Racovian Catechism*, 142.

72. Faustus Socinus, *Operum omnium*, 539–40 (*Praelectiones theologicae* 3). See also Faustus Socinus, *De statu primi hominis ante lapsum disputatio*, which treats this position at length.

73. Faustus Socinus, *Operum*, 296 (*De statu primi hominis*, 4): "Vere autem non agniturum fuisse Adamum se mortalem esse, nemine indicante, ex eo perspicuum est, quod nos ipsi de nobis id non nisi experientia ipsa, & rationibus propter experientiam animadversis, nosse potuimus. Nec mirum, Nam, ut dictum est à Philosopho; nihil est in mente, sive in intellectu, quod non prius fuerit in sensu."

74. Socinus does not claim that Adam enters the world like "an Infant." This position is reserved for Isaac La Peyrère's *Prae-Adamitae* (translated into English as *A theological systeme upon the presupposition, that men were before Adam*, 141–42), in which he argues against the "common Opinion" that "*Adam* was created by God of a full age, of the perfect stature of a man" and states instead that "*Adam* not straight, nor the first day, but by leisure, and by several stages, successively great from infancy and youth to man's

estate, by as many degrees as Christ arrived at the same state at which *Isaac* arrived at it, being himself likewise miraculously brought forth: and as other men begotten after the ordinary manner, arise from children to be men."

75. Jonathan Edwards, *Preservative Against Socinianism*, 2:16.

76. Milton, *Tetrachordon*, 604.

77. Milton, *Of Education*, 366–69.

78. For Aquinas's *quinque viae*, see *Summa theologica*, 1.q.2.a3.

79. Melanchthon, *Loci communes*. Qtd and trans. in John Platt, *Reformed Thought and Scholasticism*, 22, 24.

80. Calvin, *Institutes*, 1:43–44 (1.3.1); *Institutio*, 3:37.

81. Calvin, *Institutes*, 1:45–46 (1.3.3).

82. Socinus, *Operum; Praelectiones*, 3–4.

83. For an argument that sees this rejection of the innate idea of God as at the heart of the Socinian position and its legacies, see Sarah Mortimer, *Reason and Revelation in the English Revolution*.

84. Conrad Vorstius, *Tractatus theologicus de Deo*, 128 (translation mine). Platt discusses part of this passage in *Reformed Thought*, 206.

85. Conrad Vorstius, *Apologetica Exegesis*, 1 (translation mine).

86. Vorstius, *Apologetica*, 2; qtd. and trans. in Platt, *Reformed Thought*, 211.

87. Simon Episcopius, *Opera Theologica*, 1.6. This passage is quoted and analyzed in Platt, "The Denial of the Innate Idea of God," 221.

88. In their introduction to Milton's *De doctrina Christiana*, 1:50, nn. xi, xviii, xix, Hale and Cullington point out that most of Milton's biblical proof texts on God's unity are derived from Episcopius's *Institutiones*.

89. Hale and Cullington's translation—"pre-existence of some sovereign agent who in all these things sets himself a purpose"—seems to stack the deck a little too much in favor of a certain view about the knowledge of God's existence that I'm not certain Milton shared.

90. Calvin, *Institutes*, 1:43 (1.3.1); *Institutio*, 3:37.

91. Aquinas, *Summa theologica*, 1–2.q.103.1, translation modified. For Aquinas's notion of human "natural inclination" as it relates to the good, see 1–2.q.94.2. In his commentary on Galatians, Aquinas claims that grace is capable of working through an *instinctum interiorum* (1.4) and that humans are drawn to God by *naturali instinctu* (2.4).

92. For a history of how the notion of instinct became tangled up with synderesis and feeling, see Robert A. Greene, "Instinct of Nature."

93. Schwartz, *Remembering*, 5.

94. Rogers, *Matter*, 122–29.

95. For Satan's "fatal course" and Plato's Great Year, see Quint, *Inside "Paradise Lost,"* 130.

96. Augustine, *City of God*, 608 (14.13). See Lewis, *Preface*, 65.

97. Lewis, *Preface*, 98; William Empson, *Milton's God*, 89.

98. As Sid-Ahmad argues in "Ibn Tufayl's Hayy," Adam's story resonates with the contemporaneously translated and widely circulating Arabic story of Hayy, an infant alone on an island who eventually understands God's existence through nothing more than reason and observation. If, as Sid-Ahmed suggests, Milton knew the *Hayy Ibn*

Yaqzan, then I want to insist that he translated the impulse it records out of a rationally oriented third-person voice and into a first-person account that stresses the resources of feeling.

99. Calvin, *Institutes*, 1:36 (1.1.1); *Insitutio*, 31.

100. Calvin, *Institutes*, 1:36 (1.1.1), translation modified; *Institutio*, 31.

CHAPTER THREE

1. For scholarship dedicated to Traherne's use of prelapsarian Adam and Eve, see Martz, *Paradise Within*, 65–79; and Cynthia Saenz, "Language and the Fall." In this chapter I offer the first analysis of Traherne's obsession with Adamic awakening.

2. I refer here to Harold Bloom, *The Anxiety of Influence*.

3. For a Lacanian reading of this poem in relation to Eve's encounter with the pool in *Paradise Lost*, see Alvin Snider, "The Self-Mirroring Mind in Milton and Traherne."

4. *OED*, s.v. "seeming," n. 1a; s.v. "view," n. 4. For Traherne's tendency to treat values, ideas, and concepts as tangible "things," see Kathryn Murphy, "No Things But In Thoughts."

5. For the size and provenance of the MS, see Traherne, *Works*, 2:xi–xix.

6. *OED*, s.v. "resent," v. I.1a and 1b.

7. Traherne's Adam can perceive his essence. See *Works*, 1:421: "In the Beginning" the human "Senses were united to Rational and Intelligible Powers, and by the union did Partake of all their excellencies: Sin only broke the Bond, and canceld the Privilege."

8. For insight on the tradition standing behind this claim, see Minnis, *From Eden*, 64, on Peter Lombard, who held that Adam in Paradise "saw God without intermediary."

9. *Gratitude* was a now obsolete way of saying *grace*. See *OED*, s.v. *gratitude*, n. 2.

10. For details, see Jan Ross, "Introduction," in Traherne, *Works*, 1:xiv–xv, vii–xix.

11. Shakespeare, *Complete Pelican*, 1422 (*Othello*, 3.3.164–65).

12. *OED*, s.v. "surprise," n. 4b.

13. Calvin, *Institutes*, 1.:43 (1.3).

14. Robert Watson, *Back to Nature*, 300–301, makes a comparison between Traherne and Descartes; Webber, *The Eloquent "I,"* 220, notes that Traherne was born the year Descartes's *Discours* was published; and Carol Ann Johnston, "Heavenly Perspectives, Mirrors of Eternity," 393, sees Traherne as drawing on Descartes's optics.

15. The secondary literature on Descartes's understanding of thought and consciousness is vast. See especially Dasie Radner, "Thought and Consciousness in Descartes"; Moriarty, *Early Modern French Thought*, 50–70; Boris Hennig, "Cartesian *Conscientia*"; Vili Lähteenmäki, "Orders of Consciousness and Forms of Reflexivity in Descartes"; Boris Hennig, "'Insofar As' in Descartes's Definition of Thought"; Steven Nadler, "Consciousness Among the Cartesians"; Thiel, *Early Modern Subject*, 43–54; and Simmons, "Cartesian Consciousness."

16. Marleen Rozemond, *Descartes's Dualism*, 10.

17. As Rozemond, *Descartes's Dualism*, 11, shows, he uses mind and thought interchangeably from the *Principia* to the *Notae in programma quoddam* (1648).

18. Henry More, *Divine Dialogues*, 6. Subsequent quotations are cited parenthetically.

19. Thomas Baker, *Reflections Upon Learning*, 103; Edward Howard, *Remarks on the New Philosophy of Descartes*, 124.

20. Wallace Stevens, *The Palm at the End of the Mind*, 209.

21. For the origin of the story about how Dryden asked Milton for permission to "tag" his lines, see John Aubrey, "Minutes on the Life of Mr. John Milton," 7.

22. For the relationship between *Paradise Lost* and *State of Innocence*, see, e.g., Nicholas Von Maltzhan, "Dryden's Milton and the Theatre of Imagination."

23. John Dryden, *The State of Innocence*, 105 (2.1.1–8).

24. Jean-Luc Marion, *Cartesian Questions*, 33.

25. I have based my translation here on that provided by George Heffernan in René Descartes, *Meditations / Meditationes*, 100–101. I use this translation as a baseline for this and similar passage because of its admirably exacting literalness.

26. See Étienne Balibar, *Citizen Subject*, 60–64.

27. Since Heffernan captures this sentence more accurately, I have again used the translation in Descartes, *Meditations / Meditationes*, 100–101.

28. Heffernan, *Meditations / Meditationes*, 105.

29. Martin Heidegger, *The Basic Problems of Phenomenology*, 121.

30. See Libera, *Archéologie*.

31. I owe the concision of this formulation to conversations with Jean-Luc Marion.

32. The distinction between *what* and *who* is fundamental to the insights that Heidegger would elaborate in *Being and Time*, the grammatical contents of which were articulated in Heidegger, *Basic Problems*, 119–21. The distinction is fundamental to Arendt, *Human Condition*, and Paul Ricoeur, *Oneself As Another*. Arendt, *Human Condition*, 10, n. 2, locates the origin of this distinction in Augustine. Libera, *L'invention*, traces the history of this distinction in medieval philosophy.

33. For dating, see Jan Ross, "Introduction," in Traherne, *Works*, 5:xvii–xix.

34. For dating, see Jan Ross, "Introduction," in Traherne, *Works*, 5:xvi.

35. For a complementary analysis, see Webber, *Eloquent "I,"* 223–24.

36. *OED*, s.v. "enjoyer," n.; Pierre de Belloy, *A Catholicke Apologie against the Libels*, 136; Henry Hexham, *A Copious English and Netherlandish Dictionary*, *enjoyer* (accessed through Lexicons of Early Modern English); William Pemberton, *The Godly Merchant*, 84. For a related examination of enjoyment as a category central to Traherne's work, see Graham Dowell, *Enjoying the World*.

37. Augustine, *On Christian Doctrine*, 9 (1.3). Subsequent quotations are cited parenthetically according to page numbers for the English and chapter and section numbers for the Latin.

38. For Traherne and *De Trinitate*, see Martz, *Paradise Within*, 45–51.

39. For dating, see Jan Ross, "Introduction," in Traherne, *Works*, 1:xx–xxi.

40. For a discussion of Traherne's understanding of life and his abhorrence of mechanical "puppets," see Gary Kuchar, "Traherne's Specters."

41. For early microscopy, see Catherine Wilson, *The Invisible World*.

42. For how value inheres in hierarchical uses of animacy, see Mel Y. Chen, *Animacies*.

43. For Traherne on self-preservation, see *Works*, 1:409; 1:420.

44. For Traherne's use of the *Asclepius* and the hermetic tradition, see Carol L. Marks, "Thomas Traherne and Hermes Trismegistus."

45. On pronoun usage in the *Centuries*, see Webber, *Eloquent "I,"* 219–47.

46. *OED*, s.v. "principle," n. I 1c, 2.

47. Irenaeus, *Against Heresies*, 521. Traherne opens *Roman Forgeries*, the only treatise published during his lifetime, with a discussion of Irenaeus (indeed, the father's name is this text's first word). For Traherne and Irenaeus, see Patrick Grant, *The Transformation of Sin*, 170–97. For the increased importance of the ante-Nicene fathers in seventeenth-century intellectual life, see Jean-Louis Quantin, *The Church of England and Christian Antiquity*. For another example of infancy being aligned with Adam in seventeenth-century England, see John Earle, *Micro-Cosmographie*, 8–9: "A Childe is a Man in a small Letter, yet the best Copie of Adam before hee tasted of Eve, or the Apple; and hee is happy whose small practice in the World can only write this Character."

48. Gerrard Winstanley, *Fire in the Bush*, 72.

49. Recall Lucretius's account of birth in *On the Nature of Things*, 395 (5.222–25): "The child [*puer*], like a sailor cast forth by the cruel waves, lies naked upon the ground, speechless [*infans*], in need of every kind of vital support, as soon as nature has spit him forth with throes from his mother's womb into the regions of light [*primum in luminas oras*]."

50. Edward Phillips, *The New World of English Words*, infancy (accessed through Lexicons of Early Modern English). See also *OED*, s.v. "infancy," n. 1a. This was a common way of understanding infancy or early childhood in the period. See Phillippe Ariès, *Centuries of Childhood*, 15–49; David Cressy, *Birth, Marriage, and Death*, 15–196; and Greteman, *Poetics*, 1–17.

51. See also *OED*, "infant," n.1a.

52. Helkiah Crooke, *Microcosmographia*, 267.

53. Critics have not adequately noted how Traherne positions the birth of the ego as an event that occurs within the womb. Robert Ellrodt, *Seven Metaphysical Poets*, 93, writes of Traherne, "No poet has so subtly and sympathetically observed the awakening of the senses in early infancy." Yet although Ellrodt understands Traherne's poetry in light of Piaget's theories of child psychology, he does not notice the specificity of where and when the poet's "first impressions" take place. The critic who comes closest is the great Helen C. White, *Metaphysical Poets*, 299, who writes of "The Preparative," "The story which Traherne tells begins before birth with the embryonic mind's first glimmer of a consciousness of the members of its own body. But not even Traherne would, I think, expect this part of the story to be taken as more than a must-have-been, a reconstruction of an earlier stage from what is later apparent, something like that legendary history in which all peoples elaborate their dimly descried and passionately inferred beginnings." For recent considerations of Traherne's understanding of the "child" in a thematic sense (again, lacking the specificity of time and place so central to Traherne's depiction of originary experience), see Edmund Newey, "'God Made Man Greater When He Made Him Less'"; and Elizabeth Dodd, *Boundless Innocence*, 15–17, 172–76.

54. *OED*, s.v. "from," prep 6a; and prep. 3a.

55. Park, *Secrets of Women*.

56. Mikhail Bakhtin, *Speech Genres*, 138: "Just as the body is formed initially in the mother's womb, a person's consciousness awakens wrapped in another's consciousness."

57. D. W. Winnicott, "The Theory of the Parent-Infant Relationship," 587, n. 4.

58. This erasure of the mother belongs to discursive habits found everywhere in the period. Critics have long noted how early modern male writers appropriate the female body in order to legitimize their creative endeavors. Riffing on Ovid's claim in the *Tristia*, 152 (3.14.13–14) that his poetry was *Palladis exemplo de me sine matre creata / carmina sunt* ("Pallas-fashion were my verses born from me without a mother"), a number of British poets made similar claims, none so literal as the unacknowledged translation by Samuel Daniel, *Delia and Rosamund*, B2 ("Sonnet II," 2), who claims that he "brought foorth" his poetry "without a Mother." The most famous example appears in the opening sonnet of Sir Philip Sidney's *Astrophil and Stella*, in *Selected Prose and Poetry*, 163 (12–14): "Thus great with child to speake, and helplesse in my throwes, / Biting my trewand pen, beating my selfe for spite, / 'Foole,' said my Muse to me, 'looke in thy heart and write.'"

59. John Lydgate, *Dance of Death*, 69–70.

60. For these different treatments of *anamnesis*, see Scott, *Recollection*, 15–85.

61. This argument is advanced by Scott, *Recollection*, 87–156.

62. Scott, *Recollection*, 159–210.

63. Plutarch, *The Philosophie, commonlie called, the Morals*, trans. Philemon Holland (London, 1603), 836. The section of this collection entitled "The Opinions of the Philosophers" was long attributed to Plutarch. It was in fact written by Aëtius. A translation of the original text appears in A. A. Long and D. N. Sedley, eds. *The Hellenistic Philosophers*, 1:238.

64. See, e.g., John Wallis, *Truth Tried*, 45, who claims that he cannot "subscribe to the *Platonists*, to make *Knowledge* nothing but a *Remembrance*. (As if there were naturally in our Understanding, the Pictures or Pourtraictures of all Truths, but so obscured and covered as it were with dust, that these glorious Colours doe not appear, till such time as they be rubbed and washed over anew.) I approve rather of Aristotle's *Rasa Tabula*, (then Plato's *Reminiscientia*) making Understanding, of it selfe, to have no such *Idea* or Picture at all, but capable of all."

65. Nathaniel Culverwell, *Discourse on the Light of Nature*, 81.

66. Culverwell, *Discourse*, 81–82.

67. For Traherne's debts to various Platonists, see, e.g., Carol L. Marks, "Thomas Traherne and Cambridge Platonism"; and Sarah Hutton, "Platonism in Some Metaphysical Poets." For Traherne as Neoplatonic mystic, see A. L. Clemens, *Mystical Poetry of Thomas Traherne*; and Stanley Stewart, *Expanded Voice*. For Traherne's debts to the Aristotelian tradition, see Paul Cefalu, "Thomistic Metaphysics and Ethics." For Traherne's most explicit reflections on Aristotle, see *Works*, 3:188–207.

68. For Traherne's notebooks, see Carol L. Marks, "Thomas Traherne's Commonplace Book"; and Carol L. Marks, "Traherne's Ficino Notebook."

69. See Cefalu, "Thomastic Metaphysics," 249: "With respect to human psychology and cognition, moral philosophy, and the nature of God, Traherne is a neo-scholastic who makes use of Platonic imagery and concepts, not a Platonist who sometimes invokes scholastic terminology."

70. As Pheobe Dickerson, "'The Lathorns Sides,'" 34, points out, the "experience that Traherne describes" in this poem "is not one of total disembodiment, but rather of possessing a body before having knowledge of the fact."

CHAPTER FOUR

1. See Wilderbing, *Forms*, 133–50.

2. For an account of why Traherne criticism was, for a long time, removed from the historical context within which he wrote, see Dodd and Gorman, eds., "Traherne in Context"; and Julia J. Smith, "Traherne and Historical Contingency."

3. For abortion in early modern England, see, e.g., Cressy, *Birth*, 47–50.

4. Harvey's discoveries in the realm of fetal sensation have not been discussed at any length. See O. Temkin, "The Classical Roots of Glisson's Doctrine of Irritation," 321; Walter Pagel, *William Harvey's Biological Ideas*, 256; Walter Pagel, *New Light on William Harvey*, 34–36; and Moshenska, *Feeling Pleasures*, 289–91. Although there is more work on Descartes and infancy, so far as I know, no one has previously contextualized Descartes's understandings of thought and consciousness in relation to the history of embryology.

5. For the history of fetal *animation* (a related but different topic), see, e.g., Maaike Van Der Lugt, "L'animation de l'embryon humain dans la pensée médiévale."

6. Janel Mueller, "Donne's Epic Venture," provides this generic designation.

7. For souls in the poem, see Elizabeth D. Harvey, "The Souls of Animals."

8. John Donne, *Metempsychosis*, 192 (493–509).

9. See Needham, *History*, 18–74.

10. See Wilderbing, *Forms*, 133–50.

11. This process was reworked by Aristotle's followers. See, e.g., Aquinas, *Summa contra gentiles*, 2.89.1–23.

12. For plant life as an analogy in the history of embryology, see Brooke Holmes, "Pure Life."

13. For Galen's insistence that the liver is the principal part in embryological development, see Galen, *Clavdii Galeni Opera omnia*, 4:658 (*De foetuum formatione*, 2).

14. Dante, *Purgatorio*, 558–59 (25.52–57). Subsequent quotations are cited parenthetically according to page, canto, and line numbers.

15. On traducianism and infusionism (or creationism), see John M. Rist, *Augustine*, 317–19. Dante does not shy away from the theological difficulties that attend the infusionist position. As Billy Junker, "Fallen Nature," argues, in *Purgatorio*, Dante distances himself from the position that human beings are corrupt through natural inheritance: "'bad governance' [*la mala condotta*] is 'the cause that has made the world wicked,'" Dante writes in the voice of Marco the Lombard, "and not 'nature corrupt in you [*e non che 'n voi sia corrota*]'" (154; 16.103–5).

16. For Donne, traducianism, and infusionism, see Ramie Targoff, *John Donne*, 11–15.

17. John Donne, *Devotions Upon Emergent Occasions*, 91.

18. John Donne, *Letters to Severall Persons of Honor*, 17–18. Qtd. in Targoff, *John Donne*, 12.

19. Donne, *Metempsychosis*, 192 (506–9).

20. Galen, *Opera*, 4:476 (*De foetuum formatione*, 3).

21. For Fabricius's place in the history of embryology, see Howard B. Adelman, "Introduction"; and Needham, *History*, 105–9.

22. Fabricius, *Embryological Treatises*, 278–79.

23. Note that even if embryos were conceived as plants, that did not necessarily settle the question of whether or not they could feel, for there was an ancient controversy dedicated to precisely this question. In *De plantis* (2:1251; 815a), Aristotle summarizes various views on this topic. For Aristotle's own view, articulated in *De anima*, that plants possess life—indeed, are the primary example of life in its most basic form—but nevertheless "cannot perceive," see Aristotle, *Complete Works* 1:675; 424a–424b.

24. This is the critical consensus. See, e.g., Bruno Nardi, *Studi di filosofia medieval*, 9–68; Stephen Bemrose, "'Come d'animal divegna fante'"; and Jennifer Fraser, "Dante/Fante."

25. Donne, *Metempsychosis*, 181 (135–43).

26. Donne, *Metempsychosis*, 183 (178–83); John Carey, *John Donne*, 50. Carey also notes how Donne's description of the sparrow emphasizes his stress on the body over the soul by reworking an analogy from Plato's *Phaedrus*, in which Socrates claims that the development of desire at the sight of beauty causes the soul "that has seen the most" (526; 248d) in the other world to grow wings like those it once had: "Like a child whose teeth are just starting to grow in, and its gums are all aching and itching—that is exactly how the soul feels when it begins to grow wings. It swells up and aches and tingles as it grows them" (528; 251c). Donne jokingly deflates Plato's image by literalizing it. He takes the budding wings of a fit Platonic soul and turns them into a bodily mode of transport that enables an actual sparrow to copulate in an indiscriminate and incestuous frenzy that culminates in its early death.

27. As Hannibal Hamlin, *Psalm Culture and Early Modern English Literature*, 129, remarks, Pembroke diverged from her sources when the topic of embryology arose.

28. Mary Sidney, *The Sidney Psalms*, 130–31, ll. 43–56.

29. John Davies, *Muse's Sacrifice*, 34–35.

30. Davies, *Muse's Sacrifice*, 35.

31. *OED*, s.v. "feel," v. I.3b; and I.1a.

32. John Davies, *Nosce te ipsum*, 99.

33. Thomas Browne, *Religio Medici*, 129. Browne may have gotten this idea from Herbert, *De veritate*, 124.

34. Browne, *Religio Medici*, 44–45.

35. Fabricius, *Embryological Treatises*, 279.

36. For Placentinus's rivalry with Fabricius, see Alessandro Riva, "Iulius Casserius."

37. For Crooke and embryology in early modern England, see Keller, *Generating Bodies*.

38. Crooke, *Microcosmographia*, 648; Iulij Casserij Placentini, *Pentaestheseion hox est de quinque sensibus*, 4.

39. Davies, *Muse's Sacrifice*, 35.

40. Fabricius, *Embryological Treatises*, 279.

41. Placentinus, *Pentaestheseion*, 4.

42. For Harvey's overlap with Placentinus, see Geoffrey Keynes, *The Life of William Harvey*, 33.

43. On Harvey and Fabricius, see Keynes, *Life of William Harvey*, 25–28.

44. William Harvey, *Generation of Animals*, 20. Subsequent quotations are cited parenthetically. For Harvey's use of Aristotle and Fabricius, see James G. Lennox, "The Comparative Study of Animal Development."

45. On Aristotle's zoophytes, see G. E. R. Lloyd, *Aristotelian Explorations*, 67–82.

46. Fabricius, *Embryological Treatises*, 279.

47. This was an idea Harvey developed in his *Prelectiones anatomie universalis* (1616): "The action of the brain is sensation and the brain exists for the sake of sensation which constitutes the very definition of an animal. . . . [The brain] can experience sensation by reason of the sensations which are brought back to it, and because of this it is called the organ of sensation in general, which is but one thing and which comprises the brain, the nerves and the special sense organs. And it is necessary that it should be so, that the brain may perceive the oneness of what it is seeing or hearing and so forth, out of many things apprehended one thing comprehended" (William Harvey, *Anatomical Lectures*, 313–15).

48. Robert G. Frank, *Harvey and the Oxford Physiologists*, 26–28.

49. With the discovery of *Commentaries of Heaven* and *Kingdom of God*, we now know far more about Traherne's interest in science. But earlier critics also glimpsed the extent of his learning. For Traherne's scientific knowledge, see Marjorie Hope Nicolson, *Breaking of the Circle*, 170–75. For his knowledge of anatomy, see Jonathan Sawday, *The Body Emblazoned*, 256–65.

50. Nicolson, *Breaking of the Circle*, 120, suggests that this poem was indebted to Harvey.

51. For Traherne's theological convictions around the possibility of sharing in God's goodness, power, and desires, see Denise Inge, *Wanting Like a God*.

52. These claims echo Neoplatonic sources and reformulate an idea found in Gaster, *Chronicles of Jerahmeel*, 20: while in the womb, a "light shines upon the head of the child, by which it sees from one end of the world to another." The third person narrative found in the *Chronicles* describes the fetus's situation from the outside. Traherne, by contrast, attempts to describe the inner experience, the *consciousness* of an embryonic being.

53. On Traherne's debts to the scholastic tradition, see Cefalu, "Thomistic Metaphysics."

54. Thomas Aquinas, *Expositio libri posteriorium analyticorum*, 1:148, 3.1, translation mine.

55. Aquinas, *Expositio*, Lectio 4, Caput 2 (comments on *Post An* 71b8–72a8).

56. Nicholas Culpeper, *Directory for Midwives*, 55. See also Sharp, *Midwives Book*, 109.

57. Traherne mentions Charleton in *Kingdom of God*. See *Works*, 1:377.

58. Walter Charleton, *Natural History of Nutrition, Life, and Voluntary Motion*, 119–25.

59. Charleton, *Natural History*, 119.

60. On the connection between Harvey's idea and Glisson's work, see Pagel, *New Light*, 34–36.

61. Marin Cureau de la Chambre, *The Art How to Know Men*, 108.

62. Webber, *The Eloquent "I,"* 224.

63. Crooke, *Microcosmographia*, 648; Placentinus, *Pentaestheseion*, 4.

64. For this episode in the *Confessiones*, see especially Brian Stock, *Augustine the Reader*, 23–26.

65. For a succinct account of desire and language in Augustine's thought, see John Freccero, "The Fig Tree and the Laurel," 35–37.

66. See Henry Vaughan, *Complete Works*, 185 ("Sure, there's a tie of bodies!"), 196 ("Corruption"), 261 ("The Timber"). Subsequent citations from Vaughan's poetry are cited parenthetically by page and line number.

67. See Leah Marcus, *Childhood and Cultural Despair*; and Martz, *Paradise Within*.

68. As Marcus, *Childhood*, 153–200, notes, Vaughan's view of childhood shares much with that of Traherne. But on this point they diverge rather sharply.

69. White, *Metaphysical Poets*, 289.

70. F. E. Hutchinson, "The Sacred Poets," 44.

71. T. S. Eliot, "Mystic and Politician as Poet," 1.

72. Douglas Bush, *English Literature in the Earlier Seventeenth Century, 1600–1660*, 156–57.

73. Benjamin Norton, *New English Dictionary, those, these* (accessed through Lexicons of Early Modern English).

74. Jonathan Culler, *Theory of the Lyric*, 289.

75. Culler, *Theory*, 294.

CHAPTER FIVE

1. I here am pursuing, in quite different ways, a line of thought present in such treatments of Locke as Paul de Man, "The Epistemology of Metaphor"; and Jonathan Lamb, *The Things Things Say*, 127–72.

2. Gray, *De principiis cogitandi*, 329, lines 8–9. Subsequent quotations are cited by line number for the Latin poem and by page number for the English translation.

3. Moshenska, *Feeling Pleasures*, 281. See also S. H. Clark, "'Pendet Homo Incertus.'"

4. Thomas Gray, letter to Richard West, qtd. in Roger Lonsdale, "Introduction to *De Principiis Cogitandi*," 321.

5. William Mason, *Poems and Letters of Thomas Gray*, 160.

6. On Lucretius in the eighteenth century, see especially Richard Kroll, *The Material Word*. On poetry and Lucretius later in the eighteenth century, see Amanda Jo Goldstein, *Sweet Science*.

7. Gray, letter to Richard West, qtd. in Lonsdale, "Introduction," 321.

8. Aristotle, *Complete Works*, 2:2316 (1447b); Sidney, *Defence of Poesy*, 12.

9. For eighteenth-century attempts to represent the generality of species being, see Heather Keenleyside, *Animals and Other People*.

10. For Gray and West, see Robert L. Mack, *Thomas Gray*, 105–6.

11. Virgil, *Eclogues, Georgics, Aeneid I–VI*, 140–41 (*Georgics* 2.76–77), 584–85 (*Aeneid* 6.737–38, translation modified).

12. Kathryn Tabb, "Madness as Method," 875.

13. Milton, *Of Education*, 403.

14. Perhaps this is what Locke learned from the philosophical narrative of intellectual development articulated by Ibn Tufayl in the medieval Islamic masterpiece *Hayy Ibn Yaqzan*. For Locke's use of Tufayl, see Avner Ben-Zaken, *Reading "Hayy Ibn Yaqzan*," 101–25.

15. I take Sarah Ahmed, *Queer Phenomenology*, 35, to be making a similar point in her reading of Edmund Husserl, which shows how Husserl transitions from "this table" to "the table," from a particular table used in a particular way for a particular purpose in a particular dynamic to an object that stands in for any other object that might appear.

16. For Hume's critique of Locke, see *Enquiry*, 13, n. 10.

17. For Locke's use of the category of *historia*, see Weinberg, *Consciousness*, 52.

18. John Locke, *Drafts for the "Essay*," 79 (Draft A, section 44).

19. On the relationship between the Locke's *First Treatise* and the *Essay*, see especially Nathan Tarcov, *Locke's Education for Liberty*, which shows how the *First Treatise* speaks to rest of Locke's corpus.

20. For theories of resistance, see, e.g., Daniel Lee, *Popular Sovereignty in Early Modern Constitutional Thought*.

21. Milton, *Tenure of Kings and Magistrates*, 198.

22. Milton, *Tenure*, 202.

23. Robert Filmer, *Patriarcha and Other Writings*, 2. Subsequent quotations are cited parenthetically.

24. For Locke on slavery, see especially Mary Nyquist, *Arbitrary Rule*, 326–61.

25. For Locke and embryology, midwifery, and generation, see Peter Walmsley, *Locke's "Essay" and the Rhetoric of Science*, 59–73; and Peter R. Anstey, *Locke and Natural Philosophy*, 188–203.

26. Harvey, *Generatione animalium*, B2.

27. For Locke's ownership of *Paradise Lost*, see John Harrison and Peter Laslett, *The Library of John Locke*, 189. For Locke's reading of the divorce tracts and praise of Milton's Latin, see Sharon Achinstein, "Early Modern Marriage in a Secular Age," 372.

28. John Locke, *Some Thoughts Concerning Education*, 31, 113.

29. For Locke and Socinianism, see John Marshall, "Locke, Socinianism, 'Socinianism,' and Unitarianism."

30. Jonathan Edwards, *Socinianism Unmasked*, 50.

31. Jonathan Edwards, *Socinian Creed*, 28.

32. Edwards, *Socinian Creed*, 122.

33. Edwards, *Preservative Against Socinianism*, 16.

34. Locke makes a stronger version of this claim in *Thoughts Concerning Education*, 25–31.

35. For an example of the first position, see Vere Chappell, "Locke's Theory of Ideas." For the second position, see Antonia LoLordo, *Locke's Moral Man*, 112–22. For an overview of how these positions ramify in Locke's *Essay*, see Weinberg, *Consciousness*, 26–32.

36. Thiel, *Early Modern Subject*, 116.

37. See Weinberg, *Consciousness*, 26–51.

38. La Forge, *Treatise*, 76, translation modified; La Forge, *Traitté de l'esprit de l'homme*, 96.

39. La Forge, *Treatise*, 57, translation modified; La Forge, *Traitté*, 54.

40. See Thiel, *Early Modern Subject*, 99. For Locke's later published praise of Cudworth, see *Thoughts Concerning Education*, 146.

41. Thiel, *Early Modern Subject*, 110.

42. Cudworth, *True Intellectual System*, 1:215, 3.34. Subsequent quotations are cited parenthetically according to page, book, chapter, and section numbers.

43. For Descartes's *conscientia* and Cudworth's *consciousness*, see Thiel, "Cudworth," 89.

44. For a more extended summary of this argument, see Thiel, "Cudworth."

45. For the best account of "concernment," see Strawson, *Locke*.

46. For my grasp of this point, I am grateful to David Finkelstein, who allowed me to audit his Spring 2018 Ph.D. seminar on consciousness. Thiel, *Early Modern Subject* and Strawson, *Locke* also make similar arguments about the relationship between Person and Man in Locke's thought.

47. For the forensic nature of Locke's personhood, see especially Strawson, *Locke*.

48. Thiel, *Early Modern Subject*, 122.

49. See my discussion of Davidson in the introduction.

50. Balibar, *Identity*, 51.

51. It is important to note in passing that the alignment of *consciousness* and *experience* solidified by Locke was taken up almost immediately after Locke's *Essay*. Consider Robert Boyle, *Christian Virtuoso*, 54, who, after working through the many meanings of experience, arrives at a definition that resonates with Locke's work. Experience is, Boyle claims, "sometimes set in contra-distinction to *Reason*, so as to comprehend, not only those *Phaenomena* that Nature or Art exhibits to our Outward Senses, but those things that we perceive to pass Within our selves; and all those ways of Information, whereby we attain any Knowledge that we do not owe to abstract *Reason*." Boyle's definition complements Locke's, which positions experience as that which is perceived (either external phenomena or mental operations). Experience has become the relationship between a source of stimuli and what "passes in a man's own mind." The connection between *consciousness* and *experience* becomes explicit in locution still used today—"conscious experience"—only in 1700, when Edward Young, *Two Sermons concerning Nature and Grace*, 31, claimed that ancient Greeks "found by Conscious Experience that it was as little in a Man's Power to make himself Vertuous, as it was to make himself Fortunate." When Young used the phrase "Conscious Experience," he entered conceptual terrain that was still in the making.

52. Locke, *Essay*, 104 (2.1.2): "Our Observation, employ'd either about *external, sensible Objects; or about internal Operations of our Minds, perceived and reflected on by our selves, is that, which supplies our Understanding with all the materials of our thinking*"; and Locke, *Essay*, 105 (2.1.4): "We, being conscious of, and observing in ourselves, do from [the perception of mental operations] receive into our Understandings, as distinct *Ideas*, as we do from Bodies affecting our Senses."

53. Many scholars have taken this passage as evidence that children do not possess consciousness. For an account of why this view is mistaken, see Weinberg, *Consciousness*, 29–31.

54. See also, Locke, *Essay*, 118 (2.1.25): when it comes to perception, "the *Understanding* is meerly *passive*; and whether or no, it will have these Beginnings, and as it were materials of Knowledge, is not in its own Power."

55. In light of this notion, it must be the case that Locke believes that there is no such thing as what Harvey called sense without sensation: Harvey's novel theory must, in his view, be based on a catachrestic abuse of language.

56. I am grateful to Richard Strier for pointing out the metaphoric instability in this passage.

57. For the flexible uses to which the word *furnished* was put, see Jeffrey Todd Knight, "'Furnished' for Action." I am grateful to Ryan Campagna for referring me to this article.

58. See also Locke, *Essay*, 162–63 (2.11.17), where he writes of the external and internal senses: "These alone, so far as I can discover, are the Windows by which light is let into this *dark Room*: For, methinks, the *Understanding* is not much unlike a Closet wholly shut from light, with only some little openings left, to let in external visible Resemblances, or *Ideas* of things without."

59. *OED*, s.v. "suppose," v. I.1a.

60. Smectymnuus, *An Answer to a Booke Entitvled An Hvmble Remonstrance*, 58.

61. Edward Knott, *Infidelity Unmasked*, 212, 654; Jean Baptiste van Helmont, *Van Helmont's Works*, 1037; and John Humfrey, *A Second Discourse about Re-Ordination*, 18.

62. Thomas Pierce, *The Sinner Impleaded in His Own Court*, 171.

63. William Molyneux, "A Problem Proposed." This letter, written to Locke in 1688, was in response to the section of the *Essay* Locke published in French earlier that year in the *Bibliotèque Universelle & Historique*.

64. For a version of this claim, see Tabb, "Madness."

65. Avicenna, *Avicenna Latinus*, 36 (1.1).

66. Hobbes, *Man and Citizen*, 205; Hobbes, *De cive*, 160 (8.1).

67. Etienne Bonnot de Condillac, *Treatise on the Sensations*, xix; *Traité des sensations*, 1.1–2.

68. Condillac, *Treatise*, xxxii.

69. Condillac, *Treatise*, xxx.

70. Condillac, *Treatise*, xxxvii.

CODA

1. See Cassin, ed., *Dictionary of Untranslatables*, 165–66.

2. But see Russ Leo, "Affect Before Spinoza," which argues that affect has a history unknown, with the exception of Spinoza, by most affect theorists.

3. William Wordsworth, *Essential Wordsworth*, 147–48 ("Ode," 1–5).

4. For childhood experience in modernist literature, see, e.g., Jennifer Anna Gosetti-Ferencei, *The Ecstatic Quotidian*. For Shelley's *Frankenstein*, see my discussion in the introduction. See also Laurence Sterne, *Tristram Shandy*; and Ian McEwan, *Nutshell*.

5. See Anthony Krupp, *Reason's Children*; and Maurice Merleau-Ponty, *Child Psychology and Pedagogy*.

6. See Otto Rank, *Trauma of Birth*; Didier Anzieu, *Skin-Ego*; Julia Kristeva, *Revolution in Poetic Language*; and Thomas Ogden, *Matrix of the Mind*.

7. Chalmers, *The Character of Consciousness*, 381–454.

8. José Ortega y Gasset, "Adán en el Paraíso," 476: "Cuando Adán apareció en el Paraíso, como un árbol nuevo, comenzó a existir esto que llamamos vida. Adán fué el primer ser que, viviendo, se sintió vivir. . . . Adán en el Paraíso, es la pura y simple vida."

9. Pierre Hadot, *The Present Alone Is Our Happiness*, 5–6.

10. Ortega y Gasset, "Adán en el Paraíso," 489: "Quién es Adán? Cualquiera y nadie particularmente: la vida."

11. Anna Letitia Barbauld, *Selected Poetry and Prose*, 147–48 (1–2). Subsequent quotations are cited parenthetically by line number.

BIBLIOGRAPHY

Achinstein, Sharon. "Early Modern Marriage in a Secular Age: Beyond the Sexual Con-
tract." In *Milton and the Long Restoration*, edited by Blaire Hoxby and Ann Baynes
Coiro, 363–78. Oxford: Oxford University Press, 2016.
———. "Milton's Political Ontology of the Human." *ELH* 84 (2017): 591–616.
Adelman, Howard B. "Introduction." In *The Embryological Treatises of Hieronymus Fa-
bricius of Aquapendente*, edited by Howard B. Adelmann, 1–121. Ithaca, NY: Cornell
University Press, 1942.
Adorno, Theodor. "On Lyric Poetry and Society." In *Notes on Literature*, vol. 1, edited by
R. Tiedemann, translated by Shierry Weber Nicholson, 37–54. New York: Columbia
University Press, 1991.
Agamben, Giorgio. *Nudities*. Translated by David Kishik and Stefan Pedatella. Stanford,
CA: Stanford University Press, 2011.
Ahmed, Sarah. *Queer Phenomenology: Orientations, Objects, Others*. Durham, NC: Duke
University Press, 2006.
Aït-Touati, Frédérique. *Fictions of the Cosmos: Science and Literature in the Seven-
teenth Century*. Translated by Susan Emanuel. Chicago: University of Chicago
Press, 2011.
Almond, Philip C. *Adam and Eve in Seventeenth-Century Thought*. Cambridge:
Cambridge University Press, 1999.
American College of Obstetricians and Gynecologists. "ACOG Opposes U.S. Senate Ef-
fort to Limit Abortion Access." https://www.acog.org/About-ACOG/News-Room
/Statements/2018/ACOG-Opposes-US-Senate-Effort-to-Limit-Abortion-Access.
Amerini, Fabrizio. *Aquinas on the Beginning and End of Human Life*. Cambridge, MA:
Harvard University Press, 2013.
Anderson, Gary. *The Genesis of Perfection: Adam and Eve in Jewish and Christian Imag-
ination*. Westminster: John Knox Press, 2002.
Andreini, Giambattista. *L'Adamo*. Translated by Watson Kirkconnell. In Kirkconnell, *Ce-
lestial Cycle*, 227–66.
Ankersmit, Frank. *Sublime Historical Experience*. Stanford, CA: Stanford University Press,
2005.

Anonymous. *York Plays: The Plays Performed by the Crafts or Mysteries of York*. Edited by Lucy Toulmin Smith. Oxford: Clarendon, 1885.

Anstey, Peter R. *Locke and Natural Philosophy*. Oxford: Oxford University Press, 2011.

Anzieu, Didier. *The Skin-Ego*. Translated by Naomi Segal. London: Karnac, 2016.

Aquinas, Thomas. *Expositio libri posteriorium analyticorum*. In *Opera omnia iussu Leonis XIII edita*, vol. 1, 129–403. Rome, 1882.

———. *Summa contra gentiles*. 4 vols. Translated by Anton C. Pegis. South Bend, IN: University of Notre Dame Press, 1975.

———. *Summa theologica*. 22 vols. Translated by the Fathers of the English Dominican Province. Allen, TX: Christian Classics, 1981.

Aratus. *Phenomena*. Translated by G. R. Mair. In *Callimachus: Hymns and Epigrams; Lycophron; Aratus*, edited by A. W. Mair and G. R. Mair, 185–299. Cambridge, MA: Harvard University Press, 2014.

Arendt, Hannah. *The Human Condition*. 2nd ed. Chicago: University of Chicago Press, 1958.

———. *Love and Saint Augustine*. Edited by Joanna Vecchiarelli Scott and Judith Chelius Stark. Chicago: University of Chicago Press, 1996.

———. *The Origins of Totalitarianism*. New ed. New York: Harcourt, 1979.

Ariès, Phillippe. *Centuries of Childhood: A Social History of Family Life*. Translated by Robert Baldick. New York: Vintage, 1962.

Aristotle. *The Complete Works*. Edited by Jonathan Barnes. 2 vols. Princeton, NJ: Princeton University Press, 1984.

Aubrey, John. "Minutes on the Life of Mr. John Milton." In *The Early Lives of Milton*, edited by Helen Darbishire, 1–16. New York: Barnes and Noble, 1932.

Augustine. *De beata vita*. In *Contra academicos, De beata vita, necnon De ordine libri*. Edited by Wilhelmus M. Green. Antwerp: In Aedibus Spectrum, 1956.

———. *On Christian Doctrine*. Translated by D. W. Robertson Jr. Upper Saddle River, NJ: Prentice Hall, 1997.

———. *The City of God Against the Pagans*. Translated by R. W. Dyson. Cambridge: Cambridge University Press, 1998.

———. *Confessions*. Edited and translated by Henry Chadwick. Oxford: Oxford University Press, 1992.

———. *Confessiones*. Edited by Carolyn J. B. Hammond. Cambridge, MA: Harvard University Press, 2014.

———. *On the Free Choice of the Will*. Translated by Thomas Williams. Indianapolis, IN: Hackett, 1993.

———. *On Genesis*. Translated by Edmund Hill. New York: New City, 2002.

———. *On the Trinity*. Translated by Stephen McKenna. Cambridge: Cambridge University Press, 2002.

Avicenna. *Avicenna Latinus: Liber de anima seu Sextus de naturalibus: Edition critique de la traduction latine médiévale*. Edited by S. Van Riet. Louvain: E. Peeters; Leiden: Brill, 1972.

Bacon, Francis. *The Philosophical Works of Francis Bacon*. Edited by John M. Robertson. London: Routledge, 1905.

Baker, Thomas. *Reflections Upon Learning*. London, 1700.

Bakhtin, Mikhail. *Speech Genres and Other Late Essays*. Translated by Vern W. McGee. Slavic Text Series. Austin: University of Texas, 1986.

Balibar, Étienne. *Citizen Subject: Foundations for Philosophical Anthropology*. Translated by Steven Miller. New York: Fordham University Press, 2017.

———. *Identity and Difference: John Locke and the Invention of Consciousness*. Translated by Warren Montag. London: Verso, 2013.

Barbauld, Anna Letitia. *Selected Poetry and Prose*. Edited by William McCarthy and Elizabeth Kraft. Peterborough, ON: Broadview, 2002.

Belloy, Pierre de. *A Catholicke Apologie against the Libels*. Translated by E. D. L. I. C. London, 1585.

Bemrose, Stephen. " 'Come d'animal divegna fante': The Animation of the Embryo in Dante." In *The Human Embryo: Aristotle and the Arabic and European Traditions*, edited by G. R. Dunstan, 123–35. Exeter: University of Exeter Press, 1990.

Ben-Zaken, Avner. *Reading Hayy Ibn Yaqzan": A Cross-Cultural History of Autodidacticism*. Baltimore: Johns Hopkins University Press, 2011.

Beza, Theodor, ed. and trans. *Jesu Christi Domini nostri Novum Testamentum*. Geneva, 1598.

Birmingham, Peg. *Hannah Arendt and Human Rights: The Predicament of Common Responsibility*. Indianapolis: University of Indiana Press, 2006.

Blevins, Jacob, ed. *Re-reading Thomas Traherne: A Collection of New Critical Essays*. Tempe: Arizona Center for Medieval and Renaissance Studies, 2007.

Blom, Hans W. "Sociability and Hugo Grotius." *History of European Ideas* 41 (2015): 589–604.

Bloom, Harold. *The Anxiety of Influence: A Theory of Poetry*. 2nd ed. Oxford: Oxford University Press, 1997.

Boswell, Jackson Campbell. *Milton's Library: A Catalogue of the Remains of John Milton's Library and an Annotated Reconstruction of Milton's Library and Ancillary Readings*. New York: Garland, 1975.

Boyle, Robert. *Christian Virtuoso*. London, 1690.

Brague, Rémi. "Necessity of the Good: Why Western Culture Needs to Return to Plato." *First Things* (February 2015): 47–52.

Brigham Young EEBO Corpus. https://www.english-corpora.org/eebo/.

Brisson, Luc, Marie-Hélène Congourdeau, and Jean-Luc Solère, eds. *L'embryon: Formation et animation. Antiquité grecque et latine, tradition hébraïque, chrétienne et islamique*. Paris: Vrin, 2008.

Brouwer, René. "On the Ancient Background of Grotius's Notion of Natural Law." *Grotiana* 29 (2008): 1–24.

Brown, Francis, S. R. Driver, and Charles A. Briggs, eds. *A Hebrew and English Lexicon of the Old Testament*. Based on the Lexicon of William Genesius as translated by Edward Robinson. Boston: Houghton Mifflin, 1906.

Browne, Thomas. *The Complete Works of Thomas Browne*. Edited by Geoffrey Keynes. 6 vols. London: Faber, 1964.

———. *Religio Medici and Urne-Burial*. Edited by Stephen Greenblatt and Ramie Targoff. New York: *New York Review of Books*, 2012.

Brunschwig, Jacques. "The Cradle Argument in Epicureanism and Stoicism." In *The Norms of Nature: Studies in Hellenistic Ethics*, edited by Malcolm Schofield and Gisela Striker, 113–44. Cambridge: Cambridge University Press, 1986.

B[ullokar], J[ohn]. *An English Expositor*. London, 1616.

Buonocore, Giuseppe, and Carlo V. Bellieni. *Neonatal Pain: Suffering, Pain, and Risk of Brain Damage in the Fetus and Newborn*. Milan: Springer-Verlag Italia, 2008.

Burthogge, Richard. *An Essay Upon Reason, and the Nature of Spirits*. London, 1694.

Burton, Robert. *The Anatomy of Melancholy*. New York: *New York Review of Books*, 2001.

Bush, Douglas. *English Literature in the Earlier Seventeenth Century, 1600–1660*. Oxford: Oxford University Press, 1945.

Calvin, John. *A Commentarie of John Calvin, upon the first booke of Moses called Genesis*. Translated by Thomas Tymme. London, 1578.

———. *Institutio Christianae religionis*. Vols. 3–5 of the *Opera selecta*. Edited by Peter Barth. Monachii: Kaiser, 1959.

———. *Institutes of the Christian Religion*. 2 vols. Edited by John T. McNeill. Translated by Ford Lewis Battles. Westminster: John Knox Press, 1960.

Campbell, Gordon, and Thomas N. Corns. *John Milton: Life, Work, and Thought*. Oxford: Oxford University Press, 2008.

Carey, John. *John Donne: Mind, Life and Art*. Oxford: Oxford University Press, 1981.

Carraud, Vincent. *L'invention du moi*. Paris: Presses Universitaires de France, 2010.

Cassin, Barbara, ed. *Dictionary of Untranslatables: A Philosophical Lexicon*. Translated by Emily Apter, Jacques Lezra, and Michael Wood. Princeton, NJ: Princeton University Press, 2014.

Castelvetro, Ludovico. *On the Art of Poetry*. Translated by Andrew Bongiorno. Binghampton, NY: Medieval and Renaissance Texts and Studies, 1984.

Caston, Victor. "Aristotle on Consciousness." *Mind* 111 (2002): 751–815.

Cavarero, Adriana. "'A Child Has Been Born Unto Us': Arendt on Birth." Translated by Silvia Guslandi and Cosette Bruhns. *philoSOPHIA* 4 (2014): 12–30.

Cawdrey, Robert. *A Table Alphabetical*. London, 1604.

Cefalu, Paul. "Thomistic Metaphysics and Ethics in the Poetry and Prose of Thomas Traherne." *Literature and Theology* 16 (2002): 248–69.

Chalmers, David J. *The Character of Consciousness*. Oxford: Oxford University Press, 2010.

Chambre, Marin Cureau de la. *The Art How to Know Men*. Translated by John Davies. London, 1665.

Chapman, George, trans. *The Crowne of all Homers Workes*. London, 1624.

Chappell, Vere. "Locke's Theory of Ideas." In *The Cambridge Companion to Locke*, edited by Vere Chappell, 26–55. Cambridge: Cambridge University Press, 1994.

Charleton, Walter. *Natural History of Nutrition, Life, and Voluntary Motion*. London, 1659.

Chen, Mel Y. *Animacies: Biopolitics, Racial Mattering, and Queer Affect*. Durham: Duke University Press, 2012.

Cicero, Marcus Tullius. *On Ends*. 2nd ed. Translated by H. Rackham. Cambridge, MA: Harvard University Press, 1931.

———. *Pro Cluentio*. In *Pro lege Manilia; Pro Caecina; Pro Cluentio; Pro Rabirio Perduelli-onis*. Translated by H. Grosse Hodge. Cambridge, MA: Harvard University Press, 1927.

———. *De senectute*. In *On Old Age, on Friendship, on Divination*. Translated by William Armistead Falconer. Cambridge, MA: Harvard University Press, 1923.

Clark, S. H. "'Pendet Homo Incertus': Gray's Response to Locke: Part Two: 'De Principiis Cogitandi.'" *Eighteenth-Century Studies* 24 (1991): 484–503.

Clemens, A. L. *The Mystical Poetry of Thomas Traherne*. Cambridge, MA: Harvard University Press, 1969.

Cockeram, Henry. *English Dictionarie*. London, 1623.

Coffin, Charles Munroe. "Creation and the Self in *Paradise Lost*." *ELH* 29 (1962): 1–18.

Colby, Francis L. "Thomas Traherne and Henry More." *MLN* 62 (1947): 490–92.

Condillac, Étienne Bonnot de. *Traité des sensations*. Paris, 1754.

———. *Treatise on the Sensations*. Translated by Geraldine Carr. Los Angeles: University of Southern California Press, 1930.

Conley, Carey Herbert. "Milton's Indebtedness to His Contemporaries in *Paradise Lost*." PhD diss., University of Chicago, 1910.

Coogan, Michael D., ed. *The New Oxford Annotated Bible: with the Apocrypha*. 4th ed. New York: Oxford University Press, 2010.

Cressy, David. *Birth, Marriage, and Death: Ritual, Religion and the Life Cycle in Tudor and Stuart England*. Oxford: Oxford University Press, 1997.

Crooke, Helkiah. *Microcosmographia*. London, 1615.

Crowther, Kathleen M. *Adam and Eve in the Protestant Reformation*. Cambridge: Cambridge University Press, 2010.

Cudworth, Ralph. *The True Intellectual System of the Universe*. 3 vols. Edited by J. L. Mosheim. London: Thomas Tegg, 1845.

Culler, Jonathan. *Theory of the Lyric*. Cambridge, MA: Harvard University Press, 2015.

Culpeper, Nicholas. *Directory for Midwives*. London, 1651.

Culverwell, Nathaniel. *An Elegant and Learned Discourse on the Light of Nature*. Edited by Robert A. Greene and Hugh MacCallum. Toronto: University of Toronto Press, 1971.

D'Angour, Armand. *The Greeks and the New: Novelty in Ancient Greek Imagination and Experience*. Cambridge: Cambridge University Press, 2011.

Daniel, Samuel. *Delia and Rosamund augmented Cleopatra*. London, 1594.

Dante. *Purgatorio*. Translated by Jean Hollander and Robert Hollander. New York: Anchor, 2003.

Daston, Lorraine, and Peter Galison, *Objectivity*. New York: Zone, 2007.

Davidson, Arnold. *The Emergence of Sexuality: Historical Epistemology and the Formation of Concepts*. Cambridge, MA: Harvard University Press, 2001.

Davies, Catherine Glyn. *Conscience as Consciousness: The Idea of Self-Awareness in French Philosophical Writing from Descartes to Diderot*. Oxford: Voltaire Foundation, 1990.

Davies, John. *Muse's Sacrifice*. London, 1612.

———. *Nosce te ipsum*. London, 1599.

Dear, Peter. *Discipline and Experience: The Mathematical Way in the Scientific Revolution*. Chicago: University of Chicago Press, 1995.

de Bolla, Peter. *The Architecture of Concepts: The Historical Formation of Human Rights*. New York: Fordham University Press, 2013.

de Man, Paul. "The Epistemology of Metaphor." *Critical Inquiry* 5 (1978): 13–30.

Derrida, Jacques. *Speech and Phenomena*. Translated by David B. Allison. Evanston, IL: Northwestern University Press, 1973.

Descartes, René. *Meditations of First Philosophy / Meditationes de prima philosophia: A Bilingual Edition*. Edited and translated by George Heffernan. South Bend, IN: University of Notre Dame Press, 1990.

———. *Oeuvres de Descartes*. 13 vols. Edited by Charles Adam and Paul Tannery. Paris: Léopold Cerf, 1897–1913. Cited in text as AT

———. *The Philosophical Writings of Descartes*. 3 vols. Edited by John Cottingham, Robert Stoothoff, and Dugald Murdoch. Cambridge: Cambridge University Press, 1984–1991. Cited in text as CSM.

———. *Six Metaphysical Meditations*. Translated by William Molyneux. London, 1680.

Dickerson, Phoebe. " 'The Lathorns Sides': Skin, Soul and the Poetry of Thomas Traherne." In Dodd, ed. *Thomas Traherne and Seventeenth-Century Thought*, 31–47.

Digby, Kenelm. *Two Treatises*. London, 1644.

Dodd, Elizabeth S. *Boundless Innocence in Thomas Traherne's Poetic Theology*. Farnham: Ashgate, 2015.

———, and Cassandra Gorman. "Traherne in Context." In Dodd and Gorman, eds. *Thomas Traherne and Seventeenth-Century Thought*, 1–30.

———, and Cassandra Gorman, eds. *Thomas Traherne and Seventeenth-Century Thought*. Cambridge: Brewer, 2016.

Donne, John. *Devotions Upon Emergent Occasions*. Edited by Anthony Raspa. Montreal: McGill-Queen's University Press, 1975.

———. *Letters to Severall Persons of Honor*. Edited by M. Thomas Hester. Delmar: Scholars' Facsimiles and Reprints, 1977.

———. *Metempsychosis*. In *The Complete English Poems*. Edited by A. J. Smith New York: Penguin, 1986.

Dowell, Graham. *Enjoying the World: The Rediscovery of Thomas Traherne*. Harrisburg, PA: Morehouse, 1990.

Downame, George. *Commentarii in P. Rami Regii Professoris Dialecicam*. Frankfurt, 1601.

Druart, Thérèse-Anne. "The Soul and Body Problem: Avicenna and Descartes." In *Arabic Philosophy and the West: Continuity and Interaction*, edited by Thérèse-Anne Druart, 27–48. Washington: Center for Contemporary Arab Studies, 1988.

Dryden, John. *The State of Innocence and Fall of Man*. In *The Works of John Dryden*, vol. 12, edited by Vinton A. Dearing, 79–146. Berkeley: University of California Press, 1994.

Du Bartas, Guillaume de Salluste. *Du Bartas, His Divine Weekes and Workes*. Translated by Joshua Sylvester. London, 1611.

———. *The Works of Guillaume de Salluste, sieur Du Bartas*. Vol. 1. Edited by Tigner Holmes, John Coriden Lyons, and Robert White Linker. Chapel Hill: University of North Carolina Press, 1935.

Dunstan, G. R., ed. *The Human Embryo: Aristotle and the Arabic and European Traditions*. Exeter: University of Exeter Press, 1990.

Earle, John. *Micro-Cosmographie*. London, 1628.

Early English Books Online. https://eebo.chadwyck.com/home.

Early English Print: Text Mining Early Printed English. https:// earlyprint.wustl.edu.

Eden, Kathy. *Poetry and Legal Fiction in the Aristotelian Tradition*. Princeton, NJ: Princeton University Press, 1986.

Edwards, Karen. *Milton and the Natural World: Science and Poetry in "Paradise Lost."* Cambridge: Cambridge University Press, 1999.

Edwards, Jonathan. *A Preservative Against Socinianism*. 2 vols. London, 1693.

———. *Socinianism Unmasked*. London, 1696.

———. *The Socinian Creed*. London, 1697.

Eisendrath, Rachel. *Poetry in a World of Things: Aesthetics and Empiricism in Renaissance Ekphrasis*. Chicago: University of Chicago Press, 2018.

Eliot, T. S. "Mystic and Politician as Poet: Vaughan, Traherne, Marvell, Milton." *Listener* 64 (1930): 590–91.

Ellrodt, Robert. *Seven Metaphysical Poets: A Structural Study of the Unchanging Self*. Oxford: Oxford University Press, 2000.

Empson, William. *Milton's God*. London: Chatto, 1961.

Episcopius, Simon. *Opera Theologica*. 2nd ed. London, 1678.

Erasmus, Desiderius, ed. and trans. *Novum testamentum omne*. Basil, 1519.

Evans, J. M. *"Paradise Lost" and the Genesis Tradition*. Oxford: Clarendon, 1968.

Eyffinger, Arthur. "The Fourth Man: Stoic Tradition in Grotian Drama." *Grotiana* 22/23 (2001–2): 117–56.

Fabricius, Hieronymus. *The Embryological Treatises of Hieronymus Fabricius of Aquapendente*. Edited by Howard B. Adelmann. Ithaca, NY: Cornell University Press, 1942.

Fallon, Stephen. *Milton Among the Philosophers: Poetry and Materialism in Seventeenth-Century England*. Ithaca, NY: Cornell University Press, 1991.

Falque, Emmanuel. *The Metamorphosis of Finitude: An Essay on Birth and Resurrection*. Translated by George Hughes. New York: Fordham University Press, 2012.

Filmer, Robert. *Patriarcha and Other Writings*. Edited by Johann P. Sommerville. Cambridge: Cambridge University Press, 1991.

Fissell, Mary E. *Vernacular Bodies: The Politics of Reproduction in Early Modern England*. Oxford: Oxford University Press, 2004.

Fletcher, Harris. *The Intellectual Development of John Milton*. 2 vols. Urbana: University of Illinois Press, 1956–1961.

Flood, John. *Representations of Eve in Antiquity and the Middle Ages*. London: Routledge, 2011.

Fowler, Alastair. *Renaissance Realism: Narrative Images in Literature and Art*. Oxford: Oxford University Press, 2003.

Fox, Christopher. *Locke and the Scriblerians: Identity and Consciousness in Early Eighteenth-Century Britain*. Berkeley: University of California Press, 1988.

Frank, Robert G. *Harvey and the Oxford Physiologists: Scientific Ideas and Social Interaction*. Berkeley: University of California Press, 1980.

Frankfurt, Harry G. *Demons, Dreamers, and Madmen: The Defense of Reason in Descartes's Meditations*. Princeton, NJ: Princeton University Press, 2008.

Fraser, Jennifer. "Dante/*Fante*: Embryology in Purgatory and Paradise." In *Dante and the Unorthodox: The Aesthetics of Transgression*, edited by James Miller, 290–309. Waterloo: Wilfred Laurier University Press, 2005.

Freccero, John. "The Fig Tree and the Laurel: Petrarch's Poetics." *Diacritics* 5, no. 1 (1975): 34–40.

Froula, Christina. "When Eve Reads Milton: Undoing the Canonical Economy." *Critical Inquiry* 10 (1983): 321–47.

Gabriel, Markus. *I Am Not A Brain: Philosophy of Mind for the Twenty-First Century*. Translated by Christopher Turner. Cambridge: Polity, 2017.

Gadamer, Hans Georg. *Truth and Method*. 2nd ed. Translated by Joel Weinsheimer and Donald G. Marshall. London: Continuum, 1989.

Gadberry, Andrea. "The Cupid and the Cogito: Cartesian Poetics." *Critical Inquiry* 43 (2017): 738–51.

Galen. *Clavdii Galeni opera omnia*. 20 vols. Edited by Carolus Gottlob Kühn. Leipzig: C. Cnoblochii, 1821–33.

Gaster, Moses, ed. and trans. *The Chronicles of Jerahmeel; or, The Hebrew Bible Historiale*. London: Royal Asiatic Society, 1899.

Gellinek, Christian. "The Principal Literary Sources to John Milton's *Paradise Lost*," *Grotiana* 7 (1986): 112–18.

Gilson, Etienne. *The Christian Philosophy of Saint Augustine*. Translated by L. E. M. Lynch. New York: Random House, 1960.

———. "Les sources gréco-arabes de l'augustinisme avicennisant." *Archives d'histoire doctrinale et littéraire du moyen âge* 4 (1929–30): 5–149.

Glisson, Francis. *Tractatus de natura substantiae energetica*. London, 1672.

Goldstein, Amanda Jo. *Sweet Science: Romantic Materialisms and the New Logics of Life*. Chicago: University of Chicago Press, 2017.

Gosetti-Ferencei, Jennifer Anna. *The Ecstatic Quotidian: Phenomenological Sightings in Modern Art and Literature*. University Park: Pennsylvania State University Press, 2007.

Grand, Antoine Le. *An Entire Body of Philosophy*. Translated by Richard Blome. London, 1694.

Grant, Patrick. *The Transformation of Sin: Studies in Donne, Herbert, Vaughan, and Traherne*. Montreal: McGill-Queen's University Press, 1974.

Gray, Thomas. *De principiis cogitandi*. In *The Poems of Thomas Gray, William Collins, Oliver Goldsmith*. Edited by Roger Lonsdale. London: Longman, 1969

Green, Mandy. *Milton's Ovidian Eve*. Aldershot: Ashgate, 2009.

Greene, Robert A. "Instinct of Nature: Natural Law, Synderesis, and the Moral Sense." *Journal of the History of Ideas* 58, no. 2 (1997): 173–98.

Greenblatt, Stephen. *The Rise and Fall of Adam and Eve*. New York: W. W. Norton, 2017.

Gregorić, Pavel, and Filip Grgić. "Aristotle's Notion of Experience." *Archiv für Geschichte der Philosophie* 88 (2006): 1–30.

Greteman, Blaine. *The Poetics and Politics of Youth in Milton's England*. Cambridge: University of Cambridge Press, 2013.

Grotius, Hugo. *Adamus exul*. In Kirkconnell, *Celestial Cycle*, 96–219.

———. *Commentary on the Law of Prize and Booty*. Edited by Martine Julia van Ittersum. Indianapolis, IN: Liberty Fund, 2006.

————. *The Rights of War and Peace.* 2 vols. Edited by Richard Tuck. Indianapolis: Liberty Fund, 2005.

Hadot, Pierre. *The Present Alone Is Our Happiness: Conversations with Jeannie Carlier and Arnold I. Davidson.* Translated by Marc Djaballah. Stanford, CA: Stanford University Press, 2009.

Hale, John K., and J. Donald Cullington. "Introduction." In Milton, *De doctrina Christiana,* xix–lxiv.

Hall, Joseph. *Epistles, the second volume: Conteining two decads.* London, 1608.

Halliwell, Stephen. *The Aesthetics of Mimesis: Ancient Texts and Modern Problems.* Princeton, NJ: Princeton University Press, 2002.

Hamlin, Hannibal. *Psalm Culture and Early Modern English Literature.* Cambridge: Cambridge University Press, 2004.

Hanford, James Holly. "Dr. Paget's Library." *Bulletin of the Medical Library Association* 33 (1945): 90–99.

Hardison, O. B., Jr. *The Enduring Monument: A Study of the Idea of Praise in Renaissance Literary Theory and Practice.* Chapel Hill: University of North Carolina Press, 1962.

Harrison, John, and Peter Laslett. *The Library of John Locke.* Oxford: Oxford University Press, 1971.

Harrison, Peter. *The Bible, Protestantism, and the Rise of Natural Science.* Cambridge: Cambridge University Press, 1998.

————. "Experimental Religion and Experimental Science in Early Modern England." *Intellectual History Review* 21 (2011): 413–33.

————. *The Fall of Man and the Foundations of Science.* Cambridge: Cambridge University Press, 2007.

Harrison, Timothy M. "Adamic Awakening and the Feeling of Being Alive in *Paradise Lost.*" *Milton Studies* 54 (2013): 29–57.

Harvey, Elizabeth D. "*Samson Agonistes* and Milton's Sensible Ethics." In *The Oxford Handbook of Milton,* edited by Nicholas McDowell and Nigel Smith, 649–66. Oxford: Oxford University Press, 2009.

————. "The 'Sense of All Senses.'" In *Sensible Flesh: On Touch in Early Modern Culture,* edited by Elizabeth D. Harvey, 1–21. Philadelphia: University of Pennsylvania Press, 2003.

————. "The Souls of Animals: John Donne's *Metempsychosis* and Early Modern Natural History." In *Environment and Embodiment in Early Modern England,* edited by Mary Floyd-Wilson and Garrett Sullivan, 55–70. New York: Palgrave, 2007.

Harvey, William. *The Anatomical Lectures of William Harvey.* Edited and translated by Gweneth Whitteridge. London: Livingstone, 1964.

————. *Disputations Touching the Generation of Animals.* Translated by Gweneth Whittridge. Oxford: Blackwell, 1981.

————. *Exercitationes de generatione animalium.* London, 1651.

Hasnawi, Ahmad. "La conscience de soi chez Avicenne et Descartes." In *Descartes et le moyen âge,* edited by J. Biard and R. Rashed, 283–91. Paris: Vrin, 1997.

Hasse, Dag Nikolaus. *Avicenna's "De Anima" in the Latin West: The Formation of a Peripatetic Philosophy of the Soul, 1160–1300.* London: Warburg Institute, 2000.

Heidegger, Martin. *The Basic Problems of Phenomenology.* Translated by Albert Hof-
    stadter. Indianapolis: University of Indiana Press, 1982.
———. *Being and Time.* Translated by John Macquarrie and Edward Robinson. New York:
    Harper, 1962.
———. *Sein und Zeit.* 7th ed. Tubingen: Neomarius, 1953.
Heller-Roazen, Daniel. *The Inner Touch: Archaeology of a Sensation.* New York: Zone,
    2007.
Helmont, Jean Baptiste van. *Van Helmont's Works.* Translated by J. C. London, 1664.
Hennig, Boris. "Cartesian *Conscientia.*" *British Journal for the History of Philosophy* 15
    (2007): 455–84.
———. "'Insofar As' in Descartes's Definition of Thought," *Studia Leibnizia* 43 (2011):
    145–59.
Herbert, Edward. *De Veritate.* Translated by Meyrick H. Carré. Bristol: J. W. Arrowsmith,
    1937.
Hershinow, Stephanie Insley. *Born Yesterday: Inexperience and the Early Realist Novel.*
    Baltimore: Johns Hopkins University Press, 2019.
Hesiod. *Theogony and Works and Days.* Translated by M. L. West. Oxford: Oxford Uni-
    versity Press, 1988.
Hexham, Henry. *A Copious English and Netherlandish Dictionary.* London, 1648.
Hill, Christopher. *Milton and the English Revolution.* New York: Viking, 1977.
Hobbes, Thomas. *De cive: The Latin Version.* Edited by H. Warrender. Oxford: Clarendon,
    1983.
———. *The Correspondence.* Edited by Noel Malcolm. 2 vols. Oxford: Clarendon, 1994.
———. *Leviathan.* Edited by Edwin Curley. Indianapolis, IN: Hackett, 1994.
———. *Man and Citizen.* Edited by Bernard Gert. Indianapolis, IN: Hackett, 1991.
Hogarth, Richard. *Gazophylacium Anglicanum.* London, 1689.
Holmes, Brooke. "Pure Life: The Limits of the Vegetable Analogy in the Hippocratics and
    Galen." In *The Comparable Body: Analogy and Metaphor in Ancient Mesopotamian,
    Egyptian, and Greco-Roman Medicine,* edited by John Z. Wee, 358–86. Leiden: Brill,
    2017.
Homer. *Homeric Hymns, Homeric Apocrypha, Lives of Homer.* Edited and translated by
    Martin L. West. Cambridge, MA: Harvard University Press, 2003.
Howard, Edward. *Remarks on the New Philosophy of Descartes.* London, 1700.
Hume, David. *An Enquiry Concerning Human Understanding.* Indianapolis, IN: Hackett,
    1993.
Hume, Patrick. *Annotations on Milton's "Paradise Lost."* London, 1695.
Humfrey, John. *A Second Discourse about Re-Ordination.* London, 1662.
Hutchinson, F. E. "The Sacred Poets." In the *Cambridge History of English Literature,*
    vol. 7, edited by Sir Adolphus William Ward and Alfred Rayney Waller. New York:
    Putnam's Sons, 1911.
Hutton, Sarah. "Platonism in Some Metaphysical Poets: Marvell, Vaughan, and Tra-
    herne." In *Platonism and the English Imagination,* edited by Alan Baldwin and Sarah
    Hutton, 163–77. Cambridge: Cambridge University Press, 1994.
Inge, Denise. *Wanting Like a God: Desire and Freedom in Thomas Traherne.* London:
    SCM Press, 2009.

Irenaeus. *Against Heresies*. In *The Ante-Nicene Fathers: The Apostolic Fathers*, vol. 1, edited by Alexander Roberts and James Donaldson, 309–567. New York: Charles Scribner's Sons, 1913.

Jardine, Lisa. *Francis Bacon: Discovery and the Art of Discourse*. Cambridge: Cambridge University Press, 2009.

Jay, Martin. *Songs of Experience: Modern American and European Variations on a Universal Theme*. Berkeley: University of California Press, 2005.

Johnston, Carol Ann. "Heavenly Perspectives, Mirrors of Eternity: Thomas Traherne's Yearning Subject." *Criticism* 43 (2001), 377–405.

Junker, Billy. "Fallen Nature, Utopian Institutions, and (Radical) Medieval Christian-Aristotelianism." *Moreana* 54 (2017): 149–56.

Kahn, Charles H. "Sensation and Consciousness in Aristotle's Psychology." In *Articles on Aristotle*, vol. 4, edited by Jonathan Barnes, Malcolm Schofield, and Richard Sorabji, 1–31. London: Bloomsbury, 1998.

Kahn, Victoria. "Allegory, Poetic Theology, and Enlightenment Aesthetics." In *The Insistence of Art*, ed. Paul Kottman, 31–54. New York: Fordham University Press, 2017.

———. "'The Duty to Love': Passion and Obligation in Early Modern Political Theory." *Representations* 68 (1999): 84–107.

———. *The Future of Illusion: Political Theology and Early Modern Texts*. Chicago: University of Chicago Press, 2014.

———. *Wayward Contracts, The Crisis of Political Obligation in England, 1640–1674*. Princeton, NJ: Princeton University Press, 2004.

Keenleyside, Heather. *Animals and Other People: Literary Forms and Living Beings in the Long Eighteenth Century*. Philadelphia: University of Pennsylvania Press, 2016.

———. "Matter, Form, Idea: What Lovejoy's History of Ideas Might Have to Do With Literature." *ELH* 84 (2017): 223–57.

Keller, Eve. *Generating Bodies and Gendered Selves: The Rhetoric of Reproduction in Early Modern England*. Seattle: University of Washington Press, 2007.

Kelley, Maurice, and Samuel Atkins. "Milton's Annotations of Aratus." *PMLA* 70 (1955): 1,090–1106.

Kerrigan, William. "The Heretical Milton: From Assumption to Mortalism." *English Literary Renaissance* 5 (1975): 125–66.

Keynes, Geoffrey. *The Life of William Harvey*. Oxford: Clarendon, 1966.

Kilgour, Maggie. *Milton and the Metamorphosis of Ovid*. Oxford: Oxford University Press, 2012.

Kirkconnell, Watson, ed. *The Celestial Cycle: The Theme of "Paradise Lost" in World Literature, with Translations of the Major Analogues*. Toronto: University of Toronto Press, 1952.

Kisiel, Theodore. *The Genesis of Heidegger's "Being and Time."* Berkeley: University of California Press, 1993.

Knapp, Steven. *Personification and the Sublime: Milton to Coleridge*. Cambridge, MA: Harvard University Press, 1985.

Knight, Jeffrey Todd. "'Furnished' for Action: Renaissance Books as Furniture." *Book History* 12 (2009): 37–73.

Knott, Edward. *Infidelity Unmasked*. London, 1652.

König-Pralong, Catherine, Olivier Ribordy, and Tiziana Suarez-Nani, eds. *Pierre de Jean Olivi: Philosophe et théologien*. Berlin: de Gruyter, 2010.

Koselleck, Reinhart. *The Practice of Conceptual History: Timing History, Spacing Concepts*. Translated by Todd Samuel Presner. Stanford, CA: Stanford University Press, 2002.

Kramnick, Jonathan. *Actions and Objects from Hobbes to Richardson*. Stanford, CA: Stanford University Press, 2010.

———. *Paper Minds: Literature and the Ecology of Consciousness*. Chicago: University of Chicago Press, 2018.

Kristeva, Julia. *Revolution in Poetic Language*. Translated by Margaret Waller. New York: Columbia University Press, 1985.

Kroll, Richard. *The Material Word: Literature Culture in the Restoration and Early Eighteenth Century*. Baltimore: Johns Hopkins University Press, 1991.

Krupp, Anthony. *Reason's Children: Childhood in Early Modern Philosophy*. Lewisburg, PA: Bucknell University Press, 2009.

Kuchar, Gary. "Traherne's Specters: Self-Consciousness and Its Others." In Blevins, ed., *Re-reading Thomas Traherne*, 173–200

Kuriyama, Shigehisa. *The Expressiveness of the Body and the Divergence of Greek and Chinese Medicine*. New York: Zone, 1999.

La Forge, Louis de. *Traitté de l'esprit de l'homme*. Amsterdam, 1670.

———. *Treatise on the Human Mind*. Translated by Desmond M. Clark. Dordrecht: Kluwer, 1997.

Lähteenmäki, Vili. "Orders of Consciousness and Forms of Reflexivity in Descartes." In *Consciousness: From Perception to Reflection*, edited by Sara Heinämaa, Vili Lähteenmäki, and Paulina Remes, 177–201. New York: Springer, 2007.

Lamb, Jonathan. *The Things Things Say*. Princeton, NJ: Princeton University Press, 2016.

La Peyrère, Isaac. *A theological systeme upon the presupposition, that men were before Adam*. London, 1655.

Laslett, Peter. "Introduction." In Locke, *Two Treatises of Government*, 3–126.

Lauder, William. *An Essay on Milton's Use and Imitation of the Moderns, in His "Paradise Lost."* London, 1750.

Lazarus, Micha. "Sidney's Greek *Poetics*." *Studies in Philology* 112 (2015): 504–36.

Lear, Jonathan. "Leaving the World Alone." *Journal of Philosophy* 79 (1982): 382–403.

———. *Open Minded: Working Out the Logic of the Soul*. Cambridge, MA: Harvard University Press, 1998.

Lee, Daniel. *Popular Sovereignty in Early Modern Constitutional Thought*. Oxford: Oxford University Press, 2016.

Lennox, James G. "The Comparative Study of Animal Development: William Harvey's Aristotelianism." In Smith, ed., *Problem of Animal Generation*, 21–46.

Leo, Russ. "Affect Before Spinoza: Reformed Faith, *Affectus*, and Experience in Jean Calvin, John Donne, John Milton, and Baruch Spinoza." PhD diss. Duke University, 2009.

———. *Tragedy as Philosophy in the Reformation World*. Oxford: Oxford University Press, 2019.

Leonard, John. *Faithful Labourers: A Reception History of "Paradise Lost," 1667–1970*. 2 vols. Oxford: Oxford University Press, 2013.

———. *Naming in Paradise: Milton and the Language of Adam and Eve.* Oxford: Clarendon, 1990.

Levitin, Dmitri. *Ancient Wisdom in the Age of the New Science.* Cambridge: Cambridge University Press, 2015.

Lewalski, Barbara Kiefer. "Innocence and Experience in Milton's Eden." In *New Essays on "Paradise Lost,"* edited by Thomas Kranidas, 86–117 Berkeley: University of California Press, 1969.

———. *The Life of John Milton: A Critical Biography.* Oxford: Blackwell, 2002.

Lewis, Charlton T., and Charles Short, eds. *A Latin Dictionary.* Oxford: Clarendon Press, 1879.

Lewis, C. S. *A Preface to "Paradise Lost."* Oxford: Oxford University Press, 1942.

———. *Studies in Words.* 2nd ed. Cambridge: Cambridge University Press, 1967.

Lewis, Geneviève. *Le problème de l'inconscient et le cartésianisme.* Paris: Presses Universitaires de France, 1950.

Lexicons of Early Modern English. Edited by Ian Lancashire. Toronto: University of Toronto Library and University of Toronto Press, 2019. Online at https://leme.library.utoronto.ca.

Libera, Alain de. *Archéologie du sujet: Naissance du sujet.* Paris: Vrin, 2007.

———. *L'invention du sujet moderne: Cours du Collège de France 2013–14.* Paris: Vrin, 2015.

———. "When Did the Modern Subject Emerge?" *American Catholic Philosophical Quarterly* 82, no. 2 (2008): 181–220.

Lieb, Michael. "Adam's Story: Testimony and Transition in *Paradise Lost.*" In *Living Texts: Interpreting Milton,* edited by Kristin A. Pruitt and Charles W. Durham, 21–47. Selinsgrove: Susquehanna University Press, 2000.

———. *The Dialectics of Creation: Patterns of Birth and Regeneration in "Paradise Lost."* Amherst: University of Massachusetts Press, 1970.

Lloyd, G. E. R. *Aristotelian Explorations.* Cambridge: Cambridge University Press, 1996.

Locke, John. *The Correspondence of John Locke.* 8 vols. Edited by E. S. de Beer. Oxford: Clarendon, 1976–1989.

———. *An Essay Concerning Human Understanding.* Edited by Peter H. Nidditch. Oxford: Clarendon, 1975.

———. *Drafts for the "Essay Concerning Human Understanding," and Other Philosophical Writings.* Edited by Peter H. Nidditch and G. A. J. Rogers. Oxford: Clarendon, 1990.

———. *Some Thoughts Concerning Education.* Edited by Ruth W. Grant and Nathan Tarcov. Indianapolis: Hackett, 1996.

———. *Two Treatises of Government.* Edited by Peter Laslett. Cambridge: Cambridge University Press, 1988.

LoLordo, Antonia. *Locke's Moral Man.* Oxford: Oxford University Press, 2012.

Long, A. A., and D. N. Sedley, eds. *The Hellenistic Philosophers.* 2 vols. Cambridge: Cambridge University Press, 1987.

Lonsdale, Roger. "Introduction to *De Principiis Cogitandi.*" In *The Poems of Thomas Gray, William Collins, Oliver Goldsmith,* ed. Roger Lonsdale, 321–22. London: Longman, 1969.

Lucretius. *On the Nature of Things.* Translated by W. H. D. Rouse. Cambridge, MA: Harvard University Press, 1975.

Lydgate, John. *Dance of Death*. Edited by Florence Warren. London: Early English Text Society, 1931.

MacCallum, Hugh. *Milton and the Sons of God: The Divine Image in Milton's Poetry.* Toronto: University of Toronto Press, 1986.

Mack, Robert L. *Thomas Gray: A Life*. New Haven, CT: Yale University Press, 2000.

MacLean, Ian. *Logic, Signs, and Nature in the Renaissance*. Cambridge: Cambridge University Press, 2002.

Malabou, Katharine. *Before Tomorrow: Epigenesis and Rationality*. Translated by Carolyn Shread. Cambridge: Polity, 2016.

Maltzhan, Nicholas Von. "Dryden's Milton and the Theatre of Imagination." In *John Dryden: Tercentenary Essays*, edited by Paul Hammond and David Hopkins, 32–56. Oxford: Clarendon, 2000.

Marcus, Leah. *Childhood and Cultural Despair: A Theme and Variations in Seventeenth-Century Literature*. Pittsburgh, PA: University of Pittsburgh Press, 1978.

Marion, Jean-Luc. *Being Given: Toward a Phenomenology of Givenness*. Translated by Jeffrey L. Kosky. Stanford, CA: Stanford University Press, 2002.

———. *Cartesian Questions: Method and Metaphysics*. Translated by Daniel Garber. Chicago: University of Chicago Press, 1999.

———. *In Excess: Studies of Saturated Phenomena*. Translated by Robyn Horner and Vincent Berraud. New York: Fordham University Press, 2002.

———. *In the Self's Place: The Approach of Saint Augustine*. Translated by Jeffrey L. Kosky. Stanford, CA: Stanford University Press, 2012.

———. *Negative Certainties*. Translated by Stephen E. Lewis. Chicago: University of Chicago Press, 2015.

———. *On Descartes's Passive Thought: The Myth of Cartesian Dualism*. Translated by Christina M. Gschwandtner. Chicago: University of Chicago Press, 2018.

———. *On the Ego and on God: Further Cartesian Questions*. Translated by Christina M. Gschwandtner. New York: Fordham University Press, 2007.

Marks, Carol L. "Thomas Traherne and Cambridge Platonism." *PMLA* 81 (1966): 521–34.

———. "Thomas Traherne's Commonplace Book." *Papers of the Bibliographical Society of America* 60 (1966): 458–65.

———. "Traherne's Ficino Notebook," *Papers of the Bibliographical Society of America* 63 (1969): 73–81.

———. "Thomas Traherne and Hermes Trismegistus." *Renaissance News* 19 (1966): 118–31.

Marshall, John. "Locke, Socinianism, 'Socinianism,' and Unitarianism." In *English Philosophy in the Age of Locke*, edited by M. A. Stewart, 111–82. Oxford: Oxford University Press, 2000.

Martz, Louis. *The Paradise Within: Studies in Vaughan, Traherne, and Milton*. New Haven, CT: Yale University Press, 1964.

Mason, William. *Poems and Letters of Thomas Gray: With Memoirs of His Life and Writings*. 2nd ed. London, 1820.

Matt, Daniel C., trans. *The Zohar*. Pritzker Edition. 2 vols. Stanford, CA: Stanford University Press, 2004.

Mazlov, Boris. *Pindar and the Emergence of Literature*. Cambridge: Cambridge University Press, 2015.

Mazzoni, Guido. *Sulla poesia moderna*. Bologna: Società editrice il Mulino, 2005.

———. *Theory of the Novel*. Translated by Zakiya Hanafi. Cambridge, MA: Harvard University Press, 2017.

McColley, Diane Kelsey. *A Gust for Paradise: Milton's Eden and the Visual Arts*. Champaign: University of Illinois Press, 1993.

McEwan, Ian. *Nutshell: A Novel*. New York: Nan A. Telese, 2016.

Melanchthon, Philip. *Loci communes*. In *Corpus Reformatorum*. Vol. 15. Edited by Karl Gottlieb Bretschneider. Halle: C. A. Schwetschke, 1848.

Merleau-Ponty, Maurice. *Child Psychology and Pedagogy: The Sorbonne Lectures 1949–1952*. Translated by Talia Walsh. Evanston, IL: Northwestern University Press, 2010.

———. *Phenomenology of Perception*. Translated by Colin Smith. London: Routledge, 1962.

Migne, J. P., ed. *Patralogia cursus completus, series Latina*. 221 vols. Paris, 1844–64.

Miller, Jon. *Spinoza and the Stoics*. Cambridge: Cambridge University Press, 2015.

Milton, John. *Areopagitica*. In Milton, *Complete Prose Works*, 2:480–570.

———. *Artis logicae*. Edited and translated by Allan H. Gilbert. In *The Works of John Milton*, vol. 11, edited by Frank Allen Patterson. New York: Columbia University Press, 1935.

———. *Milton: The Complete Shorter Poems*. Edited by John Carey. 2nd ed. Harlow: Longman, 1997.

———. *The Complete Prose Works of John Milton*. 8 vols. New Haven, CT: Yale University Press, 1953–1982.

———. *Defensio secunda*. Edited by Eugene J. Strittmatter. Translated by George Burnett and Moses Hadas. In *The Works of John Milton*, vol. 8, edited by Frank Allen Patterson. New York: Columbia University Press, 1933.

———. *De doctrina Christiana*. 2 vols. Edited by John K. Hale and J. Donald Cullington. Oxford: Oxford University Press, 2012.

———. *Doctrine and Discipline of Divorce*. In Milton, *Complete Prose Works*, 2:217–356.

———. *Of Education*. In Milton, *Complete Prose Works*, 2:357–415.

———. *Major Works*. Edited by Stephen Orgel and Jonathan Goldberg. Oxford: Oxford University Press, 1991.

———. *A Masque . . . Presented at Ludlow Castle*. In Milton, *Major Works*, 44–71,

———. *Paradise Lost*. Edited by Alastair Fowler. 2nd ed London: Routledge, 2013.

———. *Pro se defensio*. Edited by Eugene J. Strittmatter. Translated by George Burnett and Moses Hadas. In *The Works of John Milton*, vol. 9, edited by Frank Allen Patterson. New York: Columbia University Press, 1933.

———. *Reason of Church Government*. In Milton, *Complete Prose Works*, 1:736–861.

———. *Tenure of Kings and Magistrates*. In Milton, *Complete Prose Works*, 3:185–258.

———. *Tetrachordon*. In Milton, *Complete Prose Works*, 2:571–718.

Minnis, Alastair. *From Eden to Eternity: Creations of Paradise in the Later Middle Ages*. Philadelphia: University of Pennsylvania Press, 2016.

Mintz, Susannah B. *Threshold Poetics: Milton and Intersubjectivity*. Newark: University of Delaware Press, 2003.

Molenaar, G. "Seneca's Use of the Term 'Conscientia.' " *Mnemosyne* 22 (1969): 170–80.

Molyneux, William. "A Problem Proposed to the Author of the *Essai Philosophique*." In Locke, *Correspondence*, vol. 3 (1978), no. 1064.

Montaigne, Michel de. *Les Essais*. Edited by Jean Balsamo, Michel Magnien, and Catherine Magnien-Simonin. Paris: Gallimard, 2007.

———. *The Complete Essays*. Translated by Donald Frame. Stanford, CA: Stanford University Press, 1957.

More, Henry. *Divine Dialogues*. London, 1668.

Moriarty, Michael. *Early Modern French Thought: The Age of Suspicion*. Oxford: Oxford University Press, 2003.

Mortimer, Sarah. *Reason and Revelation in the English Revolution*. Cambridge: Cambridge University Press, 2010.

Moshenska, Joe. *Feeling Pleasures: The Sense of Touch in Renaissance England*. Oxford: Oxford University Press, 2014.

Mueller, Janel. "Donne's Epic Venture in the *Metempsychosis*." *Modern Philology* 70 (1972): 109–37.

Murphy, Kathryn. "The Anxiety of Variety: Knowledge and Experience in Montaigne, Burton, and Bacon." In *Fictions of Knowledge: Fact, Evidence, Doubt*, edited by Yota Batsaki, Subha Mukherji, and Jan-Melissa Schramm, 110–35. Basingstoke: Palgrave, 2011.

———. "No Things But In Thoughts: Traherne's Poetic Realism." In Dodd and Gorman, *Thomas Traherne and Seventeenth-Century Thought*, 48–68.

Nadler, Steven. "Consciousness Among the Cartesians." *Studia Leibnizia* 43 (2011): 132–44.

Nagel, Thomas. "What Is It Like to Be a Bat?" *Philosophical Review* 83, no. 4 (1974): 435–50.

Nardi, Bruno. *Studi di filosofia medievale*. Rome: Storia Letteratura, 1960.

Needham, Joseph. *A History of Embryology*. 2nd ed. Cambridge: Cambridge University Press, 1959.

Nellen, Henk. *Hugo Grotius: A Lifelong Struggle for Peace in Church and State, 1583–1645*. Leiden: Brill, 2015.

Nettleship, Henry. *Contributions to Latin Lexicography*. Oxford: Clarendon, 1889.

Newey, Edmund. " 'God Made Man Greater When He Made Him Less': Traherne's Iconic Child." *Literature and Theology* 24 (2010): 227–41.

Nicolson, Marjorie Hope. *Breaking of the Circle: Studies in the Effect of the 'New Science' Upon Seventeenth-Century Poetry*. Evanston, IL: Northwestern University Press, 1950.

Noë, Alva. *Out of Our Heads: Why You Are Not Your Brain and Other Lessons from the Biology of Consciousness*. New York: Hill and Wang, 2009.

Norton, Benjamin. *New English Dictionary*. London, 1735.

Nyquist, Mary. *Arbitrary Rule: Slavery, Tyranny, and the Power of Life and Death*. Chicago: University of Chicago Press, 2013.

———. "The Genesis of Gendered Subjectivity in the Divorce Tracts and in *Paradise Lost*." In *Re-Membering Milton: Essays on the Texts and Traditions*, edited by Mary Nyquist and Margaret W. Ferguson, 99–127. New York: Methuen, 1987.

O'Byrne, Anne. *Natality and Finitude*. Bloomington, IN: University of Indiana Press, 2010.

Ogden, Thomas H. *The Matrix of the Mind: Object Relations and the Psychoanalytic Dialogue*. Lanham, MD: Rowman and Littlefield, 2004.

Olivi, Pierre Jean Olivi. *Quaestiones in secundum librum Sententiarum, Quaestiones 1–48*. In *Biblioteca Franciscana Scholastica, Medii Aevi*, vol. 6., edited by Bernardus Jansen. Quaracchi, Italy: Collegii S. Bonaventurae, 1926.

Ong, Walter. *Ramus, Method, and the Decay of Dialogue*. Chicago: University of Chicago Press, 1958.

Oras, Ants. *Milton's Editors and Commentators from Patrick Hume to Henry John Todd*. Oxford: Oxford University Press, 1931.

Ortega y Gasset, José. "Adán en el Paraíso." In *Obras Completas*. Vol. 1. Madrid: Revista de Occidente, 1946.

Ovid. *Tristia*. Translated by Arthur Leslie Wheeler. Cambridge, MA: Harvard University Press, 1988.

Oxford English Dictionary. Oxford: Oxford University Press. Available online at *oed.com*.

Pagel, Walter. *New Light on William Harvey*. Basel: Karger, 1976.

———. *William Harvey's Biological Ideas: Selected Aspects and Historical Background*. New York: Hafner, 1967.

Paget, Nathan. *Bibliotecha Medica Viri Clarissimi Nathanis Paget, M. D.* London, 1681.

Park, Katharine. *Secrets of Women: Gender, Generation, and the Origins of Human Dissection*. New York: Zone, 2010.

Pemberton, William. *The Godly Merchant*. London, 1613.

Perkins, William. *A Discourse of Conscience*. London, 1596.

Pertile, Giulio. *Feeling Faint: Affect and Consciousness in the Renaissance*. Evanston, IL: Northwestern University Press, 2019.

Petrarch, *Petrarch's Lyric Poems: The "Rime Sparse" and Other Lyrics*. Translated by Robert M. Durling. Cambridge, MA: Harvard University Press, 1976.

Phillips, Edward. *The New World of English Words*. London, 1658.

Picciotto, Joanna. "Circumstantial Particulars, Particular Individuals, and Defoe." In *Reflections on Sentiment: Essays in Honor of George Starr*, ed. Alessa Jones, 29–54. Newark, NJ: Delaware University Press, 2016.

———. *Labors of Innocence in Early Modern England*. Cambridge, MA: Harvard University Press, 2010.

Pierce, Thomas. *The Sinner Impleaded in His Own Court*. London, 1656.

Piontelli, Alessandra. *Development of Normal Fetal Movements: The Last 15 Weeks of Gestation*. Milan: Springer-Verlag Italia, 2015.

Placentini, Iulij Casserij. *Pentaestheseion hox est de quinque sensibus*. Venice, 1609.

Plato. *Complete Works*. Edited by John M. Cooper and D. S. Hutchinson. Indianapolis, IN: Hackett, 1997.

Platt, John. "The Denial of the Innate Idea of God in Dutch Remonstrant Theology: From Episcopius to Van Limborch." In *Protestant Scholasticism: Essays in Reassessment*, edited by Carl R. Trueman and R. Scott Clark, 213–26. Eugene, OR: Wipf & Stock, 2005.

———. *Reformed Thought and Scholasticism: The Arguments for the Existence of God in Dutch Theology, 1575–1650*. Leiden: Brill, 1982.

Pliny the Elder. *Natural History*. 10 vols. Translated by H. Rackham. Cambridge, MA: Harvard University Press, 1952.

Plutarch. *The Philosophie, commonlie called, the Morals*. Translated by Philemon Holland. London, 1603.

Poole, William. *Milton and the Idea of the Fall*. Cambridge: Cambridge University Press, 2005.

———. *Milton and the Making of "Paradise Lost."* Cambridge, MA: Harvard University Press, 2017.

Potts, Timothy C. *Conscience in Medieval Philosophy*. Cambridge: Cambridge University Press, 1980.

Preminger, Alex, and T. V. F. Brogan, eds. *The Princeton Encyclopedia of Poetry and Poetics*. Princeton, NJ: Princeton University Press, 1993.

Putallez, François-Xavier. *La connaissance de soi au XIIIe siècle*. Paris: Vrin, 1991.

Quantin, Jean-Louis. *The Church of England and Christian Antiquity: The Construction of a Confessional Identity in the Seventeenth Century*. Oxford: Oxford University Press, 2009.

Quint, David. *Inside "Paradise Lost": Reading the Designs of Milton's Epic*. Princeton, NJ: Princeton University Press, 2014.

———. *Origin and Originality in Renaissance Literature: Versions of the Source*. New Haven, CT: Yale University Press, 1983.

Radner, Dasie. "Thought and Consciousness in Descartes." *Journal of the History of Philosophy* 26 (1988): 439–52.

Rajan, Balachandra. "Simple, Sensuous and Passionate." *Review of English Studies* 21 (1945): 289–301.

Ramachandrán, Ayesha. *Lyric Thinking: Poetry, Selfhood, Modernity*. Forthcoming.

Ramachandran, Ayesha. *The Wordmaker's: Global Imagining in Early Modern Europe*. Chicago: University of Chicago Press, 2015.

Rank, Otto. *The Trauma of Birth*. New York: Robert Brunner, 1952.

Ratcliffe, Matthew. *Feelings of Being: Phenomenology, Psychiatry, and the Sense of Reality*. Oxford: Oxford University Press, 2008.

Ricks, Christopher. *Milton's Grand Style*. Oxford: Clarendon, 1963.

Ricoeur, Paul. *Freedom and Nature: The Voluntary and the Involuntary*. Translated by Erazim V. Kohák. Evanston, IL: Northwestern University Press, 1966.

———. *Oneself As Another*. Translated by Kathleen Blamey. Chicago: University of Chicago Press, 1992.

Rist, John M. *Augustine: Ancient Thought Baptized*. Cambridge: Cambridge University Press, 1994.

Riva, Alessandro. "Iulius Casserius (1552–1616): The Self-Made Anatomist of Padua's Golden Age." *The Anatomical Record* 265 (2001): 168–75.

Rogers, John. *The Matter of Revolution: Science, Poetry, and Politics in the Age of Milton*. Ithaca, NY: Cornell University Press, 1996.

Romano, Claude. *Event and World*. Translated by Shane Mackinlay. New York: Fordham University Press, 2009.

Rosen, Stanley. *The Quarrel Between Philosophy and Poetry: Studies in Ancient Thought*. London: Routledge, 1988.

Royal College of Obstetricians and Gynecologists, *Fetal Awareness: Review of Research and Recommendations for Practice*. Published 25 June, 2010. https:// www.rcog.org .uk/en/guidelines-research-services/guidelines/fetal-awareness---review-of-research -and-recommendations-for-practice/.

Rozemond, Marleen. *Descartes's Dualism*. Cambridge, MA: Harvard University Press, 1998.

Saenz, Cynthia. "Language and the Fall: The Quest for Prelapsarian Speech in the Writings of Thomas Traherne and his Contemporaries." In Blevins, ed., *Re-Reading Thomas Traherne*, 65–92

Sanderson, Robert. *Logicae Artis Compendium*. London, 1618.

———. *Ten Lectures on the Obligation of Humane Conscience*. London, 1660.

Sarkar, Debapriya. " 'Sad Experiment' in *Paradise Lost*: Epic Knowledge and Evental Poetics." Exemplaria 26 (2014): 368–88.

Saurat, Denis. *Milton: Man and Thinker*. New York: Dial, 1925.

Sawday, Jonathan. *The Body Emblazoned: Dissection and the Human Body in Renaissance Culture*. London: Routledge, 1995.

Schmitt, Charles B. "Experience and Experiment: A Comparison of Zabaralla's View with Galileo's in De motu." *Studies in the Renaissance* 16 (1969): 80–138.

Schoenfeldt, Michael C. *Bodies and Selves in Early Modern England: Physiology and Inwardness in Spenser, Shakespeare, Herbert, and Milton*. Cambridge: Cambridge University Press, 1999.

Schwartz, Louis. *Milton and Maternal Mortality*. Cambridge: Cambridge University Press, 2009.

Schwartz, Regina. *Remembering and Repeating: Biblical Creation in "Paradise Lost."* Cambridge: Cambridge University Press, 1988.

Scodel, Joshua. *Excess and the Mean in Early Modern English Literature*. Princeton, NJ: Princeton University Press, 2002.

———. "Edenic Freedoms." *Milton Studies* 56 (2015): 153–200.

Scott, Dominic. *Recollection and Experience: Plato's Theory of Learning and Its Successors*. Cambridge: Cambridge University Press, 1995.

Scott, Joanna Vecchiarelli, and Judith Chelius Stark, "Rediscovering *Love and Saint Augustine*." In Arendt, *Love and Saint Augustine*, vii–xviii.

Sgarbi, Marco. *The Aristotelian Tradition and the Rise of British Empiricism: Logic and Epistemology in the British Isles (1570–1689)*. Dordrecht: Springer, 2013.

Shakespeare, William. *The Complete Pelican Shakespeare*. Edited by Stephen Orgel and A. R. Braunmuller. New York: Penguin, 2002.

Sharp, Jane. *Midwives Book, or, The Whole Art of Midwifry Discovered*. Oxford: Oxford University Press, 1999.

Shelley, Mary. *Frankenstein*. Edited by Maurice Hindle. New York: Penguin, 1985.

Shklovsky, Victor. "Art as Technique," in *Russian Formalist Criticism: Four Essays*, translated by Lee T. Lemon and Marion J. Reis. Lincoln: University of Nebraska Press, 1965.

Sid-Ahmad, Muhammad. "Ibn Tufayl's Hayy and Milton's Adam." In *Milton and Questions of History: Essays by Canadians Past and Present*, edited by Feisel G. Mohamed and Mary Nyquist, 355–78. Toronto: University of Toronto Press, 2012.

Sidney, Mary. *The Sidney Psalms.* Edited by R. E. Pritchard. Austin, TX: Harry Ransom
    Humanities Research Center, 1992.
Sidney, Philip. *The Defence of Poesy.* In *Sidney's 'Defence of Poesy' and Selected Renais-
    sance Literary Criticism.* Edited by Gavin Alexander. New York: Penguin, 2004.
———. *Selected Prose and Poetry.* Edited by Robert Kimbrough. Madison: University of
    Wisconsin Press, 1983.
Simmons, Alison. "Cartesian Consciousness Reconsidered." *Philosopher's Imprint* 12,
    no. 2 (2012): 1–21.
Simon, David Carroll. *Light without Heat: The Observational Mood from Bacon to Mil-
    ton.* Ithaca, NY: Cornell University Press, 2018.
Skinner, Quentin. *Visions of Politics.* 3 vols. Cambridge: Cambridge University Press, 2002.
Smectymnuus. *An Answer to a Booke Entitvled An Hvmble Remonstrance.* London, 1641.
Smith, Christopher. *The Hermeneutics of Original Argument: Demonstration, Dialectic,
    Rhetoric.* Evanston, IL: Northwestern University Press, 1998.
Smith, Julia J. "Traherne and Historical Contingency." In Dodd and Gorman, *Thomas
    Traherne and Seventeenth-Century Thought,* xiii–xx.
Smith, Justin E. H., ed. *The Problem of Animal Generation in Early Modern Philosophy.*
    Cambridge: Cambridge University Press, 2006.
Smith, Pamela H. *The Body of the Artisan.* Chicago: University of Chicago Press, 2004.
Snider, Alvin. "The Self-Mirroring Mind in Milton and Traherne." *University of Toronto
    Quarterly* 55 (1986): 313–27.
Socinus, Faustus. *De statu primi hominis ante lapsum disputatio.* Racow, 1610.
———. *Operum omnium.* Irenopoli [Amsterdam]: 1656.
———. *Praelectiones theologicae.* Racow, 1609.
———, Valentin Smalcius, Hieronim Moskorzewski, and Johannes Völker]. *Racovian
    Catechisme.* London, 1652.
Sorabji, Richard. *Self: Ancient and Modern Insights about Individuality, Life, and Death.*
    Chicago: University of Chicago Press, 2006.
South, Robert. *A Sermon Preached at the Cathedral Church of St. Paul, Novemb. 9 1662.*
    London, 1663.
Spenser, Edmund. *The Faerie Queene.* Edited by A. C. Hamilton. New York: Longman,
    2001.
Spitzer, Leo. *Essays in Historical Semantics.* New York: S. F. Vanni, 1948.
Sponde, Jean de, ed. and trans. *Homeri quae extant omnia.* 2nd ed. Basil, 1606.
Stanley, Thomas. *History of Philosophy.* London, 1656.
Starobinksi, Jean. *Montaigne in Motion.* Translated by Arthur Goldhammer. Chicago:
    University of Chicago Press, 1985.
Sterne, Laurence. *The Life and Opinions of Tristram Shandy, Gentleman.* New York:
    Modern Library, 2004.
Stevens, Paul. *Imagination and the Presence of Shakespeare in "Paradise Lost."* Madison:
    University of Wisconsin Press, 1985.
Stevens, Wallace. *The Palm at the End of the Mind: Selected Poems and Plays.* Edited by
    Holly Stevens. New York: Vintage, 1990.
Stewart, Stanley. *The Expanded Voice: The Art of Thomas Traherne.* San Marino, CA:
    Huntington Library, 1970.

Stock, Brian. *Augustine the Reader: Meditation, Self-Knowledge, and the Ethics of Interpretation.* Cambridge, MA: Harvard University Press, 1996.

Straumann, Benjamin. "The Energy of Concepts: The Role of Concepts in Long-Term Intellectual History and Social Reality." *Journal of the Philosophy of History* 14 (2019): forthcoming.

———. *Roman Law in the State of Nature: The Classical Foundations of Hugo Grotius's Natural Law.* Translated by Belinda Cooper. Cambridge: Cambridge University Press, 2015.

Strawson, Galen. *Locke on Personal Identity: Consciousness and Concernment.* Princeton, NJ: Princeton University Press, 2011.

———. *The Subject of Experience.* Oxford: Oxford University Press, 2017.

Strier, Richard. "How Formalism Became a Dirty Word, and Why We Can't Do Without It." In *Renaissance Literature and Its Formal Engagements*, edited by Mark David Rasmussen, 207–15. New York: Palgrave, 2002.

———. "Milton's Fetters, or, Why Eden Is Better Than Heaven." In *The New Milton Criticism*, edited by Peter C. Herman and Elizabeth Sauer, 25–48. Cambridge: Cambridge University Press, 2012.

———. "New Historicism, New Formalism, and Thy Darling in an Urn." In *A Companion to Renaissance Poetry*, edited by Catherine Bates, 583–94. Oxford: Blackwell, 2018.

Struther, William. *True Happiness.* Edinburgh, 1633.

Sugimura, Noël. *"Matter of Glorious Trial": Spiritual and Material Substance in "Paradise Lost."* New Haven, CT: Yale University Press, 2009.

Tabb, Kathryn. "Madness as Method: On Locke's Thought Experiments about Personal Identity." *British Journal for the History of Philosophy* 26, no. 5 (2018): 871–889.

Tarcov, Nathan. *Locke's Education for Liberty.* Chicago: University of Chicago Press, 1984.

Targoff, Ramie. *John Donne: Body and Soul.* Chicago: University of Chicago Press, 2007.

Tasso, Torquato. *Discourses on the Heroic Poem.* Translated by Mariella Cavalchini and Irene Samuel. Oxford: Clarendon, 1973.

Taylor, Charles. *Sources of the Self: The Making of Modern Identity.* Cambridge, MA: Harvard University Press, 1989.

Temkin, O. "The Classical Roots of Glisson's Doctrine of Irritation." *Bulletin of the History of Medicine* 38 (1964): 297–328.

Teskey, Gordon. *Allegory and Violence.* Ithaca, NY: Cornell University Press, 1996.

———. *Delirious Milton: The Fate of the Poet in Modernity.* Cambridge, MA: Harvard University Press, 2006.

———. *The Poetry of John Milton.* Cambridge, MA: Harvard University Press, 2015.

Thiel, Udo. "Cudworth and Theories of Consciousness." In *The Uses of Antiquity: The Scientific Revolution and the Classical Tradition*, edited by Stephen Gaukroger, 79–100. Dordrecht: Kluwer, 1991.

———. *The Early Modern Subject: Self-Consciousness and Personal Identity from Descartes to Hume.* Oxford: Oxford University Press, 2011.

Traherne, Thomas. *Roman Forgeries.* London, 1674.

———. *The Works of Thomas Traherne.* 8 vols. Edited by Jan Ross. Cambridge: D. S. Brewer, 2005–2018.

Trinkaus, Charles. *The Poet as Philosopher: Petrarch and the Formation of Renaissance Consciousness*. New Haven, CT: Yale University Press, 1979.

Tuck, Richard. "Grotius, Carneades, and Hobbes." *Grotiana* 4 (1983): 43–62.

———. "Introduction." In Grotius, *The Rights of War and Peace*, ix–xxxiii.

Tufayl, Abu Bakr Ibn. *Hayy Ibn Yaqzan: A Philosophical Tale*. Updated Edition. Translated by Lenn Evan Goodman. Chicago: University of Chicago Press, 2009.

Turner, James Grantham. *One Flesh: Paradisal Marriage and Sexual Relations in the Age of Milton*. Oxford: Clarendon, 1987.

Van Der Lugt, Maaike. "L'animation de l'embryon humain dans la pensée médiévale." In Brisson, Congourdeau, and Solère, *L'embryon: Formation et animation*, 233–54.

Vatter, Miguel. "Natality and Biopolitics in Hannah Arendt." *Revista de Ciencia Política* 26 (2006): 137–59.

Vaughan, Henry. *The Complete Works*. Edited by Alan Rudrum. New York: Penguin, 1995.

Vickers, Brian. "Epideictic and Epic in the Renaissance." *New Literary History* 14 (1983): 497–537.

Virgil. *Eclogues, Georgics, Aeneid I–VI*. Translated by H. Rushton Fairclough, revised by G. P. Goold. Cambridge, MA: Harvard University Press, 1999.

Voltaire. *Philosophical Letters: Letters Concerning the English Nation*. Translated by Ernest Dilworth. New York: Dover, 2003.

Vorstius, Conrad. *Apologetica Exegesis sive Plenior Declaratio Locorum aliquot ex Libro ejusdem de Deo*. Leiden, 1611.

———. *Tractatus theologicus de Deo*. Steinfurt, 1606.

Wallis, John. *Truth Tried*. London, 1643.

Walmsley, Peter. *Locke's "Essay" and the Rhetoric of Science*. Lewisberg, PA: Bucknell University Press, 2003.

Warren, Christopher. "When Self-Preservation Bids: Approaching Milton, Hobbes, and Dissent." *English Literary Renaissance* 37 (2007): 118–50.

Watson, Robert. *Back to Nature: The Green and the Real in the Late Renaissance*. Philadelphia: University of Pennsylvania Press, 2007.

Webber, Joan. *The Eloquent "I": Style and Self in Seventeenth-Century Prose*. Madison: University of Wisconsin Press, 1968.

Weber, Robert, and Roger Gryson, eds. *Biblia sacra: Iuxta vulgatum versionem*. Stuttgart: Deutsche Bibelgesellschaft, 2007.

Webster, Charles. *The Great Instauration: Science, Medicine, and Reform, 1626–1660*. London: Duckworth, 1975.

Weinberg, Shelley. *Consciousness in Locke*. Oxford: Oxford University Press, 2016.

White, Helen C. *The Metaphysical Poets: A Study of Religious Experience*. London: Macmillan, 1936.

Wilderbing, James. *Forms, Souls, and Embryos: Neoplatonists on Human Reproduction*. London: Routledge, 2017.

Wilkin, Rebecca. "Descartes, Individualism, and the Fetal Subject." *differences* 19, no. 1 (2008): 96–127.

Willet, Andrew. *Hexapla in Genesin; that is, A Sixfold Commentary upon Genesis*. London, 1605.

Willey, Basil. *The Seventeenth Century Background: Studies in the Thought of the Age in Relation to Poetry and Religion.* New York: Columbia University Press, 1958.

Williams, Arnold. *The Common Expositor: An Account of the Commentaries on Genesis, 1527–1633.* Chapel Hill: University of North Carolina Press, 1948.

Williamson, George. "Milton and the Mortalist Heresy." *Studies in Philology* 32 (1935): 553–79.

Wilson, Catherine. *The Invisible World: Early Modern Philosophy and the Invention of the Microscope.* Princeton, NJ: Princeton University Press, 1995.

Wilson, Thomas. *Christian Dictionary.* London, 1612.

Winnicott, D. W. "The Theory of the Parent-Infant Relationship." *International Journal of Psycho-Analysis* 41 (1960): 585–95.

Winstanley, Gerrard. *Fire in the Bush.* London, 1650.

Wordsworth, William. *Essential Wordsworth.* Edited by Seamus Heaney. New York: Ecco, 1998.

Young, Edward, *Two Sermons concerning Nature and Grace.* London, 1700.

Yu, Esther. "Tears in Paradise: The Revolution of Tender Conscience." *Representations* 142 (2018): 1–32.

INDEX

Abdiel, angel, 65, 108–9
abortion, 162–63, 265n30
Achinstein, Sharon, 76, 98, 280–81n11, 284n67, 294n27
Acts, 48–49, 171, 277n63. *See also* Bible
Adam: in Andreini, 75, 121; in *Chronicles of Jerahmeel*, 74–75; creation of, in Genesis tradition, 81–83; creation of, in Locke, 219; creation of, in Milton, 76, 81–86; creation of, in Traherne, 146–48; as "finite universal," 17; first thoughts of, in Dryden, 131–32; first thoughts of, in Milton, 42–50, 102, 111–13; first thoughts of, in modern literature/scholarship, 254; first thoughts of, in Traherne, 119–25; nature of, 4; nature of, in Milton, 76, 82–85, 107; nature of, in South, 99–100; nature of, in Traherne, 130–31; as newly awakened, 42–45, 72–76, 108–13, 131–32, 146–47, 254; as normal human being, 101, 108, 112–13, 219–21, 222; patriarchal power of, in Filmer, 216–17; as perfect being, 120, 219; in relation to war (Grotius), 94–95; as requiring experience, 57–58; as tabula rasa (Socinus), 222; in the *Zohar*, 74. *See also* Adam and Eve; Eve
Adam and Eve: and death, 66–67, 87, 92–98, 284n63; as desiring knowledge, 46–47; as effects of divine cause, 80–81; and experience, 63–68; first impressions of (*prima naturae*), 3, 24, 42, 44–45, 86–99, 111, 119–20; first thoughts of, 21, 22, 34–35, 40–42, 102; inequality between, 54, 254;

innocence lost by, 64; language acquisition by, 55–57, 197; self-preservation of, 89, 93–95 (*see also* animal[s]); as sole humanity, 17, 269n75. *See also* Adam; Eve
Adelman, Howard B., 291n21
Adorno, Theodor, 28, 272n117
Aëtius, 157–58, 289n63. *See also* tabula rasa (*abrasa tabula, rasa tabula*)
Agamben, Giorgio, 279n109
Ahmed, Sarah, 294n15
Aït-Touati, Frédérique, 19, 270n84
Alcmaeon, 180
allegory: in Milton, 36–37, 39; in Spenser, 18
Almond, Philip C., 272n7
American College of Obstetricians and Gynecologists, 265n30
Amerini, Fabrizio, 265n29
anamnesis, 156, 160, 289n60
Anderson, Gary, 272n7
Andreini, Giambattista, 75, 121, 280n8
angels: fallen, 44, 275n40; origins of (Satan), 108–9. *See also individual names*
anima, 83, 211
animal, 83
animal(s): Adam discovers in Eden, 45–46; Adam names, 55–57, 120–21; Aristotle on, 61, 67–68, 157; creation of, *vs.* human creation, 81–82; distinction between humans and, 15–16; as egos (Traherne), 138–40; instinct in relation to Adam (Milton), 45–46; limitations of, 61, 67–68, 141–42; nonviolent in Milton's Eden, 96; as part of soul, 45, 164–68, 172–75, 181; as sentient, 48, 93–95, 139–40, 276n62

Du Bartas, Guillaume de Salluste, 73–74, 82,
94, 146, 280n3, 282n28, 284n61
Dunstan, G. R., 265n29

Earle, John, 288n47
Early English Books Online (EEBO), 267nn48,
50
Early English Print, 267n48
Eden. *See* Garden of Eden
Eden, Kathy, 269n78
education: in Eden, 36; in Milton, 21, 102; in
Traherne, 191
Edwards, Jonathan, 101, 221–22, 285n75,
294nn30–33
Edwards, Karen, 277n69
ego(s), 15, 28, 38, 71, 204, 235; in Augustine,
5, 144–45; birth of (Traherne), 151–62,
182, 288n53; in Descartes, 9, 23–24, 117–
18, 132, 184; in Milton, 37–38, 76–86,
117–18; *vs.* Traherne on, 117–18 (*see also*
soul); in Traherne, 123–24, 128, 132–48,
149, 150, 180–83, 186–87, 189, 202–3,
204. *See also* consciousness; knowledge;
self; thought
Eisendrath, Rachel, 270n87
ekstasis, 141–43, 202. *See also* thought
Eliot, T. S., 198, 293n71
Ellrodt, Robert, 288n53
embryos, 3, 8–9, 11, 151–55, 160–61, 162–204,
207, 210–12, 230–31, 241–43, 252–54.
See also consciousness; fetuses
Empedocles, 18, 209
empeiria, 50, 60–62, 66, 67, 68, 71, 118, 278–
79n104, 279n113, 280nn115–16
Empson, William, 111, 272n117, 285n97
enjoyer: fly as (Traherne), 139–40; *vs.* animal[s]); as legal term, 136; Traherne
on, 136–48. *See also* enjoyment
enjoyment: Adamic, 69; Traherne on, 135–37,
199; *vs.* use (Augustine), 136; of world
(Traherne), 148–49, 190, 193. *See also*
enjoyer; happiness
epic poetry, 20, 21, 163; causes mind to wonder
(Tasso), 22; as developed in *Paradise Lost*,
34, 36, 39, 69, 108, 197, 204; thought in,
270n98. See also poetry; *poiesis*
Epicureans, 97–98. *See also* Stoicism
Episcopius, Simon, 105, 108, 285nn87–88
epistemology, 3, 4, 9, 23, 28, 207–8, 213, 215,
222; Edenic, 68, 100, 221. *See also* Locke,
John

Erasmus, Desiderius, 282n36
Erfahrung, vs. *Erlebnis*, 66
Erlebnis, 108; vs. *Erfahrung*, 66
error, 11, 55, 67, 128; and inexperience or
experience, 53, 57–58, 65, 118 (*see also*
experience; inexperience); *logos* precondition for, 68. *See also* Eve; Satan
Evans, J. Martin, 280n4, 281n25, 283n50
Eve: and experience, 63, 64–67; on experiment
vs. experience, 67 (*see also* experience);
and the Fall, 64–67; and immortality,
97, 100; in Locke, 218; and originary
experience, 3, 17, 21, 22, 50–58, 73, 118;
tempted by Satan, 63–64, 100; in Traherne, 118–19, 120; and "unexperienced
thought," 50–58, 66, 68, 70. *See also*
Adam; Adam and Eve; neonatal maturity;
Satan
existence, 40–42, 76, 109, 121; in Avicenna,
23; in Descartes, 128, 132–33; of God,
27, 48–49, 63, 73, 102–8, 111, 113, 125–
26; individuation and (Locke), 216; in
relation to preexistence, 156, 160–61; in
Traherne, 195, 198
experience: Aristotle on, 50, 60–62, 66, 67,
68, 71, 118, 278–79n104, 279n113,
280nn115–16; conceptual history of,
50–51, 71; and consciousness, 51, 66,
70–71, 235–37, 295n51; and Eve, 50–58,
63, 64–67, 68, 70; and innocence, 64; and
knowledge, 61, 213, 227, 235–36, 244;
and *logos*, 68; Milton's concept of, 58–63;
in Plato, 60. *See also* Adam and Eve;
originary experience; thought
experience, originary. *See* originary
experience
experientia, 50, 62–63, 101, 279n113
Eyffinger, Arthur, 284n58

Fabricius, Hieronymus, 162, 167–68, 171–73,
175, 282n46, 291n22, 291n35, 291n36,
291n40
Fall, the, 64–68, 76, 91–92, 100, 101–3, 191–
92. *See also* Adam and Eve; Eve; Grotius,
Hugo; Milton, John; Satan
Fallon, Stephen, 282n34
Falque, Emmanuel, 264n20
feeling, 86, 107, 150, 183; in Harvey, 181–82;
in Milton, 43–50, 76, 112–13, 276–77n62;
in Traherne, 124–26, 161, 187–89. *See
also* knowledge; sensation; thought

Mason, William, 208, 293n5
Matt, Daniel C., 280n6
maturity, neonatal. *See* neonatal maturity
Mazlov, Boris, 39, 274n22
Mazzoni, Guido, 16–17, 263n2, 269nn72–73, 270n90, 270n92
McColley, Diane Kelsey, 272–73n7
McEwan, Ian, 296n4
Melanchthon, Philip, 103, 285n79
memory: of Adam and Eve's beginnings, 3, 34, 35; in Aristotle, 59, 61–62, 156, 158–59; in Augustine, 5–7, 9, 108, 144–45; in Condillac, 249; in Locke, 223, 237, 238, 239; in Milton, 51, 67–68; of originary experience, 3, 4, 10, 149–50, 200–202, 209–10, 222 (*see also* originary experience); of Satan, 33, 37, 109–10; in Traherne, 149–50, 177, 183, 188–89, 200–202
mental presence, 2–3, 16, 162, 181, 225, 232, 241, 252
Merleau-Ponty, Maurice, 296n5
Michael, angel, 38, 69
Migne, J. P., 272n4
Miller, Jon, 283n44
Milton, John: on Adam's awakening, 42–50; and Aristotle, 46, 55, 58–63, 67–68, 76–80, 83, 86, 278n97; as blind, 44–45, 51; on Death, 39–41, 274n23; on ego, 76–86; on Eve's "unexperienced thought," 51–58; and experience, 50–71, 279n113, 280n115; and genesis tradition, 73–76; on Greek myth *vs.* Bible, 41–42; and Grotius, 87–99, 283n50; on human knowledge, 55, 102; on human nature, 72–113, 281n12; on joy, 75–76; on knowledge of God, 99–108; on logic and reason, 58–63; on mindedness, 3, 33–38, 52; on neonatal maturity, 35–36, 273n11, 37, 42–50, 52, 68, 73, 88, 109–11, 113, 118–19, 149, 207, 219; on originary experience, 17, 19–20, 22, 26–27, 34, 36, 41, 73–76, 86, 88, 98, 108, 119–20, 197, 202; and patriarchy, 54; on poetry, 21, 214, 269n74; and *Racovian Catechism*, 101–2, 284n71; on Sin, 36–42, 274n23; on soul as one with body, 76, 81, 82–86, 212; and South, 99–101; on time, 54–55; and Traherne, 26–27, 117–26 (*see also* Traherne, Thomas)
Milton, John, works of: *Areopagitica*, 49, 277n64; *Artis logicae*, 58–63, 80, 276n51, 278n94, 278n98; "At a Vacation Exercise

in the College," 78–79, 196–97, 281n19; *De doctrina Christiana*, 56, 76, 82–86, 105–6, 273n14, 278n86, 281n18, 282n38, 283nn40–41, 283n43, 285n88; *Defensio secunda*, 51, 277n77; *De idea Platonica*, 17; *Doctrine and Discipline of Divorce*, 87, 219; *Of Education*, 21, 102, 270nn94–95, 270n98, 285n77; *Masque Presented at Ludlow Castle*, 44, 275n38; *Paradise Lost*, 3, 17–19, 21, 22, 24, 26, 27, 33–58, 62, 63, 64–65, 69, 70, 72–86, 87, 88–89, 95–113, 117–21, 125, 130–32, 153, 197, 202, 207, 210, 219, 220–21, 254, 264n9, 273–74n17, 275n40, 279n109, 281n24; "Paraphrase of Psalm 114," 88; *Pro se defensio*, 51, 278n79; *Reason of Church Government*, 270n97; *Samson Agonistes*, 275n43; *Tenure of Kings and Magistrates*, 217, 294nn21–22; *Tetrachordon*, 56, 87, 102, 278n86, 278n88, 283n47, 285n76; "To Mr. Cyriack Skinner Upon His Blindness," 51, 278n80. *See also* Adam; Adam and Eve; Aristotle; Eve; Milton, John: *Paradise Lost*; Traherne, Thomas
mimesis: defined, 16, 208–9; and fiction, 20, 25, 245–47; in Locke, 213–15, 243–49; in Milton, 34, 131; and natality, 211; and origins, 36–42; and particularity, 16–18, 20–22, 24; and supposition, 245–47; in Traherne, 189, 193. *See also* fiction; poetry, *poiesis*
mindedness: and consciousness, 1–2, 4, 7–8, 14, 16, 28, 214, 252–53; embryonic, 9–11; Gray on, 209–10, 212–13; and knowledge of God (Milton), 105–6; in Milton, 3, 33–38, 52; and natality, 15, 209, 251, 252; and phenomenal world, 20–21; and poetry, 18, 214; in Traherne, 3, 22, 126–32, 153. *See also* consciousness
Minnis, Alastair, 94, 284n62, 286n8
Mintz, Susannah B., 274n29
misogyny, 8–9, 164, 167–68, 254–55
Molenaar, G., 267n44
Molyneux, William, 13, 245–46, 296n63
Montaigne, Michel de, 4, 51, 263n8, 280n1; on philosophy as poetry, 213–14; on pleasure and pain, 72
More, Henry, 83, 129–30, 286n18
Moriarty, Michael, 281n17, 286n15
mortality: in Arendt, 4–5; in Grotius, 89–93; and immortality, 86–87, 92, 97–98; in

Wilson, Thomas, 268n60

Winnicott, D. W., 154, 289n57

Winstanley, Gerrard, 151, 288n48

wisdom, 56–58, 101, 112, 222. *See also* experience; thought

wonder, 21–22, 34, 46, 74, 121, 124–26, 148–49, 190–91, 193, 198

Wordsworth, William, 25, 253

York Plays, 280n5

Young, Edward, 295n51

Yu, Esther, 267n48

Zabarella, Giacomo, 51, 59, 63

Zechariah, 84. *See also* Bible

Zeus, 36–38, 274n19

Zohar, 74–75